Medieval History and A

General Editors
JOHN BLAIR   HELENA HAMEROW

Parks in Medieval England

'the seminal work on the subject for future generations and a milestone in medieval scholarship'

Aleks Pluskowski, *Reviews in History*

'Beg, borrow or otherwise acquire a copy, read it and learn. A *tour de force*, not only covering every aspect of parks but also dealing with medieval society and landscapes'

Chris Taylor, *Landscapes*

'[Mileson] makes good use of topographical evidence in particular (the book has some excellent maps); but its bedrock is written evidence, both documentary and literary, and its strength is that it makes a major contribution to integrating the study of parks into the wider perspective of English medieval social history'

David Rollason, *English Historical Review*

'This is a seminal work. It familiarises those new to the subject with previous approaches and theories, questions past assumptions, comes to novel conclusions and points the way forward'

Amanda Richardson, *Southern History*

MEDIEVAL HISTORY AND ARCHAEOLOGY

General Editors
John Blair   Helena Hamerow

The volumes in this series bring together archaeological, historical, and visual methods to offer new approaches to aspects of medieval society, economy, and material culture. The series seeks to present and interpret archaeological evidence in ways readily accessible to historians, while providing a historical perspective and context for the material culture of the period.

PREVIOUSLY PUBLISHED IN THIS SERIES

ANGLO-SAXON DEVIANT BURIAL CUSTOMS
Andrew Reynolds

BEYOND THE MEDIEVAL VILLAGE
The Diversification of Landscape Character in Southern Britain
Stephen Rippon

WATERWAYS AND CANAL-BUILDING IN MEDIEVAL ENGLAND
Edited by John Blair

FOOD IN MEDIEVAL ENGLAND
Diet and Nutrition
Edited by C. M. Woolgar, D. Serjeantson, and T. Waldron

GOLD AND GILT, POTS AND PINS
Possessions and People in Medieval Britain
David A. Hinton

THE ICONOGRAPHY OF EARLY ANGLO-SAXON COINAGE
Anna Gannon

EARLY MEDIEVAL SETTLEMENTS
The Archaeology of Rural Communities in North West Europe 400–900
Helena Hamerow

PARKS IN MEDIEVAL ENGLAND

S. A. MILESON

OXFORD
UNIVERSITY PRESS

Great Clarendon Street, Oxford, OX2 6DP,
United Kingdom

Oxford University Press is a department of the University of Oxford.
It furthers the University's objective of excellence in research, scholarship,
and education by publishing worldwide. Oxford is a registered trade mark of
Oxford University Press in the UK and in certain other countries

© S. A. Mileson 2009

The moral rights of the author have been asserted

First published 2009
First published in paperback 2014

Impression: 1

All rights reserved. No part of this publication may be reproduced, stored in
a retrieval system, or transmitted, in any form or by any means, without the
prior permission in writing of Oxford University Press, or as expressly permitted
by law, by licence or under terms agreed with the appropriate reprographics
rights organization. Enquiries concerning reproduction outside the scope of the
above should be sent to the Rights Department, Oxford University Press, at the
address above

You must not circulate this work in any other form
and you must impose this same condition on any acquirer

Published in the United States of America by Oxford University Press
198 Madison Avenue, New York, NY 10016, United States of America

British Library Cataloguing in Publication Data
Data available

ISBN 978–0–19–956567–2 (Hbk.)
ISBN 978–0–19–872314–1 (Pbk.)

Links to third party websites are provided by Oxford in good faith and
for information only. Oxford disclaims any responsibility for the materials
contained in any third party website referenced in this work.

Acknowledgements

This book is a revised version of my doctoral thesis and has been a number of years in the making. During the time I have spent researching and writing about medieval parks I have benefited greatly from the help and generosity of others and it is a pleasure to record my gratitude to them here. Two individuals deserve special mention. John Watts, my former supervisor, has given support and encouragement throughout, interlacing profound insight and analysis with wit and practical advice. His rigorous thinking has challenged me to ask the right kinds of questions and his patient feedback has helped me to answer them with some semblance of clarity. I also owe tremendous thanks to John Steane, my other mentor, who has been a continuing wellspring of ideas, archaeological expertise, and assistance on field trips. I cannot adequately repay my debt to either of them, but I hope that they enjoy what they read in this book, to which they have both contributed so much.

Besides the two Johns, several others have been kind enough to read and comment on draft text at various stages. They are: my two thesis examiners, Professor Christopher Dyer and Malcolm Vale; Paul Brand (Chapter 5); Robert Liddiard; Christa Stigter; and the anonymous readers appointed by Oxford University Press. Their time and constructive criticism are much appreciated. My thanks also go to Professors John Blair and Helena Hamerow for supporting the inclusion of the book in their series, and to John in particular for providing all sorts of assistance along the way. Needless to say, any remaining errors of fact or interpretation in the finished product are entirely my own.

I am also grateful to a wider circle of scholars who have provided ideas, references, and material for illustrations, including the late Professor Maurice Beresford, James Bond, Rosemary Canadine, Professor Leonard Cantor, Charles Coulson, David Crook, C. S. L. Davies, the late Professor Sir Rees Davies, Chris Fletcher, John Gallagher, Mark Gardiner, Dick Greenaway, Gerald Harriss, Harry Hawkins, Rosemary Hoppitt, Maurice Keen, Hannes Kleineke, David Lewis, Jennifer Nuttall, Mark Page, Andrew Prescott, Brian Rich, Amanda Richardson, Professor B. K. Roberts, Anne Rowe, Shelagh Sneddon, and David Stone.

Help of a different kind has come from the staff of various institutions, who have dealt with my queries in a friendly and efficient manner. I would particularly like to thank Stephen Coleman (Bedfordshire HER), James Collett-White (Bedfordshire and Luton Archives Service), Robin Darwall-Smith (Magdalen College, Oxford), Keith Elliott (Northumberland HER), Nigel James and colleagues (Bodleian Library Map Room), Susan Lisk (Oxfordshire HER), and Jo Mackintosh (Cumbria HER). In the later stages of the project, Rupert Cousens, Kate Hind, and their colleagues at OUP steered the book through the publication process smoothly and efficiently.

Finally, I would like to take this opportunity to acknowledge the financial support provided by the AHRB, Keble College, Oxford, the Greening Lamborn Trust, and the Marc Fitch Fund. The latter two bodies generously provided grants towards the production of maps and illustrations, most of which have been expertly worked up from my draft versions by Cath D'Alton.

Contents

List of Figures viii
Abbreviations ix

Introduction 1

I. THE PURPOSE OF THE PARK

1. Hunting 15
2. Economy 45
3. Landscaping 82
4. Status 99

II. PARKS AND SOCIETY

Introduction to Part II 119
5. Parks and the Crown 121
6. Parks and the Aristocracy 146
7. Parks and the Community 158

Conclusion 180

Bibliography 183
Index 211

List of Figures

1. A medieval hunting horn	16
2. St Eustace hunting mural in Canterbury Cathedral	19
3. Lothrok, king of the Danes, hawking and hunting with a dog	19
4. Royal itinerary, 1199–1307, with forests, residences, and roads	23
5. Bow and stable hunting from the *Livre de Chasse*	31
6. Odiham (Hants.): castle and park	35
7. Park bank in woodland at Fingest (Bucks.)	43
8. The distribution of woodland and parks in medieval England	50
9. Parks and farming areas in Sussex	52
10. Woodstock park (Oxon.)	55
11. Beckley park (Oxon.)	57
12. Deer parks at Restormel castle and Boconnoc (Cornw.)	85
13. De La Beche (Berks.): park and manor house	87
14. Helmsley castle and parks (Yorks.)	90
15. Ravensworth castle (Yorks.)	94
16. Huntington castle and park (Herefs.)	100
17. Merdon park (Hants.)	105
18. (1)–(4). Park licences and royal forests, 1201–1300	125
19. The chronology of park licensing	128
20. (1)–(8). Park licences and royal forests, 1301–1500	129
21. Devizes (Wilts.): castle, town, and parkland	162
22. Little Preston (Northants.): park, settlement, and farming	165
23. Windsor (Berks.): town and park	174

Abbreviations

Abbrev. Plac.	W. Illingworth (ed.), *Placitorum in Domo Capitulari Westmonasteriensi Asservatorum Abbreviatio* (London, 1811)
AgHR	*Agricultural History Review*
BAR	British Archaeological Reports
Beds. RO	Bedfordshire and Luton Archives
Berks. RO	Berkshire Record Office
BL	British Library
Bucks. RO	Buckinghamshire Record Office
CChR	*Calendar of the Charter Rolls preserved in the Public Record Office*, 6 vols. (London, 1903–27)
CCR	*Calendar of Close Rolls*, 46 vols. (London, 1892–1963)
CIM	*Calendar of Inquisitions Miscellaneous,* (London, 1916–)
CIPM	*Calendar of Inquisitions Post Mortem* (London, 1904–)
COS	Centre for Oxfordshire Studies, Westgate Library, Oxford
CPR	*Calendar of Patent Rolls*, 54 vols. (London, 1891–1916)
CRR	C. T. Flower, D. Crook, and P. Brand (eds.), *Curia Regis Rolls* (London, 1922–)
EcHR	*Economic History Review*
(ed.) / (eds.)	Editor(s). Where this abbreviation precedes the date of a publication in a footnote reference it indicates an edited primary source; where it follows the date it denotes a secondary work.
EETS	Early English Text Society
EHR	*English Historical Review*
EPNS	English Place-Name Society
EYC	W. Farrer and C. T. Clay (eds.), *Early Yorkshire Charters, being a Collection of Documents anterior to the Thirteenth Century*, Yorkshire Archaeological Society Record Series, 12 vols. (Edinburgh, 1914–65)
Hants. RO	Hampshire Record Office
HCCAHBR	Hampshire County Council Archaeology and Historic Buildings Record
HER	Historic Environment Record
HKW	H. M. Colvin *et al.* (eds.), *The History of the King's Works,* 5 vols. (London, 1963–76)

Abbreviations

HMC	Historical Manuscripts Commission
MCO	Magdalen College, Oxford
New DNB	*Oxford Dictionary of National Biography*, 12 vols. (Oxford, 2004)
NMR	National Monuments Record, Swindon
ORO	Oxfordshire Record Office
Peerage	G. E. Cokayne *et al.*, *The Complete Peerage of England, Scotland, Ireland, Great Britain, and the United Kingdom*, 13 vols. (London, 1910–59)
PQW	W. Illingworth (ed.), *Placita de Quo Warranto temporibus Edw. I, II & III* (London, 1818)
RCHM	Royal Commission on Historical Monuments
Rot. Hund.	W. Illingworth and J. Caley (eds.), *Rotuli Hundredorum temp. Hen. III & Edw. I*, 2 vols. (London, 1812 and 1818)
Rot. Parl.	J. Strachey (ed.), *Rotuli Parliamentorum*, 6 vols. (London, 1767–77)
SR	*Statutes of the Realm*, 10 vols. (London, 1810–28)
TNA: PRO	The National Archives: Public Record Office
VCH	*Victoria County History*, various editors and writers (London, 1899–)
YAJ	*Yorkshire Archaeological Journal*

Introduction

In 1570 Herstmonceux park in East Sussex was described as three miles in circumference, a third of it open grassland, the rest 'well set with great timber trees'. Besides Herstmonceux castle in its western corner it contained some two hundred fallow deer, four well-stocked fishponds, a heronry ('Hern wood'), a rabbit warren, and a thatched lodge and (ruined) stable. Two roads led through the park to the church, market, and townships adjacent.[1] This extensive parkland had evolved from a much earlier park, established by the thirteenth century when the manor was the main seat of the Monceux family, who perhaps had a house on the site of the later castle.[2] The earlier park was transformed into something resembling its sixteenth-century successor by Sir Roger Fiennes in the early fifteenth century. Sir Roger shut off a road through the park in 1413 and replaced it by a new route skirting the western and northern perimeter. Then in 1441, two years after being appointed treasurer of the royal household, he obtained licence to extend the parkland by 600 acres and to build the castle, which became the first major brick building in the south-east of England.[3]

Herstmonceux park was just one of many similar enclosures created in medieval England. Over the last fifty years a great deal of research has been devoted to these landscape features, and interest in them appears to be growing rather than diminishing. Recent work has adopted a variety of methodological approaches, used a wide range of historical, archaeological, and landscape evidence and started to engage in more wide-ranging and theoretical analysis.[4] Yet until very recently the study of parks has been something of a historical backwater. Most of the research on the subject has had a local or regional focus, producing specialized studies that have been difficult for those with broader interests to combine into a coherent whole. Individual scholars have started to build larger interpretations based on this detailed work, but these have mainly grown up separately from one another and there have been few general surveys. As long ago as 1979 Leonard Cantor noted what he called the 'considerable scope for an up-to-date and systematic book on medieval parks', which might

---

[1] Parry 1833: 246–9.   [2] *VCH Sussex*, ix. 133–4; Venables 1851: 133–4.
[3] *CPR, 1413–16*, 133; *CChR, 1427–1516*, 13–14; *New DNB* (s.v. James Fiennes); Emery 1996–2006, iii. 343–54.
[4] See e.g. the various contributions in Liddiard 2007 (ed.).

'co-ordinate and relate the growing volume of material that is now available'.[5] Thirty years later, after much new work and increasingly divergent interpretations of many aspects of the subject, no such book has yet been attempted. Consequently, a great deal about the nature and development of parks is still uncertain or disputed and their significance in medieval society is only partially understood.

These circumstances seem to provide an ideal opportunity to present a general study of parks which both returns to first principles and also seeks to understand these institutions in a wider context. This book offers such a study, looking at the parks of kings, nobles, great churchmen, and gentry across the country, in upland and lowland areas alike, from the twelfth century to the early sixteenth.[6] It focuses on what appear to me to be the most important of the many questions which have still to be resolved in this well-established and increasingly lively subject. Namely, when and why did parks first appear? What precisely was their purpose? Did common features outweigh differences between them? Did their function generally stay the same throughout this long period, or did it undergo major change? What was the impact of these numerous enclosures on the crown or on relations amongst the aristocracy? To what extent did the establishment of these private reserves affect local populations? Most of these questions are quite basic ones and have received at least some attention from previous scholars, but for all the research that has been done, current writing is very far from providing clear answers to them. In fact, as will become clear, in some areas there seems to be growing uncertainty and disagreement.

This is not to deny or undervalue the considerable achievements of modern research on parks. Above all, local studies have mapped out scores of medieval parks and set out details of their histories in dozens of articles. The best of them follow W. G. Hoskins's and Maurice Beresford's emphasis on the need to combine documents with map and fieldwork evidence to identify and date features on the ground and understand their context.[7] In so doing they have provided a useful picture of the location of parks in the landscape. At a general level, it has been demonstrated that they were often located in areas of high medieval woodland cover, and were less common where woods were scarce, including in champion districts and on barren moorland.[8] Within particular localities, it has been shown that they tended to be located on higher or more sloping ground near the boundaries of manors, parishes, and townships (at least until land became more available in the later middle ages).[9]

---

[5] Cantor and Hatherly 1979: 84.
[6] Parks existed elsewhere in Britain, Europe, and indeed further afield, but these areas are largely beyond the scope of this survey.
[7] Hoskins 1955: 14; Beresford 1971: 19, 25.
[8] e.g. Rimington 1970: 9; Cantor and Hatherly 1979: 74–6; Cantor 1982: 78–81; 1983; Rackham 1986: 123–5; Neave 1991: 5; 1996: 60–1; Higham 2004: 122–3; Winchester 2007: 165–7.
[9] Rowe 2007: 135 (fig. 49), 143–4; Hoppitt 2007: 162; Moorhouse 2007: 102–6.

This sort of work has also made it possible to suggest something about the chronology of parks and their overall numbers. Cantor's pioneering trawl for evidence of parks in published calendars, antiquarian works, field names, and the *Victoria County History* produced his still highly useful county-by-county gazetteer of medieval parks[10] and enabled him to estimate that there were at least 1,900 parks in existence at one time or another during the middle ages, most, he thought, created in the thirteenth and early fourteenth centuries.[11] A subsequent estimate by Oliver Rackham posits a much larger number of parks: about 3,200 in the early fourteenth century, the period he takes to be the highpoint in their numbers.[12] This higher figure was reached by taking into account further discoveries, separating out individual parks found in close groups, and allowing for the existence of parks that are less well-documented in government records, quite a number of which were missed out by Cantor and other early searchers.[13]

Detailed studies have at the same time usefully illustrated the variety of parks. These fenced-off areas differed greatly in size: a fairly typical extent may have been around one to two hundred acres, but some small parks were under fifty acres and the biggest several thousand.[14] Larger parks were usually owned by kings and nobles, often as part of wider forests or chases, and sometimes as part of a group of parks; smaller, isolated parks tended to be owned by gentry or religious houses. Though these enclosures were above all associated with wood-pasture, some were to be found in other landscapes, including upland moors and heaths, as well as champion belts and coastal areas; the majority were located in the Midlands and south-eastern England, but there were also large numbers in the northern counties and the south-west.[15] Given these differences in size and location, it may not be surprising that lords appear to have used their parks in a number of different ways. Apart from deer herds and lodges for the parkers who supervised them, many parks also housed other game, especially rabbits in artificial warrens, as well as fishponds. In some there is evidence for the cutting of timber and exploitation of fuel wood, in others an apparent focus on the pasturing of cattle or breeding of horses. Certain parks were even partly put under the plough for arable farming.[16] The way individual parks were used often seems to have altered over time, something no doubt related to the fact that many grew or shrank over the course of their existence.[17]

Besides these fundamentals, parks have been set within a wider context of hunting and game-keeping. Particular attention has been paid to the various ways in which hunting was regulated by the crown, and how parks fitted into a

---

[10] Cantor 1983.   [11] Cantor and Hatherly 1979: 71.   [12] Rackham 1980: 191; 1986: 123.
[13] For further discussion about park numbers see below, p. 109.
[14] Cantor and Hatherly 1979: 74.   [15] Cantor 1983.
[16] Stamper 1988: 145–7; Roberts 1988: 74–5.
[17] For an interesting reconstruction of the development of different areas of parkland at Lathom (Lancs.) see Bradley and Gaimster 2004 (eds.): 276.

larger schema of game reserves.[18] Norman and later kings made a special claim to hunting by setting up forest law over large swathes of the country. The establishment of the royal forests secured these rulers an exclusive right to hunt large game, principally deer, in many well-wooded districts, moors, and heaths. The forests, which included settlements and fields as well as woods and wastes, were watched over by a hierarchy of officials and special courts were used to amerce those poaching deer or felling trees within the forest bounds. Rulers sometimes allowed favoured subjects limited hunting opportunities in the forest, but more often they permitted them to establish hunting reserves of their own, albeit apparently under strict royal control.[19] Occasionally they granted forest rights over certain areas to important subjects, typically by the new name of 'chase'.[20] More commonly they gave lords licences to have 'free warren', or exclusive rights to hunt lesser game on their demesne lands outside forest areas.[21] The main beasts of the warren were hares, game birds, foxes, wild cats, badgers, and other small animals,[22] and lords with warren rights could prosecute those hunting these animals on their lands in the royal courts. Sometimes kings also acknowledged lords' rights to make parks in which to keep deer, including on estates which were under forest jurisdiction. Parks differed from forests, chases, and warrens in being fully enclosed, and to enter (or 'break') a park without permission was an act of trespass.

Nonetheless, for all this valuable information, the predominance of local studies and the close interest in the formalities of forest law and niceties of hunting franchises have tended to bring with them a slight narrowness of focus. The emphasis on topography carries on Hoskins's vision of the landscape as an object worthy of serious study, potentially, indeed, the 'richest historical record we possess',[23] but, on its own, it can actually only tell us so much about parks. At the same time, the concentration on individual parks and those of particular counties, allied to the differing interests and approaches of particular scholars, has contributed to the problems in reaching any coherent conclusions about parks as a whole. This applies to many areas but is particularly evident in terms of the crucial question of the function of parks.

At first glance it might seem simple enough to provide an answer to the question of what parks were for: those who created parks wanted somewhere to hunt. This has long been a favoured interpretation, fitting in well with the traditional assumption that medieval kings and lords were obsessively keen hunters who established and maintained forests and chases as hunting grounds.[24]

---

[18] Turner (ed.) 1901: pp. i–cxxxix; Cantor 1982.   [19] Petit-Dutaillis 1930: 149–54.
[20] Ibid. 154.   [21] Turner (ed.) 1901: p. cxxiii; Crook 2001: 36–7.
[22] In practice, deer were sometimes preserved by rights of warren, and the roe deer at least may have been formally recognized as a beast of the warren in the earlier 14th cent.: Turner (ed.) 1901: pp. cxxvii–cxxxii; Roberts 1988: 67; *CChR, 1427–1516*, 8.
[23] Hoskins 1955: 14.
[24] Petit-Dutaillis 1930: 151–4, esp. 154; Warren 1961: 140; Stenton 1965: 100.

Introduction 5

The prime quarry in the forest was the deer and so it would seem logical to suppose that parks full of deer were likewise areas put aside for great men's hunting.[25] However, some time ago Oliver Rackham provided a strong challenge to this view by asserting that the idea of forests and parks acting primarily as hunting grounds is a myth.[26] Others seem to have backed this claim up, not least by pointing out the limited evidence of aristocratic participation in hunting and by raising particular objections to the role of parks as lordly playgrounds because of the relatively confined area of many of these enclosures.[27]

The questioning of older assumptions about parks and forests as lords' hunting grounds has had a mixed impact. Many recent writers continue to stress aristocratic recreational hunting, perhaps unconvinced by the objections, or unaware of them. For them the park remains, quite simply, the 'hunting-park', part and parcel of the elite's shaping of the landscape for the pleasures of the chase, a miniature version of the forest.[28] Some though have felt the need to provide alternative explanations for the purpose of parks, perhaps because of the doubts about hunting, perhaps simply through examination of the other activities that went on in and around them.[29] A number of historians still lay great stress on deer, but in a rather different way, seeing the main purpose of parks as breeding deer to supply luxury fresh meat, to be unceremoniously culled by the lords' officials.[30] The park may thus be seen as a 'deer farm', or at least some kind of storage area and collection point for game, with any real hunting going on in forests and chases outside.[31] In this way park-making was an activity that had much to do with aristocratic tastes, hospitality, and social networking, but little connection with more active leisure pursuits.

Others, though, have focused their attention elsewhere. For instance, it has been claimed that parks were partly a means of preserving and controlling valuable woods and grassland for their economic use, rather than just for hunting.[32] Or, especially among some recent landscape historians, there is an increasing tendency to view parks of all periods as having been an integral part of lords' concern with the appearance of their residences and estates, providing a carefully arranged, in some sense landscaped, backdrop to castles and manor houses.[33] This kind of use of parkland is sometimes suggested as having significant 'aesthetic', decorative functions,[34] but has also been interpreted as part of lords' demonstration of power and sophistication.[35] The latter interpretation draws heavily on an older and frequently repeated idea that parks served a less

---

[25] Shirley 1867: 13, 15; Platt 1978: 47; Saul 1986: 189.
[26] Rackham 1986: 125, 133; 1989: 51.   [27] Below, pp. 15–16.
[28] Crouch 1992: 309–10; Thompson 1998: 152; Emery 1996–2006: ii. 225; Short 2000: 136.
[29] See e.g. Creighton 2002: 190–1.
[30] Rackham 1980: 197; Birrell 1992: 113, 122; Bond 1997: 25; 1998: 24. For an early anticipation of this view see Crawford 1953: 189.
[31] Liddiard 2000b: 51.   [32] Britnell 1977: 109; Hoppitt 1992: i. 278.
[33] For an up-to-date discussion of parks and landscaping see Liddiard 2005: 97–121.
[34] Taylor 2000: 39, 50; Bond 1994: 144.   [35] See e.g. Liddiard 2000a: 182.

tangible, but nonetheless important, role as status-symbols, hand in hand with—or perhaps above and beyond—more functional uses.[36]

To add to this complexity, many writers have drawn a sharp distinction between the purpose of high and later medieval parks, usually taking the Black Death as the watershed. According to this view, the function of parks was transformed in the later middle ages. New parks created in that period little resembled their predecessors and the use made of older parks was likewise changing. A focus on deer-keeping and hunting was increasingly giving way to 'landscaping'—with new parks apparently being established as settings for grand houses more frequently than ever before—and to 'mixed-use', chiefly stock fattening and wood production.[37] This idea of transition seems to chime in with what is often perceived as a general shift in the later middle ages away from militaristic architecture and residences as defensive structures, towards the country house, with a greater concern for decorative gardens and parkland.[38] It may also seem to be supported by the suggestion that in this era of reduced pressure on land and fewer people there were more abundant game supplies, perhaps implying that nurturing and protecting deer was less necessary.[39] The changes in purpose were allegedly signposted by an alteration in the nature of park perimeters, with more impenetrable barriers of ditches and pales on mounds of earth being replaced by simple fences, which, it is argued, could not have so effectively retained deer.[40] Nonetheless, despite its general currency, the idea of a late-medieval shift in the function of parks is as yet unproven and may actually present several problems.

All this leaves us with an interesting but rather disorderly range of suggestions about why these enclosures were set up and how the priority of various factors may have shifted over the course of the middle ages. In the absence of any real consensus, various supposed roles are frequently lumped together, with emphasis on the individual ingredients according to preference or awareness of particular interpretations or local examples. The latest scholarship, far from moving towards any consensus about the function of parks, has actually started to question whether these enclosures really formed a coherent group at all. It was long assumed that the use of the word 'park' (or its Latin or French equivalents) to describe part of a lord's demesne signified a special kind of enclosure for deer.[41] But confidence in this idea is rapidly diminishing. One recent approach has been to suggest that there were different 'types' of lordly parks, including not just deer reserves but also places devoted entirely to wood production or livestock.[42]

---

[36] Below, pp. 101–3.
[37] Cantor and Hatherly 1979: 79; Platt 1978: 47; Rackham 1986: 128–9; Bond 1998: 26; Stamper 1988: 146–7; Hoppitt 1992: i. 91; Bailey 2007: 101.
[38] For a recent exposition of this view see Johnson 2002: 39–40, 44–5.
[39] Almond 2003: 169; Pollard 2004: 89.
[40] Cantor 1964: 61–2; Cantor and Hatherly 1979: 74.
[41] See e.g. Turner (ed.) 1901: p. cxvi n. 1.   [42] Winchester 2007: 166.

Introduction

A slightly different, though related, tendency has been to see parks as fundamentally multi-purpose enclosures, where deer-keeping was just one among a number of uses, and not necessarily the most important.[43] If these kinds of ideas are accepted, the parks owned by kings and aristocrats, or at least many of them, seem to differ more in scale than in substance from the ordinary field or woodland closes which were sometimes also called 'parks' (especially in the west of England).[44] The very identification of parks as a distinctive and meaningful category of enclosure, so long taken for granted, might thus appear to be endangered.

Similarly, there are strongly divergent interpretations of the chronology of park-making, another central issue, with several different views about when parks were introduced and when they started to decline. Whatever their ultimate Roman or Arab roots, parks have traditionally been claimed as a Norman innovation in England, and late Anglo-Saxon references that might imply parks have been played down.[45] The main growth in park numbers is usually thought to have occurred a considerable time after the Conquest, but there is uncertainty about exactly when. Some see the twelfth century as the likely period when park-making really started to take off on a large scale,[46] but others focus much more on the thirteenth and early fourteenth century.[47] More recently, however, it has been argued that parks were widespread in late Anglo-Saxon society and may have had their origins there.[48] The later chronology of parks is likewise rather unclear. Park creation and maintenance is generally thought to have been in decline after the Black Death, but even this has not been fully established. Many have claimed that there were very large falls in park numbers after 1350,[49] suggesting that the rising cost of wages and decline in tenant labour services may have made it too expensive to maintain existing parks or to create new ones,[50] or that worsening climatic conditions and disease badly affected deer stocks.[51] But others have given a more positive view of the level of later medieval park-making,[52] sometimes arguing that economic conditions could be favourable to imparking in this period.[53]

However, just as significant as disagreements over the function of parks or their chronology is the fact that the wider importance of the subject has seldom been adequately conveyed. A good deal of work is still required to show that

---

[43] Liddiard 2007 (ed.): 1. See also Muir 2006: 128.
[44] Cuhn 1981 (ed.): 627–8; Latham 1965 (ed.): 332; Rothwell *et al.* 1992 (eds.): 496; Field 1993: 25–6; Adams 1976: 125; Hoskins 1955: 143, 146; Lock (ed.) 1998, 2002: ii. 340; Shirley 1867: 14 n. 1; *VCH Oxon.*, x. 50; *CPR, 1345–8*, 73.
[45] Cantor and Hatherly 1979: 71; Rackham 1986: 122–3; Rowley 1997: 130. Cf. Shirley 1867: 3–4, which ventures less firm conclusions.
[46] Rackham 1986: 123; Hoppitt 1992: i. 76.
[47] Cantor and Hatherly 1979: 73; Dyer 1994: 20. [48] Liddiard 2003: 4.
[49] Cantor 1970–1: 12; Platt 1978: 46–7; Rowley 1986: 135; Squires and Humphrey 1986: 9; Taylor 1998: 19; Hoppitt 1999: 66; Emery 1996–2006: ii. 226.
[50] Cantor and Hatherly 1979: 79. [51] Hoppitt 1992: i. 82–3.
[52] e.g. Bond 1994: 134; Stamper 1988: 146.
[53] Beresford 1971: 207; Britnell 2004: 41; Cantor and Hatherly 1979: 79; Hoppitt 1992: i. 86.

park-making, besides being a significant social practice in itself, could cast light on other better-studied aspects of the development of medieval society. For instance, although it has long been claimed that these big and costly enclosures were 'status-symbols', this is an idea which has seldom been tested or developed further.[54] In fact, if it is accepted that parks really were a central part of the package of gracious living, essential to the lifestyle and image of an aristocrat, their creation and use ought to be closely related to lords' interests and sense of identity and, therefore, to questions of social standing and authority. Particular episodes in the history of individual parks certainly suggest that contemporaries closely identified these enclosures with power and lordship. At Herstmonceux in 1243, for instance, servants of the countess of Eu apparently attempted to assert her overlordship of the manor against a rival claimant on the death of the lord, William de Monceux, by hunting deer in the park.[55] A generation later, Henry III and his army took revenge on Waleran de Monceux (William's son) for supporting the rebellious Simon de Montfort by wrecking the same park and killing the deer.[56]

In an insightful couple of paragraphs, David Crouch has suggested that knights created parks as part of their self-conscious assertion of aristocratic credentials in the later twelfth and thirteenth century, providing them with places to hunt in emulation of greater lords in their wide forests.[57] He sees this as part of the same process of 'social diffusion' illustrated by their adoption of heraldic devices and improvement of their residences in the same period.[58] Viewed in this way, parks may offer a new approach to analysing the definition and assertion of status within the aristocracy, one that has a wide applicability, relevant to the whole of the middle ages. In other words, if parks really were status-symbols, and given that status competition has been suggested in other areas, should they not form part of the historiography on aristocratic competition? If parks moved down the social scale, as has been suggested, what was the effect of this? Did poaching become a sublimated form of private warfare? Should some alleged aristocratic attacks on or misuses of parks be interpreted in this way? How far were park-makers attempting to affirm, or indeed assert, pre-eminence by managing the use of space? And how far did this involve manipulating the wider setting and appearance of major residences through surrounding parkland?[59] As well as adding significance to the spatial relationship between parks and residences, this last question raises further problems about how status and, indeed, how parks themselves were understood. How important, for instance, were they in projecting a visual image compared to gardens? A clearer perspective is evidently required on parks' role in elite leisure, culture, and social competition.

[54] Cf. Birrell 1992: 126.   [55] *CRR, 1242–3*, 422–3.   [56] Venables 1851: 134.
[57] Crouch 1992: 309–10.
[58] See also Coss 2003: 34–8 on the wider emulation of the attributes of nobility over the course of the 12th cent.
[59] Cf. Johnson 2002: ch. 3, esp. pp. 48–52.

Equally importantly, the extent to which parks affected men and women of different classes has received only very limited attention from a literature where comments on the social effects of imparking on the wider community have tended to be scattered and brief.[60] This is partly because of the focus of many older studies on forests and the royal licensing of parks, which can make it seem that park creation was purely of concern to the crown. Some recent work has begun to develop a more nuanced and sophisticated approach, particularly by exploring the meanings which contemporaries from various social groups may have vested in parks and the hunting and other activities that went on within their bounds.[61] As we shall see, lords and their servants seem to have wished to impress ordinary people with their parks and hunting exploits, and they necessarily involved a few of them in their hunts. But quite how lesser folk typically looked upon reserves which so often interfered with their traditional land uses is uncertain.

A number of areas need to be addressed if we are to better appreciate the impact of parks on wider communities. Among these is the extent to which parks represented an affront to traditional peasant hunting activity, since hunting was actually practised at all social levels. In other words, did park-making bring an end to the activities of lesser local huntsmen or did they manage to carry on with their hunting and trapping more or less unmolested, in the park or elsewhere? This issue may be illuminated by examining the motivation of the lesser individuals who often took part in poaching raids on parks. But besides hunting, there is the important question of how far parks affected the use of land for other activities. After all, these enclosures were very widespread, if unevenly distributed, and in the most densely imparked counties they were created in as many as one parish in three.[62] Despite this, their agricultural impact has usually been neglected by general surveys of medieval farming.[63] Where wider agrarian issues have been touched upon, the significance of parks has been downplayed, and the focus has generally been on how the control of resources may have been important to lords making parks, rather than on the effects of park-making on local inhabitants. As one recent writer has put it, medieval parks are 'very much under-researched as an aspect of enclosure' and their 'effect on local economies and populations is still largely unknown'.[64] To progress beyond this limited understanding, parks clearly have to be more closely fitted into an analysis of the wider enclosure movements of the middle ages: in other words, all those changes in farming practices and rural life

---

[60] Manning 1993: 116; Beresford 1971: 192–5, 204–6; Hoskins and Stamp 1963: 37–8; Franklin 1989: 149, 165; Neave 1991: 11–13; Crook 1976: 35–6. Way 1997 is more substantial, but geographical rather than historical in methodology; reviewed by Stamper 1998.
[61] Marvin 1999; Johnson 2002; Herring 2003; Liddiard 2005.
[62] Cantor and Hatherly 1979: 74–5 (esp. fig. 1); Rowe 2007: 144.
[63] See e.g. Hallam 1988a (ed.); Miller 1991 (ed.), apart from e.g. 80–1, 118–19; Thirsk 2000 (ed.), except Dyer, 110, and Short, 136–7. Campbell 2000 considers the distribution of wood-pasture (94–101), but provides no specific discussion of parks.
[64] Hollowell 2000: 1.

associated with the growth of population, spread of arable farming and intensification of land use in the twelfth and thirteenth century, and the different types of enclosure which accompanied the radically changed economic climate of the late middle ages.[65]

It should be clear, then, that many significant and interesting questions about parks are open for debate. In attempting to provide answers to these questions this book contends that parks, for all their variety, can be understood as a special and distinctive kind of land use. Ultimately, perhaps, a general study is needed to counteract the inherent shortcomings of the pursuit of the individual park through local studies, which, like the search for the individual baron, puts us 'in danger of losing our sense of the class as a whole'.[66] Some will no doubt disagree with the conclusions presented here, a few perhaps even with the idea that general conclusions of any kind can be reached, but the aim of the book is to stimulate further debate and provide it with some focus rather than to claim definitive solutions.

A broad chronological spread has been adopted to provide a longer view of supposed key periods of transition, such as the Black Death of the mid-fourteenth century. The particular start and end points have been selected for a variety of reasons. The choice about where to start presents some difficulties, as the earlier discussion of origins might suggest.[67] But the twelfth century has been selected as the main departure point based on the belief that it marked the real beginnings of medieval park-making, distinct in character and scale from related activities that had come before.[68] The conclusion of the study in the early sixteenth century is based mainly on the view that the social changes taking place in the second quarter of the sixteenth century significantly affected the purpose and function of parkland. In any case, there are already a number of studies of the evolution of hunting and parks in the sixteenth and seventeenth centuries, and a vast literature on the landscape parks of the eighteenth century.[69] The 'post-history' of the medieval park can safely be left to others.

The rest of the book is divided into two parts. Part I comprises four chapters (Chapters 1 to 4), each looking at different aspects of the function of parks and their social meaning. The overall aim of this section is to suggest an answer to the fundamental question of why parks were created and maintained. Chapter 1 looks at the place of hunting in aristocratic social life and how far it motivated park-making; it is here that the continued survival of parks in the later middle ages is closely addressed. Chapter 2 examines the evidence for the economic exploitation of parks and provides an assessment of its significance. Chapter 3 explores the extent to which parks were laid out or landscaped to provide a contrived stage for aristocratic living. Chapter 4 deals with the important issue

---

[65] Cf. Miller and Hatcher 1978: 33–41; Birrell 1987; Dyer 2006.
[66] Carpenter 1992: 6.   [67] Above, p. 7.   [68] Below, pp. 134–6.
[69] See e.g. the following and the further works cited therein: Shirley 1867: 27–51; Prince 1967; Hyams 1971; Lasdun 1991; Manning 1993; Bond 1998; Williamson 1998 and 2000.

of how far parks were created as status-symbols, looking at the particular social circumstances of various park-makers and how these may have affected their decision to impark.

Part II approaches parks from the other direction, looking at the effects that they had on society as a whole, both on the king at the centre and on individuals and communities in the localities. It starts, in Chapter 5, with an investigation of how and to what extent parks affected the crown and what the royal response was. This chapter provides a discussion of the early chronology of park-making as part of an analysis of the supposed royal stringency over park creation. The subject of Chapter 6 is the impact of park-making on the aristocracy, on their leisure, jurisdiction, self-perception, and estate economy. Chapter 7 looks at the effects of parks on wider society. A short conclusion follows.

I
The Purpose of the Park

1

Hunting

...a good hunters horn shuld be dryve of ii span of lengthe, and nought moche more ne moch lasse; and nought to crokyng neither to straught...

(Practical advice for the aristocratic huntsman: Edward, duke of York, *The Master of Game*, c.1406–13)[1]

General histories of the middle ages have long suggested that hunting was an important part of royal and aristocratic leisure and hospitality,[2] and a tradition of specialist studies continues to develop, increasingly turning to more speculative examinations of the link between hunting and the construction of group identities and social hierarchies.[3] But, for all the interest in the subject, it remains difficult to fully understand the place of hunting in medieval society. Arguments which assume the importance of hunting to the aristocracy often rely a good deal on literary and artistic representations, which are mainly French and later medieval. Historical and material evidence has generally proved to be more diffuse and less malleable, with much more information available about the preservation of game animals and creation of regulations controlling hunting than about actual lordly participation.[4] Given this background, it is perhaps not surprising that the significance of hunting as an elite pastime in the middle ages has been questioned.[5] Oliver Rackham has proposed, for instance, that most medieval kings were too busy to hunt very often, that 'a royal hunt was an occasion of symbolic significance, like a coronation, and about as rare',[6] and the idea of hunting as an aristocratic recreation has been questioned in a similar way.[7] In fact, there seems to be much more evidence

---

[1] Baillie-Grohman and Baillie-Grohman (eds.) 1904: 72. See Cummins 1988: 160–71 and Fig. 1, below.
[2] Bartlett 2000: 238–41 and Harriss 2005: 116 are good recent examples. See also Steane 1993: 146–55 and sources cited above, Introduction, nn. 24–5.
[3] Savage 1933; Thiébaux 1967; Barlow 1983*a*; Cummins 1988; Hanawalt 1988; Orme 1992; Birrell 1994; Marvin 1999; Almond and Pollard 2001; Almond 2003: 167–71; Harvey 2004; Pluskowski 2007; Sykes 2005*b*, 2007*a*.
[4] Hatcher 1970: 184; Roberts 1988: 70; Pollard 1990: 199–200; Birrell 1992: 113; 1994: 37–9; Franklin 1989: 156–7; Cantor and Wilson 1968: 241. One writer resorts to asserting that the popularity of hunting is 'well nigh self-evident': Gilbert 1979: 72.
[5] Above, p. 5.
[6] Rackham 1986: 133. This view is stridently repeated in Rackham 2002: 22.   [7] Hunt 1997: 110.

Fig. 1. A medieval hunting horn.
Source: Bodleian, MS Douce, 335, f. 47.
Reproduced with permission.

of servants hunting for their lords than of these men engaging in the activity themselves. What is more, on top of these general doubts about the importance of hunting to the aristocracy, there may be more specific difficulties relating to parks in terms of their suitability as hunting grounds, particularly in accommodating lengthy chases on horseback.[8] Perhaps then we have to concur that although parks 'could be the scene of hunts... a confined space full of trees offers little scope for a good hunt', and that it is 'an error to call parks "hunting preserves"'.[9] For all these reasons there might appear to be some justice in claims that hunting was far less important to royal and aristocratic lifestyles than usually assumed.

This chapter is not the place for a full account of the practice and significance of medieval hunting, but some re-examination of its popularity as an elite pastime is clearly in order since it lies at the heart of the question of what parks were for. It may therefore be useful to start off by reconstructing a general picture of the importance of hunting to the medieval aristocracy, before looking more specifically at the role of parks.

THE IMPORTANCE OF HUNTING

It ought to be said straightaway that it is quite wrong to think that the fairly limited number of direct documentary references to aristocratic hunting indicates that it was an uncommon activity among this class. Instead, the many gaps in the evidence should prompt us to think carefully about what particular

---

[8] Cantor and Wilson 1963: 142; 1968: 241; Drury 1976: 141; Rackham 1986: 125; Neave 1991: 8; Richardson 2005: 28; Sykes 2007a: 50–1.

[9] Rackham 1986: 125.

sources can and cannot tell us about hunting by different groups and, above all, to look at a wider range of material. Many records that might have most clearly indicated lordly hunting activity have been lost, including the great majority of household accounts.[10] Those that do survive have not been studied systematically for evidence of hunting, but even so it seems that the costs of hunting and hawking accounted for a consistent and far from negligible part of kings' and lords' personal expenses.[11] On the other hand, it is hardly surprising that some other sources which exist in greater bulk do not show much of relevance since lords did not usually need to record their actual hunting forays. Manorial accounts, for instance, only very seldom reveal anything directly about lords' pastimes, whether in hunting or anything else. Likewise, to try to find evidence of royal hunting in forest records, as Rackham seems to have done, is fairly futile since these documents were far more concerned with unauthorized hunting by subjects.[12]

In fact, when a variety of sources are examined, and the insights from documentary, landscape, and literary evidence are combined, the position of the doubters becomes completely untenable. Hunting emerges as a prominent common interest among the English aristocracy, as long assumed, if not fully demonstrated, and notwithstanding attempts at revisionism. A careful consideration of the evidence suggests that many lords participated on a regular basis, and this is apparent in a number of ways. First, we can readily establish the dominance of hunting in aristocratic culture and its presence in the artefacts purchased by kings and lords. This alone makes it seem highly likely that they would have wanted to recreate the world of the hunt in the territory available to them. Beyond this, there is evidence that more directly confirms hunting as an important and often frequent activity for many kings, lords, and gentry. Indeed, it may have played a more significant role than usually allowed even by its apologists.

Hunting deeply permeated aristocratic culture, and this is reflected by its prominent place in medieval literature and visual arts, as well as in aristocrats' actual language and behaviour. A number of contemporary literary works were devoted entirely to hunting. At least four manuals on the subject were produced in medieval England, mainly adapted from French models, and more may have existed.[13] A French huntsman of Edward II (William Twiti) compiled one in the early fourteenth century and three more were written in the fifteenth century, including the *Master of Game*, composed by Edward, duke of York, Henry IV's master of hart-hounds, for the young Prince Henry, later Henry V. The popularity of these works is difficult to assess, since we have very inadequate sources for judging which books and manuscripts were actually owned by aristocrats, let

[10] Woolgar (ed.) 1992–3: i. 5–6; Dyer 1989: 49–50.
[11] Given-Wilson 1986: 14, 61; Dyer 1989: 75; Botfield (ed.) 1841: 277–80.
[12] Rackham 1976: 154. On the focus of forest records see Young 1979: 97.
[13] Rooney 1993: 7–11.

alone read by them.[14] But there are indications that hunting treatises were popular, particularly in the later middle ages,[15] including the fact that in 1421 Henry V paid for twelve books on hunting, perhaps for distribution among his courtiers.[16]

But far from being a narrow, specialist topic, hunting was a regular theme in a wide range of medieval writing. Besides the dedicated manuals, many other more general literary works contained extended hunting-related passages, usually featuring aristocrats and their servants. Hunting was a major theme in romance literature, a genre extremely popular with the aristocracy.[17] The activity featured particularly prominently in the hugely popular twelfth-century *Tristan* story, reproduced throughout the middle ages.[18] Hunting was important too in a number of fourteenth-century English works, such as the anonymous northern poem *Sir Gawain and the Green Knight*, *The Parlement of Three Ages*, and Chaucer's *Book of the Duchess*.[19] Many other texts referred to the subject in passing or made use of hunting allusions.[20] Apart from being part of a good story or being used to teach some moral or theological lesson, medieval writers often recommended hunting as a practical preparation for war, inculcating tracking skills, hardiness, the use of bows and swords, and horsemanship.[21] Participation was seen to be an important part of the education of young noblemen, as military training but also as an essential part of the manners of an aristocrat, with its most ardent literary apologists urging moral as well as physical benefits.[22]

From the Bayeux Tapestry onwards, hunting also pervaded medieval art, showing how far kings and aristocrats—always among the major patrons—were steeped in the imagery of the chase. In 1256, for instance, Henry III commissioned a painting for his washroom in Westminster Palace showing a king being rescued by his faithful hounds from the plots of his own men, perhaps showing his fear of some of the barons and trust in his Poitevin friends (the loyal hounds).[23] Later medieval secular artworks, particularly ever-popular Continental tapestries, contain abundant depictions of hunting aristocrats,[24] and greyhounds and game animals were notably popular heraldic devices among English royalty and nobility.[25] A great deal of art was, of course, commissioned for religious purposes, and hunting symbols were prevalent here too. Deer, game animals, and hunting scenes

---

[14] Scattergood 1983: 29–30, 35–6; Carpenter 1992: 205; Pollard 1990: 199.
[15] Hands (ed.) 1975: pp. xiii, xvii, xxi, xxxii–xliv.
[16] Rooney 1993: 7 n. 1; Alexander 1983: 158.   [17] Scattergood 1983: 36.
[18] Fedrick (ed.) 1970. The Tristan story was a favourite of Richard III's: Sutton and Visser-Fuchs 1997: 90.
[19] Barron (ed.) 1998: 91 ff.; Offord (ed.) 1959; Benson (ed.) 1987: 334–5.
[20] Orme 1992: 142–7; Rooney 1993: 6.
[21] Cummins 1988: 3–4 and n. 15; Sutton and Visser-Fuchs 1997: 89. See also Gilbert 1979: 72.
[22] Thiébaux 1967: 260–1.   [23] Clanchy 1998: 162.
[24] Cummins 1988: plates between 150 and 151; McKendrick 1995: 49; Marks and Williamson 2003 (eds.): 290; Wingfield Digby 1971: 43–55; *Eighth Report of the Royal Commission on Historical Manuscripts*, appendix, part 1 (1881, reissued 1909), 628b; Stansfield 1987: appendix 2, pp. 317–18. Cf. Syson and Gordon 2001: 75–85, 156–89.
[25] London 1959: 139, 146–7, plates and appendices; Roberts 1997: 116–17; Brooke-Little 1970 (ed.): 69–70; Marks and Williamson 2003 (eds.): 204–5; Gwynn-Jones 1988: 89.

Fig. 2. Detail of the fifteenth-century mural in Canterbury Cathedral depicting a suitably aristocratic-looking St Eustace and his vision of Christ crucified between the antlers of a hunted stag.

Source: photo by author.

Fig. 3. Lothbrok, king of the Danes, hawking by the river and hunting with a dog in a park. From the *Lives of Saints Edmund and Fremund*, presentation copy to Henry VI.

Source: BL, Harley MS 2278, f. 43v. © British Library Board. All rights reserved.

were popular images on floor tiles in abbeys and churches;[26] they appeared in wall-paintings, like the beautiful fifteenth-century mural in Canterbury Cathedral (see Fig. 2); and they featured in objects and places associated with lords' most private devotions, including books of hours, portable altars, and chapels (see Fig. 3).[27]

By the later middle ages hunting had become part of the language and ritual of high politics. The pageantry for Henry VI's coronation in Paris involved setting up a 'forest' in the street, where a stag was hunted by horsemen and hounds to the feet of the young king's horse, so that he could graciously spare its life.[28] Much of the communication between Edward IV and Louis XI of France during the tense period in the lead-up to Edward's invasion in 1475 centred around the imagery of wild and fantasy creatures and their chivalric connotations. Edward responded to an insulting gift of animals from Louis by declaring his intention to 'hunte throughe the parties of Fraunce' with his nobles (loosely represented by their heraldic beasts) and let loose his 'howndes', asserting that he was 'mastir of the game'.[29] During the celebrations for the coronation of Henry VIII and Catherine of Aragon at Westminster in 1509, eight bramble-clad knights presided over a group of men dressed as foresters or park-keepers, all in green clothes and complete with horns, who arranged a 'pagente like a park', with artificial trees, undergrowth, and fallow deer. The unfortunate deer were released from the enclosure and chased down by greyhounds in the palace grounds, their bodies presented to the queen and ladies.[30]

To some extent, the prominence of hunting in all these areas was related to its use as a vehicle for narrative or tool for allegory and is not necessarily to be taken as a literal reflection of lords' love of the chase. The hunt allowed the fictional hero to be drawn into the wild to experience danger and adventure; the skill of the hunter, the qualities of his quarry, and the travails of the chase could be used to explore a range of ideas, from religious conversion or the sufferings of Christ to courtly love and sexual fulfilment.[31] But it is hard to avoid the conclusion that the reason hunting was so much used was precisely because the landed elite *were* directly involved in it. After all, kings and lords often had much time to fill: only so many hours could be spent at business, prayer, or table.[32] Individual preferences and physical capabilities might vary, but there were fairly limited options for leisure, and hunting had all sorts of attractions.

Most simply, hunting was an outlet for atavistic violence: the desire to catch, to control, and to kill. But there was also pleasure in the sociable potential of the hunt. Hunting provided fertile opportunities for the lord of a great household to engage in an activity that involved his fellows and followers in a common

---

[26] Eames 1980: i. 224, ii, designs 1899–1935; Eames 1985: 16, 44, 46–7, 54, 119, 134, 141; Wight 1975: 22 (fig. 21), 44 (fig. 53), 109.
[27] Warner (ed.) 1912: 29, 131, 187–91, 201, 204, 210 (Queen Mary's Psalter); Pluskowski 2007: 71 (Macclesfield Psalter); Roberts 1997: 117 and n. 57; *HKW* ii. 1007–9; Wylie 1968: i. 214 n. 6.
[28] Wolffe 2001: 61.   [29] Kekewich *et al.* (eds.) 1995: 69, 266.
[30] Ellis (ed.) 1809: 512.   [31] Cummins 1988: ch. 4.   [32] Keen 1995: 308 ff.

enterprise, sometimes in intimate groups, sometimes *en masse*. It combined well with other outdoor activities, and it might be concluded with a feast. The organization and structuring of the hunt reflected the aristocratic participants' wealth and social pre-eminence, and the distribution and consumption of the spoils would have allowed them to display largesse and hospitality.[33] Just as importantly, hunting was greeted with general approval and acceptance among the secular elite: Theodore of Antioch went as far as to suggest that it was the only amusement appropriate for kings.[34] The moral criticisms of some churchmen and (later) humanists simply suggest the prevalence of hunting—among clerics as much as laymen—and were resisted, or simply ignored.[35]

Few other leisure activities seem to have had the same potential or to have met with similar approbation. Tournaments and jousting were popular but participation on a suitably grand scale required even more time and money; and in earlier periods rulers were suspicious of tournaments as a potential cover for rebellion.[36] Gambling, often combined with chess or other board games, and, of course, drinking were popular, but tended to be associated with lewdness, violence, and impropriety.[37] Interests in books, literary recitation, and courtly love could demonstrate cultural accomplishments, but these were held in rather variable esteem. As John of Salisbury scathingly put it in the twelfth century, 'in our days, the scholarship of the aristocracy consists in hunting jargon'.[38]

ROYAL HUNTING

Across western Europe, kings and their relatives and courtiers often led the way among hunting enthusiasts.[39] According to the medieval chroniclers, England was no exception to this: William I, William Rufus (killed while hunting), Henry I (nicknamed 'stag-foot'), Henry II, John, Edward I, Edward III, and Edward IV were all devotees of the chase, and other kings are recorded as taking part on particular occasions.[40] Of course, the chroniclers were often critical of these kings, and were not above using hunting as an example of how, as they saw it, rulers neglected the serious business of government. But it would be absurd to dismiss this very strong contemporary association between kings and hunting as sheer rhetorical construct. In any case, other evidence points to the same conclusion, that kings really did hunt frequently.

[33] See Ch. 4, below.
[34] Cummins 1988: 5. Cf. Trigg (ed.) 1990: 13–14, ll. 402–6, and Orme 1992: 143.
[35] Pollard 1990: 207; Orme 1992: 142–7; Mertes 1994: 55.
[36] Crouch 2005; Vale 2001: 184–200.
[37] Vale 2001: 170–9; Steane 2001: 271–2; Huchard *et al.*, n.pl., n.d., 120–1.
[38] Bartlett 2000: 239.   [39] Vale 2001: 179–84, esp. 182; Cummins 1988: 1–2.
[40] Whitelock (ed.) 1961: 165; Barlow 1983*b*: 22–3, 119; Hollister 1985: 131; Wright (ed.) 1839: 4; 1863: 250; James *et al.* (eds.) 1983: 477; Prestwich 1988: 115; Riley (ed.) 1863–4: i. 328; Luce and Raynaud (eds.) 1869–99: v. 225; Giles (ed.) 1845: 146 n. 3.

A love of hunting seems to have been inculcated early on, as the educationalists recommended, and active participation was regarded as an important rite of passage for young princes.[41] The considerable efforts kings made to obtain hunting equipment and maintain large hunting staffs suggest that the passion for the chase often continued into adulthood.[42] Hunting-related services and the supplying of hawks, bows, hunting arrows, and other similar items were made part of the feudal dues of certain tenants-in-chief;[43] some kings, like Richard II, paid for expensive and personalized hunting knives and horns,[44] and perhaps even had arrow heads decorated for visual effect.[45] That many rulers regularly used this equipment and their hunt servants to aid them in their own sport, as well as to send them off to cull meat for the table, seems almost certain. Their inseparability from the pleasures of the chase is implied by the fact that they might take their huntsmen, hunting dogs, and hawks with them even when they went off to war, sometimes, like King John, going so far as to have wild animals sent overseas to ensure a supply of quarry when they arrived.[46] But their attachment to hunting is just as clearly suggested by their more regular itineraries.

Medieval English kings lived much of their lives in places designed for hunting. Like their Anglo-Saxon forebears, the Norman and later kings built the great majority of their residences in rural settings, close to the woods and wastes which formed the core of the royal forests and away from the major road networks (see Fig. 4).[47] Their locations might have been partly determined by high land or otherwise defensible terrain, but this would not explain why kings went to them so often.[48] Apart from the solace of relative isolation, the major attraction of these places must have been hunting, especially at the less elaborate houses. Many of the smaller royal homes, often occupied on a day-to-day basis by foresters or parkers, can best be interpreted as hunting lodges, and even the great palaces, like Clarendon (Wilts.), seem to have developed out of such buildings.[49] The early royal interest in securing space to set up these hunting bases is reflected in William I's reversal of the Confessor's earlier grant of the manor of Old Windsor (Berks.) to Westminster Abbey, which was said to have been partly motivated by the 'nearby water and wood which was suitable for hunting'.[50]

---

[41] Orme 1984: 192–3.
[42] Crouch 1992: 306–7; Roberts 1997: 112–13; Topham (ed.) 1787: 304–9; Byerly and Byerly (eds.) 1986: 319–40; Given-Wilson 1986: 61–2; Myers (ed.) 1959: 113; CPR, 1485–94, 124; TNA: PRO, E101/586/30, 33.
[43] See e.g. CIPM i. 431, ii. 704–5 (index entries); Beresford 1971: 194.   [44] Steane 1993: 147.
[45] James 1990: 9 (fig. 1).   [46] Warren 1961: 95, 140; Chalmers 1936: 188.
[47] HKW i. 42–8, 81–5; Creighton 2002: 185–7.
[48] For an indication of the frequency of visits see Green 2006: 299; Warren 1961: 136 and n. 1; Prestwich 1988: 164; Safford (ed.) 1974–7; Hallam (ed.) 1984.
[49] On Clarendon see HKW ii. 910–18 and Bartlett 2000: 138. For other examples of royal hunting lodges see HKW i. 82–4 and the many entries listed in the index of HKW ii, s.v. 'lodges, hunting'; Roberts 1995: 98–103.
[50] Bates (ed.) 1998: 870 (no. 290), 873–5. The document recording this transfer is a 12th-cent. fabrication, but it is based on material written in William's reign and shortly after.

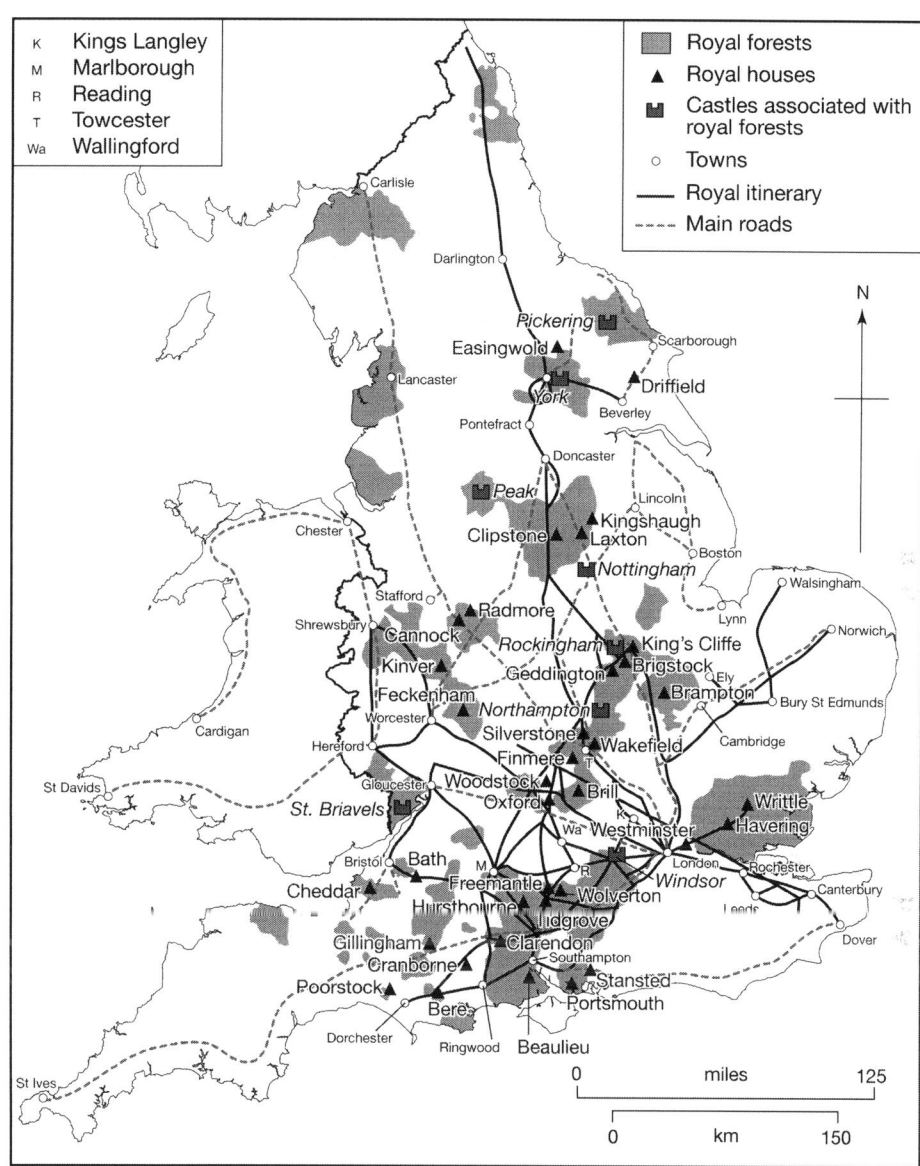

Fig. 4. A simplified royal itinerary, 1199–1307, showing frequent visits to castles and houses in the royal forests. The residences depicted are those existing 1154–1216; the main roads are taken from the Gough Map of *c*.1360.

Sources: *HKW* i. 85; Saul 1994 (ed.): 156.

The same kingly preference for hunting retreats is evident in the later middle ages, although by this time the royal itinerary was even more focused on London, the Thames Valley, and the south-east than earlier. Edward III, for example, spent much of his time in southern lodges and country houses and when he went as far afield as the Midlands and the west his excursions often seem to have been hunting trips, as in August 1375 when he arranged a visit to Rutland forest 'for sport there in the present hunting season'.[51] Richard II's summers were planned around stays at houses and park lodges in Windsor forest and at Woodstock (Oxon.), Easthampstead (Berks.), and Henley-on-the-Heath (Surrey); he spent over £450 on work based around improving the lodges his father had set up in the New Forest (Hants.) in 1387–90 and £1,164 on the old manor house in Windsor park in 1394–6.[52] Fifteenth-century kings likewise favoured rural retreats, well-served with parks and forests, especially Eltham (Kent), Windsor, and Sheen (Surrey), but also Havering (Essex), King's Langley (Herts.), Berkhamsted (Herts.), Henley-on-the-Heath, Easthampstead, and Woodstock.[53]

The evidence suggests that royal participation in hunting at these places and elsewhere would have occurred more or less all year round. The summer was a particularly important time for deer hunting, with the male deer, the favoured prey, at their fittest and fattest from around mid-June until September, the 'time of grease'.[54] This is reflected in recorded royal involvement, which tended to be greatest in these months, especially after the fawning time (or 'fence month') around Midsummer, when the female deer and their young required special protection.[55] But hunting seasons were flexible and varied according to local custom and some quarry was always available.[56] Female deer could be hunted during the close season for stags and bucks, roughly from mid-September to early February, and other game species at different times of the year.[57] In any case it seems unlikely that kings would necessarily feel too much bound to stick to formalities. Certainly they hunted in the spring and winter too. King John and his queen spent much of March and April 1207 moving between various lodges and forests in central and south-western England, closely followed by the king's chief forest justice and master of hounds, Hugh de Neville, and his pack.[58] Edward III's winter itinerary was also shaped by visits to hunting seats, as in January and early February 1367.[59]

---

[51] *CCR, 1374–7*, 154.   [52] Saul 1997: 449 n. 70; *HKW* ii. 986 and 1008.
[53] Harriss 2003: 14–15; Wolffe 2001: 361–71 (royal itinerary, 1436–61); Kleineke 2009: 180.
[54] Baillie-Grohman and Baillie-Grohman (eds.) 1904: 188–9; Cummins 1988: 33.
[55] McDonnell 1992: 115; Ormrod 1990: 57–8; Saul 1997: 449; Hector and Harvey (eds.) 1982: 342; Chalmers 1936: 192; Baillie-Grohman and Baillie-Grohman (eds.) 1904: 137.
[56] Tilander (ed.) 1956: 50.
[57] Baillie-Grohman and Baillie-Grohman (eds.) 1904: 3, 189; Richardson 2005: 26; Cummins 1988: 56; Cox 1905: 50–2.
[58] Woolgar (ed.) 1992–3: i. 114–16.   [59] Tout 1920–33: iv. 180–1.

ARISTOCRATIC HUNTERS

The great enthusiasm for venery spread far beyond a narrow court circle: many of the nobility and gentry were keen hunters too, despite formal royal restrictions over hunting in many forest areas. Their activities are often less well recorded than those of their rulers, especially before the thirteenth century, but aristocratic enjoyment of hunting has left its traces even in the poorly documented period after the Conquest. Domesday occasionally refers to lordly hunting activity,[60] and in the twelfth century, greater and lesser lords alike seem to have been keen hunters.[61] Great churchmen, often individuals from aristocratic families, hunted too, despite the church's official disapproval, and they were the most frequent recipients (or at least preservers) of early royal charters conceding hunting rights.[62] Bishop Hugh du Puiset of Durham (1153–95), for example, was an avid hunter and the complex arrangements for his hunts are shown in the *Boldon Book* (1183), which lists his tenants' hunting-related obligations and services.[63]

The growth of evidence from the thirteenth century onwards makes it readily apparent that hunting was a frequent occupation for many lords.[64] By this time it is clear that important landholders had subinfeudated manors in return for hunting equipment, like Shirburn (Oxon.), held of the honor of St Valery in exchange for three barbed arrows (the kind used for hunting) and an unstrung bow rendered every year.[65] Bows, horns, dogs, hawks, and other hunting items were common objects in aristocratic as much as royal purchases and gift-giving, and lords seem to have taken great pleasure in the accoutrements of the hunt, buying fine silk collars for their greyhounds and providing their dogs with sophisticated kennels.[66] In 1304–5, for instance, Henry de Lacy, earl of Lincoln, purchased a green tent and robe for hunting trips.[67] Ninety years later Roger Mortimer, earl of March, bought green hunting gowns for himself, his brother Thomas and a group of the king's chamber knights, also buying a new bow, bow strings, arrows, and gilding for his freshly sharpened hunting knife.[68] Later medieval bishops, abbots, priors, and monks likewise continued the interest in the chase shown by their predecessors;[69] Bishop Anthony Bek of Durham (1283–1311) was just as keen a huntsman as Hugh du Puiset.[70]

---

[60] Darby 1977: 202.   [61] Crouch 1992: 305–8; Bartlett 2000: 238–41.
[62] Bates (ed.) 1998: e.g. nos. 20, 76, 343; Johnson and Cronne (eds.) 1956: nos. 629, 709, 774 ff.
[63] *VCH Durham*, i. 259–341, 327–41, 327, 329, 331, 333, 334, 335, 337, 338.
[64] See e.g. Birrell 1994; Fowler 1969: 194–5.
[65] *CIPM* vii. 23 (no. 48); *VCH Oxon.*, viii. 183. See also Beresford 1971: 194 for the hunting-related service owed by the lord of Bromley to the bishop of Lichfield when he came to hunt at Eccleshall (Staffs.).
[66] Woolgar 1999: 193–5; Cummins 1988: pl. 15; Denholm-Young 1932–4: 392; Greatrex (ed.) 1978: 3 (no. 10); *CIPM* xx. 45 (William Bonville's supposed purchase of 12 hunting bows for £2 in 1391); ORO, P328/F/1.
[67] Miller and Hatcher 1978: 203.   [68] Woolgar 1999: 195.
[69] Turner (ed.) 1901: pp. lxxxvii–xciii; Orme 1992: 134–5; Bond 2004: 171–3; Spufford 2000: 295; Coulton 1960: 215–17; *VCH Oxon.*, ii. 88–9.
[70] Drury 1978: 93.

The sport influenced the shape of aristocrats' itineraries as much as it did those of their rulers. Apart from generally favouring rural over urban houses, lords seem to have often chosen to reside mainly in wood-pasture areas, sometimes even building residences within or on the fringes of isolated wooded territories and wastes. The barren expanse of Charnwood forest in north-west Leicestershire, for example, attracted a string of minor lordly houses and lodges.[71] The main attraction at Charnwood was presumably terrain for hunting, and the importance of this activity is confirmed by detailed arrangements about hunting there made by Roger de Quincy, earl of Winchester, and Roger de Somery in 1247, including over access to Bradgate park.[72] Finite game supplies in individual localities also played their part in prompting aristocrats to move between residences. Thus, hunting opportunities seem to have been among the few things that lured the Marcher lords to their Welsh lands.[73] Likewise, when the earl of Kent went to Yardley (Northants.) in 1467 he went to hunt in the large chase there and spent over £9 doing so.[74] The gentry could not compete on the same scale, but hunting might equally help determine where they spent their time. When a knight toured round his manors, he might well pause longer where game was available, like Ralph son of William Fitzralph, who hunted at Pontes (Essex) in 1341–2.[75] Thus leisure considerations as well as estate management encouraged a peripatetic lifestyle.

Not surprisingly, hunting appears to have been an important part of aristocratic social life. In 1375, for instance, the young Robert de Vere, earl of Oxford, then a boy of 13, spent the whole of September hunting with the prior of Lewes, Sir John St Clair, and others at his manor of Laughton, Sussex.[76] Such group activities are only occasionally recorded, but the references that do survive—often from records of the prosecution of unauthorized hunting in royal forests—conjure up something of sociable pleasures of the chase, with aristocrats hunting with family members, friends, and associates as well as hunt servants.[77] The Northamptonshire forest pleas of 1251, for instance, include a presentment against Gilbert de Clare, who allegedly uncoupled his hounds after a red deer while walking in one of his woods after dinner; also presented were Robert de Mares, Robert Basset, Robert de Longchamp, and John Lovet (a forest verderer), who had apparently dined with him.[78] More legitimate sport of a similar kind was enjoyed by the 'gentiles' who joined a hunting expedition in Windsor forest in 1388 to take eight does for the abbot of Westminster for the feast of St Peter in Chains (1 August).[79] And nor was participation reserved to men. Like their queens, noblewomen and female gentry were involved too, perhaps especially by the later middle ages. Some were spectators, like the ladies

---

[71] Squires and Humphrey 1986: *passim*; Emery 1996–2006: ii. 172, 211.
[72] Shirley 1867: 16–19.   [73] Davies 1978: 120.   [74] Jack (ed.) 1965: 75.
[75] Britnell 1987: 232.
[76] Saul 1986: 191–2; BL, Add. Roll 32141, m. 6; Fryde *et al.* 1986 (eds.): 476.
[77] Birrell 1982: 12–13; 1994: 55–8, 64–5; 2001: 148–9.   [78] Turner (ed.) 1901: 34.
[79] TNA: PRO, SC6/754/21, m. 4.

who were splendidly entertained in tents during Edward IV's summer hunts,[80] but others were more active participants, sometimes from an early age.[81]

The role played by hunting as a social gel and common interest in local gentry society is particularly well illustrated by two late-medieval poems. The first, the anonymous 'Lament for Sir John Berkeley', was probably written for a northeast Midlands gentry audience shortly after Sir John's death in 1375. It opens with a party of lords out hunting and depicts their sorrow at the death of a man who had been a keen huntsman and regular companion, showing the grief of the poet, probably one of Sir John's servants, at the passing of a much-admired master.[82] The second poem, by Lydgate, was addressed to Thomas Chaucer in the 1410s, when Chaucer, apparently the lynchpin in the local hunting set, was about to set off for France, perhaps for the Agincourt campaign.[83] Besides his family and best friend, the poet tells us that others will miss him too: for the gentlemen living around his residence at Ewelme (Oxon.) it was 'Farwel huntyng and hawkyng bothe tweyne,/ and farewel now cheef cause of your desport'. In all likelihood, hunting was the 'chief disport' of many local aristocratic communities besides the Chaucer and Berkeley circles.

Like their rulers and the nobility, such gentry groups seem to have been interested in killing a wide range of animals, in different kinds of locations, and in a variety of ways. There is extensive evidence that their quarry included not just deer (of various species) but also otters, hares, and other smaller game (and in earlier periods wolves and boar), all of which could be chased with dogs, netted, or shot at with arrows, and game birds, which could be snared, trapped, or targeted with hawks or falcons.[84] Nevertheless, deer were perhaps the single most favoured prey, where available, and were usually regarded as the noblest,[85] with the preference apparently shifting towards fallow deer. The greatest lords could hunt these creatures in their own forests, chases, or parks, but landowners of all ranks seem to have often hunted deer in the royal forests too, for all the prohibitions against this.[86]

PRESSURES ON DEER AND HUNTING

This brief survey suggests something of the importance of hunting as a royal and aristocratic pastime in medieval England. But how, we might ask, do parks fit

---

[80] Giles (ed.) 1845: 146 n. 3.
[81] Orme 1983: 83–4; 1992: 137; Thiébaux 1967: 262, 263; Cummins 1988: 8 and plates, 9, 13, 32, 34, 41, 44; Almond 2003: 143–66; Woolgar 1999: 194; Spence 1994: 41.
[82] Turville-Petre 1982: 336.   [83] Gray (ed.) 1985: 61.
[84] Cummins 1988; Oggins 2004; Moorhouse 2007: 121–2; *VCH Oxon.*, xii. 444; Woolgar (ed.) 1992–3: ii. 517, 543; Rackham 1986: 34–40; Wrottesley (ed.) 1885: 130; Johnson and Cronne (eds.) 1956: p. xxi; Barron (ed.) 1998: 91–5, 101–5, 107–9, 115–19, 121–3, 133–5; Greenwell (ed.) 1857: pp. xvii–xviii.
[85] Girouard 2000: 14–15.
[86] Birrell 1982: 11–13; Orme 1992: 133; Saul 1986: 191–2; *VCH Derbyshire*, i. 418; Pollard 1992: 199; Jones and Page 2006: 122.

in? At first sight they seem to provide the perfect solution for the keen royal or aristocratic hunter. By putting deer in a park a lord could guarantee a convenient supply of his favourite quarry and, perhaps, a place to hunt it. This would have been especially important given the growing pressure on wild animals and the spaces where they could be nurtured and hunted thanks to the growth of population and spread of agriculture. Most calculations suggest that the population of England more than doubled and perhaps even trebled in the two hundred years between the late eleventh and the late thirteenth century.[87] The growth of population inevitably put a premium on cereal production, encouraging the clearance of woods and cultivation of rough pastures.[88] According to one estimate, the area of England covered by woodland (mostly wood-pasture rather than a solid mass of trees) was probably reduced by a third from an already fairly low 15 per cent in 1086 to about 10 per cent by *c*.1300,[89] and in many places only small areas of wood and wastes were left.[90] At the same time, a developing economy encouraged increasing use of remaining wood-pasture and upland areas for grazing and wood production.[91] In both royal and lordly forests, religious houses and laymen were granted land and rights to chop down trees, cultivate ground, and graze animals and over time this thinned wooded cover and limited the areas unexposed to human activity.[92] Ironically, the gift of parks to monks for the foundation of religious houses, which became quite common from the twelfth century, is indicative of this spread of people and farming: these were among the few places where a house of a more strenuous order could be set up free from lay development and interference, in the seclusion of a fenced-in 'wilderness'.[93]

The intensifying use of the landscape had a considerable effect on deer populations. The native species, the red and the roe, seem to have been in decline in England probably from as early as the twelfth century, and certainly by the thirteenth,[94] although they remained more common in the north of England than the Midlands or south.[95] The large-scale introduction of the fallow deer from overseas in the twelfth century seems to have been a response to this decline in native deer, as well as being related to changing hunting practices.[96] But even the importation of fallow deer does not seem to have provided a complete solution to inadequate deer numbers, especially in the open

---

[87] Harvey 1988: 46–9; Prestwich 2005: 531–2.   [88] Britnell 2004: 72.
[89] Rackham 1986: 88.   [90] Miller 1964: 23; Britnell 2004: 312.
[91] Hallam 1981; Britnell 2004: 73. Cf. Hallam 1988*c*: 510–11.
[92] Rackham 1986: 138; Stamper 1988: 129; Jones and Page 2003: 74–83; McDonnell 1992: 114; Cantor and Squires 1997: 9; Gowland 1936–8: 381–9; Drury 1978: 92; *VCH Durham*, ii. 378 ff.; Roberts 1968: 102, 104, 106, 111; Mason (ed.) 1980: 171, 172.
[93] Aston 2000: 81–2, 88, 97; Pantin 1941: 22–3; Purvis (ed.) 1936: p. x; Stenton (ed.) 1922: 91; Bond 2004: 175 (fig. 48). For the story of the foundation of Meaux abbey (Yorks.) in a park which was still under construction, see Bond (ed.) 1866–8, i. pp. xiii–xvi, 77, 80, 81.
[94] Rackham 1986: 39–40; Creighton 2002: 19.
[95] Brentnall 1949–50: 194–5; Short 2000: 134.
[96] Sykes 2007*b*: 66–75, 78–9; Rackham 1986: 49, 123, 125; 1989: 46–7.

forest outside of enclosed hunting grounds.[97] In the areas of the countryside beyond the bounds of the forests and other designated game reserves, there was little or no protection for deer from hunters and they would not have flourished.[98] All this would have made park-based deer herds more and more important, and pressure on land use seems to have encouraged the move to preserve deer inside parks even in more remote areas like Charnwood and the north of England.[99]

Nor did the picture change all that much in the later middle ages. The contraction of farming may have promoted some regeneration of deer numbers, but this is far from certain: a contrary tendency was the decline of forest administration, which all but removed the protection afforded to these creatures. Stocks of red deer were in crisis in the forests of northern England in the late fifteenth century thanks to overhunting, and, according to a statute of the late 1480s, there were no deer at all left in Inglewood forest (Cumberland), due to the negligence and corruption of forest officials.[100] Roe deer, far from recovering, seem to have been almost extinct from southern England by the fifteenth century, perhaps because of their lesser protection under forest law in the later middle ages,[101] perhaps because changing woodland management reduced the roe's access to hazel, an important part of its diet.[102]

In other words, deer-hunting would not have been feasible in most areas by the later thirteenth century (or even earlier) without parks to protect deer stocks and, presumably, to provide a space for undisturbed hunting in an increasingly busy landscape.

THE PARKLAND HUNTING GROUND

These circumstances suggest a strong link between parks and royal and aristocratic hunting and seem to make it safe to assume that aristocrats hunted the deer in parks. But a remaining difficulty is presented by awkward doubts about the practicality of recreational hunting in parks—the idea that most of these enclosures were simply too small for the kind of hunting favoured by the aristocracy. However, this uncertainty can in fact be resolved, and it can be shown that aristocratic hunting practices were central to the growth in park numbers. The evidence leaves us in no doubt that parks partly acted as larders for luxury food and that lords regularly sent their servants to them to unceremoniously

---

[97] Stamper 1983: 48–51; Roberts 1988: 78.
[98] TNA: PRO, C143/1, no. 19; C143/231, no. 21; Cam 1930: 251, article 11 (on the bounds and landmarks of chases and warrens).
[99] Squires and Humphrey 1986: 15, 23–4; Pollard 1990: 202 and n. 17; Todd (ed.) 1997: 13; Tupling 1927: 15–16.
[100] Pollard 1990: 200–1; Bond 1998: 23; 4 Hen 7, c. 6: SR ii. 531.
[101] Turner (ed.) 1901: pp. xi, cxxviii, cxxx.   [102] Bond 1998: 24.

cull deer, but the importance of lords' own hunting has been underestimated. In fact, most park creators intended their parks as hunting grounds; they and their heirs and successors used them as such over long periods; and, contrary to the prevailing view, those parks newly established in the later part of the period were also intended for hunting. As with lordly hunting in general, a relative paucity of direct documentary references does not necessarily mean that park-based hunting was rare: indeed, there was usually even less reason for owners' use of their own parks for hunting to prompt any written record than hunting in open territory outside. In any case, and importantly, the significance of aristocratic hunting as a motivation for park creation and maintenance was not necessarily directly dependent on the regularity with which this activity occurred in individual parks.

How then are we to deal with the objection that the park was unsuitable for the aristocratic chase? The answer seems to lie in the fact that there were a variety of ways of hunting and that those most favoured in parks were perfectly attuned to their size.[103] Although *par force* hunting on horseback, which potentially required many miles of open terrain, was much referred to by French hunting manuals (and later historians), there is little reason to assume that this was the only kind of hunting that aristocrats engaged in. It may be that Norman and Angevin lords enjoyed hunting deer across large open spaces (perhaps mainly red deer, which are great straight-line runners), in headlong chases that could not be accommodated in any but the largest parks,[104] but this was not the end of the story.

First of all, the *par force* chase could be modified to fit into a smaller space and for use with fallow deer, which made up the large majority of park-based deer herds in the middle ages. In other words, the finding of a single deer in the woods and chasing it over miles of countryside could be condensed into the chasing (or 'coursing') of a single animal, separated from the rest of the herd, with hounds in parkland clearings, the mounted hunter or hunters perhaps riding up to assist in the final kill.[105] This seems to have been the kind of hunting that went on in the parks of the abbot of Bury St Edmunds (Suffolk): Abbot Samson (elected in 1182) 'created several parks which he stocked with game, and he retained a huntsman with hounds. If any important guest was being entertained, the abbot would sit with his monks in a woodland clearing to watch the hounds giving chase...'[106] William Beauchamp, earl of Warwick, likewise appears to have been coursing in his park of Beoley (Worcs.) on

---

[103] The various hunting methods are described in Gilbert 1979: 52–60.

[104] Roberts 1988: 73; Cummins 2002: 47; Sykes 2007b: 68, 70–5. The greater suitability of red deer for this kind of hunting may explain Norman kings' willingness to grant away rights to the hunting of roe deer, the other native species.

[105] Gilbert 1979: 55–6. Nicholas Trivet (1258?–1328) claimed that Edward I used a sword when hunting on horseback: Hog (ed.) 1845: 282.

[106] Greenway and Sayers (eds.) 1989: 26.

Fig. 5. Bow and stable hunting from a manuscript of Gaston de Foix's *Livre de Chasse*.

Source: Bibliothèque nationale de France, MS Fr. 616, f. 111v.

Christmas Day 1270, when the single deer he was chasing with his huntsmen and dogs escaped from the park into Feckenham forest.[107] In the fifteenth century, royal correspondence attests to the practice of this kind of coursing in parks, amongst other hunting methods.[108]

It also appears that English kings and lords often hunted by a method called bow and stable (or the 'drive'), where beaters drove a group of deer towards a trap or waiting archers (see Fig. 5).[109] This method required significant manpower but it was eminently suited to the park landscape, and indeed it may even have been instrumental in the development of the park itself. Historians sometimes present the drive as having been more important from the fifteenth century onwards,[110] but actually the driving of quarry across the country towards armed men, pits, nets, or other traps is a very ancient method of hunting game, including deer of all kinds. It seems to have been the preferred method of hunting in pre-Conquest Britain, where hedges or 'hays' were often utilized as traps,[111] and was used by the Normans after the Conquest.[112] The close link between parks and bow and stable is suggested by the fact that one medieval Latin word meaning 'to hunt' or 'to shoot' (*bercio, bersare*) shared the same root as a word for a fence enclosing a park (*bersa*), and that a *bersarius* could refer to a park-keeper or forester as well as a hunter.[113]

Other techniques could be practised in parks too. Even in smaller, steeper, or more heavily wooded enclosures it would still have been possible to stalk deer on foot.[114] This kind of hunting was not grand, but it might provide opportunities to hone skills and socialize, and Henry V is supposed to have particularly

---

[107] Birrell (ed.) 2006: 100. [108] Monro (ed.) 1863: 101; below, p. 40.
[109] Cummins 1988: 53. [110] Ibid. 56; Cummins 2002: 47; Almond 2003: 82–3.
[111] Hagen 1995: 134–5; Gilbert 1979: 52–4. 'Hays' are discussed further below, p. 134 n. 44.
[112] Barlow 2006: 828. [113] Martin 1982: 198; Latham 1965 (ed.): 49.
[114] Cantor and Wilson 1968: 242.

enjoyed it.[115] Besides deer, other game kept in parks could be hunted within a limited space, including hares, which could be coursed on park launds, as well as foxes and game birds.[116]

It seems plausible then that as the population grew and space was reduced in the twelfth and thirteenth centuries, *par force* chases became less common and the alternative methods of coursing, stalking, or driving of deer towards traps became more and more widely taken up by the aristocracy, and that these methods were then transferred into enclosed parks, where hunting might continue, on a smaller scale. Gaston de Foix, the great French huntsman of the late fourteenth century, did not approve of park-based hunting because he and many other Frenchmen seem to have continued to prefer more vigorous *par force* hunting in the larger open spaces still available in many parts of France. But the reality was that in smaller and more crowded England the contemporary English lord could less readily allow his hunting to be 'a daily devastation of his lands', as the hunting activities of Hugh of Avranches, first earl of Chester (d. 1101), were unsympathetically described over two hundred years earlier.[117] Here the park-based hunt became, necessarily, more acceptable, and, in any case, it could be developed, should the lordly huntsman wish, into a grand, ceremonial affair, which could involve many men and game animals, like Edward II's bow and stable hunts at Clarendon and elsewhere or those of the bishop of Winchester in Merdon park (Hants.).[118]

A virtue, in other words, could be made from an increasing necessity. The parkland landscape after all was one which provided plentiful opportunities for enhancing the sport, whatever style of hunting was carried out. Within the enclosed park, the landowner had great freedom to manipulate the scenery to facilitate hunting.[119] In the early seventeenth century, Gervase Markham recommended a variety of land uses within parks to improve hunting: coppices and undergrowth for beasts to make lairs, tall woods to echo the joyous sounds of hound and hunting horn, open launds for deer grazing and for greyhounds to course, and hay meadows for winter feed.[120] It seems likely that similar ideas already had currency in the middle ages, albeit Markham's may be a slightly romanticized, bucolic view. There are several medieval references to the felling of trees in 'trenches' (clearings, paths, or rides cut through woodland). This was perhaps an appropriate way to take timber and at the same time improve access for woodland management, but it may also have been designed to provide a suitable arena for hunting (either coursing or the drive).[121] Edward I ordered this kind of planned felling in Woodstock and Clarendon parks in the mid to

---

[115] Shirley 1867: 16 n.; Allmand 1997: 61.   [116] *CPR, 1301–7*, 186; Rackham 1976: 147.
[117] Chibnall (ed.), 1969–80: ii. 263.
[118] Vale 2002: 180; Roberts 1988: 73; below, p. 105 (Fig. 17). Cf. Benson (ed.) 1987: 184.
[119] Cummins 1988: 59–60.
[120] Roberts 1988: 73. Cf. Neave 1991: 8 for a similar late 16th-cent. source.
[121] Latham 1965 (ed.): 492 (s.v. *trenchea*); Richardson 2005: 27, 49, 147. Cf. Blanning 2007: 397.

later 1270s.[122] The king's personal involvement suggests that his leisure interests were crucial: he visited both palaces frequently and the felling at Woodstock started after a visit at Christmas 1274. Likewise, when Edward III ordered the construction of a park for Queen Philippa at Brigstock in Rockingham forest (Northants.) in 1350, he took a close interest in its layout, specifying that trenches were to be cut through the woodland, as well as that the new enclosure should be provided with lodges and deer-leaps (gaps in the perimeter fence with pits on the inside, allowing deer to jump into the park, but not to get back out).[123] It seems likely that other lords were likewise manipulating their park landscapes, planting trees to provide cover, using hedges or fences as barriers, and clearing launds and wide paths at least in part for chasing or driving deer.[124]

Existing natural features in parkland could also be used to aid in the hunt. Suitable slopes within parks would have helped guide the deer towards a place where archers were stationed, as well as making the hunting visible from higher ground.[125] In fact, the presence of gradients or valleys may even have played a part in determining the choice of site for a park: the great majority of parks contained areas of sloping terrain.[126] In some cases the conscious use of topography is suggested by the selection of permanent sites for the establishment of traps or standings. The 'King's Standing' in Lancaster Great Park—a park visited by Edward II and enlarged by John of Gaunt—was an area on rising ground where the king might shoot at deer driven before him.[127] In 1334 Edward III ordered a watermill to be removed from inside Woodstock park and a 'certain suitable hay' to be put in its place: this may have been a trap for deer to be driven into.[128] Certainly Edward was keen on the drive style of hunting in his later years: in August 1375, while at Yardley (Northants.), he gave orders for the sheriff of Leicestershire to conscript men to 'make a sufficient stable' (to act as beaters) for his hunting in Ridlington park (Rutland).[129]

Leaving aside this question of how hunting in parks was carried out, there are—when one looks hard enough—many direct indications of its importance as a motivation for park-making and park maintenance. Occasionally record sources provide very clear confirmation that parks were, as the evidence about abbot Samson might suggest, being created to provide hunting grounds. Thus in December 1347 an order was given to the chamberlain of Chester by the Black Prince and his council to enclose two woods in Flintshire and make them parks 'for the preservation of the prince's covert and deer-hunting there'.[130] Similarly, requests for royal or baronial authorisation of parks sometimes show that lords,

---

[122] Bond 1997: 42; Richardson 2005: 27, 69 (fig. 34).
[123] CPR, 1348–50, 552–3 (quoted by Steane 1993: 148–9). For deer-leaps see Higham 2003.
[124] Cummins 2002: 46–7.   [125] Richardson 2005: 28.
[126] The other, economic, context of this choice of land is discussed in Ch. 2, below.
[127] Shirley 1867: 68.   [128] CCR, 1333–7: 243.   [129] CCR, 1374–7: 154.
[130] Stamp (ed.) 1930–3: i. 159, 93–4.

including churchmen, wanted these enclosures as places to hunt in,[131] and a number of park licences formally authorize hunting within park bounds, presumably in response to the petitioners' requests.[132] Occasionally we can more fully reconstruct the hunting enthusiasm of the individuals who developed parks, including Roger de Quincy, earl of Winchester (d. 1264),[133] and, in the following century, a number of individuals who received blanket pardons for hunting in royal forests and parks and were also licensed to create their own parks in various places. The latter group included the chancellor, Bishop Burghersh, at the end of Mortimer and Isabella's regime in October 1330, and royal favourites such as William Montague, John Molyns, and Nicholas de la Beche in the first decade of Edward III's personal rule.[134] Their contemporary, the worldly Abbot Godfrey of Crowland, who set up a deer park in Oundle (Northants.) in the early fourteenth century, was just as keen a huntsman.[135] Even where clerics were too pious to hunt in their own parks they might, like Abbot Samson, set them up to entertain important guests, who were already in the later twelfth century doubtless becoming used to hunting in their own and others' parks.

More common than documents showing the park conceived as a hunting reserve are those which confirm hunting as a favoured use of existing parks. According to Matthew Paris, for instance, in the early 1250s Hugh of Northwold, bishop of Ely (1229–54), had a 'hunting enclosure' (*indaginem*), 'which is commonly called a park'.[136] Very often hunting forays were still going on long after a park was first set up. King John, for example, went to Odiham (Hants.) for his 'disport', having built a new castle (replacing an older residence) next to the large park which had been established there in the early twelfth century or before (Fig. 6, opposite).[137] A similar case is provided by a 1322 survey of the manor of Manchester (Lancs.), which shows that at Blackley, where a park was recorded in the thirteenth century, there were two hundred deer 'for the lord's pastime with the deer-leap'.[138] This deer-leap was presumably created at a spot on the edge of the park where the lords of the manor, the de la Warres,[139] liked to hunt. When the earl of Oxford and his companions hunted at Laughton in 1375 they almost certainly did their hunting in the long-established and well-stocked park, which had been extensively refurbished in preparation for their visit and the lodge repaired.[140] Numerous other instances of park-based hunting could be cited from across the country and indeed in France beyond, including those where kings took advantage of hunting in their

---

[131] TNA: PRO, C143/6/14; Todd (ed.) 1997: no. 201; *CChR, 1257–1300*, 481.
[132] *CChR, 1226–57*, 28–9, 114, 115, 220. Cf. also *EYC* ii, no. 1098, and TNA: PRO, C143/6, no. 14.
[133] Crouch 1992: 308–9.
[134] *CPR, 1327–30*, 70; *1330–4*, 16, 18, 166, 563; *1334–8*, 88, 190, 548, 567; *1338–40*, 62, 429; *CChR 1327–41*, 342, 353–4.
[135] Raban (ed.) 2001: xxvi, xxviii.   [136] Luard (ed.) 1872–83, v. 343–4; *VCH Herts.*, iii. 99.
[137] Brown 1954: 192; *HKW* ii. 766; *VCH Hants.*, iv. 90.
[138] Higham 2004: 121–2; Farrer (ed.) 1907: 56 (*ad ludum domini cum saltorio*); Cantor 1983: 44.
[139] *VCH Lancs.*, i. 333–4 and iv. 230; *Peerage*, iv. 141–3.
[140] BL, Add. Roll, 32141, m. 4; above, p. 26.

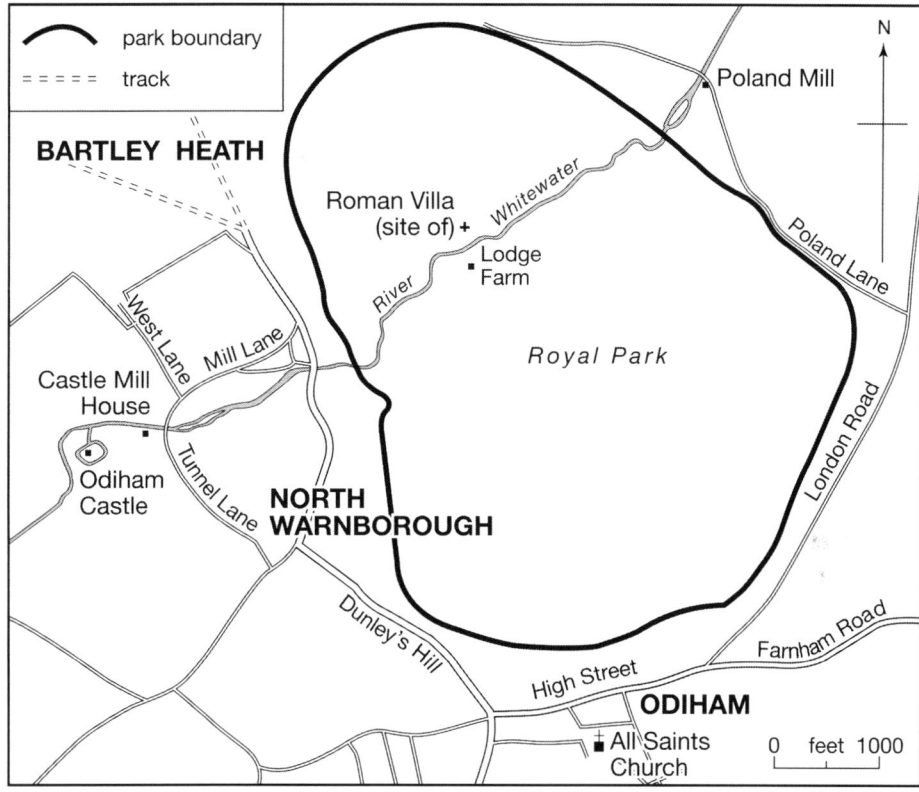

Fig. 6. The royal castle and park at Odiham (Hants.).
Sources: 1st edn. 1:10,560 OS map (1875); MacGregor 1983: 29.

subjects' parks or where lords loaned their reserves to their fellows, and such activities often no doubt went unrecorded.[141] And, as we will see in Chapter 6, aristocratic disputes over parks tended to centre on the question of hunting rights.

Other non-documentary sources of various kinds point to the same long-lasting focus on hunting. Literary texts require careful interpretation but can be highly revealing, like the mid or later fourteenth-century *Wynnere and Wastoure* poem, which strongly implies that much aristocratic hunting went on in parks. Wynnere's description of the hunting trips of the present generation's 'forefathers' refers to buck hunting taking place in 'broad launds' on their estates, and launds (woodland clearings) on private estates would probably most often have been found within parks. Place-names are also important, with minor local names for fields and lanes often indicating that lords kept kennels for hunting dogs in or near their parks, in northern and southern England alike.[142]

[141] Richardson 2005: 60, 82; Roberts 1988: 71; Byerly and Byerly (eds.) 1977: p. xv; Coulson 1979: 75; Crouch 1992: 309; *CCR, 1302–7*, 21; *CPR, 1334–8*, 426.
[142] Moorhouse 2007: 115–17; Roberts 1988: 74 (fig. 3); Richardson 2005: 80; *CPR, 1391–6*, 49. Cf. MacGregor 1983: 64, 140, on the kennels at Odiham park (Hants.).

FREQUENCY OF USE

But what about the question of how often parks were utilized for hunting? After all, it has been suggested that lords and their privileged guests made only occasional hunting forays in particular parks, perhaps every few years, or even less often.[143] This tends to be seen as another reason to minimize the importance of hunting, but, in fact, such a view is rather misleading. First, it seems doubtful that lordly hunts really were so rare. It has to be emphasized once again that infrequency of references in most surviving sources cannot be taken as evidence of infrequent use. Almost all parks were sited at major residences (many established at pre-existing hunting grounds) that were visited fairly frequently, whatever the rank of the owner. For the king and great lords there were more of these, each visited less often, for lesser lords there were fewer, each visited more regularly. But the principle was the same: the park was put where the owner would be most able to use it.[144] Parks were created near residences because lords wanted to hunt in them, not because lords were gravely concerned about transport costs for moving venison and timber to their households. The fact that economic exploitation of parks is better documented than their use as hunting grounds does not mean that it was necessarily more important.[145]

Sometimes hunts in parks may have been very infrequent, for example where the owner was a minor, old, infirm, not a keen huntsman or huntswoman, or, most significantly, where a park or the vestige of one was maintained at a residence that was no longer much visited.[146] In such cases parks might decay, be turned to breeding grounds for game, or be used mainly for grazing or wood production. But there is no reason to suppose that this was the norm. Active adult park owners, especially male ones, might hunt in their parks regularly, like Henry Wakefield, bishop of Worcester (1375–95), who maintained a number of parks at Alvechurch, Blockley, and Hartlebury (Worcs.) and Henbury and Stoke Bishop (Glos.) and hunted in them when he visited. Henbury was a particularly favoured spot and Wakefield usually spent up to three months a year there, hunting in the parks of Pen and Sneyd.[147] When deer numbers in particular parks ran low hunting might have to be suspended, but this was only temporary: in 1490 or 1491 Ralph Ryther seems to have called a halt to the taking of deer from his park at Ryther (Yorks.), but in one of his letters he promised to invite Sir Robert Plumpton to come and kill a buck with him once the summer was past.[148] And even where a lord did not himself visit very often, the park could be used, as we have seen, by allowing others to hunt in it, providing a source of patronage.

---

[143] Birrell 1992: 122.   [144] Platt 1978: 47.   [145] See Ch. 2 below.
[146] Liddiard 2000b: 55 (Buckenham, Norfolk, by the early 14th cent.); Richardson 2005: 37–8 (Clarendon by the later 15th century); MacGregor 1983: 115 (Odiham by the 15th cent.).
[147] Dyer 1980: 133, 202–3.   [148] Stapleton (ed.) 1839: 106–7 and n.; Kirby (ed.) 1996: no. 97.

In any event, the significance of seigneurial hunting as a reason for making parks was not directly related to the frequency with which it occurred in individual places. Like the Black Prince in Flintshire, other lords might be prepared to set aside ground for hunting and spend money on reserves and residences even if they did not use them that often. Leisure was a very important consideration, not necessarily to be bound by the ordinary rules of estate economy. Great lords in particular had numerous estates and large incomes and might maintain parks in many places in case they wished to hunt there. Having multiple parks allowed them to hunt more often by increasing the number of places at which they had a supply of deer.[149] On royal estates especially, no expense was spared to ensure good sport whenever the king might choose to visit, as the lavish provisions for deer and dog food at Cornbury park in Wychwood forest, near Woodstock (Oxon.), demonstrate.[150] While the owner was absent deer could be drawn from a park, salted, and transported for his table, and other farming uses could take place. When he drew near the focus switched to the lordly hunt,[151] which was fundamentally the park's raison d'être.

CONTINUITY IN THE LATER MIDDLE AGES?

So far it has been argued that hunting was central to the establishment and maintenance of the majority of parks. But does this hold good for the period after the Black Death? Or was the later middle ages characterized by the general decline and decadence of the park so often assumed by historians, either for economic reasons, with landlords less able to afford hunting parks, or because of a shift in focus towards 'amenity' areas and landscaping?[152] Here it will be argued that many parks survived into the later middle ages, that they very often retained their role as hunting grounds, and that the new creations of the later period were still designed as much as ever with hunting in mind.

The frequent scholarly emphasis on the decline of parks in the later middle ages is exaggerated, perhaps in part because the decline in park licensing is too readily equated to a decline of parks.[153] While it is true that some old parks had been abandoned or converted to farmland, many existing parks remained intact. Probably around 70 per cent of parks that were in place at the turn of the fourteenth century were still there in the late fifteenth.[154] What is more, several hundred new parks were made and other existing parks extended in the fifteenth and early sixteenth centuries, partly making up for

---

[149] Cf. below, p. 79.   [150] Watney 1910: 34, 37.   [151] Hatcher 1970: 180.
[152] Above, pp. 6, 7.   [153] For the chronology of park licensing see below, p. 128 (Fig. 19).
[154] This conclusion is based on my study of Oxfordshire and Bedfordshire parks, as well as Hoppitt 1992: i. 70 (fig. 4.2); Squires and Humphrey 1986: 17; Rowe 2009: 9.

the losses.¹⁵⁵ It is significant that contemporaries had the perception that there were numerous parks around in the late middle ages, even if the accuracy of their estimates of overall park numbers might be doubtful. A Venetian visitor in the 1490s put park numbers at 'more than 4,000, all enclosed with timber fences'.¹⁵⁶ In the early sixteenth century, Polydore Vergil suggests that a third of England was uncultivated and that much of this was given over to parks, so that 'allmoste everie where a man may se clausures and parckes paled and enclosed'.¹⁵⁷ The decay of a park could happen at any time and the modern focus on the later middle ages is misleading in this respect. The main causes of decline and disparkment were in operation in the thirteenth century as much as the fifteenth: changes in family fortunes, shifts in residential patterns, alterations in agricultural priorities, and the compromising of deer herds through overuse, disease, or poaching, the last a particular problem during times of unrest.¹⁵⁸ And, as we shall see in the next chapter, the late medieval aristocracy were in general far from being too poor to afford to maintain their parks.¹⁵⁹

Beyond the fact that parks remained an important feature of the later medieval landscape, there is much evidence to show that parks across the country continued to be stocked with deer in the late middle ages—a first pointer to their continued role as hunting grounds. Parks that were created by the crown or came into royal hands provide most detail on their continued presence, thanks to the larger amount of surviving written evidence.¹⁶⁰ But it was not just kings and their relatives with many parks and wide tracts of forest and chase who managed to keep up their deer stocks. The majority of late fourteenth- and fifteenth-century inquisitions *post mortem* referring to parks specify that they contained 'beasts of the chase' (and, of course, in inquisitions where deer are not mentioned their absence cannot be assumed). This applied not just to parks belonging to great lords, who had many parks and hunting grounds, but also to those possessed by members of the gentry, and it was true in northern and western England¹⁶¹ as much as in the Midlands,¹⁶² the Home Counties and the south,¹⁶³ or East Anglia.¹⁶⁴ Similarly, references to actions over park-breaking

---

¹⁵⁵ In some counties new creations may have entirely made up for disparkments: Rowe 2009: 7–9.
¹⁵⁶ Sneyd (ed.) 1847: 39.   ¹⁵⁷ Ellis (ed.) 1846: 5.
¹⁵⁸ On the link between poaching and political disorder see below, pp. 156–7.
¹⁵⁹ Below, p. 76.
¹⁶⁰ e.g. TNA: PRO, SC6/962/4 ff. (Woodstock); Watney 1910: 31, 34, 37, 38 (Cornbury); *VCH Oxon.*, v. 56 (Beckley); *VCH Berks.*, ii. 343, Pearman 1894: 25 (Caversham); *VCH Wilts.*, x. 245–6 (Devizes); *VCH Wilts.*, xv. 126 (Ludgershall); Kerr 1925: 153–6 (Higham Ferrers); Drage 1989: 65 (Nottingham castle park); Birrell 1962: 121 (parks in the honor of Tutbury, Staffs. and Derbs.); TNA: PRO, E101/593/35–44 and 593/52–595/28 (costs of the deer in Clarendon park).
¹⁶¹ *CIPM* xvi, nos. 211, 452, 736, 739, 744, 1069, 1083; xxii, nos. 34, 303, 433, 446, 736; xxiii, nos. 109, 119, 451, 483, 506, 577, 705.
¹⁶² *CIPM* xvi, nos. 205, 323, 548; xxii, nos. 25, 30; xxiii, nos. 101, 373, 403, 701.
¹⁶³ *CIPM* xxii, nos. 75, 81, 99, 168, 186, 219, 236, 302, 347, 424, 426, 761, 778–9; xxiii, nos. 52, 220, 260, 275, 303, 706.
¹⁶⁴ *CIPM* xvi, nos. 25–6; xxii, nos. 309, 440, 441, 499, 504; xxiii, nos. 120, 704, 709, 713, 714.

across the country show that deer remained the main targets.[165] There seems little reason to doubt Polydore Vergil's description of the many parks that he saw 'all about' at the beginning of the sixteenth century as being 'fraughte with .. venerie'.[166] After all, with the right conditions and a little luck, a viable deer population could be sustained over a long period. Careful breeding could help maintain the herd (there is some evidence of stud animals), and depleted herds could be restocked from outside, either through deer-leaps, opportunistic capture, the owners' other reserves, or royal or aristocratic gift.[167] And even where ruin had occurred it was far from irreversible: parks could be refurbished, as at 'Mouncheseys' park at Stansted (Essex), which was refenced to contain a herd of deer in 1414.[168]

But if parks still had their deer, is there clear evidence that they remained in use as hunting grounds? The answer is a resounding 'yes'. Despite the supposed shift towards the more intensive use of parks for agricultural purposes—which will be examined later on—all the indications are that park-based hunting maintained and even increased in its popularity and developed in sophistication. For a start, and importantly, contemporaries continued to readily associate parks with hunting. In a fifteenth-century French polemic, the *Débat des héraulx d'armes*, the English herald makes a direct link between the presence of parks and the quality of hunting in England, saying that 'the kingdom of England is adorned with fine hunting, for there is such abundance of parks, full of venison'.[169] Bow and stable hunting, perfect for parks, was said to be a 'way of life' in late fourteenth-century England,[170] and in the early fifteenth century, Edward of York added a long chapter on how this kind of hunt should be organized for the king to his translation of Gaston de Foix's hunting treatise. This new chapter made it quite clear that it could just as well take place in parks as in forests.[171] More concrete evidence is also available to confirm these impressions and demonstrates that a variety of hunting methods continued to be used in parks.

Throughout the later middle ages, kings were just as focused on expanding their existing parkland as their predecessors had been in setting up parks, and their interest clearly centred on hunting. The evidence that survives gives the impression of an often fairly full hunt diary, although particular jaunts tended to be recorded in detail only where important guests were entertained. Henry VI's assertive wife Margaret of Anjou was particularly vocal in expressing her concerns to ensure her and her husband's 'disporte and recreacion' in various

---

[165] TNA: PRO, CP40/526, rot. 341; CP40/806, rot. 72; CP40/818, rot. 46; CP40/840, rot. 50 d.; E13/160, rot. 20 d.; C1/6/347; C1/27/430.
[166] Ellis (ed.) 1846: 5.
[167] Birrell 1992: 116; Kirby (ed.) 1996: 133; TNA: PRO, E101/540/28; Rackham 1989: 52, 54, 55, 56; Armitage-Smith (ed.) 1911: ii, no. 1513; Greatrex (ed.) 1978: no. 10; Cummins 1988: 262, 264; Roberts 1988: 79; MacGregor 1983: 77; Lumby (ed.) 1889–95: ii. 74; *VCH Oxon.*, xiv. 200.
[168] Woodger 1974: 214.   [169] Cummins 1988: 62.   [170] Ibid. 53.
[171] Baillie-Grohman and Baillie-Grohman (eds.) 1904: pp. xlviii–xlix, 107–12.

parks, through special orders to parkers to maintain deer stocks and stop others hunting.[172] Evidence about later kings' park hunts is often more sporadic, but sometimes more descriptive. In 1472, for instance, Edward IV entertained Louis de Gruthuyse, his host during his recent exile, at hunting in Windsor Little Park, which he had extended in around 1466, as part of a wider series of celebrations; they apparently chased deer on horseback, using greyhounds and buckhounds.[173] Three years later he was again hunting at Windsor, this time with George Neville, archbishop of York, and they had 'ryghte good chere', Edward promising to go to Neville's manor of Moor (Herts.) to hunt in its park.[174] Henry VII took an interest in deer stocks in parks like Castle Donnington (Leics.) and Higham Ferrers (Northants.), and this was because he wanted to hunt in them.[175] In May 1496 he was intending to go to Higham and was concerned that unauthorized hunting was eating into the game supply. He desired 'the replenysshyng of our said game ther for oure disport and pleasour', and ordered that no one else was to 'have shotte suete ne course within oure seid parke' without full authority.[176] On 3 February 1505 Henry went on a post-prandial hunt with King Philip of Castile in Windsor park, the two kings killing deer with their crossbows.[177]

There is no reason to suppose that the later medieval aristocracy as a whole was any less fond of hunting in their parks than their rulers or their own predecessors. For instance, when he visited Winchester College in 1415 Henry Beaufort, bishop of Winchester (1405–47), was given a gift of bows and arrows, which were specifically said to be for his use when he went hunting in the Hampshire parks of his see.[178] An extant series of accounts from the 1460s and 1470s suggests that John Howard, first duke of Norfolk, did much of his hunting in parks.[179] The comments of one knight from fifteenth-century Cumberland probably sum up the position of many park owners. The rather splendidly named Sir Lancelot Threlkeld was apparently wont to say that he had 'three noble houses'. One, Yanwith nigh Penrith (Yanwath, Westmorland), where he resided in winter, was for warmth; one, his home manor of Threlkeld (Cumberland), was well stocked with tenant followers for war; and the other, Crosby Ravensworth (Westmorland), where he had a park full of deer, was 'for pleasure'.[180] And men like Lancelot were still lending out their parks for other local worthies to hunt in too.[181] Like their queens, noble ladies seem to have been particularly keen on hunting in parks in this period. In the late 1370s the countess of Hereford and her retinue hunted in the bishop of Lincoln's park of

---

[172] Monro (ed.) 1863: 100–1, 106, 137.
[173] Anon. (ed.) 1836; *CPR, 1461–7*, 551; Harwood 1929: 104.
[174] Halliwell (ed.) 1839: no. 10. See also Whitehead 1950: 30 on Edward's supposed hunt in Thomas Burdett's park at Arrow (Warks.).
[175] Somerville 1953: i. 269. [176] Kerr 1925: 155. [177] Tighe and Davis 1858: i. 440.
[178] Roberts 1993: 478. [179] Botfield (ed.) 1841: 277–80, 558.
[180] Nicholson and Burn 1777: i. 498.
[181] Kingsford (ed.) 1919: ii, no. 255; Armitage-Smith (ed.) 1911: ii, no. 1092; Cummins 1988: 261–3.

Buckden (Hunts.).[182] It seems likely that Anne of Burgundy had a part in the enclosure of 'Le Parke de Madame' at the property of her husband, John, duke of Bedford, at Penshurst (Kent) after *c*.1424.[183] Lady Margaret Beaufort, meanwhile, worried about her and her son Henry VII's recreation in Madeley park (Staffs.).[184] According to the English *Débat* herald, ladies went to parks for entertainment and took 'singular joy in shooting with the bow and killing ... beasts'; a special ladies' crossbow was designed for the purpose.[185]

Royal park owners and a few of their richest subjects may even have further developed facilities for the formalized watching of hunts in their reserves in the later middle ages. Increasingly elaborate arrangements were sometimes made for the drive style of hunt, as in the 'new park' in the New Forest (Hants.) in the 1480s where hundreds of deer were gathered from the wider forest in anticipation of royal visits, and a stand was provided for deer-slaughtering jaunts.[186] It may even be that the parkland 'deer-course', once assumed to have been a post-medieval creation, was actually developed in the later middle ages, although at present topographical clues do not seem to be supported by direct medieval documentary evidence.[187] In the sixteenth century, and perhaps earlier, these demarcated courses were venues for a rather specialized kind of 'hunting' (more like greyhound racing), which was closely stage-managed, with formal rules and spectator stands; deer were released at the top and dogs chased them down the course, sometimes to be killed, sometimes to be allowed to survive. Much of the interest was probably in socializing and gambling on which would be the winning dog.[188]

All of this suggests that parks were just as integral to royal and aristocratic hunting in the later fourteenth and fifteenth century as in earlier periods. This is attested by the continued development of the bow and stable hunt, and by widespread participation, not just amongst men but, it seems, increasingly amongst women too. If the park was not the only hunting venue, it was a frequent, and probably typical location.[189] In this light, it seems rather unlikely that the new parks of this period really had as little to do with hunting as has often been supposed.

NEW PARKS OF THE LATER MIDDLE AGES

Contrary to the usual suggestion, there is actually no reason to assume that those creating parks in the later fourteenth or fifteenth century did not have hunting in mind. In fact, these new parks were not so different in function from

---

[182] Canadine 2003: 43.   [183] Stratford 1993: 112.
[184] Jones and Underwood 1992: 73.   [185] Cummins 1988: 62.
[186] Stagg (ed.) 1983: pp. ix, 23, 24.
[187] Taylor 2004: 47–50; Herring 2003: 42; Roberts 1997: 137; Richardson 2005: 80–2.
[188] Some idea of the post-medieval arrangements is given by Musty 1986: 131–2; Taylor 2004: 45–7. Cf. also Blanning 2007: 404–5.
[189] For some examples of hunting outside parks see Birrell 1962: 121; Somerville 1953: i. 269; Mosley 1832: 132–4.

earlier ones. They were certainly stocked with deer: park licences as well as the 1517 enclosure inquiry make it clear that fifteenth- and early sixteenth-century parks were created for deer or 'wild beasts'.[190] Archaeological excavations can sometimes provide another kind of confirmation, as at Moor Park, Rickmansworth (Herts.), where deer bones (fallow) first appear in deposits dating after the time when construction of the park was licensed (1426).[191]

The great size of most of the parks created or proposed in the fifteenth century was probably closely related to the desire for good hunting facilities.[192] The availability of land meant that large areas of varied terrain could be enclosed, including open country as well as woods,[193] providing excellent opportunities to design areas for drives, stationing bowmen, or even perhaps for *par force* chases on horseback. For instance, the steep valley running through Minster Woods (Oxon.), which Sir William Lovell was licensed to impark in 1442, would have been ideal for a bow and stable hunt or deer-course.[194] Sites could also be chosen which made it easier to watch the deer and the hunt. The major extension of the royal park at Rockingham castle in the 1480s enclosed what has been called a 'large natural amphitheatre'.[195] The same description could be applied to the mile-long valley added to Ewelme park (Oxon.), visible from the plateau in the middle of the existing enclosure.[196] The example of Ewelme also neatly demonstrates the continuing interest in hunting which the creation or extension of parks in the later middle ages represented. The owner (and possible creator) of the park in the early fifteenth century was none other than Thomas Chaucer, leader of the local hunting set celebrated by Lydgate,[197] and the park itself was close to an earlier park at Huntercombe ('the huntsmen's valley').

In light of this, the idea that later medieval parks were too insecurely enclosed for hunting appears highly doubtful.[198] First, it seems that high, deer-proof fences or walls were a sufficient alternative to palings or hedges mounted on banks.[199] Just as importantly, there are grounds for questioning the idea that early parks invariably had large banks whereas later ones did not. While a significant proportion of earlier parks display the remains of impressive banks

---

[190] *CChR, 1427–1516*, 30; *CPR, 1441–46*, 261. In the 1517 records imparking for wild beasts is always distinguished from other forms of enclosure, save, for some reason, in Cheshire (see e.g. Leadam (ed.) 1897: ii. 418).

[191] Biddle *et al*. 1959: 193; *CPR, 1422–9*, 351. Pheasant bones first survive from this period too.

[192] For instance, in 1469 Ralph Wolseley was licensed to impark his entire manor of Wolseley (Staffs.) and to make deer-leaps there and to have free warren and chase of hares, rabbits, pheasants, partridges and other birds, fish, and deer: *CPR, 1467–77*, 184.

[193] See e.g. *CPR, 1408–13*, 425 (Stockholt (Bucks.), 1412).

[194] OS Map 1:25000, sheet 180 (1999 edn.), 328129.

[195] RCHM *Northants*., ii. 128–9; Brown and Taylor 1974: 72–4; *CPR, 1485–94*, 7.

[196] Buckley n.d.: 2, 4; OS Map 1:25000, sheet 171 (1999 edn.), 6591.

[197] Above, p. 27.   [198] Above, p. 6.

[199] Beresford 1971: 203. See also the reference to the 'deer fence' put up at Barley Park, Ducklington in the early 16th cent. (*VCH Oxon*., xiii. 130).

Fig. 7. An early fourteenth-century park bank in woodland at Fingest in the Buckinghamshire Chilterns. The park boundary outside the woodland is much less clearly defined.

Source: photo by Christa Stigter.

and ditches, some may have had much more modest perimeters;[200] and a number of fifteenth- and sixteenth-century parks were certainly enclosed with sizeable banks and ditches.[201] The real relationship is more likely to be geographical rather than chronological: between surviving banks and wooded areas. Later medieval parks were often created in more open, champion areas and their banks are therefore more likely to have been ploughed out in the post-medieval period than those of earlier parks which were predominantly located in wood-pasture areas, where stretches of perimeter bank are often preserved in woodland (see Fig. 7).

All of this evidence points to the conclusion that the new parks made by the aristocracy of late medieval England were just as much intended for hunting as earlier established ones or, indeed, later medieval Continental parks.[202] An inscription tablet formerly above the tomb of Sir Thomas Cokayn at Ashbourne (Derbs., late 1530s) provides a very succinct confirmation of this. After proudly reporting Thomas's martial exploits, it recorded that 'Three Parks did he impale, therein to chase the Deere'.[203] Early sixteenth-century sources show the popularity of hunting in parks among royalty and aristocracy,[204] and there is no reason to assume that this was a new departure from late fourteenth- or fifteenth-century practices, any more than it was from those of earlier periods.[205]

In summary, there seems to be a very strong case for seeing hunting as being central to park-making throughout the middle ages. More stress is needed on the unfashionable fact that aristocrats were eager to hunt and that this seems to have been the primary motivation for park creation up and down the country, in northern and southern counties alike. Of course, this is not to suggest that hunting was either devoid of more complex social meaning or divorced from more calculated intentions relating to the way lords used their land or even, perhaps, to how they presented themselves. Still less does it mean that parks were used solely as hunting grounds. To consider the other functions of parks we have to leave behind the baying of the hounds and the bloodlust of the kill. The meeting of the lord with his estate officials may be a good place to start.

---

[200] Ryan 1999: 182, 190 (Essex and Suffolk). For more substantial banks see below, p. 104.
[201] *CChR, 1341–1417*, 467 and *1427–1516*, 8, 98 (references to 'dikes'); Cantor and Squires 1997: 19 (photo); Stevenson and Squires 1999: 54; NMR, ID No. SS61NE9 (King's Nympton, Devon).
[202] Syson and Gordon 2001: 80; Cummins 2002: 48. The background of a 1446 painting by Konrad Witz shows a hunt in a park on the shores of Lake Geneva: Taylor 2000: 45.
[203] Dugdale 1730: ii. 1121. See also Cox 1875–9: ii. 385.
[204] For particularly compelling evidence from Warwickshire in the 1520s see the *MSS of Lord Middleton*, HMC (1911), 346–7, 358–9.
[205] For a different view see Rackham 2002: 22.

2

Economy

Parks were typically large enclosures, and many of them encompassed hundreds of acres of varied terrain. Such land provided a mixture of resources which could potentially be put to productive use, and, in fact, economic activities can often be shown to have gone on within park bounds, sometimes on an appreciable scale. It might thus be thought that parks were created at least partly to facilitate material exploitation. Yet historians have devoted limited attention to the economic motivations which may have informed the creation and maintenance of parks. The work which has been done suggests no clear conclusions, producing instead two quite different strands of opinion about the significance of the agricultural and industrial activities which were carried out inside parks, one which highlights and another which downplays them.

Thus, on the one hand, it has been suggested that the 'economic contribution' of parks may have outweighed their 'sporting value'.[1] In particular, it has been proposed that parks helped preserve woods and wastes as important resources, especially in the face of a rapidly expanding population in the 250 years or so before the Black Death.[2] In a like way, it has been claimed that 'the imparking movement of the twelfth and thirteenth centuries owed much to the desire of landlords to control pasture rights',[3] and that the renting of pasture ('agistment') in parks was a 'frequent and important item of revenue in manorial accounts'.[4] We are not surprised to hear, then, that parks might be created partly as 'profitable assets' because of the amount of wood and pasturage that they could provide.[5] Although there was not the same pressure on woods and wastes after the Black Death, it is often said that falling agrarian profits and a shift in emphasis towards pastoral farming and woodland management prompted lords to use parkland more efficiently in this period.[6]

On the other hand, it has been claimed—sometimes by the same writers—that parks were largely unaffected by economic imperatives. They were an expense and a drain on resources, but this was accepted for the pleasure they

---

[1] Cantor 1982: 77. Cf. Rackham 1990: 153–5.
[2] Liddiard 2003: 19–20; Dyer 1980: 70–1; Hoppitt 1992: i. 278; Glasscock 1973: 167.
[3] Britnell 1977: 109.   [4] Cantor and Hatherly 1979: 80.   [5] Dyer 1980: 70–1.
[6] Stamper 1988: 145–7; Bond 1998: 29.

brought. One historian suggests that the aristocratic parks which proliferated in the thirteenth and fourteenth centuries had 'irrational functions', taking land that could be farmed out of production, with minor profits from grazing and so on providing scant compensation.[7] Looked at in this way, parks were a luxury, a manifestation of increased wealth associated with the profits of demesne farming in the thirteenth century.[8] Certain features of parks certainly seem to provide support for this kind of view. It is notable, for instance, that since they enclosed deer, which damage young growth, their creation cannot necessarily be assumed to have helped preserve woodland.[9] Perhaps then the supposed creation of parks on 'inferior terrain' and 'unimproved land' on the edge of lords' manors was simply a kind of damage limitation?[10]

These contrasting interpretations leave us with an apparent paradox: the park as an attempt to preserve and exploit valuable resources and at the same time a waste of land. Resolving this contradiction is essential before we can approach the way in which medieval park-makers, owners, and administrators understood the place of these reserves within the running of their estates. To understand the relationship between parks and estate management better we need to consider a number of issues. What kind of land was enclosed and what value did it have? Precisely how close was the link between pressure on resources and imparkment? And then the questions that bring us closest to park-makers' (and owners') motivations: how intensively were agrarian resources within parks managed and how far was exploitation driven by maximizing production or profit? Finally, could the resources enclosed within parks be preserved or controlled by other means? By answering these questions we should be able to more clearly distinguish between economic value and economic rationale, bringing us closer to understanding whether these enclosures were essentially created and maintained for economically productive purposes or only incidentally so.

Perhaps not surprisingly, there are no easy answers: assessing the financial value of parks to their owners is a difficult business. It is made particularly complex by trying to work out the productivity and costs of deer-keeping. It has been suggested by some scholars that venison provided an important contribution to the aristocratic household's diet, especially in providing fresh meat in the winter, and even that it might sometimes have been produced on a commercial basis, as at Barnard Castle (Durham).[11] Yet cultural attitudes meant that deer were regarded as a special kind of animal and this makes it seem unlikely that they were normally managed in quite the same business-like way as cows or sheep bred for everyday household use or commercial sale. An indication of the unusual position of deer is that the costs of their keeping, which, as we shall

---

[7] Dyer 1994: 20. For a similar view see Liddiard 2000*b*: 51.   [8] Platt 1978: 46–7.
[9] Cantor and Hatherly 1979: 72.   [10] Ibid. 71, 74, 79.
[11] Rackham 1990: 153; Lasdun 1991: 5–6; Cantor and Hatherly 1979: 72; Austin 1984: 75; Creighton 2002: 19–20.

see, could be very considerable, were not fully comprehended in manorial accounts.[12]

But even when deer-keeping is not factored in, we have to consider the balance that was struck between the long-term conservation of occasionally utilized but valuable resources (like timber) and the level of regular returns. Simply adding up profits from timber, grazing, or other sources and subtracting the potential income from rents or grain sales does not give a realistic interpretation of this terrain's economic dimension. In all sorts of ways, wood-pasture could have an importance beyond potential raw profit levels. Since lords' use of this terrain was often geared towards domestic consumption or use on the estate rather than production for market, the revenue that it generated is only a partial measure of its usefulness. Aristocratic households and monasteries had considerable requirements for timber, fuel, and feed for domestic animals.[13] In an age of less developed transport and communications, maintaining these everyday necessities near major residences could save a good deal of inconvenience, especially for sedentary monastic communities. At the same time, timber and venison provided their owner with much-sought-after items of patronage, something which cannot be understood in purely financial terms.[14]

Parks differed considerably in terms of size, topography, and location and this too must have affected their potential for mixed uses. The question of how economic parks were, or could have been, therefore has to be considered in relation to each locality; it cannot be accurately judged on a generalized global level, as it often is. In the lowlands most land had at least some utility for arable farming, whereas many upland areas had little long-term suitability for growing crops and could be used only for rough grazing. But even in the lowlands, particular soils could pose problems for cereal production.[15] The size of the lord's household, the density of the local population, and the extent of market opportunities were also factors that affected what might be profitable. Where existing demesne met domestic cereal requirements and there were few tenants pushing to clear new ground and no large local market there may have been little incentive for arable expansion. In such circumstances the creation of parkland might be a way of making use of poorer land, adding deer to other uses.[16] Whether it was the best way we will consider later. In other areas there might be more demand for land to be farmed, especially in the lowlands, and even marginal soils could attract cultivators. In such places the release of wood-pasture for clearance and cultivation could generate significant new incomes from rent, particularly in the thirteenth century.

These elements of variation were further complicated by change over time. The medieval period saw profound long-term economic changes which would have

---

[12] Birrell 1992: 112–15; Farrer (ed.) 1907: 56. [13] Woolgar 1999: 39, 76–7, 110, 191–2.
[14] Harvey 1997: 6–7; Bond 1997: 26, 39; Stamp (ed.) 1930–3: iv. 301.
[15] Muir 2004: 36–7. [16] Rackham 1986: 50.

had a significant impact on land-use possibilities and priorities. The increasing importance of markets and commercial transactions from the later twelfth century introduced a very different environment for the management of rural resources than that which had prevailed earlier. Likewise, the options for land use were very different in the period of demesne farming, population growth, and high land demand in the thirteenth and early fourteenth centuries than in the period of reduced population, high labour costs, low commodity prices, and seigneurial leasing that followed. The later middle ages also saw a shift in the regional pattern of wealth, from the Midlands grain belt to the south-east (buoyed by the London market) and the industrial south-west.[17] Besides these general economic trends, patterns of use might evolve as the park passed through the hands of succeeding owners with differing estate management priorities.[18]

A final complication is introduced by the nature of the surviving evidence on the economic use of parkland. The management of the majority of parks is poorly recorded. Only a few parks are well-documented in long runs of surviving manorial accounts, like those belonging to the crown or the bishops of Winchester; many others are provided with little or no equivalent material, particularly those belonging to the gentry. This makes it difficult to determine accurately how far the differing financial circumstances and estate-management practices of various types of owner affected the running of their parks. We might suspect, for example, that resident gentry park owners may have placed more emphasis on efficient exploitation than their absentee royal or magnate counterparts, but this is seldom possible to prove. Another more general problem is that profits from parks are not always clearly distinguished from those from other woods and pastures. Nonetheless, for all these complexities and potential elements of variation, certain significant features can be discerned.

THE NATURE OF PARK TERRAIN

The most basic question concerning parks as economic units is the kind of land that they incorporated. There is no denying the broad correlation suggested by much of the literature between parks, woodland, and inferior soils.[19] Place-names and Domesday data illustrate a regional link between woodland districts and imparking, in upland and lowland regions alike,[20] while the texts of park licences, earlier ones in particular, appear to give ready confirmation of the woody nature of the actual ground enclosed.[21] By contrast, where woods were few, parks also seem to have been thin on the ground, as in west Norfolk, most of Cambridgeshire,

---

[17] Bolton 1980: 229, 232–3.   [18] See e.g. Holmes 1957: 101.   [19] Above, pp. 2, 46.
[20] Rackham 1986: 123; Cantor and Hatherly 1977: 432; 1979: 74–6; Neave 1991: 5. There are difficulties in using the Domesday evidence for reconstructing woodland levels in individual manors, but the broad picture is tolerably accurate: Ford 1979: 149.
[21] For a few examples see *CPR, 1216–25*, 135; *CChR, 1226–57*, 114, 227, 333; *1257–1300*, 28.

Fenland Lincolnshire, and in much of a long stretch of open country running down from the Yorkshire Wolds to Salisbury Plain, including south-east Warwickshire and north-west Berkshire (Fig. 8, below).[22] This brings us to the link with poor soils, since on the whole woodland was most prevalent in localities which were less attractive to medieval farmers, with the woods themselves often occupying higher ground, steeper terrain, and poorly draining, acidic or infertile soils.[23]

Nonetheless, it is important to realize that these environmental links were broad rather than absolute ones and must not be exaggerated. For a start, the general link between more wooded areas and poor soils has to be qualified, and this has important implications for our understanding of the arable potential of land enclosed in parks. Woodland districts varied a good deal in their geology, topography, and soils. Some—often the most densely wooded—occupied inferior terrain with limited farming potential and had low population densities, including the Weald and the Chilterns. But others contained extensive areas of fertile soils and were much more densely settled, like north Essex and eastern Hertfordshire. Just as significantly, the potential of woodland districts for arable farming does not always seem to have been fully exploited during the middle ages. This is suggested, for instance, in the case of the forests of Wychwood, in west Oxfordshire, and Whittlewood, on the Buckinghamshire–Northamptonshire border, by evidence of extensive Roman settlement and farming in places which reverted to scrub and woodland in the early Anglo-Saxon period and were only very partially cleared for farming in the high middle ages. It seems then that woodland regions were not *necessarily* less fertile than their champion counterparts and that the extent to which individual areas were used for cereal farming in the middle ages was not purely related to their suitability for crop growing. The development and survival of distinctive 'wood-pasture' landscapes cannot therefore be explained simply by physical and environmental characteristics. It also has to be understood in terms of a range of other factors, including the formation of early territorial units, the development of patterns of landholding, settlement, and agrarian exploitation, and cultural priorities, including the creation of forests and other hunting grounds.[24]

Just as importantly, the correlation between parks and woodland was not as overwhelmingly strong as sometimes supposed. Although parks generally clustered around wooded regions, the presence of extensive woodland did not ensure heavy imparking and nor did its absence necessarily preclude it. Thus some of the most thickly wooded areas, including the Weald, had little more than an average density of parks, and others, like the west Hertfordshire Chilterns, had fewer than less wooded places nearby. By contrast, certain districts with more moderate levels of woodland cover saw the creation of

---

[22] Campbell 2000: 82–3.
[23] Rowley 1986: 113; Rackham 1986: 98; Roden 1968: 62; Short 2000: 123.
[24] Williamson 2003: 57 ff.; Bond 1986: 152; Jones and Page 2006: 107–8.

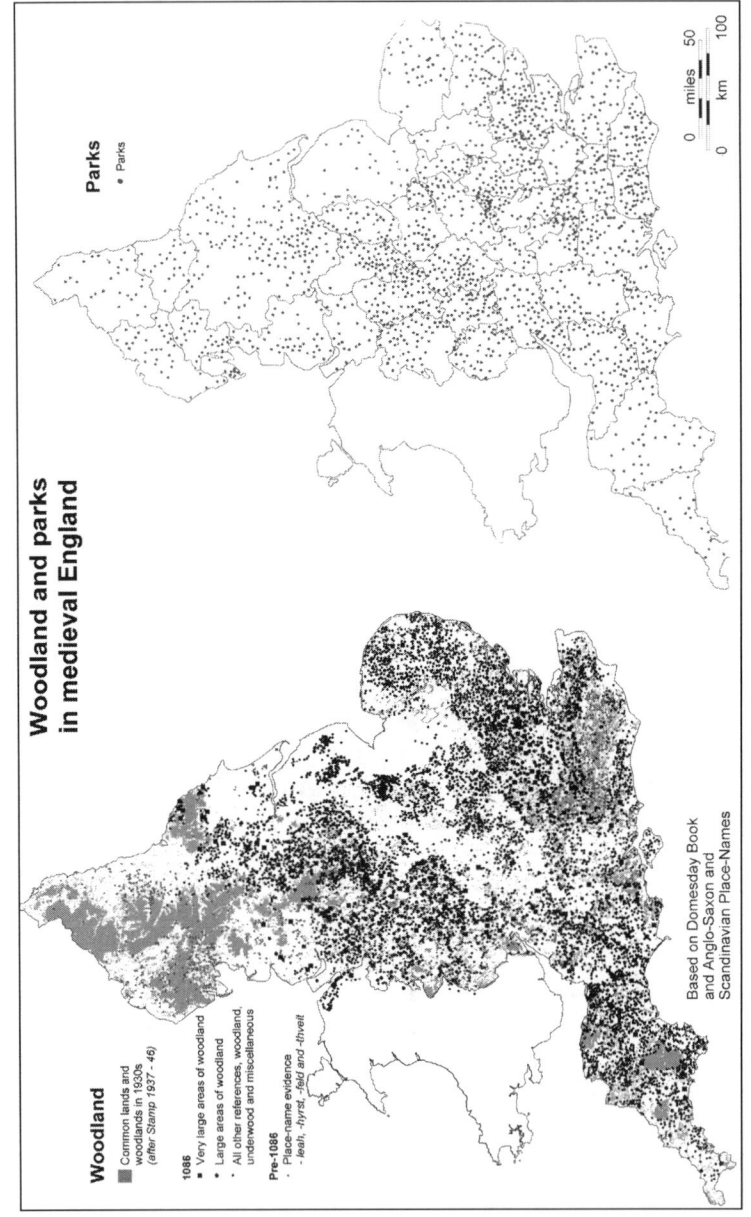

Fig. 8. The distribution of woodland and parks in medieval England.
Sources: Roberts and Wrathmell 2002: 28 (by permission of English Heritage); Cantor 1983: 4.

considerable numbers of parks in the twelfth and thirteenth centuries, including not just eastern Hertfordshire and north Essex, but also areas like non-Wealden Sussex (Fig. 9, overleaf) and parts of Leicestershire. A number of parks were even created in places with almost no woodland, including north-east Gloucestershire.[25] Recent investigation of Cornwall provides a similar caveat to the link between parks and heavily wooded areas since it suggests that around fifty parks were created in this poorly wooded county in the middle ages, rather than the eighteen or twenty previously identified.[26]

Given these complexities in the relationships between parks, woodland districts, and soils it is perhaps unsurprising that parks themselves seem to have enclosed land of varied quality, rather than being confined to the worst areas. In fact, quite frequently parks incorporated soils that were average or even good compared to the local norm, as is shown by evidence from Cambridgeshire, Hampshire, Staffordshire, and elsewhere.[27] Occasionally they even appear to have included some of the best land in their area: at Henley (Oxon.) in 1300, for example, sixty acres of parkland were being used (perhaps temporarily) for arable worth 4d. per acre,[28] a value which compared very favourably to other arable land on this part of the Chiltern dip slope.[29] Some of the early parks of the bishops of Winchester and Bath in Hampshire and Somerset likewise appear to have taken in prime local land.[30] In Cornwall, parks were mainly established in the county's 'agricultural heartland', rather than in high and bare uplands less suitable for farming, settlement, or park-making, and usually included sizeable areas with arable potential.[31] Much the same could be said about the parks of North Yorkshire or the Lake District.[32]

In other words, although further investigation is called for, we can already suggest that the enclosure of parks, even in early periods, regularly kept potentially cultivable soils out of arable use. This rather more nuanced picture is strengthened by several further points. First, since many parks covered large areas it was almost inevitable that they would incorporate some cultivable land. Indeed, the very nature of the park usually required that not all should be thick wood or steep hillsides: after all, grass formed the main foodstuff for the deer and hunting required open spaces and at least some stretches of fairly level ground. In any case, gradients could actually make heavy soils more workable since they

[25] Campbell *et al.* 1992: 12; Rowe 2007: 135–40; Williamson 2003: 57; Rackham 1986: 123–5; Cantor 1983: *passim*; above, p. 50 (Fig. 8).
[26] Herring 2003: 35; Cantor 1983: 18–19. Cf. below, p. 140 on landownership and park distribution.
[27] Way 1997: 36–7; Roberts 1988: 75–6; Hodder 1988–9: 41, 45, 48, 50; 1992: 180. Cf. Squires 1992: 48; Richardson 2005: 13–14; Rimington 1971: 6.
[28] TNA: PRO, C133/95, no. 24.
[29] Demesne arable at nearby Rotherfield Greys, Rotherfield Peppard, and Bolney was valued at only 2d. per acre in the early 14th cent.: TNA: PRO, C134/26/10, no. 9; C134/14, no. 23; E142/32, rot. 13. For arable values more generally see Campbell *et al.* 1992: 16 (table 8).
[30] Roberts 1988: 76; Aston 1988: 87. [31] Herring 2003: 37. Cf. Caseldine 1999: 32.
[32] Muir 2006: 133, 137 (figures).

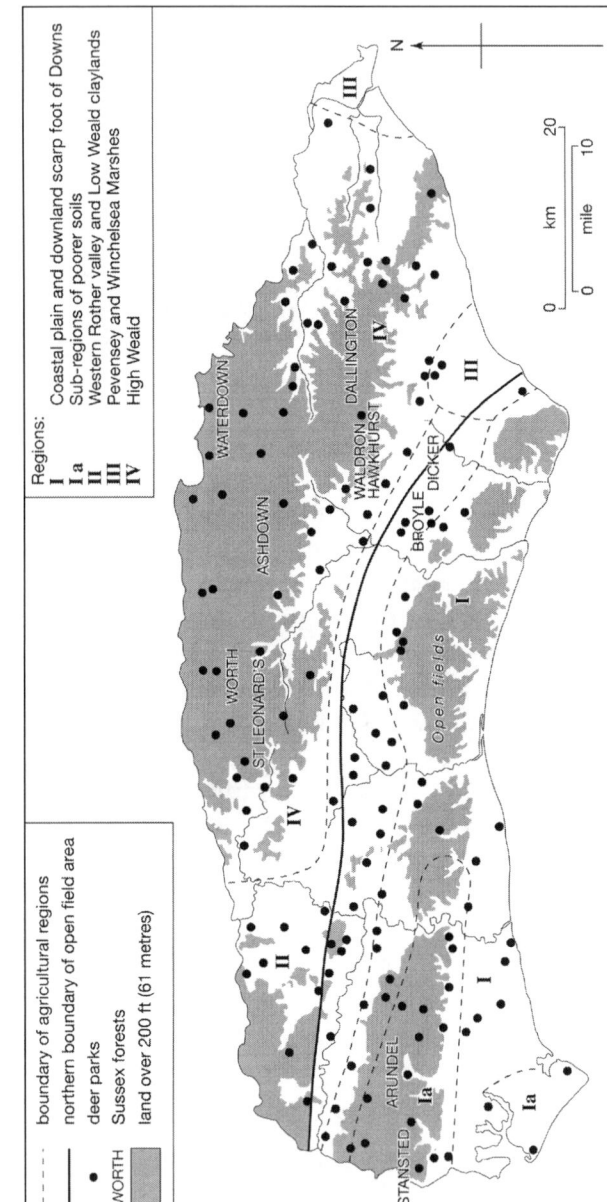

Fig. 9. Parks and farming areas in Sussex.
Source: Gardiner 1999: 38–9.

aided drainage, and horse-drawn ploughs in particular could tackle quite steep slopes.[33] Evidence of prehistoric, Romano-British, and Anglo-Saxon settlement and field systems in areas converted into parkland in the middle ages also testifies to parks' farming potential.[34] As the example of Henley suggests, recognition of the cultivable quality of land in parks was sometimes demonstrated in the middle ages by total or partial disparkment and conversion to farmland or by the cultivation of small areas of crops in carefully fenced off compartments inside active parks, as at Blackley park in Manchester (Lancs.) in 1322.[35]

More than this, we can actually show that parks did not simply occupy *potentially* cultivable land that was deliberately kept out of productive use, but that significant numbers of them took in land that was, or had recently been, under the plough. All the evidence suggests that cultivated land taken into parks was overwhelmingly converted into deer pasture, rather than cultivation continuing, not least because to grow crops near deer required costly additional fencing.[36] Importantly, this imparkment and conversion of arable was not solely a product of the decline in the value of this land in the later middle ages, but occurred in the high middle ages too. In the lowlands in particular, early parks entirely formed from vacant ground were probably not as common as has been suggested; perhaps they were even the exception rather than the rule. Twelfth- and thirteenth-century lords were engaged in a complex process of estate and settlement redesign rather than creation, and they were prepared to carry out major changes in already populated landscapes to establish their residential complexes and home farms, shifting peasant holdings and taking arable land out of productive use. As Ros Faith has perceptively suggested, 'many of the old cultivated inlands around the lord's house may have been replaced by deer parks'.[37]

The enclosure of arable land within parks can be demonstrated by a combination of landscape and documentary evidence. Modern field surveys, like the large-scale RCHM project in Northamptonshire, show ridge and furrow and former plough headlands in land which must once have been in parks, at least some of which probably derived from medieval cultivation prior to imparkment.[38] But ridge and furrow is uneven in its survival and difficult to date, so other types of evidence have to be employed too, including topography. For instance, the bishop of Bath's park at Westbury (Somerset) occupied a fertile,

---

[33] Rackham 1986: 98.
[34] Bellamy *et al*. 1983: 15–16 (Brigstock, Northants.); *VCH Berks*., iv. 503 and Oxon. HER, Parks and Gardens Register (Ashdown, Berks.); Wade-Martins and Yaxley 1980: 18–19 (North Elmham, Norf.); RCHM *Dorset*, iii. 298; above, p. 35 (Fig. 6).
[35] Farrer (ed.) 1907: 52 (13 acres of arable worth 8s. 8d.). See also e.g. *VCH Shrops*., viii. 162; *VCH Oxon*., xiv. 200; Winchester 2007: 182; TNA: PRO, SC8/44/2191; SC6/1248/13, m. 6.
[36] Below, p. 70.
[37] Faith 1997: 194. The effects of parks on peasant farming are discussed further in Ch. 7, below.
[38] Taylor 1980: maps 17 and 18; RCHM *Northants*., iii. 165. Ridge and furrow can still be seen on the ground in the area of the medieval park at Kirtlington (Oxon.): personal observation, Apr. 2004. Features preserved in Beche Park Wood, near Aldworth (Berks.), may be former headlands: fieldwork by Dick Greenaway, 2003.

and presumably early-settled valley site in the parish and it seems highly likely that the creation of the park would have displaced existing cultivation.[39] But it is when there is also documentary material that the analysis can usually be taken much further. For some places it is actually possible to give an indication of how much cultivated ground particular parks took in during the twelfth and thirteenth centuries and to see something of the financial costs. In 1130, for instance, the sheriff of Gloucestershire claimed a reduction in his farm to take into account loss of earnings amounting to £3 12s. through the imparking of *terra lucrabili* (presumably arable) into the royal park of Alveston.[40] The enclosure of the early park at Framlingham castle (Suffolk) seems to have necessitated a wholesale takeover of land, including arable, meadow, and pasture as well as woodland and common waste.[41] In the late thirteenth century Hugh de Courtenay created a large deer park next to his *caput* at Okehampton (Devon), on the edge of Dartmoor, clearing away farmsteads to the south of the castle, as well as converting part of the demesne arable to parkland.[42] At King's Langley (Herts.) 120 acres of land 'which was arable' and eight acres of meadow 'which used to be mowed before deer were placed therein' were enclosed in a new royal park by 1290.[43] Many other examples could be cited from elsewhere in the country, in lowland and upland areas alike.[44]

We can gain a better sense of the way park-making could directly interfere with arable cultivation in the twelfth and thirteenth centuries by looking in more detail at a couple of south Midlands counties, Oxfordshire and Bedfordshire. The process of enclosure and conversion of farmland in these two counties was well under way in the twelfth century. At Woodstock (Oxon.), for example, there was major land-use change, perhaps occurring in two main stages, and this almost certainly involved some appropriation of tenant arable land as well as enclosure of wood, waste, pasture, and meadow. A very large part of the northern half of the park was taken out of the lands of Wootton parish (Wootton village is a mile and a half north of Woodstock), probably in or before the early twelfth century, and some of this was likely to have been farmland.[45] Certainly, the majority of the northern part of the park has always been suitable for corn growing,[46] and an area of slight ridge and furrow north of the site of the former royal palace may represent the vestige of part of the open fields of Old Woodstock (see Fig. 10).[47] Slightly later, the park seems to have been extended to the south-east of the palace, perhaps when New Woodstock was founded in the later twelfth century,[48] thereby incorporating the northern area of the open fields of Hensington (in Bladon parish), part of a Templar estate.[49]

---

[39] Aston 1988: 87.   [40] Hunter (ed.) 1833: 77; *VCH Gloucs.*, ii. 264 ff.
[41] Hoppitt 1992: i. 105.   [42] Austin 1978: 195–6.   [43] Munby 1977: 132.
[44] Slade (ed.) 1962: 236–9; *CIPM* iii. 463–4; *VCH Berks.*, iii. 211; HMC, *Various Collections*, i (1901), 364; *CChR, 1226–57*, 463; Hoppitt 1992: i. 59; Richardson 2005: 42; Winchester 2007: 182.
[45] *VCH Oxon.*, xii. 16, 443.   [46] Ibid. 430–1; Orr 1916: 61.   [47] Bond 1997: 49–50.
[48] *Rot. Hund.*, ii. 839.   [49] *VCH Oxon.*, xii. 14, 16 (map), 441. Cf. Bond 1997: 48–9.

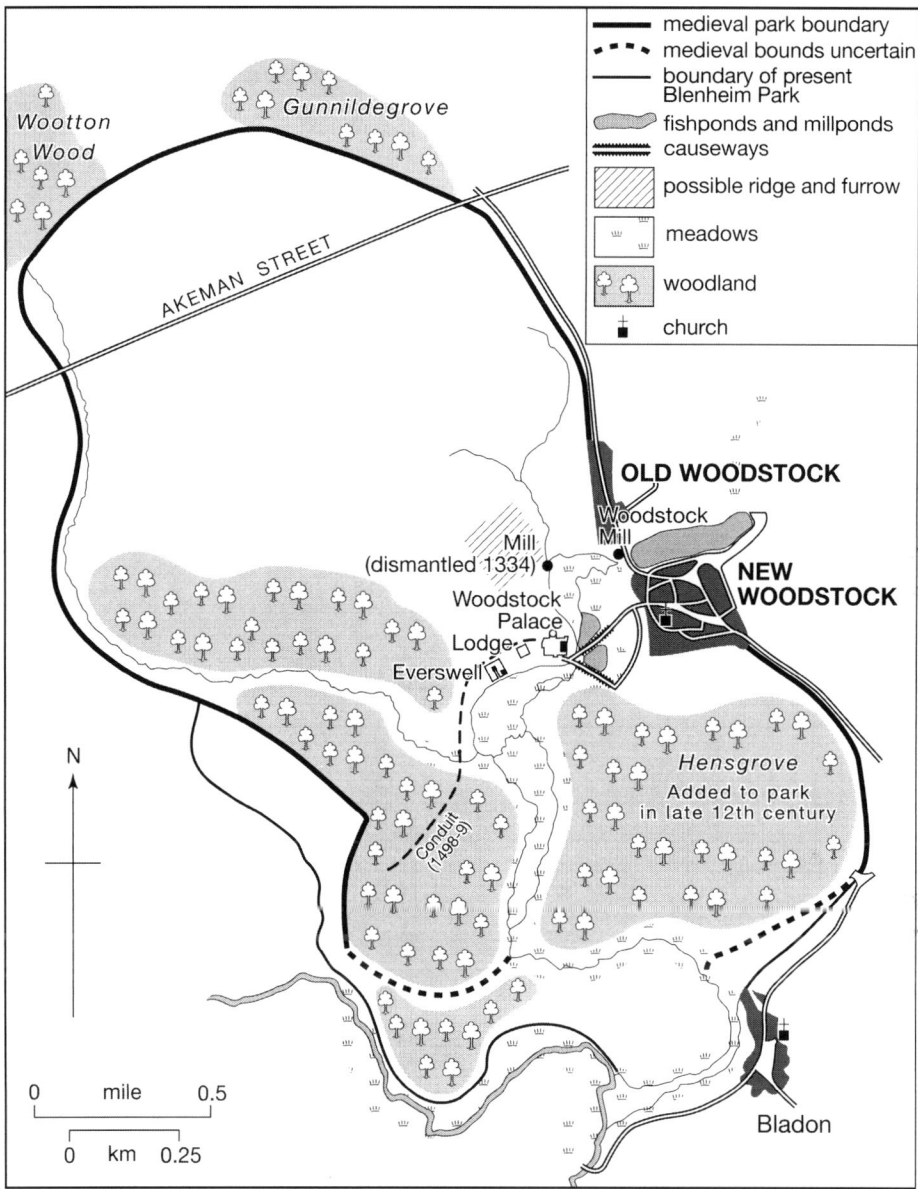

Fig. 10. Woodstock park in the middle ages.
Source: Bond 1997: 29.

At Thame (Oxon.), as at Woodstock, it seems that meadow and arable lands were enclosed as well as woodland and pasture. Before 1146 there had been a neat division between the abbey's demesne inside the park and the lands of the peasants around the outside (*circa parcum*), probably involving the reorganization of holdings. This had presumably occurred when the park was first set up by the bishop of Lincoln some years earlier: certainly an extension of the park while it was still in his hands in 1131 required an exchange of land with Richard de Vernon.[50] This park may have functioned as more of a home farm than a game preserve under the abbots, but there is no reason to believe that the bishop of Lincoln set it up as anything other than a deer park.[51]

Segenhoe (Beds.) provides similar evidence of large-scale farming reorganization. Here the twelfth-century (or earlier) park was part of a ten-hide estate, which was gradually broken up into small manors during the middle ages; the early park itself was succeeded by two parks within what became the two main manors (Brogborough and Beckerings).[52] In the later twelfth century the lord of Odell, the main landholder, was involved in a major reorganization of land with the lord of 'La Leigh', during which he seems to have shown more interest in maintaining the integrity of his park and perhaps extending it than retaining arable land or the peasant cultivators. In order to retain the whole park and the demesne at Brogborough for himself, Odell seems to have been persuaded to give away a quarter of the arable land in the manor (two out of eight hides), and, at the same time to eject all the villeins who lived next to the wood at 'Bechebury'.[53]

In other cases there is no known documentary record but topographical evidence strongly suggests early interference with farming and landholding. For example, at Beckley (Oxon.) a detailed reconstruction of the later medieval settlement pattern and field boundaries can be used to conjecture about the effects of the creation of a large baronial park in the later twelfth century. Given the early presence of settlement here, it seems highly likely that the enclosure of the park would have taken in parts of the open fields of the neighbouring communities of Beckley, Horton, and Woodperry (Fig. 11, opposite).

Similar disruption to cereal farming and consequent loss of profits seems to have continued into the thirteenth century and beyond. At Stevington (Beds.), for instance, Roger de Quincy apparently took over twenty acres of arable into his park, giving Harrold priory 2½ acres of arable in exchange for lost tithes.[54] At Eaton Bray (Beds.) the landscape evidence shows a c.100-acre park just a few hundred metres from the site of the medieval village and it seems likely that the park enclosure caused considerable disruption to land use, possibly involving the displacement of existing farming.[55] At Kirtlington (Oxon.), the Bassets' park, first referred to as 'recently constructed' in 1279, appears to

---

[50] Salter (ed.) 1947–8: i 143; Johnson and Cronne (eds.) 1956: no. 1707.
[51] For the granting of deer parks to monastic communities see above, p. 28.
[52] VCH Beds., iii. 320–2 (the manorial history is complex and this old account rather inadequate); VCH Beds., ii. 147; Beds. RO, H/DE 433 (1728 map).
[53] BL, Harley 1885, f. 7. Cf. Vinogradoff 1892: 233–4, 457.   [54] Fowler (ed.) 1935: 41.
[55] Schedule of Ancient Monuments, Park Farm (1995): copy in Bedfordshire HER.

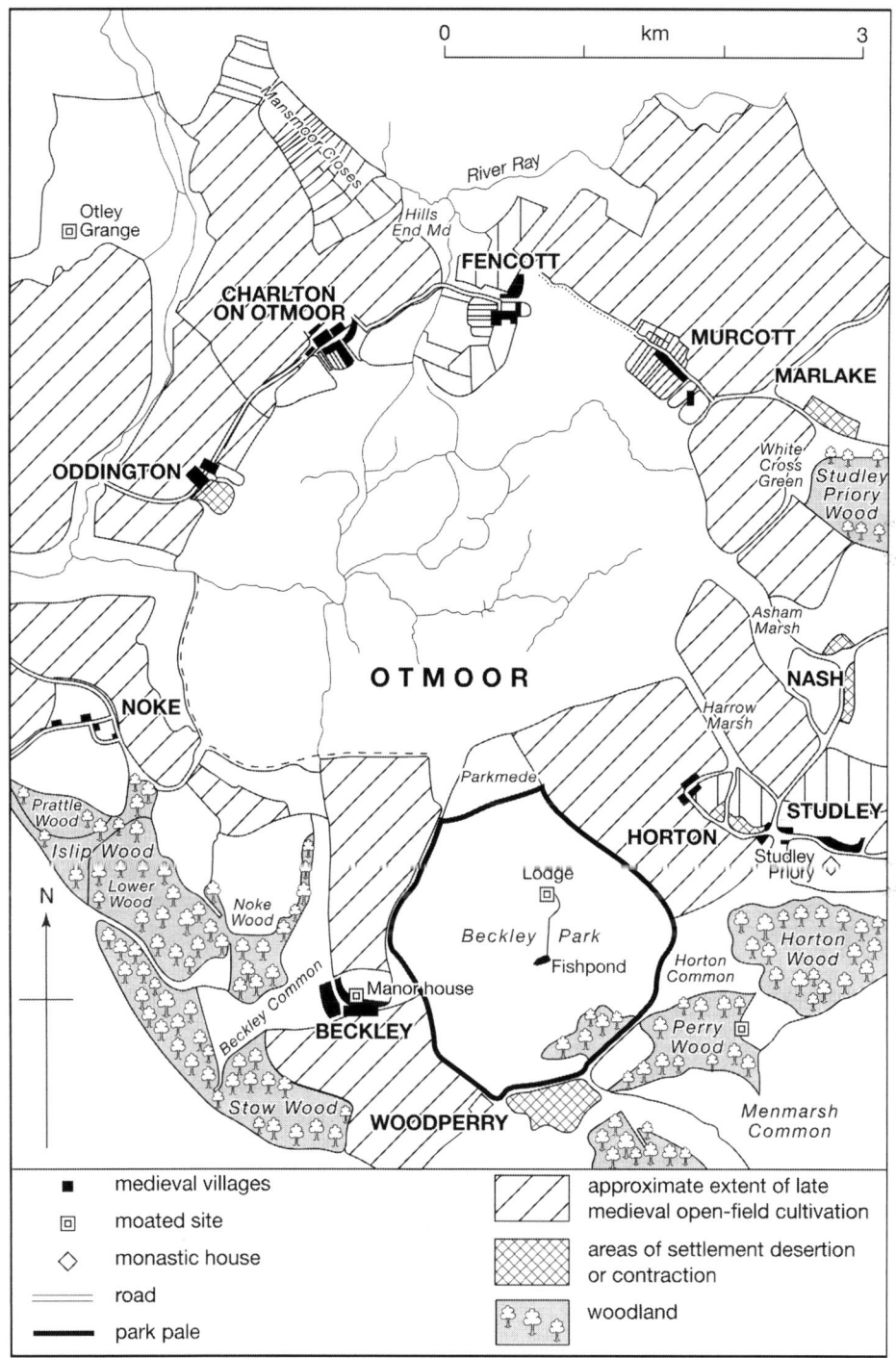

Fig. 11. Beckley park in the later middle ages.
Source: Bond 1981: 119.

have been at least partly created out of the open fields.[56] At Henley (Oxon.) £1 3s. worth of arable land formerly in hands of three tenants had been taken into Richard, earl of Cornwall's park before 1269, the rents lost.[57] In 1296–7 a tenant at Watlington was absolved of 10d. rent for three acres of land taken into a park belonging to Richard's son and successor, Edmund.[58]

These instances provide nine certain or very probable cases of parks taking in arable (as well as pasture and valuable meadowland) in twelfth- and thirteenth-century Oxfordshire and Bedfordshire, each of which counties had around thirty parks by 1300. Yet it would be wrong to assume that the fairly limited number of known documentary or archaeological indications of imparking taking in arable represent the full extent of the interference, either in these counties or elsewhere. The very proximity of many parks to villages, hamlets, and their fields suggests otherwise,[59] and where we do have the rare luxury of good documentary evidence, there are indications of quite widespread addition of arable land to parks, as on the bishop of Winchester's estates in southern England.[60] In fact, it seems likely that some kind of initial interference with cultivated land or later extension onto it occurred in a considerable proportion of cases; in the lowlands it may even have been a majority. By the thirteenth century the continuing spread of agriculture would have made disruption more likely than in earlier periods, although high profits from increasing demesne cultivation would have been some discouragement to large-scale reorganization of cultivated ground.

It seems then that lords were willing to give up the prospect of farming potentially cultivable land for the sake of their parks, even ground that was currently under crops or had recently been so. No doubt they acted within limits, probably rarely sacrificing the most productive areas. In this respect it is notable that the later thirteenth-century spurt in imparkment in Wealden Sussex, which included the enclosure of land previously improved by marling, came at a time when landowners there were shifting the agricultural focus to their champion estates, where the use of legumes was increasing productivity.[61] More generally, the imparking of arable seems to have been particularly extensive in the twenty years or so before the Black Death,[62] at a time when lords' profits from cereal farming were reduced by a fall in grain prices not matched by a fall in labour costs and, in some areas, by increasing rural poverty and soil exhaustion.[63]

---

[56] *VCH Oxon.*, vi. 225; *Rot. Hund.*: ii. 822; St John's College, Oxford MS: Kirtlington Survey, 1750.
[57] TNA: PRO, SC6/1095/9; Midgley (ed.) 1942 and 1945: i. 99.
[58] Midgley (ed.) 1942 and 1945: i. 84.
[59] Figs. 6, 10, 11, 13–14, 17, 21–3. See also the useful local reconstructions in Currie 1997: 16 and RCHM, *Northants.*, iii. 165.
[60] Hants. RO, 11M59/B1/42, rot. 2d.; Page (ed.) 1996: 33, 105, 277.
[61] Brandon 1974: 104.
[62] See e.g. Vanderzee (ed.) 1807: 8, 172, 332, 334, 376, 380; *VCH Sussex*, ii. 295–6; *VCH Oxon.*, xii. 14 and 441; Steane 1994: 455 and 457 (fig. 4); Lyth 1986: 20.
[63] Miller and Hatcher 1978: 52, 61, 66; Dyer 2002: 239–40; Britnell 2004: 289 (fig. 14.2).

Nonetheless, on the whole, the use of cultivable ground for parkland seems to be a first pointer to the uneconomic motivations behind imparking. This land generally had the potential to deliver higher profits under crops than as deer pasture, particularly before the second quarter of the fourteenth century. Its enclosure, like the enclosure of meadow, suggests that lords were not totally bound by land quality and optimum use in determining where to establish their parks. And, quite apart from the enclosure of existing fields, it has to be remembered that the creation of parks in woodland and waste could also serve to block the further expansion of farming in the thirteenth and early fourteenth centuries.[64]

THE PRESSURE ON WOODLAND AND WASTE

But might it have been that at certain times there was so much pressure on wood-pasture that lords wished to retain it, including where land had some agrarian potential, or even to extend it by enclosing farmland? After all, while twelfth- to fourteenth-century lords might benefit from woodland clearance and increased farming activity, the reduction and overuse of wood-pasture was clearly sometimes a cause of concern for them.[65] Rather than being proto-environmentalists, these men were worried about securing supplies of timber, fuel, and fodder. These commodities were costly to transport and not always readily available on the local market, with prices fluctuating considerably according to supply and demand. Royal gifts of timber for building and dead trees for fuel were very numerous by the thirteenth century and seem to indicate that lords could not always obtain sufficient supplies of these materials. Even those with wood stocks of their own might have to undertake long-distance transport from one manor to another, especially where large building timbers were involved.[66] Part of the problem was that tenants required these same resources: where locals had common rights, they often gradually denuded woods and overused pastures and hindered effective lordly management and exploitation.[67]

In the light of this, it seems reasonable to suggest that the creation of parkland was, at least in part, a way of preserving and managing wood-pasture as a useful resource. Indeed, a broad correspondence between the spread of imparking and the pressure on wood-pasture is clear enough. If the twelfth to early fourteenth century was probably the period of most clearance for cultivation and greatest

[64] The effect of this on local communities is discussed below, p. 164.
[65] Rackham 1986: 301; Rowley 1986: 115.
[66] Farmer 1991: 409–10; 1995: 105, 119; Dyer 1980: 70; Rogers 1866–1902: i. 249–51, 424, 445–7; Johnson and Cronne (eds.) 1956: no. 774.
[67] Birrell 1987: 41; TNA: PRO, C133/22, no. 1; C133/118/17, no. 4; C134/97/4, no. 3; CPR, 1330–4, 18; CIPM xxi, nos. 627, 629.

use of wood for building and firewood, it also appears to have been the period of greatest park creation,[68] and by the turn of the fourteenth century it may be that as much as a fifth of all remaining wood-pasture was enclosed inside deer parks.[69] But was there really a close match between pressure on resources and the creation of individual parks? To answer this, the precise chronology and location of woodland clearance compared to imparking has to be assessed, even if, inevitably, this can only be done on a localized basis.

No single county or region can represent the whole picture, but Oxfordshire may serve as a case study to start a more detailed reconstruction. Here, as elsewhere, many parks were set up in areas where there was probably increasing competition for wood-pasture resources, between lord and lord and lord and tenant, for example at Elsfield.[70] Rather than pursue individual examples, it might be useful to try to distinguish common features in the well-wooded districts that saw particularly heavy imparkment: west Oxfordshire and the upland Chilterns in the far south.

In the west of the county considerable wood and unused ground remained in the late eleventh century. But woodland and waste was not evenly spread, and woodland in particular was concentrated in Wychwood forest and in sizeable pockets at Stanton Harcourt, Ducklington, Hanborough, and Bladon. Some local populations were growing rapidly, putting more pressure on pasture, timber, and fuel and in places considerable assarting was going on (usually directed by the manorial lords).[71] At the same time it is notable that there were many imparkments. In Wootton hundred, for instance, it seems probable that Henry II extended Woodstock park by the incorporation of Hensgrove Wood around the time he founded the adjacent borough of New Woodstock on waste ground, which would have brought an increased local population and made closer control of the adjacent woodland more desirable.[72] In the same hundred, parks were also created at Eynsham, Cornbury, and perhaps at Hanborough by the thirteenth century and at Stanton Harcourt in the earlier fourteenth. Moving further west, Bampton hundred experienced the greatest population growth in Oxfordshire between 1086 and 1334;[73] in the manor of Witney, for instance, the population seems to have more than doubled during the thirteenth century.[74] Bampton also saw a notable concentration of imparking, with parks created at Standlake, Ducklington (where the lord was assarting too), and Witney in the thirteenth century.

The well-documented manor of the bishop of Winchester in Witney provides a particularly useful example for analysis. Here the terrain was predominantly open-field, marsh, meadow, and rough pasture, with woodland mainly in the

---

[68] For more on the chronology of park-making see above, p. 7, and below, pp. 134–6.
[69] If, as Rackham suggests, wood-pasture then covered 10% of England and parks 2%: Rackham 1986: 88, 123. But note below, p. 109.
[70] Clark 1977: 2–3, 6.   [71] Schumer 1999: 33, 37–8.   [72] *VCH Oxon.*, xii. 333.
[73] Martin and Steel 1954 (eds.): 111.   [74] Titow 1962: 4–5.

north.[75] In 1086 twenty-five ploughs were in operation, which would suggest that around 3,000 acres were already under cultivation (at roughly 120 acres per plough). Titow estimated that up to the early fourteenth century a further 1,770 acres were reclaimed from the waste and cultivated; 1,110 acres by 1256 and another 660 acres by 1306, when reclamation more or less ended.[76] That would put almost 5,000 acres under cultivation. Since the size of the manor was around 7,000 acres, this would mean that there was a diminishing amount of uncultivated ground outside the park and adjoining chase by the later thirteenth and early fourteenth century, once settlement, roads, and water are taken into account.[77] The creation of the park, in the mid-thirteenth century, might thus plausibly appear to have been an attempt to conserve part of the remaining wood-pasture.

Looking south-east, there were broadly comparable developments in the Chilterns. The dip slope of the hills had a large quantity of woodland,[78] but it was shared among many lords and neighbouring lowland communities as well as the upland hamlets in the hills themselves. Nor was wood cover unlimited or ubiquitous even here: 'feld' names such as Rotherfield were chosen by the Anglo-Saxons to denote open pasture plateaux in the woods, and settlement and arable farming was well established by the eleventh century.[79] Parts of the Chilterns apparently saw considerable population growth (from a fairly low base) and quite widespread assarting in the high middle ages.[80] The area also witnessed park-making on a large scale and sizeable chunks of woodland were enclosed within parks as a result. For example, at Stonor probably half the woodland in the manor was imparked in the early fourteenth century.[81] Just as significantly, in many Chiltern parishes decent pasture for animals was meagre and a good deal of it enclosed in parks, including in Rotherfield Greys and Rotherfield Peppard.[82] Imparking here too could thus be interpreted as a response to spreading cultivation and intensifying use of wastes, as at Watlington, on the scarp face, where the park was formed in the eastern part of the parish around the mid-thirteenth century, at a time when settlement and farming had for quite some time been spreading onto the higher ground in this area.[83]

Finally, to look briefly elsewhere in the county, in some of those places where there was less wood-pasture there might seem to be an even stronger link between pressure on resources and imparking. Banbury hundred was very densely settled from an early date and the park created at Banbury in the

---

[75] *VCH Oxon.*, xiv. 1–3; Gelling 1953–4 (ed.): ii. 333. The very large wooded area attributed to this manor in 1086 may be partly explained by the existence of use-rights in neighbouring Wychwood: *VCH Oxon.*, i. 401; Schumer 1999: 35, map 10.
[76] Titow 1962: 8–9.
[77] The park seems to have been around 180 acres in extent: *VCH Oxon.*, xiv. 199–200.
[78] Rackham 1986: 77 (fig. 5.4).
[79] Blair 1994: pp. xxii, 126 (fig. 74); Hepple and Doggett 1994: 68–9.
[80] Stamper 1988: 129; *VCH Oxon.*, xvi. 11, 210, 247.   [81] Steane 1994: 456–7.
[82] Roden 1969: 11.   [83] *VHC Oxon.*, viii. 225; Emery 1974: 78.

early thirteenth century enclosed what was probably the only area of remaining woodland.[84] Likewise, there was very little woodland in Finmere where a park had been set up by the early thirteenth century. At Hook Norton Domesday suggests that arable cultivation was already extensive and there was only a small wood; the park there probably enclosed much of the remaining uncultivated ground, largely meadow and pasture near the stream.[85]

Nonetheless, if the Oxfordshire evidence reinforces the general link between pressure on wood-pasture and imparking, it also shows a more complex picture: the relationship was not direct or all-important and must not be overstated. At Witney much of the known high-medieval assarting was carried out in the north-east (Hailey township), whereas the park was set up in an area in Curbridge township, west of the borough, with more stable, longer established open fields. Chunks of woodland remained in the north in any case, in the purlieu of Wychwood forest, especially in the north-west (in Crawley township), and lord and tenants alike enjoyed common rights in the forest itself.[86] For all the assarting in well-wooded areas like Wychwood or in the Chilterns, there was no danger of a total denuding of woodland or conversion of all untilled ground to arable.[87] If there was pressure on wastes in parts of these less intensively farmed areas, it had its limits. It is also notable that the chronology of assarting did not necessarily closely match that of imparking. This is demonstrated in areas around Wychwood where much assarting started after the formal removal of forest law at the beginning of the fourteenth century, but failed to prompt any related spurt in park-making.[88] What is more, in certain places parks were created where the population seems to have been hardly growing at all and there can only have been slight pressure on large wastes, as at Middleton Stoney and Bucknell.[89]

The same mixed picture applies to other parts of the country. In places park-making probably helped to preserve dwindling woodland in the face of expanding populations and growing pressure on resources, as in the Stort Valley in Hertfordshire in the thirteenth century.[90] But the situation was apparently very different in other times and places. Many of the manors that Domesday Book shows already had parks in 1086 were then heavily wooded and largely made up of soils that would have discouraged early cultivators.[91] In subsequent centuries parks might likewise be created in locations where plenty of untilled ground remained. For instance, Kent and Hampshire were full of parks by the early fourteenth century, but their creation cannot necessarily be linked to any

---

[84] *VCH Oxon.*, x. 50. Domesday records 50 hides of land with no woodland; pasture was a mere three furlongs by two. For the many settlements, especially hamlets, see *Rot. Hund.* ii. 705–10.
[85] Tiller 2000: 282, 285.   [86] *VCH Oxon.*, xiv. 1, 178–9, 199–200, 206–7, 214–15 (map).
[87] Schumer 1999: 59, 62.   [88] On these clearances see Schumer 1999: 56.
[89] Rahtz and Rowley 1984: 12–13; *VCH Oxon.*, vi. 75 (Bucknell).
[90] Rowe 2007: 143.   [91] Liddiard 2003: 9–10.

threat to the survival of woods and pastures. In fact, although these two counties were far from immune to the general population growth of the period, wood-pasture remained so abundant in many locations that it was probably often omitted from manorial extents because not scarce enough to be worth recording.[92]

These examples have so far been drawn from lowland areas, but similar caveats apply, and often more strongly, to upland areas, where, despite population growth and the spread of farming, in many places human activity remained much more restricted. In Durham, for instance, there was still plenty of waste in the eighteenth century and not all of it could have been cultivated or heavily grazed even when population was at its peak of medieval growth in the late thirteenth century.[93] The same was probably true in the north Midlands in the Ferrers' forests of Needwood (Staffs.) and Duffield Frith (Derbs.), where there was some expansion of arable and pastoral activity, but where the local population remained low in the twelfth and thirteenth century, when most of the parks in the forest were probably created. In sum, there was a correlation between rapidly growing population and park-making, but it was far from absolute. Parks were created in some manors being rapidly denuded of remaining wood-pasture, but not in others, as well as being established in other places where this resource was more plentiful.

If the park is to be seen as a means of preserving wood-pasture resources, these great variations in chronology and in the terrain enclosed—sometimes arable as well as wood and waste—are surprising. They suggest that the desire for a means of managing deer and providing a convenient place to store, nurture, hunt, and cull them was not necessarily directly linked to a larger goal of saving wood-pasture for its own sake. On many occasions, after all, lords only decided to make or extend a park after certain targeted areas of ground had already been turned over to arable, perhaps long ago. Most significantly of all, even if the evidence is taken to broadly support the idea that lords wanted to impark to preserve wood-pasture, this does not necessarily show that this imparking was motivated by anything other than the desire to preserve deer habitat and hunting ground. The only way to really find out how far the park was a way of retaining and exploiting wood-pasture as an economic resource is by looking at the way it was managed once created, and this is what we shall turn to next.

EXPLOITATION OF PARKLAND RESOURCES

There is no denying that parks were sometimes put to a wide range of agrarian and even industrial uses, from an early date and across the middle

[92] Hallam 1988c: 510, 524; Campbell 2000: 84–5.   [93] Dunsford and Harris 2003: 35, 53–4.

ages. Parks were used for pasturing demesne and tenant livestock; they provided firewood and peat and might be used for charcoal production; they could be a source of raw materials such as timber and stone; they often protected fishponds and rabbit warrens; some housed smithies, potteries, and mines; and, as we have seen, areas of parkland were occasionally given over to growing crops.[94] Many of the writers who cite examples of such uses emphasize their significance.[95] It is sometimes also pointed out that these kinds of exploitation might be made more productive by the practice of creating internal compartments, which, we might infer, was a sign of landlords trying to make their parks work economically.[96]

Certainly none of these functions must be discounted. The park could provide a relatively secure location for putting valuable horses and other livestock, sometimes containing scores or even hundreds of these animals,[97] and at the very least park enclosures provided handy pounds for tenants' or other locals' stray animals or for storing heriot beasts before their sale.[98] We may in fact sometimes underestimate the use of parks for livestock because estate records often focus on pasture rents paid by tenants, which represented only one part of their pastoral utilization: demesne use, which was often the priority, might only be recorded where it interfered with the agistment of peasant animals.[99] What is more, from an early period a number of larger parks provided venues for carefully managed horse-breeding and the king's stud was mainly based within royal parks.[100]

Parks could also be a major source of timber for their owners' or others' building projects.[101] Occasionally, park timber sales brought very large returns, like the 800 marks generated for the Black Prince at Peckforton (Ches.) in the late

---

[94] Fisher (ed.) 1946: nos. 18 and 42; Hoppitt 1992: i. 132; Watkins 1989: 13–15, 24; 1997: 22, 25; Moorhouse 2003a: 332–4; Le Patourel (ed.) 1957: 23, 24, 54, 61; Bellamy et al. 1983: 16; Britnell 1977: 107–12; Beresford 1971: 187; Riall 1997; Gaimster et al. 1989 (eds.): 189; Cantor and Moore 1963: 48; Roberts 1988: 74–8; Dyer 1994: 111; Woolgar (ed.) 1992–3: ii. 544–5; Stamp (ed.) 1930–3: i. 151; *CPR, 1301–7*, 278; *1446–52*, 57; *1485–94*, 130, 189.

[95] Cantor and Hatherly 1979: 80–1; Stamper 1988: 145–7; Lomas 1992: 158; Hey 1986: 82–3; Hunt 1997: 113–16; Dyer 1980: 151–2; Roberts 1988: 75; Britnell 1977: 111 nn. 23–4.

[96] Tudor and later depictions of compartmentalization in parks help to convey how this practice might have aided wood-pasture management in the middle ages: Roberts 1988: 76–7, esp. 76 (fig. 5); Stamper 1988: 142 (fig. 7.5).

[97] See e.g. Farmer 1995: 131: 108 peasant animals agisted in the c.600-acre episcopal park at Bishopstoke (Hants.) in 1301–2, and 175 in the following year (at 6d. a head).

[98] Pittman 1990: 20. Cf. Sumner 1917: 104.

[99] Kerr 1925: 66; Farmer 1995: 131; TNA: PRO, SC6/955/20 (Beckley, 1283–4). For other examples of demesne beasts in parks see *CRR, 1237–42*, 265; Slade and Lambrick (eds.) 1990 and 1992: i. 299–300; Page (ed.) 1996: 62 (Downton park, Wilts.: lord's livestock only), 80 (Merdon, Hants.: 27 demesne yearlings, but no tenant animals, 800-acre park), 223–4 (Fareham, Hants.: 24 demesne animals, along with some tenant livestock, 300-acre park), and *passim*.

[100] Birrell 1962: 119; Davis 1989: 40–1, 80–2; Neilson 1940: 437–44; Watney 1910: 28; MacGregor 1983: 47, 96, 100; *VCH Hants.*, iv. 90; Rimington 1971: 11–12; TNA: PRO, E101/102/1, 14, 20, 27.

[101] McIntosh 1986: 16–17; Harding and Lambert 1994: 6–7; *VCH Oxon.*, v. 67; Stamp (ed.) 1930–3: i. 1 ff.; Bond 1997: 37–42; *CCR, 1242–7*, 162.

1350s.[102] And a few exceptional parks seem even to have been created mainly or entirely as wood reserves. This seems particularly to have been the case with parks associated with wooded 'hays', found in royal forests and elsewhere. In Clarendon forest (Wilts.) Melchet park or 'hay' seems to have been enclosed in the early thirteenth century to provide timber, and the lodge built there in 1357 may have been primarily intended to guard this valuable resource.[103] Some parks produced underwood too. Estate surveys show that woodland in parks might be managed as coppices, sometimes divided into compartments cut on a planned rotation, with the length of cutting cycles determined by local growth rates and the size of shoots required. Much of the fuel wood and fencing material produced probably went to provide for the needs of the lord's household, although information on this is often hard to recover.[104] But there were also fairly frequent sales to locals to raise cash or dispose of excess, as appears to have occurred at Haynes (Beds.) in the later fourteenth century.[105]

In the larger parks there was sufficient space to fit in quite a considerable amount of grazing or fuel production, and this is reflected in profit levels. Some big parks appear to have been much utilized for pasturage, including Vastern Great Park (c.1,900 acres) in Wiltshire, the agistment of which was valued at as much as £10 per year in 1334.[106] In the uplands, large stone-walled parks were often closely connected with monastic and other grazing farms, such as the parks of Furness abbey, licensed in the early fourteenth century.[107] These pasture-based parks could support large numbers of livestock and turn in a significant proportion of estate profits, like the bishop of Durham's park at Bishop Auckland.[108] Here in 1338–9 the total receipts were just under £60, discounting arrears of £21. About 25 per cent of the receipts came from pasture, which was mainly in the very large, internally compartmented park. With wood sales and perquisites from the park realizing another £1 or so, the parkland brought in about £15 that year and cost only £1 10s. 5d. in maintenance. Other more wooded parks produced quantities of wood: the sale of timber and underwood from the earl of Gloucester's c.1,265 acres of parkland at Thornbury brought in a mean annual income of over £12 before the Black Death (with large yearly fluctuations).[109] Some produced particularly sizeable amounts of

---

[102] Booth 1981: 131. The great oaks in the park, which apparently remained untouched, were valued at a further £900. Cf. *VCH Oxon.*, v. 67: Edward I raised 400 marks from timber sales in Beckley park in 1301. See also Watkins 1997: 22, 25.

[103] Richardson 2005: 47, 49.   [104] Watkins 1993: 24, 25; TNA: PRO, C135/98, no. 8, m. 2.

[105] Thompson (ed.) 1978 [Beds. RO]: 6, 10, 14.

[106] *VCH Wilts.*, iv. 404. Cf. the bishop of Winchester's 1,000-acre park at Bishop's Waltham (Hants.): Page (ed.) 1996: 250–1, and the lords of Caus's 300-acre park of Minsterley (in Westbury), said to be worth £6 in 1300: *VCH Shrops.*, viii. 317.

[107] Waites 1997: 57–9; Aston 2000: 140; Atkin 1994: 12; Cumbria HER, 2804–6 (Crosby Ravensworth, Westml.).

[108] Greenwell (ed.) 1857: 201–6.

[109] Franklin 1989: 159 (and 162, 164 for estimated acreages of the two parks).

fuel: in the late 1380s the large archiepiscopal park at Beverley (Yorks.) was apparently made to yield 12,200 faggots a year, worth just over £18 net;[110] one year in the 1340s the Black Prince's household used some 7,275 faggots (valued at over £7) from the substantial park at Byfleet (Surrey).[111] Clarendon park's extensive coppice woods, primarily established in the early fourteenth century, were exceptionally valuable, raising £20–£35 per annum from 25–40 acres in 1330–3.[112]

Nonetheless, all these activities have to be quantified and put into perspective, rather than generalized claims being made from individual cases. The extent and frequency of productive use varied considerably, but when the evidence is looked at in more depth, it is possible to draw some general conclusions. Concentrating first on the period up to 1350, it becomes clear that economic activities were typically subsidiary, only a part of efforts to meet domestic requirements or, with the developing but limited commercial activities, designed to help offset something of the high costs associated with deer-keeping, rather than to generate profit in their own right. At best, parks were managed 'with an eye to general economic advantage', being expected to make a contribution towards paying for themselves.[113] As suggested earlier, we must resist the temptation to assume that because we have a considerable amount of documentary and archaeological evidence for the economic exploitation of parks, this means that such exploitation was their primary function.[114]

For a start, although internal fences used to separate different activities were probably common, they were far from ubiquitous, especially in earlier periods: according to one estimate, based on a wide study, only around half of parks were compartmentalized.[115] For many park-makers putting up such fencing was probably not an initial priority and it may have appeared gradually over time rather than all being erected when the park was first enclosed. It is notable, for instance, that the abbot of Abingdon only inserted details about preserving enclosed coppices in Radley park (Berks.) into a fourteenth-century confirmation of a thirteenth-century agreement about the custody of the park: the original charter just referred to timber and wind-fallen branches.[116] Without these internal compartments it was much harder to sustain mixed use. Domestic stock could not be very effectively managed without segregation, to control breeding and keep them separate from the game.[117] Only with fences could woodland be better preserved from the particularly destructive eating habits of the deer: left to their own devices these creatures destroy all but mature

---

[110] *CIPM* iv. 214.
[111] Stamp (ed.) 1930–3: i. 151. In 1607 the park was said to be over three miles in circuit (*VCH Surrey*, iii. 402).
[112] Richardson 2005: 49–51, 55–6. [113] Roberts 1988: 78; Stamper 1988: 145.
[114] Above, p. 36. [115] Rackham 1986: 126.
[116] Slade and Lambrick (eds.) 1990 and 1992: i. 299–300.
[117] Cantor and Hatherly 1979: 80.

trees.[118] Without internal fencing, underwood shoots could not be cut at ground level ('coppiced') but could only be produced more inconveniently by lopping tree trunks at a height ('pollarding'), in this case just above the deer's browsing reach.[119] Like any other fences internal park barriers required regular upkeep, and many must have decayed over time.

The serious limitations to the economic exploitation of parks become even clearer when we look at each area in detail. Frequently park pastures were said to be worth nothing at all because the presence of wild beasts precluded any stock grazing or mowing, and sometimes even pig pannaging.[120] In most parks the presence of deer greatly restricted grazing use, especially in the winter,[121] and any grazing by domestic stock was most often assessed at a low value, from a few shillings to two or three pounds.[122] Even at Alvechurch (Worcs.), where pasturage brought in a respectable £2 9s. 8d. in 1299, the bishop of Worcester's estate surveyor stated that the park pasturage was worth 'so little' because the wild beasts grazed most of the grass.[123] The fact was that many small and medium-sized parks had too little excess pasture to support any but a few domestic animals, presumably often demesne stock. And even with big upland pasture parks we must not forget the deer: at Bishop Auckland (Durham) in 1350–1 there were no receipts from the pasture by the east gate or by the hall, which was reserved for the deer (*ad bestias de venacione*).[124]

The use of parks for livestock was extremely variable, and often has every appearance of being *ad hoc* and unsystematic as well as relatively minor. Stock levels in parks fluctuated according to the season, deer numbers, and the

---

[118] This was no doubt why many parks seem to have had no underwood: Bond 2004: 179; VCH Oxon., vi. 243; TNA: PRO, C133/43, no. 5; C139/59/38, m. 8.

[119] Bond 1997: 41–2; Hepple and Doggett 1994: 131.

[120] Hants RO, 11M59/B1/51, rot. 14d. (Farnham, Surrey, 1291–2: nothing from pasture in park because of wild beasts); TNA: PRO, E142/32, rot. 12 (Enfield, Middx., 1322: pasture in two parks belonging to the earl of Hereford not valued because of wild beasts); C134/97, no. 4, m. 3 (Penn, Bucks., 1325: yearly value of pasture in park not accounted for because the wild beasts depasture it); C132/42/1, no. 6 (Watlington, Oxon., 1272: pasture worth 5s. pa when no wild beasts); C133/95, no. 23 (Watlington, 1300: 10s. per annum in herbage and pannage, if wild beasts removed); Fowler (ed.) 1937: 136 (Millbrook, Beds., 1285: a large park, with pannage, pasture, and underwood worth £5 yearly, unless wild beasts prevent); Hull (ed.) 1971: 2, 24, 121–2; Page (ed.) 1996: 133; Morris (ed.) 1978: 19: 3; Richardson 2005: 41.

[121] McIntosh 1986: 18; Hull (ed.) 1971: 41–2; TNA: PRO, C132/31, no. 2; C133/105, no. 8; C133/43, no. 5; C134/26/10, no. 9; C135/21, no. 24. Estate surveys referring only to the value of woodland may represent parks where deer required all the pasture, or at least where any excess was not otherwise used. See e.g. C134/82, no. 11 (Harrold, Beds., 1324) and C134/89, no. 1 (Cainhoe, Beds., 1325).

[122] Clough (ed.) 1969: 2, 9, 35 (1301: Arundel (Sussex), grazing of small park worth 5s., and of large park £1, plus 5s. pannage; Stansted (Sussex), park grazing brings in £1 10s., and pannage 10s. in years with mast; Mileham (Norf.), a park worth £2 as grazing); TNA: PRO, C145/108, no. 2, m. 4 (Middleton Stoney (Oxon.), 1328: pasture worth 6s. 8d.); ibid., SC6/1095/10 (Watlington, 1278: 8s. 6d. pasture sold in the park; £1 14s. 4d. from pig pannage, although presumably only a share of this in the park; park pasture or underwood may or may not have contributed to the 15s. raised by the sale of animal feed); Midgley (ed.) 1942 and 1945, i. 84 (Watlington, 1296–7: 15s. 9d. from sale of park pasture after the tithe was taken; 16s. 6d. levied from the owners of 99 pigs at 2d. a pig for letting them feed off the mast in the park).

[123] Hollings (ed.) 1934–50: ii. 209. [124] Greenwell (ed.) 1857: 212.

frequency of lordly visits,[125] and where business-like decisions were made about whether to put demesne or tenant beasts in parks, this did not necessarily mean that livestock were the most important use. Park pastures were not usually as useful or valuable as other demesne meadows and pastures without deer, and any use or income raised from park pastures has to be put in perspective by comparison with the revenues from similar resources elsewhere in the manor. For example, in 1300 the herbage and pannage of Henley park, probably several hundred acres in extent, was said to be worth 13s. 4d. a year, but this was less than the value of a mere 4½ acres of high-quality demesne meadow in the manor.[126] Lest this comparison be thought unfair, it might be noted that the 8s. 6d. of pasture rented in the park at Watlington in 1278 compared unfavourably with the 18s. raised from pasture in the 'moor' there.[127]

Parks were more important in the history of horse-breeding than the other way round: if many, even most, studs were in parks, it does not follow that most parks had studs. Individual studs in parks might well be fairly short-lived enterprises,[128] and even the relatively well-run park-based royal studs did not meet the king's need for horses, some of which had to be purchased from abroad.[129] Pig pannaging, meanwhile, was more or less an accidental by-product of mature nut-bearing trees: supply could not be readily increased and profits from sales depended on variable local demand.[130] Pannage was also a particularly unreliable income source. Occasionally it could bring in respectable sums of several pounds,[131] but decent pannage in any given locality was unusual, a cause of remark, as in the Chilterns in 1296, which probably helps explain the large numbers of pigs pannaged in Watlington park that year.[132] Even in heavily wooded areas there was usually only sufficient nuts and mast to collect fees every five to seven years.[133]

The timber in park woods was also very variably exploited, with resources tending to be overused in times of need and ignored or neglected in other periods.[134] As with many other woods, the focus on commercial management of woodland in parks was distinctly limited. This was especially the case in areas away from river transport links and large market or industrial centres, where profitable extraction was very difficult, but it also applied to a surprising extent in some places closer to major outlets or waterways (including the south-west Chilterns).[135] The price of timber certainly remained stable and probably tended to rise over the thirteenth and earlier fourteenth centuries, but in most places it was not a steady market with consistent demand and lords did not

---

[125] Kerr 1925: 162.   [126] TNA: PRO, C133/95, no. 24 (meadow worth 13s. 6d.)
[127] TNA: PRO, SC6/1095/10.   [128] Booth 1981: 94–5.
[129] Prestwich 1988: 177; MacGregor 1983: 97; Neilson 1940: 439.
[130] Farmer 1995: 106–7.   [131] Cannon (ed.) 1918: 140; Farmer 1995: 106.
[132] Luard (ed.) 1866: 408.
[133] Preece 1991: 61; Roden 1968: 66; Rackham 1986: 121–2; Richardson 2005: 40–1; TNA: PRO, SC6/754/11 (Windsor and other parks).
[134] Dyer 1980: 175–6; Booth 1981: 130–2.   [135] Hatcher 1996: 254–5; Roden 1968: 64–5.

often focus on supplying it, partly no doubt because growth cycles were so long.[136] In any case, although parks often contained much fine timber, supplies were not inexhaustible and most of the trees had to be preserved to maintain a suitable environment for deer and hunting. Repairs to the perimeter and lodges had to be the top priority for the use of trees in the park, or for the income generated from their sale if these trees were themselves not suitable.[137] As a result, sale of parkland timber was infrequent and usually small-scale where it occurred. Often park timber was sold only in financial need, as the liquidation of an asset (which, after all, would take several lifetimes to regenerate, and only if properly protected). The fact that wind-blown timber and branches or 'old oaks' were the first target for sale or use outside the park suggests, at best, a concern for conservation, but perhaps also simply a reactive rather than proactive approach.[138]

Park-based fuel production had serious limitations too. Organized commercial growing of firewood in parks seems to have been limited, especially in noble parks (although resident gentry and religious houses might have made more effort).[139] Despite the significant rise in fuel prices in the thirteenth century, a worthwhile return for planned production of this relatively bulky, low-value product was dependent on good access to larger domestic markets or export centres.[140] And there is no evidence that parks were created or even very often managed to supply demand. It is notable, for instance, that there was no close correlation between the manors that produced more substantial profits from wood sales in the south-east and Home Counties in the later thirteenth and fourteenth centuries and the location of parks.[141] Where wood was sold, the few shillings or pounds brought in were fairly small beer, probably mainly useful in helping towards park upkeep.[142] The more sizeable sums sometimes given in accounts typically represent revenue from five or seven yearly fellings, or even one-off sales, rather than representing a steady annual income.[143]

The reason why fuel production often remained at a low level was directly related to parks' function as deer reserves and hunting grounds. In many parks fuel production could not be fully exploited because open launds interspersed with large trees were more suitable for hunting, perhaps also more aesthetically

---

[136] Rackham 1986: 89; Farmer 1991: 411, 414–15; 1995: 105, 119, 131; Birrell 1990–1: 40.
[137] Kerr 1925: 160; Neave 1991: 9–10; Roberts 1997: 249; Squires 1996: 24; Hepple and Doggett 1994: 133; *CIPM* xxi, no. 280; *CPR, 1388–92*, 4, 14.
[138] Slade and Lambrick (eds.) 1990–2: i. 299–300; Greenwell (ed.) 1857: 200–1; Armitage-Smith (ed.) 1911: ii. 207; Page (ed.) 1999: 91; Richardson 2005: 50.
[139] Watkins 1993: 25.   [140] Witney 1990: 37; Hatcher 1993: 20–1.
[141] Galloway *et al.* 1996: 460, 461 (fig. 2), 462 (fig. 3 and text); Cantor 1983: *passim*.
[142] The value of park coppices was often only £1 or £2 a year or less: *VCH Worcs.*, iii. 340; Clough (ed.) 1969: 9, 35 (Stansted (Sussex), underwood up to £2 in value may be sold every year without damage; Mileham (Norf.), up to £5 of wood may be sold from within and without the park); TNA: PRO, C134/82, no. 11; C134/89, no. 1; C135/35, no. 33; E142/32, rots. 2 (underwood worth 4s.), 12 (underwood in two parks worth £2 per annum).
[143] Kerr 1925: 161–2; Farmer 1995: 127–8.

pleasing. It was actually convenient to let the deer eat much of the underwood to improve access and views. Wood produced in protected park coppices was often primarily intended for maintaining the park fences, rather than for sale, or even for the household.[144] This helps to explain why even in localities where there were parks and substantial local charcoal and other fuel production was going on, much of it might be focused in woods outside park perimeters, as on the royal estates around Bolsover and Shuttlewood (Derbs.) in the fourteenth century.[145]

In general, the handling of fish and small game was similarly unbusiness-like. As long as the lord had enough to meet his needs when in residence, there was relatively little incentive for maximizing productivity. Fishponds and rabbit warrens in parks, like those elsewhere, were mainly used for the lord's table and for occasional gifts, rather than being set up primarily for the market. Effective fish-farming was labour-intensive and many ponds were not regularly cleaned or the fish fed sufficiently to increase output.[146] Commercial production was mainly carried out by non-aristocrats who leased ponds in the later middle ages.[147] Rabbits, which had been introduced to the mainland in the early thirteenth century as a source of meat and fur, took a good deal of nurturing, protecting, and looking after. Before 1350 most warrens produced small numbers of rabbits, only some of which were sold for profit.[148]

Finally, cultivation in parks was usually strictly limited. Although barns were sometimes found in parks, which might be taken as a sign of cereal farming, these seem most often to have been used to store hay grown in park meadows for the use of the deer.[149] Crop-production could only happen where there was sufficient internal fencing or where deer stocks were low or non-existent.[150] And, in fact, estate surveys make no reference to cultivation in the vast majority of parks, and any arable brought into parks was normally turned over to pasture for deer.[151] What limited cultivation did go on was usually small in extent and sporadic in duration, carried out when the demesne required it or market conditions were right, since it was not usually the best soil for the landlord to farm.[152] Where parkland was cultivated it seems often to have supported lower value crops that could be sown on poorer soils, like barley, oats, or peas, rather than higher value ones like wheat.[153] On the other hand, the decision not to cultivate larger areas of parkland was not necessarily strictly economic, it was simply that the space was wanted for deer and hunting.

---

[144] Witney 1990: 30.   [145] TNA: PRO, SC6/1297/13.
[146] Dyer 1994: 101–11, esp. 107–8; Roberts 1986: 126–30.   [147] Currie 1991: 100.
[148] Veale 1957; Bailey 1988: 1–12; Campbell 2000: 415–16, 423; Campbell and Bartley 2006: 116–17.
[149] Moorhouse 1981: 692; Roberts 1988: 74; below, p. 77.
[150] Cantor and Hatherly 1979: 81; Stamper 1988: 146; Rackham 1990: 155–6. Cf. perhaps the 'Park Field' in Elmore Park in Applehanger, Goring (Oxon.): Kift *et al.* 1989: 59–60.
[151] See e.g. Vanderzee (ed.) 1807: 172. For an indication of a lack of medieval cultivation provided by archaeological fieldwalking see Germany 2001.
[152] Britnell 1977: 110.
[153] Salzman (ed.) 1955: 6, 9, 13, 26, 35, 36, etc.; Britnell 1977: 107; Roberts 1988: 75.

When compared to estate revenue as a whole, the income produced by parks was typically very small. Revenue from pasture and wood sales comprised only a small part of the total income in most manors, especially in the lowlands, with rents and sale of demesne cereal produce usually providing the bulk of receipts. Wood-pasture in turn accounted for only a small proportion of all demesne pasturage, around 6–10 per cent by value nationally in the first half of the fourteenth century,[154] and parks usually made up only part of the wood-pasture in the manors where they were present. In an average year in the late thirteenth century grain sales from his many estates brought the bishop of Winchester well over £1,000 a year, wool sales several hundred, and wood sales somewhere in excess of £100. Pasture sales were worth only about £70, with hay sales bringing an additional £15–£20 or so and pannage about £40.[155] And this was a lord with many estates in Hampshire and other areas with large amounts of wood-pasture, including numerous large parks. Around the same time the Kent and Sussex manors of the archbishop of Canterbury, many of them with extensive parkland, achieved only around 3–8 per cent of their profits through pasture, hay, underwood, pannage, and garden produce.[156] A study of inquisitions *post mortem* in the ten counties around London in the late thirteenth and early fourteenth centuries showed that parks were usually found on large, valuable manors with extensive demesnes, yet their mean estimated value was just £1 14s. 2d. each.[157] Pasture accounted for a higher proportion of profits in the west and north of England, but here too in this period usually only a minority of overall revenue, and parks themselves produced only a fraction of the income.[158]

All this underlines the fact that twelfth- to early fourteenth-century lords created and maintained their parks primarily as leisure assets, rather than economic resources.[159] They were loath to turn them into humdrum farms, especially in places they visited often. Most parks were not fully exploited even for demesne use, let alone for commercial purposes. In this respect it is notable that parks receive little mention in the late thirteenth-century treatises on estate management.[160] For officials to refer to the missed opportunities that parks represented was exceptional: a rare example is to be found at the very end of an early fourteenth-century treatise on husbandry in the Mohun cartulary, relating to an estate at Dunster and Carhampton (Somerset), and this simply indicates the possible scale of the profits being spurned. Here the writer recommended a total reorganization of land use in Marshwood park, based on

---

[154] Campbell 2000: 85.   [155] Farmer 1995: 110, 112–14.
[156] These figures are calculated from Du Boulay (ed.) 1964.
[157] Campbell *et al.* 1992: 12. It should also be noted that the values given for parks in inquisitions sometimes represent gross or potential revenues rather than net profits.
[158] Holmes 1957: 96–7; Campbell and Bartley 2006; Farrer (ed.) 1907.
[159] For a telling individual example of the lordly attitude see Davies 1978: 120.
[160] Birrell 1992: 113–14; Oschinsky (ed.) 1971: 269, 433, 437.

the introduction of cereal farming. It was suggested that the launds of the 400 acre park be ploughed up and cultivated and the deer enclosed in the reduced space remaining. Apparently, this and the introduction of cow houses and storehouses might make the park yield more profit than the entire existing cultivated demesne of the manor.[161] We cannot be sure whether this advice was followed,[162] but this example raises a more important question of whether there was a wider realization of park costs in the later middle ages, at a time when harsher agrarian conditions and falling profits might conceivably have forced a greater focus on maximizing parks' productive potential.

CHANGES IN THE LATER MIDDLE AGES?

There has been a great deal of emphasis on the increasing economic exploitation of parkland in the later middle ages. We are told that in the lean times after the Black Death landowners were under pressure to increase revenue and cut costs. With less demand for land and less market for grain than before there was little incentive to cultivate parkland, but there were other ways that it could be made more profitable, or at least less costly. The most drastic measure was to cease keeping deer, stop maintaining expensive enclosures, and turn the land to another use, perhaps renting it out to tenants.[163] Some parks were disparked in this way, but elsewhere lords kept their parks but apparently allowed more extensive grazing and coppicing, as well as selling more timber.[164] The creation and extension of parkland to produce much larger parks has sometimes been interpreted in terms of increasing space for these mixed uses, especially grazing.[165] These purported changes would seem to fit in with what we know of the profound agrarian reorganizations in the later fourteenth and earlier fifteenth centuries. In other words, first, the almost total abandonment of what was left of demesne arable farming, which led to large parts of estates being leased out, and, secondly, the growing importance of less labour-intensive activities, including livestock husbandry, and woodland management, which seems to have been becoming more sophisticated.[166]

However, the reality seems to have been that there was considerably less intensification of agrarian use of parkland than usually suggested. As we have seen, plenty of parks in the later fourteenth and fifteenth centuries remained full of deer,[167] and this actually meant the continued disregard of increasing profits.

---

[161] Lyte 1909: i. 324.
[162] The size of the park was estimated at only 270 acres in 1428 (TNA: PRO, C139/33, no. 32, m. 10), but it is difficult to know how accurate this figure was.
[163] Cantor and Hatherly 1979: 79.
[164] Bond 1998: 29; Bond 2004: 179; Pollard 1990: 204; Winchester 2000: 82–3.
[165] Above, p. 6 and sources cited in n. 37.
[166] Dyer 2002: 330–46; Roden 1968: 65–6; Britnell 2004: 411.
[167] Above, pp. 38–9.

Across the country, income, which was often mainly from pasture, frequently remained at around the same fairly low levels.[168] It was clear that park pastures would have been worth more if the deer were removed, and sometimes the emphasis on providing for the deer meant that they were worth nothing at all.[169] Even where park resources were farmed out in a more organized way, tenants' economic extraction often had to fit round the game animals.[170] It does seem that in some areas, notably in the northern uplands and parts of the north and west Midlands, a proportion of parks were used to house larger numbers of livestock, particularly in the late fourteenth and earlier fifteenth centuries.[171] But this was far from an entirely novel development in areas where agrarian conditions had long favoured animal husbandry and where there had sometimes been sizeable profits from park grazing earlier on,[172] nor was it a universal trend even in these areas.[173] In fact, by the mid to later fifteenth century growing deer herds seem to have been responsible for falling revenue from agistment in many northern parks, including those of the Percies in Northumberland.[174]

Nor is there much indication that the exploitation of underwood or timber within parks became much more systematic. Although coppices and internal fencing were probably more common by this period, profits from wood generally remained fairly small items of income in manorial accounts, including

---

[168] Compare Page (ed.) 1996 with Page (ed.) 1999; Newton (ed.) 1960: 69, 82, 94 (Thaxted Great and Little parks: 38s. 3 1/2d. in 1361–2, 13s. 4d. in 1377–8, and 10s. 6d. in 1380–1); Hatcher 1970: 180–4; Cantor and Moore 1963: 40–1, 46–7; Canadine 2003: 44–6, 53; Jack (ed.) 1965: 106 (Ampthill (Beds.), agistment in two parks £7, where manorial rents totalled more than £115), 129 (Badmondisfield (Suffolk), agistment of a park farmed to parker for £2), 136 (Winfarthing (Norf.), agistment of parks farmed for £5); TNA: PRO, SC6/966/3; SC6/966/20; SC6/1846; SC6/908/10; SC6/971/7; SC6/966/20; SC6/HENVII/1448, m. 6. Many inquisitions *post mortem* state that parks were worth nothing after the maintenance of the deer, enclosure, and parker's fee (e.g. *CIPM* xxii and xxiii *passim*). Others typically refer to small profits of £1 or so, and often less, e.g. *CIPM* xx, nos. 186, 424, 441; xxiii, nos. 52, 101, 259, 260, 374, 404, 405, 483, 484; TNA: PRO, C139/74/27, m. 4; C139/75/30, m. 4; C139/75/32, m. 4 etc.

[169] Newton (ed.) 1960: 82, 94; *CIM 1377–88*, nos. 395–6; *CIPM* xx, no. 499 (agistment worth £2 yearly after maintenance of beasts of the chase, for whom a meadow was also reserved to provide winter feed); Toomey (ed.) 2001: p. xix; TNA: PRO, C139/75/30, m. 4; SC11/271, m. 1; Field (ed.) 2004: 156–7 (1462: 60s. rent for park herbage and other pasture rents relaxed because reserved for beasts of the chase this year).

[170] *CPR, 1485–94*, 97; Le Patourel (ed.) 1957: 51, 68; Hatcher 1970: 181, 184; Coates 1964–9: 139; *VCH Oxon.*, xii. 432; TNA: PRO, DL25/3516 (Halton, Ches.).

[171] Stamper 1988: 146; Pollard 1990: 204; McDonnell 1992: 119; Moorhouse 2003*a*: 329, 332, 334; Spence 1994: 61–4; Bean 1958: 14 and n., 39, 47; Drury 1976: 141 ff.; Birrell 1962: 121; TNA: PRO, DL 43/15/11 (Duchy of Lancaster valor, north parts, 1417–18). For other regions see e.g. TNA: PRO, SC6/754/11, mm. 1–2; SC6/754/21, m. 3 (large income from agistment in Windsor park, late 14th cent.), and Berks. RO, D/EZ 77, 1/1–7 (demesne use of Chamberhouse park (Berks.) for horses and cows, 1447–68).

[172] See e.g. Dyer 1988: 375.

[173] In February 1437 one inquisition *post mortem* stated that a 300-acre park in the barony of Greystoke (Cumbl.) was worth the large sum of 20 marks, but the two other parks there were assessed at only £3 (for a 120-acre park) and £1 (for a 200-acre park): TNA: PRO, E149/152/2, m. 3. See TNA: PRO, C139/76/35, m. 35 and C139/77/36, m. 43 on the lack of profits from agistment in Aston Cantlow and Fulbrook parks (Warks.) in the 1430s. See also Holmes 1957: 96–7, 160.

[174] Bean 1958: 44 n.; Birrell 1962: 121.

where there were parks.[175] Only a small minority of parks produced large incomes from wood sales and probably even fewer on anything approaching a consistent basis.[176] Despite the fact that parks were sometimes created where there was a strong market for wood (including places well-connected with London), or in areas which remained wooded where tree cover had been cleared elsewhere in the vicinity (as in parts of the Yorkshire Dales), there is, as in earlier periods, rarely any indication that the wood was enclosed or managed to supply this market.[177] Where some park woods proved useful for industrial purposes, this might be more or less accidental. The bishop of Durham was involved in mining and smelting lead for household use and for sale, and it so happened that his (long-existing) parks were the only source of fuel wood for the smelting, yet the ore had to be transported up to eleven miles to the parks.[178] Where timber extraction went on, almost absurd measures sometimes had to be taken to do this around the deer: in the late 1370s at the bishop of Lincoln's park of Buckden (Hunts.) special wooden cages had to be constructed and put over twenty-four felled oaks to prevent damage by the 'beasts of the chase' that filled the park.[179] As earlier, most parkland timber was probably used on an *ad hoc* basis for repairing the pale or for demesne and tenant buildings.[180]

For much of the fifteenth century, wider conditions would have posed considerable difficulties for the successful economic use of parks, especially during the deep slump which permeated almost all sectors of the economy from *c*.1440 to 1470.[181] The picture varied a good deal from place to place, but even the most resilient wood-pasture regions, like Warwickshire, were affected. Despite generally higher standards of living, total demand for fuel wood and timber would almost certainly have been reduced in an era of continuing low population.[182] The evidence is patchy but all the indications are that both timber and fuel prices were at a fairly low ebb throughout the period *c*.1390–1540;[183] higher labour costs would also have brought problems for commercial production in many areas by raising transport costs and shrinking the zone of profitable extraction.[184] By the later 1430s harsh weather and disease seem to have checked the earlier expansion of stock farming. In the mid-century pastures were unprofitable and difficult even to lease, and this sector of the economy did not recover substantially until late in the century or early in the next.[185] Likewise, large-scale commercial rabbit farming, which developed

[175] Galloway *et al*. 1996: 460; Godber 1969: 136; Canadine 2003: 49 (table 3.3); Newton (ed.) 1960: 39, 69, 82, 94; Rackham 1989: 78–80; Alston 1992: 7.
[176] Rowe 2009: 24–6; Watkins 1993: 25 (large sales in the earl of Warwick's park at Wedgnock, close to Coventry, in the early 15th cent.).
[177] Wright 2003: 73; Moorhouse 2003*a*: 320.   [178] Lomas 1992: 203.
[179] Canadine 2003: 43.   [180] Alston 1992: 3, 7; TNA: PRO, SC6/962/30.
[181] Hatcher 1996: 244–6.
[182] Dyer 1989: 177–8; Galloway *et al*. 1996: 455–6, 469–70; Hatcher 1993: 28; 1996: 255.
[183] Brown and Hopkins 1981: 44–51; Hatcher 1993: 28.
[184] Galloway *et al*. 1996: 470; Mate 1984: 348.
[185] Hatcher 1996: 252–3, 271; Dyer 2002: 338; Birrell 1962: 121.

thanks to increased consumer demand for luxuries after the Black Death, seems to have generally declined in the fifteenth century.[186] And besides the market difficulties in all of these areas, lords' own households were probably making somewhat lower overall demands for provisions, timber, and fuel thanks to the reduction in the number of residences and trend towards slightly smaller establishments (the continuing growth in size of the royal household was exceptional).[187]

Perhaps unsurprisingly, it is often hard to find active efforts to increase the productivity or profits of parks in the later middle ages. Changes in the form of resource exploitation—for example, leasing whole pastures to single individuals rather than charging various men for access[188]—should not necessarily be taken as a sign of an increase in exploitation *per se*. Where park resources were farmed out, this was often on long and fixed leases and frequently to officials, perhaps because kings and lords were looking to provide favour rather than maximize profits, or perhaps because of limited local demand.[189] Where additional revenue-generating activities were introduced in less often visited royal and noble parks, local gentry officials might be the instigators and at least partial beneficiaries.[190] For all that some larger or better-run parks could be profitable (along with those where the deer were neglected), most probably remained a net expense in the later middle ages.[191] Again and again there seems to have been no profit from parks beyond the feeding and supervision of the 'wild beasts' and the costs of enclosure.[192] Indeed, if a park was worth 'nil beyond the maintenance of the game, the wages of parker and the costs of enclosure', it had done its job, economically speaking.[193]

However, for all the economic difficulties of the period, it seems that the relative lack of exploitation of parks remained largely a conscious decision, rather than being unavoidable. A Venetian visitor who commented on English deer parks in the later 1490s suggests that some noble lands lay barren and waste because of the agrarian problems of the time, but parks do not seem to be

---

[186] Hatcher 1996: 254; Bailey 1988: 10–14.   [187] Woolgar 1999: 10–15.
[188] For a mid-15th-cent. example see Bucks. RO, AR1/93/1/2: five-year lease of the herbage of Fawley park (Bucks.) with the dovecote inside and a croft adjacent for £2 a year.
[189] Hatcher 1970: 181, 184; *VCH Oxon.*, xii. 432.
[190] See e.g. Richardson 2005: 38, 40, 45, 46, 51, 136, 151.
[191] Hatcher 1970: 179–80; Rowe 2009: 24–5. For small net profits see Cannadine 2003: 45 (table 3.1), 46 (table 3.2), 53 (table 3.4). Thompson (ed.) 1978 [Beds. RO], gives a mixed impression, with profits of a few pounds in some years and similar losses in others. There are many source problems which make it difficult to work out net profit levels (partly because these were not the main concern). Later inquisitions *post mortem* probably tend to underestimate income, whereas other sources, like valors, may well overestimate it. It is also difficult to measure the value of demesne use as opposed to sales or rental income, or to put precise figures on some of the costs, such as perquisites going to officials.
[192] *CIPM* xxi, nos. 516, 627; xxii, nos. 25, 30, 34, 47, 75, 81, 99, 168, 219, 302, 309, 347, 426, 433, 440, 761, 778, 779; xxiii, nos. 109, 220, 275, 280, 303, 404, 451, 484, 506, 577, 705, 706, 709, 713, 714; TNA: PRO, C139/74, no. 20, mm. 2, 3; C139/74, no. 21, m. 5; C139/77, no. 36, m. 44.
[193] *CIPM* xx, no. 243 (Belvoir, Leics.).

in this category.[194] Instead, these particular 'uncultivated' grounds were deliberately set aside, 'all enclosed with timber fences'. Often the underuse of parkland was a quite deliberate choice, as with the duchy of Cornwall parks where deer herds were prioritized until the extensive disparking of the sixteenth century. If this disparking was partly 'a sensible economy', it was more a recognition of the lack of sporting use made of these particular parks.[195] Early seventeenth-century writers confirm the impression of hunting and deer-keeping only giving way to a drive to greater profitability after the middle ages, in Cornwall and elsewhere.[196]

In the later middle ages, as before, lords tended to create and maintain parks as hunting grounds and sylvan areas managed for pleasure, with other functions in the background. When Edward IV took an interest in his Nottinghamshire and Staffordshire parks it was to reduce tenant cattle numbers to increase the number of deer for him to hunt.[197] Where a lord was a regular visitor the general net losses of a few pounds made by parks were not hard to bear. Even where visits were intermittent the build-up of arrears might be accepted or little noticed, as at Beckley and many other royal and aristocratic parks.[198] The continued prioritization of leisure is hardly surprising. The fifteenth century may have witnessed a lowering of aristocratic revenues, but the aristocracy was not impoverished by the reduction in profits from individual estates.[199] Many lords and gentry maintained high incomes through acquiring further estates, marriage, and service to the crown. Their building projects, park-making, and other lavish expenditures are testimony to their continued liquidity and taste for fine living.[200] Parks were retained, much as they always had been, as accoutrements of the aristocratic lifestyle. Perhaps because they were increasingly costly in terms of labour they were ever more impressive demonstrations of the disdain for financial worries shown by men of high status.

DEER-KEEPING

We cannot conclude an examination of the park economy without looking at the deer themselves. And when we do this, it confirms that keeping a deer herd was a very expensive enterprise and that the productivity of what has been called 'deer farming' in parks can be readily overestimated.

Deer were the focus of great attention and required a large financial outlay. To start with, the cost of building lengthy, deer-proof fences was extremely high. Even park deer were at least semi-wild and far more agile than domestic

---

[194] Sneyd (ed.) 1847: 39.   [195] Hatcher 1970: 179–84. Cf. Lomas 1992: 159.
[196] Pett 1998: 255; Camden 1610: 293.   [197] Drage 1989: 65; Birrell 1962: 121.
[198] VCH Oxon., v. 67.   [199] Dyer 1989: 32–6; Britnell 1997: 189–90; Woodger 1974: 203–13.
[200] Dyer 1994: 260–1, 266.

livestock, making their management much more costly. The most athletic or terrified deer can leap up to three metres vertically and six metres horizontally: the sheep or cow that could match this was a rare specimen.[201] Deer therefore required higher and sturdier barriers than other animals, along with deer-leaps and funnels to arrange their movement through forest into park or between park compartments, not least for the cross-breeding that was recognized as beneficial.[202] The enclosure and fitting out of a large royal park at Clipstone in 1178–80 cost £89.[203] In 1251 the bishop of Winchester spent over £48 on construction work at Witney park, including the digging of an eight-foot wide, six-foot deep perimeter ditch and the erection of freshly cut timber palings.[204] Within the next two years he spent £31 on the digging of 22 furlongs of bank in and around the park at Bishop's Sutton (Hants.) and further sums on carts to carry timber and on five carpenters working for twelve weeks making two park gates and deer-leaps.[205] When the earl of Lancaster constructed a new park at Musbury (Lancs.) in the early fourteenth century it cost him over £92.[206] Most staggeringly of all, Edward III's enclosure of the 'new park of Windsor called Wychemere' in c.1359–63 cost almost £400.[207] And besides initial construction, parks required occasional major repairs: in 1283–4, ditching, repairing stonework, and putting up 458 perches of hedge ('haye') around Beckley park cost £13 14s. 1d., this sum representing almost two-thirds of the total spent on the manor that year (£21 16s. 11d.).[208] Minor maintenance represented a further expense, perhaps averaging out at a pound or so a year for a medium to large park.[209]

Feeding and caring for deer was also a potentially costly business. Fallow deer were still relative newcomers to the cold British climate and took a great deal of looking after, particularly in the winter. The records show the construction of shelters and provision of winter hay for various park herds from at least the mid-twelfth century.[210] The onset of poorer weather conditions in the early fourteenth century must have made things harder for them.[211] The sheer expense of providing fodder for deer herds in the biggest and best-stocked royal parks is rather breathtaking. In the two years up to Michaelmas 1380, 340 cartloads of hay had been used to feed the king's 'wild beasts' in Woodstock and Cornbury parks, and 178 cartloads were left in the barns that were apparently more or less dedicated to this purpose.[212] From September 1378 to September 1379, 180 carts of hay were used for the deer, at a total cost of £31

---

[201] Stamper 1988: 141. [202] Higham 2003: 59, 63, 65; Birrell 1992: 120; Roberts 1988: 79.
[203] Crook 1976: 35. [204] Hants. RO, 11M59/B1/23, rot. 6; *VCH Oxon.*, xiv. 199.
[205] Roberts 1988: 69–70. [206] Higham 2003: 60. [207] Hatherly and Cantor 1979–80: 78.
[208] TNA: PRO, SC6/955/4, m. 1. Sale of the old hedges raised only £1. Cf. Midgley (ed.) 1942 and 1945: ii. 192 (repairs to palings at Haverah (Yorks.) after strong winds).
[209] Birrell 1992: 119; TNA: PRO, SC6/1122/19, m. 2d.; Hyde 1955: 333 ff.
[210] Roberts 1988: 79; Midgley (ed.) 1942 and 1945: ii. 192; Birrell 1992: 117; *VCH Oxon.*, xiv. 200; Kerr 1925: 156–7; Rimington 1971: 9–10; TNA: PRO, SC6/1122/19, m. 2d.; SC6/971/7.
[211] Dyer 1989: 259. [212] TNA: PRO, SC6/962/24.

10s.; carriage costs, stacking in the barns, and carrying to the deer took the amount spent to £38 5s. 11d. The same exercise the following year cost £35 8s. 2d. In 1379–80 a cart was used to ferry hay from barn to deer for 101 days (at a cost of 6d. a day). During these two years men were also paid to cut brushwood to provide additional sustenance, for 92 days and 101 days respectively (at a total cost of over £4).[213] The outlay on deer food at these two big parks would have supported a fairly substantial gentry family. But tending for deer was clearly a labour of love: during a visit to Odiham (Hants.) in 1276 Edward I ordered part of a meadow in the park there to be enclosed to produce fine hay for winter sustenance for the deer: all the thorns and briars had to be eradicated and the area fenced and gated. The hay was placed in specially constructed cradles for the deer to feed from.[214]

If fences and feed represented a considerable outlay, the cost of personnel was just as significant. Park-keepers had to be provided to look after the deer and these men were usually housed in sturdy lodges, often surrounded by moats, and had to be supplied with bows, nets, and other hunting equipment.[215] At larger parks sub-parkers, gate-keepers, and other officers were also employed.[216] Parkers' wages may often have amounted to less than £1 a year in the later thirteenth or early fourteenth century, but they could be as much as £2 or £3, and they increased later.[217] At any rate, even quite humble parkers were paid more than those who looked after ordinary farm livestock,[218] and many of them also received a sizeable plot of land, pasture rights in the park, a share of windfallen wood, and off-cuts of venison. Besides these working officials, larger royal and noble parks sometimes had sinecure parkerships associated with them, usually granted to absentee gentry or even noble 'parkers', who were given special privileges in the park and, usually, substantial wages of several pounds a year. Their appointment, rather than being a necessary cost, acted as a way of rewarding friends or followers and cultivating a following.[219]

The way that lords paid for these deer-related expenses varied, but there was no way round them. In earlier periods great lords had tenants who owed them labour services and even possessed a few feudal rents that could be directed towards park construction and maintenance.[220] But labour services were

[213] The long-term commitment to provisioning deer in Woodstock park is well illustrated in *VCH Oxon.*, xiv. 445–6.
[214] MacGregor 1983: 76–7.
[215] For archaeological evidence of lodges see e.g. RCHM *Northants.*, i. 69, ii. 86; Rowe 2009: 35–6. Very few lodges have been excavated, and the few which partly survive as standing buildings deserve further investigation.
[216] Newton (ed.) 1960: 8, 11 and n.
[217] Midgley (ed.) 1942 and 1945: i. 87 (6s. 8d., Watlington, 1296–7); ii. 192 (£4 11s. for two parkers at Haverah (Yorks.) and £1 10s. 4d. for a parker at Bilton (Yorks.), 1296–7); Roberts 1988: 80; Hoppitt 1992: i. 165, 242–3; Watney 1910: 38; *CIPM* xvii, no. 543; Saul 1986: 190 n. 119.
[218] Midgley (ed.) 1942 and 1945: i. 87; Page (ed.) 1999: 95 (park-keeping combined with many other offices, Witney, 1301–2).
[219] See below, pp. 146–7.
[220] Harding and Lambert 1994: 5; *VCH Sussex*, vi/2. 106; *CIPM* i, nos. 411, 609; *Rot. Hund.* ii. 34; Purvis (ed.) 1936: 197–8; Bond 2004: 177; *CChR, 1427–1516*, 61 ('pyrksilver').

usually not that extensive and were unevenly spread around the country and between estates, featuring disproportionately on the property of the greatest lords.[221] In any case, the use of these services on parks meant that they could not be used elsewhere, for more productive ends. Park construction and maintenance was very time-consuming work,[222] and, as with other services, enforcement was always a potentially contentious issue and could result in serious local disputes.[223] By the later middle ages, when labour services were commuted for money payments and workers became scarce and expensive, lords had to spend more or find new ways to secure their park enclosures.[224] Some resorted to bartering resources: in 1404 Richard Woodville made a grant of all the underwood in Wick Park in his manor of Wick Hamon (Northants.) to William Furtho and two others, who, in exchange, were to make a fence round the park at their own expense.[225] In 1501 the bishop of Lincoln went further, granting Freefolk manor (Hants.) for thirty years in return for the maintenance of the pale around the park there and finding winter hay for the deer.[226]

In return for all this outlay and organization, deer supplied only a very modest amount of meat. Large and well-run parks could be fairly efficient venison producers, certainly far more so than open forests: the 1,000 acre royal park of Havering (Essex) produced as much venison (about forty fallow deer a year in the earlier thirteenth century) as the 10,000 acres of forest in south-west Essex.[227] In the later middle ages park-based herds probably became even more important as forest deer populations declined: the bishop of Coventry took more deer from his parks than from his chase when staying around Cannock in 1461–2.[228] But, nonetheless, overall returns were unimpressive compared to the amount of land and effort given over to these animals. Deer were inefficient stock animals which consumed a large amount of grass relative to their body weight, while, it seems, suffering just as badly from disease and theft as other species.[229] Perhaps only about 10 per cent of a park herd could be taken each year on a sustainable basis (without resupplying), and since most parks were smaller and less well-stocked than Havering, this represented only a very modest return. A 200-acre park with a hundred deer might have produced as few as ten deer a year.[230] Not surprisingly, where it was present at all, venison usually provided for only a fraction of an aristocratic household's meat consumption:

---

[221] Kosminsky 1956: 289–91.   [222] Roberts 1988: 69–70.
[223] Baigent (ed.) 1891: 13–17; Liddiard 2003: 16–17; Page (ed.) 1999: 86.
[224] Hatcher 1994: 3–35, esp. 13–20.   [225] VCH Northants., v. 418.
[226] Bilikowski 1983: 4.
[227] Rackham 1980: 193. Cf. Rackham 1989: 55; Bond 1998: 24.
[228] Woolgar (ed.) 1992–3: ii. 463, 464, 466, 468, 469, 472, 475, 481 (from parks); ii. 453, 457, 460, 463, 466 (from the chase).
[229] Chapman and Chapman 1975: 185, 191; Roberts 1988: 79; Kerr 1925: 157; Richardson 2005: 33–4, 122–7; Rackham 1980: 193; Mate 1985: 24–5; Birrell 1992: 115, 118; 2006.
[230] Birrell 2006: 187. Cf. Roberts 1988: 79; Clough (ed.) 1969: 2, 3, 9, 35.

bone finds suggest around 5 or, at the very most, 10 per cent.[231] Only in areas with very extensive wastelands and hunting grounds did it provide lords with any more substantial a source of protein. The idea of widespread commercial production is thus a non-starter. In any case, contemporary aristocratic attitudes would have made this unacceptable: venison was a special food for feasting and gift-exchange.[232] The small number of known sales apparently resulted from black-market activities by foresters or poachers. Craft use of skins, bone, and antler was of very minor importance.[233] Small wonder that the Cistercian Chapter General took the stern view in the twelfth century that deer (like cranes) were animals which 'usually arouse curiosity and show off their own vanity rather than serve any useful purpose'.[234]

In summary then, in choosing to introduce deer, lords knowingly accepted additional costs and problems in the management of wood-pasture. They were prepared to make this compromise because they wanted deer and hunting more than they wanted to optimize their use of untilled ground. In other words, we must not lose sight of the fact that parks were overwhelmingly created as deer reserves. There was a link between pressure on woods and wastes and the establishment of parks, but the timing of park-making was more affected by the presence of a lord who wanted a large game reserve and had the resources to create one than by the desire to retain dwindling non-arable resources for their own sake. Thus although the creation of a park normally increased lordly control—by excluding common rights and thereby helping to protect timber, underwood, and pasture[235]—the enclosure itself was a very special kind of place. Its creator was motivated by concerns besides the purely agrarian, and although deer produced meat and might be carefully nurtured, they were not 'farmed' like ordinary stock animals.

It also has to be remembered that parks were far from the only means of organizing and exploiting woods and pastures, still less the most effective. Lords made many attempts to define and limit common rights, and parks were only one part of this. Foresters, woodwards, haywards, and other officials enforced restrictions on the use of woods, hedgerows, and pastures throughout manors, with or without parks, gathering fines and payments.[236] Woods, meadows, or pastures were frequently enclosed or otherwise demarcated as 'demesne' or 'several' in many locations outside parks.[237] And even in 'common', 'foreign', or 'out' woods, where common rights were often exercised, there might be enclosure or other attempts to tighten regulation.[238] Where a

---

[231] Dyer 1989: 59–61; Creighton 2002: 18 (fig. 2.6); Bond 2004: 182; Sykes 2005*a*: 117 (fig. 59).
[232] Birrell 1992: 114–15; 2006: 177; Acheson 1992: 180; Edelen (ed.) 1968: 255; below, p. 106.
[233] MacGregor 1991: 355–78.   [234] Pullen (ed.) 1966: 82.   [235] See below, pp. 168–9.
[236] Birrell 1987: 31–3; Ault 1972: 65, 158, 168–70; Douglas and Greenaway (eds.) 1981: 884, 893, 896; *CChR, 1226–57*, 274; TNA: PRO, SC6/1095/10; Davies (ed.) 1963: 71–3.
[237] *Extenta Manerii: SR* i. 242–3; Hart and Lyons (eds.) 1884–93: i. 283 ff.; *CPR, 1330–4*, 23; TNA: PRO, C135/21, no. 24; Rackham 1986: 86, 98, 101.
[238] Moorhouse 1979: 51–2; 1981: 685–92; Roden 1968: 67 (Shirburn, Oxon.).

lord's desire was purely to preserve and manage wood-pasture, especially for profit at market, then these other forms of control were introduced, not game parks. Even on manors with parks, lords typically possessed additional areas of waste, wood-pasture, and coppice outside the park fence and these quite commonly provided more important sources of materials or revenue.[239]

[239] So much is made clear by numerous manorial accounts and inquisitions *post mortem*. One striking example is provided by an inquisition relating to Eaton Bray (Beds.) in 1274, where a 27-acre wood in the park was valued at £40 10s., but the total value of woodland in the manor was £283 8s.: TNA: PRO, C133/2/7, m.2. Cf. above, p. 68.

3

Landscaping

> ...the fairest castle that ever a knight owned, erected in a meadow, surrounded by a park, set about by a palisade of close set spikes, which enclosed many trees in its circuit of more than two miles.
>
> (Gawain approaches Bertilak's castle)[1]

Until relatively recently, the idea that medieval parks might have been laid out for visual effect was treated with condescension. The long-accepted view drew a sharp line between the 'practical' medieval park and 'aesthetic' post-medieval one.[2] Medieval parks were 'essentially functional',[3] 'simply private enclosures... in which to keep deer'.[4] Any leisure aspect focused solely on the pleasures of the chase or the provisioning of the banqueting table. It was believed that these earlier parks, unlike later parks and gardens around country houses, were not associated with any interest in shaping the land for visual appeal. On the contrary, in fact, they could not be taken to show that 'medieval lords had even the slightest interest in the appearance of the countryside'.[5] This analysis drew support from the claim that, since medieval parks were set up to make use of poor land on the edge of manors and parishes, they were usually quite some distance from the owner's local residence.[6] The only building likely to be found in a park was a utilitarian lodge for the parker.[7]

During the last couple of decades, however, there has been a considerable reassessment of the presence and significance of aesthetic sensibilities in medieval lords' estate planning,[8] and this has had a direct impact on the understanding of parks. Thus visual impact has been added to strategy and defence as an early and long-lasting motivation in castle planning: even early twelfth-century castles might be put on false-crests where they stood out most clearly, rather

---

[1] Barron (ed.) 1998: 72–3.
[2] Creighton 2002: 73. For examples of the traditional view see, for instance, Cantor and Hatherly 1979: 71; Thomas 1983: 202–3; Lyth 1986: 14.
[3] Williamson and Bellamy 1987: 71.   [4] Neave 1996: 60.
[5] Williamson and Bellamy 1987: 71.   [6] Platt 1978: 47; Cantor 1983: 3.
[7] Cantor 1970–1: 13.
[8] Much has been made of contemporary sources that seem to show an aesthetic response to landscape, like Gerald of Wales's admiring description of the setting of his family castle at Manorbier (Pemb.) in the 1180s: Harvey 1981: 10; Taylor 2000: 44; Creighton 2002: 4.

Landscaping 83

than on higher ground better for a fortress but less prominent.[9] According to this newer perspective, many of the features lords set up around their homes were laid out at least partly to enhance the visual effect. Approach routes to houses might be carefully planned so that visitors were given slowly unravelling or suddenly appearing views of the residence.[10] Moats and ponds were not simply barriers or fish tanks, but provided shimmering reflections and the illusion of buildings floating on water; aristocratic gardens provided carefully contrived sights and scents, as well as produce.[11] Parks themselves have been thoroughly caught up in this stream of reinterpretation and are increasingly seen as an important part of the setting of major residences.[12]

This new approach has derived much of its inspiration from the way houses and their surrounding landscapes are described in medieval literature. In particular, it has been supposed that literary and artistic ideal types influenced a contemporary concept of 'landscape' and helped to shape real landscapes.[13] Some writers imply that the Classical and Islamic idea of the paradise-like garden or park provided a template,[14] but most have seen the western European romances as the most direct influence.[15] Thus it has been suggested that the many moats and ponds in parks may have been linked in the aristocratic mind with visions of Excalibur and the lake in the tale of King Arthur,[16] and even that the later fourteenth-century northern poem *Sir Gawain and the Green Knight* created an image of the 'perfect residence' which subsequent park-makers tried to reproduce in their own house and park complexes.[17] In this apparently sophisticated, even playful, guise, park-making appears as a self-conscious ordering, beautification, and taming of the wild, parallel perhaps to the romanticization of the 'wild forest' in medieval romance.[18]

Besides suggesting such possible sources of inspiration and means of transmission, scholars have offered a variety of explanations of why such landscaping might have appealed to medieval aristocrats. Some have emphasized a genuine aesthetic interest: that, from an early date, medieval parks had, like gardens and orchards, 'an ornamental function as well as a practical and prestige value'.[19] Certainly, fourteenth- and fifteenth-century poets and writers often describe parks as beautiful, or as *The Parlement of Three Ages* has it, 'full faire'.[20]

---

[9] Liddiard 2000*a*: 175–6; Creighton 2002: 80–1. [10] Liddiard 2000*b*: 60–4.
[11] Creighton 2002: 75–6, 79, 83; Harvey 1981: *passim*.
[12] Liddiard 2005: ch. 5; Herring 2003: 38–41; Everson *et al.* 2000: 105. Taylor 2000 provides a fairly recent summary of the ever-growing corpus of examples of what are seen as 'landscaped parks'.
[13] Taylor 2000: 45–6, 48; Liddiard 2000*a*: 182, 184; Creighton 2002: 4.
[14] Harvey 1981: 58; Rackham 1986: 122–3.
[15] The seminal article here is Hagopian van Buren 1986 (e.g. 118, 125, 130–4).
[16] Liddiard 2000*b*: 118. The chivalric Garter fraternity was based at Windsor, where the knights would have been surrounded by parks and artificial lakes and moats: Roberts 1997: 9–10; Hatherly and Cantor 1979–80: 78.
[17] Liddiard 2000*b*: 118; above, epigraph to this chapter.
[18] On the forest as literary device see Saunders 1993. [19] Bond 1994: 144.
[20] Offord (ed.) 1959: 5.

Manicured parklands are shown in a stylized fashion in late-medieval manuscript illustrations and wall paintings, and some writers have suggested that such representations were genuine reflections of reality.[21] This apparent appreciation of beauty has helped prompt the idea of parks as pleasure grounds used for a variety of entertainment, besides hunting, including picnicking, dancing, and walking,[22] and this might seem to be backed up by contemporary literature.[23]

This approach plausibly suggests for the middle ages something of the interest in the design of parks and gardens made so familiar by studies of the Renaissance and, above all, the eighteenth century.[24] Although their mentality and milieu was different, medieval aristocrats clearly had a refined aesthetic sense, which they could, potentially, have brought to bear on parks. After all, if the park could be shaped to enhance not just the hunt but also the watching of the hunt, might it not be positioned and designed for other kinds of visual appreciation and activities? And if an emphasis on purely aesthetic interest might seem potentially naïve, the possibilities of conveying complex social meaning perhaps make this scenario more plausible. Underlying much of the recent literature on medieval landscapes is the idea that the shaping of the environment was related to the projection of status by demonstrating material wealth, control over resources, and refined taste.[25] According to this view, the carefully laid out park provided a very concrete proclamation of the power of its owner by creating a 'landscape of lordship'.[26]

This newer kind of interpretation of medieval parks offers exciting possibilities, but it also presents considerable difficulties. A number of crucial issues remain unclear. Ideas about landscaped settings around lords' residences have to be reconciled with the traditional picture of parks typically being distant from castles and houses.[27] The archaeological reconstructions that seem to show parkland conceived as part of residential centres usually come from a fairly narrow range of better-known royal and ecclesiastical sites, so that it is difficult to tell whether this purported interest spread beyond a limited circle. Indeed, some of those most interested in 'ornamental landscapes' have been cautious about how often parks were involved.[28] We clearly require a better idea of how many parks were near to or surrounded residences, and also some sense of the number that may have been laid out specifically with an eye to enhancing the appearance of these complexes. A firmer sense of the chronology has to be built up too. As Liddiard points out, many taking this view of parks have focused on the later middle ages, and, as we have seen, some writers see a

---

[21] Harvey 1981: pp. xii, 46, fig. 20 and colour plate III B, between 114 and 115; Landsberg 1995: 12–13, 21–5, 54. See also Girouard 2000: 32 (plate); and Fig. 2 above.
[22] Dyer 1994: 20; Creighton 2002: 73; Woolgar 1999: 165; Taylor 2000: 50; van Buren 1986: 120–4, 131; Howes 2002: 195.
[23] Benson (ed.) 1987: 174, 184; Cuhn 1981 (ed.): 627; Landsberg 1995: 23–4.
[24] Cf. Liddiard 2005: 97.   [25] See Ch. 4, below.   [26] Liddiard 2000a: 182.
[27] Above, p. 82.   [28] Taylor 2000: 50.

Fig. 12. Deer parks at Restormel castle and Boconnoc in Cornwall.

Source: Henry VIII map of Fowey harbour.

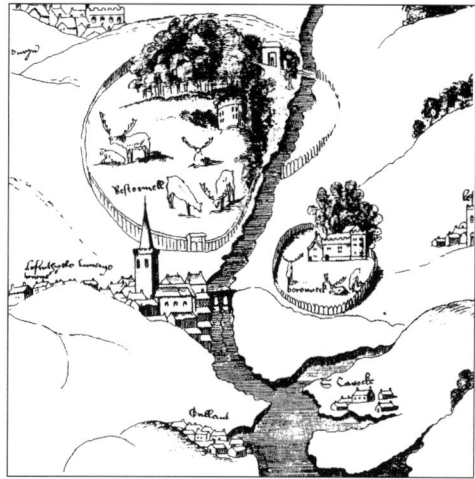

shift from the 'medieval' deer park towards the very different 'modern' landscape park or garden as occurring in the fifteenth century.[29] Yet we have already questioned the idea that later parks were so very different from earlier ones: certainly this does not seem to have been the case with hunting, so was it actually the case with this purported landscaping?

Our assessment of the extent to which park-making involved the manipulation of the landscape to convey power and authority depends on how much weight we are prepared to give to arguments based primarily on topography and literary and artistic sources, since direct corroborating documentary evidence is so rare. The nature of the sources means that the researcher has to provide a good deal of interpretation and inference, necessarily bringing to bear his or her own preoccupations. There is perhaps a danger that approaches developed in relation to eighteenth-century evidence are too unquestioningly transferred to the middle ages. Clearly it is important to try to determine how important any contemporary interest in visual effect was compared to other factors in the planning of landscape features and, indeed, how much unified planning went on (as opposed to piecemeal development), and this requires a good deal of further collection and comparison of evidence.[30] But, at the same time, real progress will ultimately require a clearer definition of the rather blurry concept of 'designed landscape', rather than a focus solely on building up the corpus of supposed examples.

This chapter aims to provide a firmer sense of how far conscious landscaping may have affected parks and of its significance compared to hunting and agrarian uses. First it examines the idea of parks as carefully designed elements in residential settings, looking at the spatial proximity of parks and houses and

---

[29] Liddiard 2000*a*: 169–70; above, p. 6.
[30] These kinds of issues are discussed in Liddiard 2005: 119–21.

the case for their establishment next to, surrounding, or in sight of residences as part of a landscaping plan. The concern to offset houses and organize views and approach routes is considered, as well as the extent to which there may have been an interest in providing views of sylvan spaces from inside houses. Following this is an examination of how far parks themselves may have been organized for aesthetic effect or to facilitate activities other than hunting, in particular how often they had some garden-like features. Evidence of possible landscape appreciation from the high middle ages as well as the later period is considered, in an attempt to redress the usual focus on the latter.

THE PARK AS RESIDENTIAL SETTING

It is certainly true that medieval houses and parks could be more closely related spatially than traditionally thought, even in very early periods. Across the country many royal and lordly castles built in the late eleventh and twelfth century had parks immediately adjoining them by the thirteenth century.[31] In Norfolk, for example, eight out of thirteen early castles probably had parks in their immediate vicinity, most commonly adjacent to one side; only the short-lived field castles of Stephen's reign seem to have been without such parks.[32] With few if any documentary references most of these parks are impossible to date with precision. Landscape evidence sometimes suggests that the parks were enclosed after the castles were constructed,[33] but at least some were apparently conceived at the same time, like Geoffrey de Clinton's at Kenilworth (Warks.) in the early twelfth century.[34] By the later twelfth and thirteenth centuries knights too were increasingly setting up parks and some of these were close to their residences. In some cases these gentry parks were adjacent to houses, but more often the houses were located inside the parks themselves, typically close to the boundary fence, as at De La Beche, Aldworth (Berks.) (see Fig. 13).[35] Equally, a number of twelfth-century and later bishops' palaces, monastic precincts, and abbatial manor houses had adjacent or surrounding parks.[36] We may suspect that many of these houses were established before the parks, but this was probably not always the case.

The spatial relationship between residence and park seems to have strengthened over the course of the thirteenth and fourteenth centuries. This development involved all ranks of park owners and occurred in a variety of ways.

---

[31] Crawford 1953: 189; Creighton 2002: 188–9; Winchester 2007: 168. Cf. Crook 2002: 73 (Laxton, Notts.); Somerset HER, 11402 and 17901 (Nether Stowey, Som.).
[32] Liddiard 2000b: 17, 25.   [33] Winchester 2007: 168; below, Fig. 16.
[34] Below, pp. 111, 113.
[35] Fenner 1990: 46–9; Winchester 2007: 181–2; Ryan 1999: 183, 190.
[36] Bond 2004: 177–8, esp. 178 (fig. 50); Roberts 1988: 74–6, figs. 3–5; Taylor 1989: 223; Page 1898: 335; Bigmore 1979: 96 (and Hardy (ed.) 1837: 204).

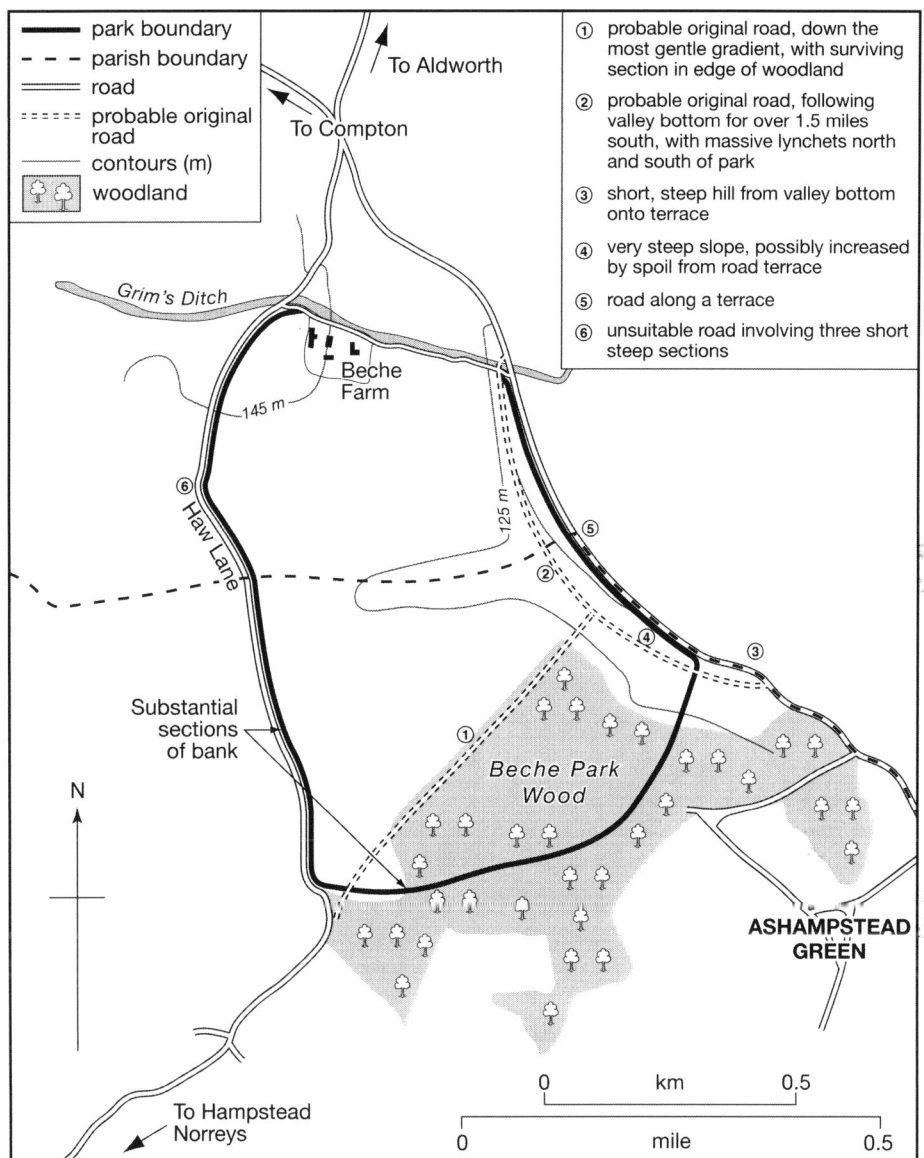

Fig. 13. De La Beche, Aldworth (Berks.). The medieval manor house was located at Beche Farm, at the northern end of the park, where an Iron-Age earthwork ('Grim's Ditch') was probably used as part of the park boundary. The creation of the park (which was licensed in 1335) appears to have led to the diversion of two stretches of road along steeper and less suitable routes.

Sources: 1st edn. 1:10,560 OS map (1882); fieldwork by Dick Greenaway, 2003.

As earlier, some new parks were created around existing or new-built houses; in places they joined or replaced older parks located further from the residence, as at Castle Bolton (Yorks.) and Hoxne (Suffolk).[37] Another pattern, more common than in earlier periods, was for lords to shift their residential focus from castles or other sites outside already established parks to new homes entirely within their bounds. Such were the actions of Henry III at Windsor in the 1240s,[38] the lords of Goltho (Lincs.), Walsall (Staffs.), and Kendal (Westmorland) around the same period,[39] and others elsewhere slightly later.[40] This process was sometimes a gradual one, occurring in stages, for example where existing park lodges were converted into principal residences. At Guildford (Surrey), for instance, there was a progression from a royal castle facing towards the town and away from the park (which existed before 1086) to an early thirteenth-century palace facing towards the park, and finally to a lodge within the park, first mentioned in 1318 and the king's main local residence by the 1390s.[41] Finally, existing parks were sometimes extended to bring nearby residences within their bounds, or to bring them from a peripheral to a central position within the park.[42]

But, as long suspected, it was in the fifteenth century that the spatial relationship between parks and houses seems to have become strongest. There was a great fashion for building new homes within freshly created or newly extended parkland, especially towers, which had come back into vogue, no doubt inspired by the flat-topped towers developed at the English and French royal complexes of Windsor and Vincennes in the later fourteenth century.[43] This enthusiasm for imparked tower-houses can be seen in projects such as John, duke of Bedford's stone and brick castle in his new park at Fulbrook (Warks.) created in the early 1420s.[44] This was the era of the 'castellated-pavilion' or tower-house in the deer park, writ large in great projects such as Cromwell's at Tattershall (Lincs.).[45] Across the country, from Westmorland to Kent and Devon to Norfolk, men signalled similar designs in applications for licences simultaneously to create parks and build crenellated residences, often styled 'lodges' or 'fortresses' and increasingly often built in brick, like Herstmonceux castle.[46] And, as in the previous century or so, new parks were also

---

[37] Moorhouse 2003a: 329; Hoppitt 2007: 155.   [38] Roberts 1997: 249; Astill 2002: 10–11.
[39] Everson *et al.* 1991: 97; Wrathmell and Wrathmell 1974–5: 21, 52; Winchester 2007: 168.
[40] Bond 1998: 30; Saul 1986: 190; Rowe 2009: 12–14.   [41] Richardson 2007: 34–5, 36 (fig. 8).
[42] One or other of these processes seems to have occurred at Pinley (Warks.) in 1251: *CPR, 1247–58*, 100. See also Rowe 2009: 64 (Berkhamsted castle, *c.*1340).
[43] Emery 1996–2006: ii. 349–53; Creighton 2002: 81–2; Liddiard 2000b: 118–19; Wilson 2002: 64–5; Chapelot 1994: 40–1, 45, 71.
[44] Hearne (ed.) 1745: 123; TNA: PRO, C139/77/36, m. 43.
[45] The phrase is Charles Coulson's, used by him in relation to Bronsil castle (Herefs.): Coulson 1979: 75 n. 8.
[46] *CChR, 1341–1417*, 427, 467; *1427–1516*, 1, 13–14, 38, 72, 80–1, 94–5, 100, 102, 137, 188, 214–15, 242; *CPR, 1422–9*, 351; *1429–36*, 446; *1467–77*, 392, 421; *1476–85*, 151, 162, 203–4; *1485–94*, 367; *1494–1509*, 43, 163–4; Shirley 1867: 61, 77.

enclosed around existing houses and older parks further from residences tended to be abandoned more often than those which were nearby.[47]

What is more, there also seems to be some direct evidence that parkland was regarded by contemporaries as having potential to enhance the visual impact of a residential complex. For instance, parks themselves were sometimes directly associated with words denoting beauty. In 1267 the prior of Durham was permitted to impark a wood called 'Beaurepaire' ('beautiful retreat')—now called Bearpark—and fill it with deer, and in 1369 Bernard Brocas was licensed to impark a similarly named house at Sherborne St John (Hants.).[48] A park was likewise created around the castle at Beaudesert in Warwickshire by the thirteenth century, if not before.[49] Perhaps in such cases the setting up of parks was seen as augmenting the attractions of places that were regarded as beautiful (or that their owners liked to think of as such).

Such an idea might be supported by examples of the apparent use of parks to control the scenery. Where a castle or house was actually inside a park, this potentially gave the landowner greater freedom to develop views and plan complex approaches, as at Woodstock (Oxon.) and Stow (Lincs.) in the twelfth century, where the residences were reached by causeways across artificially dammed pieces of water.[50] A similar effect could be created in cases where the park was in front of the house: it created an enclosed space across which travellers would have looked as they approached the residence, like at Devizes (Wilts.) in the early twelfth century.[51] At Helmsley (Yorks.) those going towards the castle from the south in the thirteenth century were apparently led on a deliberately circuitous route between a park ('la Haye') and the most impressive residential range (Fig. 14, overleaf).[52] Parkland perhaps also provided a backdrop when stretching out across higher ground beside or behind the residence, as with the castle parks at Greystoke and Cockermouth (Cumberland) in the thirteenth century and Ravensworth (Yorks.) by the late fourteenth century.[53]

Besides playing a part in how the residence appeared from the outside, some parks may have provided views for those inside, looking out. This was especially the case since lordly lodgings were usually on upper floors, with ground floors used for communal space, servants, and storage: the higher storeys of towers and castles would have offered natural vantage points to look into gardens and parks when these were set out nearby.[54] But, more than this, the desire for a view was sometimes actively incorporated into building plans,

---

[47] Hoppitt 1992: i. 63–5.   [48] *CChR, 1257–1300*, 141; *CPR, 1367–70*, 188.
[49] The castle here was called 'Castellum de Bello Deserto' in the 1140s: Gover *et al.* 1936 (eds.): 199. In the mid-1260s there was a park and small moor, and a 'great park' and a 'little park' were mentioned in the early 14th cent.: *CIPM* iii. 225; *VCH Warks.*, iii. 45.
[50] Everson *et al.* 1991: 185; Taylor 2000: 39, 44, 46; Bond 1997: 33, 43; above, Fig. 10.
[51] Taylor 1998: 32; below, Fig. 21.   [52] Everson and Barnwell 2004: 24–5.
[53] Ryder 1979: 85, 97–100.   [54] Taylor 1998: 40; Creighton 2002: 227.

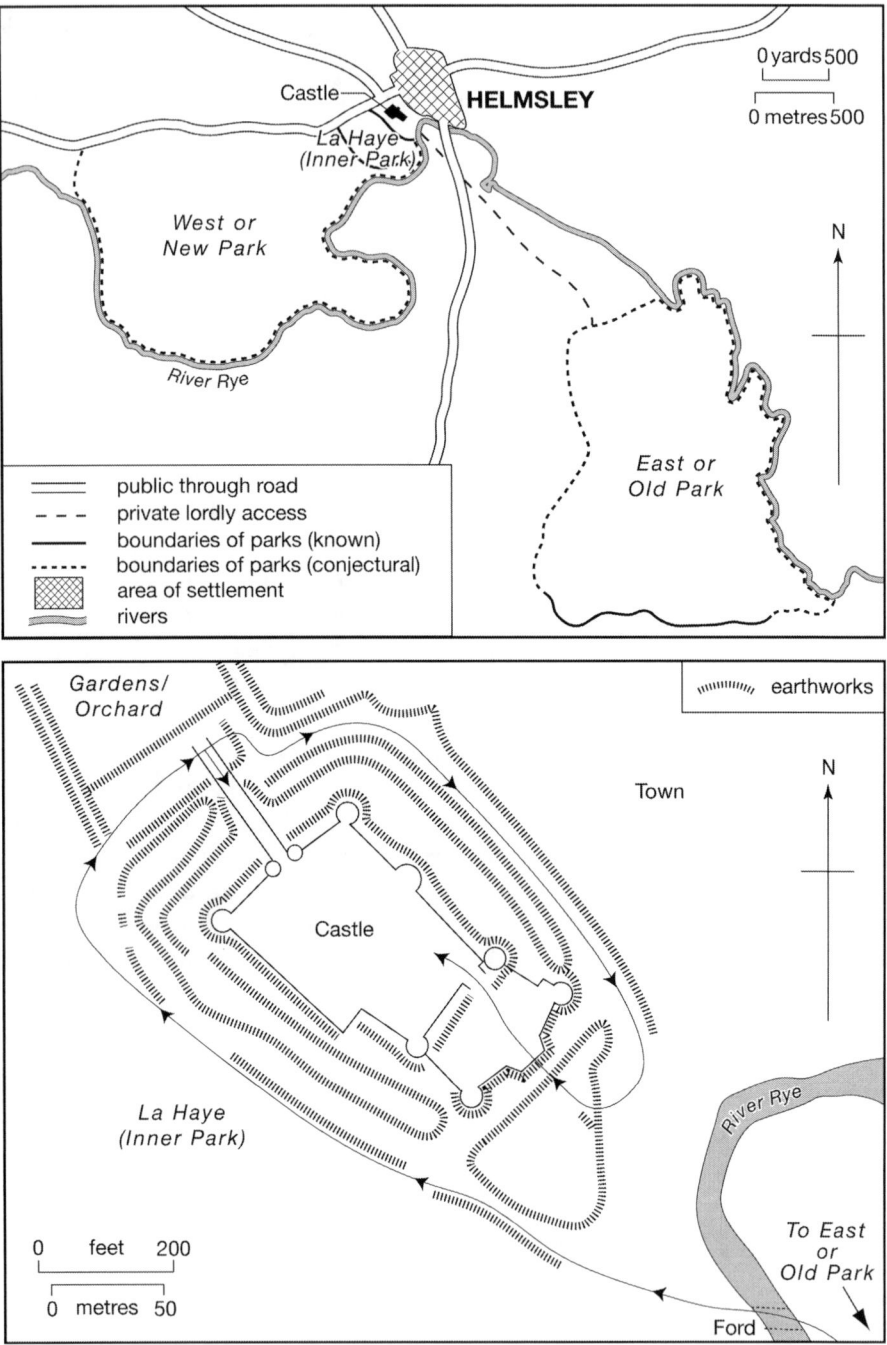

Fig. 14. Castle and parks at Helmsley (Yorks.). The approach route to the castle from the south, probably intended for the lord and his guests, seems to have been planned in order to display surrounding parkland and gardens to full advantage. The atmosphere provided by the private parkland south of the castle would have been very different from that in the busy streets of the town to the north.

Source: Everson and Barnwell 2004.

reinforcing its importance. It was not just at Helmsley that the windows from the lord's apartments looked out over the park. As early as the twelfth century, the private chambers in some castles seem to have been aligned to face nearby parks, while the more public area of the hall faced the adjacent settlements.[55] In the thirteenth century, Henry III's building works showed a greater emphasis on developing windows and window seats in castles than those of his predecessors.[56] For example, at Clarendon a reference of 1252 to the building of a chamber 'towards the park' suggests that the royal apartments faced the gardens and parkland to the north and that the view of the park was taken into account in the planning of this arrangement.[57] Hugh de Courtenay's grand rebuilding of Okehampton castle (Devon) at the end of the thirteenth century included the creation of a suite of sumptuous new domestic buildings with large windows equipped with window seats, from which the new parkland could be viewed, uninterrupted by any curtain wall, which was restricted to the northern part of the building.[58] At Woodstock a balcony was created outside Princess Isabella's chamber in 1354, to overlook the park (*ad respiciendum versus parcum*).[59] A fifteenth-century window at Barnard Castle (Durham) likewise looks out over the deer park.[60]

Archaeologists are also increasingly identifying raised terraces, walkways, or viewing platforms in gardens next to great houses that would have provided views into parks.[61] At Clarendon a platform was created outside the royal apartments, most likely perhaps in the fourteenth century. Likewise, at the royal castle developed at Ludgershall (Wilts.) from the twelfth to fourteenth century, a large, wide bank at the north of the site may have been a garden walk accessed directly from the royal lodgings to look out into the elongated park below, which was set up before 1203.[62] In *c*.1500 Abbot Richard Beere of Glastonbury created a walled garden at his manor of Mells (Som.), with mounts at each end of the north terrace probably designed to give views over the park beyond.[63] In this light, it might be noted that when Matthew Columbers was licensed to impark his wood of Chisbury, in Little Bedwyn (Wilts.) in 1260, the woodland was 'below' (next to) his garden (*subtus gardinum suum*).[64]

Taken together, this evidence suggests that some parks may indeed have acted as a wider visual backdrop to houses and their immediate surroundings. This function appears to have been rather more common than the usual focus on a handful of examples might suggest, and it seems to have been present across the country and in earlier periods as well as later ones.

---

[55] Liddiard 2005: 113–14.   [56] Jansen 2002: 105.   [57] Richardson 2005: 63.
[58] Creighton 2002: 67.   [59] *HKW* ii. 1016–17 and n.   [60] Johnson 2002: 40 (fig. 2.9).
[61] Oosthuizen and Taylor 2000: 70–4.   [62] Everson *et al.* 2000: 101–2, 104–5.
[63] Harvey 1981: 138–9.
[64] TNA: PRO, C53/50, m. 4. The calendared text omits this information (*CChR, 1257–1300*, 28).

THE PLEASURE PARK?

There is also some limited evidence of parks themselves being organized as aesthetically pleasing recreational areas, with provision for activities besides hunting. The idea of the park as a garden-like area of contrived beauty and as a stage set for courtly entertainment was apparently sometimes put into effect. Certainly this was the case on the Continent. For instance, already in the twelfth century, the Norman rulers of southern Italy constructed gardens, lakes, and pavilions inside the parks attached to their country palaces around Palermo; and there were similar developments in France.[65] A century later, from around 1290, a complex, landscaped parkland was created at Hesdin by Count Robert II of Artois (d. 1302) and later came into the possession of the dukes of Burgundy.[66] Here the walled park extended over three miles north of the castle. Fourteenth-century and later descriptions show that it was divided into three main sections: the first was an area of gardens, orchards, a pond, menagerie, and stables, near the castle; the middle section was a hilly wooded area with roads running through it; and finally, at the far northern end, was a marshy area ('li Marés') with fountains, pools, and a large pavilion. In the later middle ages, compartmented, artificially manicured parks could be found in Italy: in the late fifteenth century the Gonzaga park, which stretched between Marmirolo and the family's *castello* of Goito, was divided into three zones: pleasure grounds, a space for small game and domestic animals, and then the area for the more important bigger game.[67] In 1520 Albrecht Dürer described the great park of Brussels as 'like a paradise', with its lodges, places for jousting and other games (including tennis), garden, and maze in one area and vineyards, fruit trees, and 'pretty little woods and grazing areas' full of game animals in another, all visible from the main buildings.[68]

It seems likely that this conception of the park had an influence in England.[69] In a cosmopolitan aristocratic society, Continental parks probably inspired some of the more ambitious English park-makers, just as French and other gardening styles seem to have informed English gardening.[70] Edward II visited Hesdin in July 1313;[71] it was around this year that he extended the parkland at Windsor, and by *c.*1317 he had greatly increased the size of Clarendon park.[72] Perhaps he laid out the Little Park and garden near the palace at Clarendon as part of a scheme to create a wider and more varied area of parkland like that at Hesdin? Certainly, mid-fourteenth-century and later alterations to the parkland around Brigstock (Northants.), Kenilworth, and Windsor suggest the same interest in creating varied zones of activity; at Kenilworth Henry V built a

---

[65] Harvey 1981: 10, 48. [66] Hagopian van Buren 1986: 125–9.
[67] Syson and Gordon 2001: 80. [68] Cummins 2002: 48.
[69] Richardson 2007: 27–31; Pluskowski 2007: 71–3. [70] Stratford 1993: 109–10.
[71] Vale 2001: 229. [72] Harwood 1929: 167; Richardson 2005: 60; *CCR, 1313–18,* 507.

new banqueting house or 'pleasance' set in a marsh within the park complex.[73] The idea of recreating a 'paradise' seems to have caught on too: contemporaries called Henry V's magnificent imparked palace at Sheen a 'second paradise'.[74]

In particular, the setting up of multiple separate parks or sections of parks may sometimes have related to a landscaping or mixed-leisure interest similar to that which can be seen on the Continent. Some smaller parks in the immediate environ of residences, often called 'little parks' in contemporary documents, seem to have been more like gardens or general leisure spaces than parks for deer.[75] In the thirteenth century, the smallest of the three 'parks' at Helmsley ('Rapark', on the north side of the castle) actually appears to have been only the size of a garden or orchard.[76] Likewise the little park next to the bishop of Lincoln's palace at Buckden has been interpreted as a garden-like part of the grounds, with the larger deer-filled park beyond.[77] This was perhaps not so different from the garden that stood to the immediate south of the bishop of Ely's palace at Somersham by the twelfth or thirteenth century, in the north-eastern corner of a wider park.[78] The 'Little Park' that Edward II created near the palace at Clarendon had an external ditch, presumably to keep deer out.[79] Such parks were perhaps similar to the gardens surrounding many castles in Yorkshire and elsewhere by the later middle ages, which were divided from parkland beyond by moats or canals (see Fig. 15).[80]

Some larger parks also contained detached gardens within their bounds.[81] That these gardens had an aesthetic function may be suggested by the fact that putting them in parks necessitated costly fencing or ditch-digging and exposed them to damage from game animals. Nonetheless, such a function can only be clearly demonstrated in a small number of cases, mainly where gardens were associated with more sophisticated lodges in royal parks. Henry II's Everswell complex in Woodstock park is the best-documented example, with its close resemblance to the bower and orchard described in the Tristan story.[82] But Edward III also turned several of his park lodges into pleasances towards the end of his reign. At Odiham (Hants.), for instance, he upgraded the garden near the lodge, apparently for Queen Philippa.[83] The work here included the enclosure of what can only be described as a fenced pleasure garden, accessed by no less than five doors; inside were seats with turf-covered roofs and a screened toilet. Edward also greatly improved the lodge in Beckley park after the Black Prince gave him the manor in 1373, surrounding it with a garden and vineyard laid out within triple moats.[84]

[73] Bellamy *et al.* 1983; Harvey 1981: 98, 106–7; Astill 2002: 10–11.   [74] Wylie 1968: i. 212.
[75] Landsberg 1995: 12–13, 21–5, 54; Dyer 1994: 114.
[76] Everson and Barnwell 2004: 24–5.   [77] Bigmore 1979: 96. Cf. Taylor 1998: 18.
[78] Taylor 1989: 211.   [79] Richardson 2005: 118.
[80] Moorhouse 2003*b*: 200–1; 2003*a*: 329–32.
[81] Richardson 2005: 62; Salzman (ed.) 1955: pp. xxx, 6; *CPR, 1343–5*, 190; Lyte 1909: ii. 343; Dale (ed.) 1950: p. xxxi.
[82] McLean 1981: 99–101; *VCH Oxon.*, xii. 438; *HKW* ii. 1015–16.
[83] MacGregor 1983: 102.   [84] *HKW* ii. 899; Oxon. HER, Parks and Gardens Register.

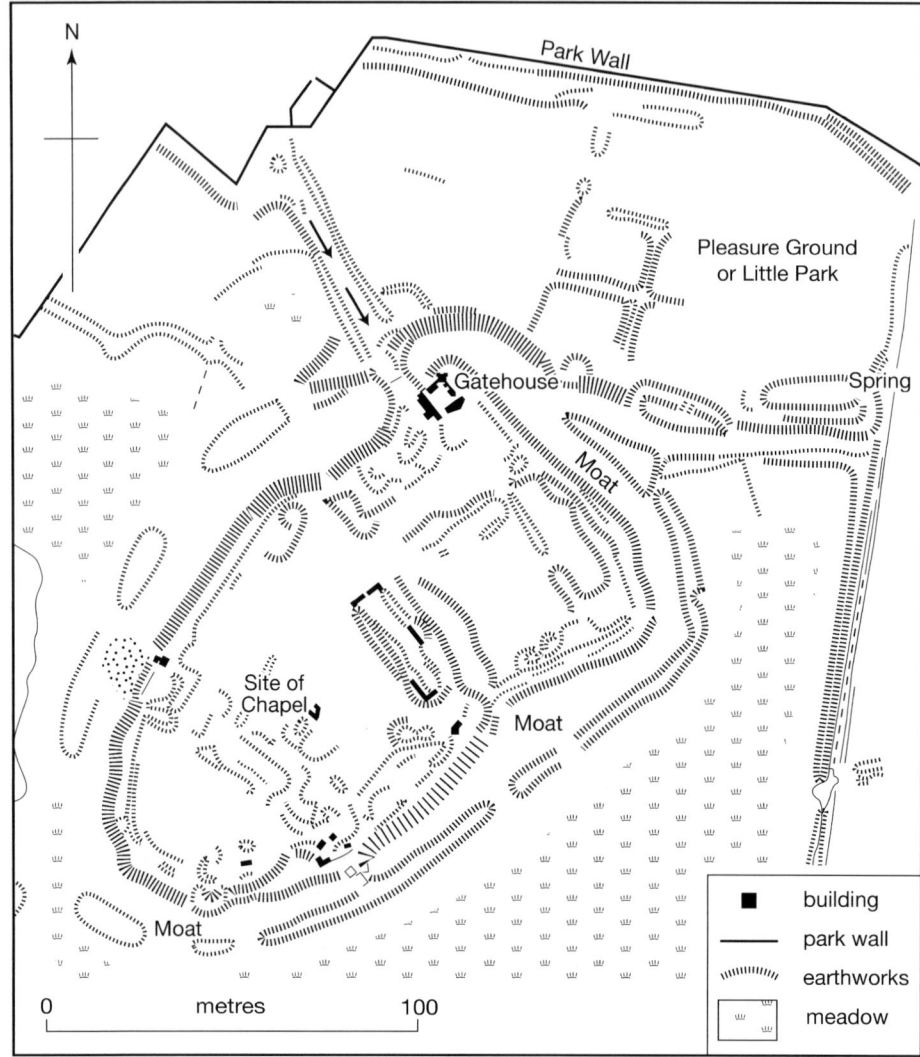

Fig. 15. Ravensworth castle (Yorks.), with a pleasure ground or 'little park' by the main approach route from the north.
Source: Liddiard 2005: 99.

This kind of work on lodges and gardens suggests that the purpose of parkland did not always revolve entirely around deer-keeping and hunting. Occasionally other uses of parkland were actually recorded. Some large royal parks were used to accommodate major festivities. Windsor park hosted a tournament in 1278, and Woodstock likewise in 1355 (on the occasion of a royal birth) and 1389.[85] Certain inner parks near castles may have had a particular function as stages for

[85] Lysons (ed.) 1814; *VCH Oxon.*, xii. 436.

games or jousts, probably because of convenience of access and provisioning as well as because they afforded the best views from the lord's window.[86] But besides these more formal activities, medieval aristocrats seem to have enjoyed *al fresco* living, and parks and their buildings could provide a suitable setting. Towers, lodges, and other ancillary buildings within parks were sometimes apparently used for meals and feasts,[87] and in the later fifteenth century a 'house of boughs' was created for Lady Margaret Beaufort in the 'little park' at her London residence of Coldharbour, where she could take supper. The same lady greatly extended Collyweston park (Northants.) in order to provide an enlarged space for her household's recreation, and sometimes that of her son. A complex of house, garden, ponds, and park was created running down to the water meadows in the Welland valley below. On one occasion there, the boys from the chapel performed 'ballets' for Lady Margaret 'by the woodside'.[88] Likewise, monastic parks sometimes seem to have provided outdoor relaxation and recreation for monks and their guests, including perhaps Bearpark, where the priors of Durham built a sizeable manor house in the 1250s.[89]

THE SIGNIFICANCE OF 'LANDSCAPING'

There are indications, then, that a conscious desire to create a visual stage for gracious living did exist and that it sometimes incorporated parks. In a sense this is not surprising. The royal and aristocratic residence represented a lordship and administrative centre as well as shelter and protection for the owner and his family. It was a place where important meetings were held, and influential guests courted and entertained, and its internal arrangements helped direct and limit access to the lord.[90] There seems no reason why the social ordering should not have continued outside. Some features of this ordering appear to have existed earlier than often suggested, and no doubt future archaeological research will uncover further plausible examples of 'designed landscaping' involving parks. But, nonetheless, these concerns and, more particularly, the place of parks in them must be kept in perspective.

First, the relationship between parks and houses needs to be considered very carefully. We should not necessarily assume that any apparent spatial link between park and residence was the result of deliberate location for visual effect. Given the relatively small size of most manors a substantial number of parks and residences would inevitably have been within sight of each other, and many parks would have been visible from the roads and lanes which approached castles and manor houses. Where parks were located in high and prominent

---

[86] Creighton 2002: 190; Richardson 2005: 63.
[87] Moorhouse: 2003*a*: 332; Woolgar 1999: 165; *HKW* ii. 918; Elliott 1975: 6.
[88] Jones and Underwood 1992: 155–6.   [89] Lomas 1992: 159. Cf. Cantor and Wilson 1963: 144.
[90] Given-Wilson 1987: 91; Thompson 1995: 151–2.

positions in the landscape this may sometimes have been more or less accidental: it was simply that suitable wood-pasture for making into parks tended to remain on the higher ground away from early settled centres. In any case, although some parks were located right on the doorstep of residences, this was far from an overwhelming trend.[91] The picture was more complex. On large estates some parks were close to castles and houses but others were in more remote areas, often in forests or chases.[92] The fact that many, even most, major castles had an adjacent or surrounding park does not mean that the majority of royal or baronial parks were positioned close to such residences. Nor did gentry parks necessarily surround or lie next to their owners' manor houses.

A very detailed investigation of the relationship between parks and houses in Hertfordshire starts to provide a more secure statistical footing.[93] In this county it has been possible to identify the spatial relationship between some fifty parks and residences. Of forty-one pre-fifteenth-century parks, nineteen (just under 50 per cent) were located a kilometre or less from their associated residence. Some of these parks would have been visible from the residence or vice versa, but this was far from always the case. Only eight of the houses (or around 20 per cent) were actually within or immediately adjacent to a park. The proximity between park and house seems, not surprisingly, to have become much stronger in the fifteenth century, when all or almost all of the ten new parks created were developed in association with houses, either adjacent to or within the park, and two other existing parks had new houses built within them. A good deal more work remains to be done, but the evidence available from a number of other lowland counties, including Dorset, Hampshire, Somerset, and Suffolk, suggests a broadly similar picture;[94] in upland regions, like Cumberland and Westmorland, a slightly larger proportion of parks may have been close to houses,[95] if only because of the limited availability of flatter land. At any rate, it seems likely that only a minority of parks created in the twelfth to fourteenth centuries had residences within or immediately adjacent to them (excluding minor lodges).

Just as importantly, the make-up of the parkland itself suggests significant limits to the prevalence of sophisticated landscape-gardening. Topography and the finite nature of owners' resources set certain basic practical restraints on the appearance of real-life landscapes which were absent from the world of the romances. This was especially the case below the level of the king and richest magnates and prelates. Rough wood-pastures could not readily be transformed into sylvan resorts, still less bare upland valleys with small pockets of woodland, like Alston (Cumberland), where Robert de Vieuxpont was licensed to impark in 1337.[96] Most parks comprised a mixture of open lawns, wood-pasture,

---

[91] See e.g. Bond 1986: 153 on parks several kilometres from their associated residences.
[92] Winchester 2007: 168–70.   [93] Personal communication from Anne Rowe.
[94] Bond 1994: 141 (fig. 6.10); Roberts 1988: 74; personal communication from Rosemary Hoppitt.
[95] Winchester 2007: 167 (fig. 62); personal communication from Harry Hawkins.
[96] Hutchison 1794–7: i. 213; *CPR, 1334–38*, 550.

enclosed woods, and small pasture closes: they were not closely tended and manicured gardens like the 'garden of love' in the thirteenth-century *Romance of the Rose*.[97] In all likelihood only a small minority had enclosed gardens within their bounds, let alone pleasances or fountains. And if the medieval parkland landscape of open grassland interspersed with large trees looked like an eighteenth-century 'landscape park', this was mainly because the creators of the latter often altered medieval parks or copied their style in a self-conscious recreation of 'pseudo-medieval' parkland.[98]

The Hertfordshire evidence does reinforce the observation that the fifteenth century saw a pronounced tendency for lords to build homes entirely within parks. It is hard to escape the conclusion that this shift was related to an interest in what these residences looked like and how they were experienced. Part of the aim was probably to create social distance by shutting ordinary people out and restricting access: a desire to reinforce an exclusive aristocratic identity had perhaps replaced earlier efforts to overawe locals and others with castles located in prominent positions. It is possible, perhaps, to detect a degree of refined revulsion at ordinary country dwellers and a desire to shut out the world of field and farm in the professed motivations of John of Wheathampstead, abbot of St Albans, for his enclosure of a park beside his manor house at Tyttenhanger (Herts.) in the late 1420s. The new park closed the area to local graziers and created a peaceful spot for the abbot, monks, and their guests to walk amongst meadows and grazing deer and calves where previously there had been bushes, briars, and the shouts of shepherds.[99]

Even so, the late-medieval trend towards closer proximity between parks and residences probably also reflected more prosaic motives of convenience and security. These motives had perhaps influenced those earlier lords who had put houses and parks close together, or the greater number who had been concerned to shut off roads or paths running through their parkland, perhaps with the aim of reducing opportunistic poaching or theft of livestock.[100] With farmland in less demand in the late middle ages it was increasingly easy to have one's hunting ground and game supply close at hand, making the deer, and perhaps to some extent the residence itself, more readily watched over. This may have been increasingly desirable in a period which saw more defined tension between classes.[101] If there was actually a wish for personal privacy, this did not necessarily have any complex social meaning. Some may simply have wanted a space where they could escape from the social performance of public life and lordship with friends and family, as had apparently been part of Henry I's motivation for enclosing Woodstock park centuries before.[102]

---

[97] McLean 1981: 99; Dahlberg (ed.) 1995: 39 ff.   [98] Rackham 1986: 129.
[99] Riley (ed.) 1870–1: i. 261.   [100] See below, pp. 166–7.
[101] Cf. below, pp. 176–7.   [102] *VCH Oxon.*, xii. 436.

Overall, it seems reasonable to suggest that an interest in the visual appearance of residences and their surrounding landscapes was subsidiary to the main purpose of the majority of medieval parks: keeping deer for hunting and as a luxury meat. Hunting normally remained the focus of attention, even in the late middle ages, for all that hunts might become increasingly stylized or be accompanied by other entertainment and festivities.[103] As suggested in Chapter 1, where landscape alterations were carried out within parks they were probably mainly designed to facilitate hunting and the watching of hunting.[104] Most often the planting of trees in parks (which was rare anyway) would have related to creating covert for deer, rather than leafy avenues for aesthetic effect. Medieval park fences were mainly designed to control the movement of game animals, and moats and ponds were there to help protect lodges and provide water for deer; they may have added to a sense of privacy and mystique, but this is largely unknowable. Lodges, towers, or residences in high or central positions were presumably thus located mainly to help watch over the deer and observe hunting forays. Internal divisions in parks were presumably more often made to separate deer and hunting from young trees and crops, rather than for aesthetic or amenity value.[105] Closely related groups of parks would often have been designed for different deer-keeping or hunting purposes, including some of the larger 'little' parks.[106]

Of course, it would be false to draw a clear distinction between 'functional' characteristics relating to hunting and aesthetic beauty: deer almost certainly had the effect of creating an image of aristocratic power and privilege. In the middle ages it was the special place of deer and hunting in contemporary culture that did most to make parks impressive accoutrements of lordship and sometimes important elements in residential landscapes, rather than any interest in landscaping parkland for its own sake. A telling confirmation of this is provided by the justificatory pronouncements relating to Henry VIII's intrusive project of building, enclosure, and land-use change at Hampton Court in the early sixteenth century, presenting a programme that may not have been unfamiliar to a twelfth-century king or great lord. The associated statute opined that the king had decided to build a 'goodlie sumptuous beautifull and princelie Mannor, decent and convenient for a Kinge', 'ornated with Parkes Gardens Orchardes and other things of great comoditie and pleasure... requisite for the prosperous continuance of his most Royall parson'.[107] The large enclosed park (known as Hampton Court Chase) was not just part of the impressive scenery, however. Its essential function remained the provision of a space full of game where Henry could indulge in the pleasures of the chase, which were his 'disporte pastime comfort and consolacion', and its impact no doubt primarily derived from this function.

---

[103] Dickens and Myers (eds.) 1951: 54. [104] Above, pp. 32–3.
[105] Above, p. 66.   [106] Above, p. 40.   [107] 31 Hen 8, c. 5: *SR* iii. 721.

4

Status

> Disparked my parks, and felled my forest woods,
> from my own windows torn my household coat,
> Raced out my impresse, leaving me no sign,
> Save men's opinions and my living blood,
> To show the world I am a gentleman.
>
> (Bolingbroke rails against his opponents' abuse of his
> property during his exile: *Richard II*, Act III, Scene I)

In the autumn of 1302, a small delegation of men, including sub-escheator Nicholas de Wedergrave, took seisin of Huntington castle (Herefs.) and went hunting in the castle park (see Fig. 16).[1] Their task was to complete a formal take-over of Humphrey de Bohun's estates and obtain the fealty of the tenants for their royal master, Edward I. Humphrey's father, who had died a few years previously, had been one of Edward's chief opponents and the marriage between the old earl's son and Edward's daughter, Elizabeth of Rhuddlan, and the entail of lands associated with it, was an important part of the king's efforts to link the great fiefs to the royal family. This was a policy aimed at enriching himself and his kin, but was also, necessarily, an assertion of royal power.[2] Given these circumstances, the deputies' hunting foray may seem a purely incidental activity, perhaps even a rather frivolous one, but, according to an unsigned report written by one of them, it was actually carefully conceived with this larger situation in mind. As the writer put it to the king: 'because there is a fine (*beau*) park, we hunted barren does (*deymes baraignes*) therein the better to publish and solemnize your lordship (*seigneurie*) and seisin before the tenants and people of the country'.

Such a detailed record of an individual hunt is unusual enough in itself, but this episode is lent particular interest by its apparent use as a theatrical vehicle for propaganda. Here we seem to have a carefully thought-out attempt to use a game reserve to reinforce the king's new control over a power-centre of one of his great tenants-in-chief, a place made more significant by its position on the

---

[1] TNA: PRO, C145/61, no. 1, m. 6; *CIM, 1219–1307*, 508–10. This chapter is largely based on Mileson 2007.

[2] *DNB* ii. 771; McFarlane 1973: 261–7.

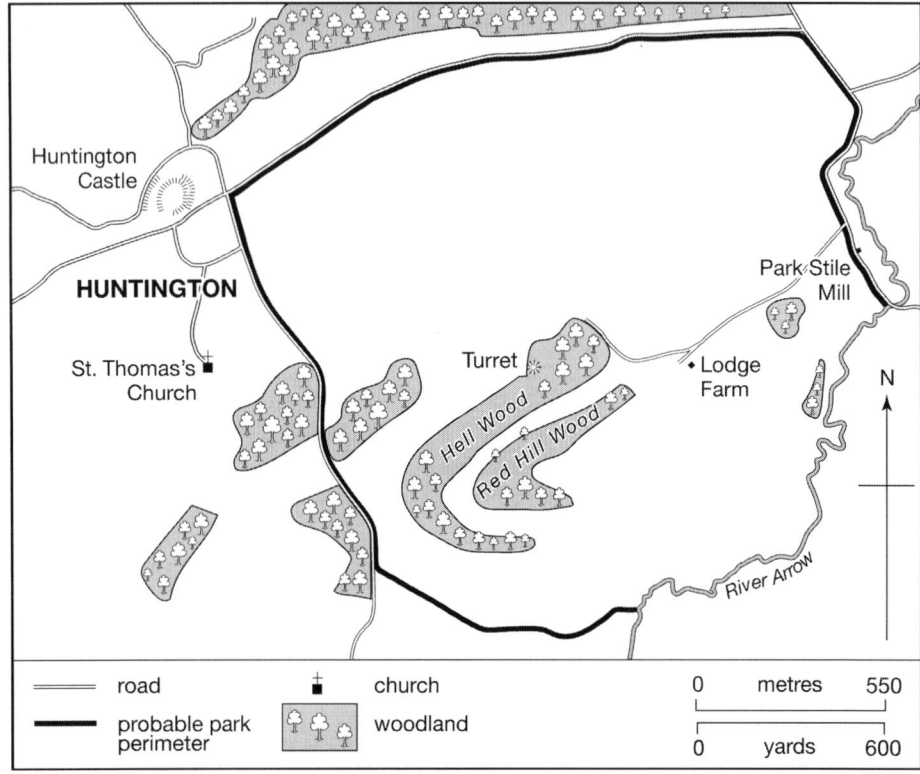

Fig. 16. Huntington castle (Herefs.), with its large park. The park, which enclosed the ruin of an abandoned motte and bailey (the 'Turret'), seems to have ballooned out from a point to the south-east of the castle, suggesting that it was enclosed after the castle had been built. The castle, first referred to in 1228, possibly existed by the earlier twelfth century; the park may have been established in the late twelfth or early thirteenth century.

Sources: 1st edn. 1:10,560 OS map (1891); King 1983: i. 206–7; Whitehead and Patton 2001: 220–1.

edge of the Welsh March, where Edward had striven to underline his authority in the 1290s.[3] Beyond the specific circumstances, this hunt also seems to be highly suggestive about the more general symbolic role of parks and hunting within medieval society. It appears to fit in well with the modern idea that part of the motivation for the creation and maintenance of parks in the middle ages was the desire to assert or reinforce lordship and high social standing. The events at Huntington may, for instance, offer a parallel to, and help to explain, the hunt conducted by the servants of the countess of Eu at Herstmonceux in 1243.[4] They also suggest why Herstmonceux park was such a natural target for Henry III's rowdy followers a couple of decades later.

[3] Davies 1987: 377–9. [4] Above, p. 8.

Yet, for all its potential implications for the social meaning of parks and hunting, the episode at Huntington has its share of complexities. The idea that hunting in fine and public style within a park might signify lordship is plainly expressed, but even if this hunt was really a planned effort to demonstrate royal power (rather than a perk for royal agents), we cannot be sure how far it would have carried real social resonance for those who witnessed it. The outcome of the hunting-trip also suggests that creating the desired impression may well have been far from straightforward: in the event, the party did not manage to catch any deer, 'but only took a hare in returning to the castle'. The whole exercise thus seems to have been a flop, and perhaps rather an embarrassing one given the kind of message about royal power that these men were apparently trying to put across. And quite what should be made of the reference to barren does is unclear. Was it simply anticipating the accusation that they had been heedless about preserving the deer herd?[5] Or was there some other more symbolic meaning, clearer to a medieval audience than to a modern one?

These kinds of questions and uncertainties are symptomatic of the difficulties which surround our understanding of the cultural role of medieval parks. Recent work has begun to explore the meanings that contemporaries may have vested in parks and the hunting and other activities that went on within their bounds.[6] An important aspect of this has been to investigate what ordinary people—apparently the mainstay of the audience at Huntington—may have thought about reserves which so often interfered with their use of the landscape and access to resources. Yet the central issue of how far conscious efforts to project high status informed park creation still remains uncertain. As suggested earlier, the idea of parks as status-symbols remains in many ways only partly developed, having been more often stated than argued in depth.[7] Some features of parks would seem to fit in with status assertion better than others and this, in turn, may raise questions about its significance in the initial decision to impark. We might wonder, then, how far parks really can be understood as status-symbols? The following pages are an attempt to answer this question, and they consider both the case which can be made in favour of this idea and the problems with it.

THE PARK AS STATUS-SYMBOL

The medieval perception of parks as status-symbols has long been accepted as one of those firmly established historical 'facts', and the repetition of this idea

---

[5] Slightly later sources suggest that barren (non-pregnant) female deer were particular—and legitimate—targets for huntsmen during the autumn and winter period, after open season for male deer had finished: Barron (ed.) 1998: 93, 101; Baillie-Grohman and Baillie-Grohman (eds.) 1904: 21, 189.

[6] Marvin 1999; Johnson 2002; Herring 2003; Liddiard 2005.   [7] Above, p. 8.

has done a great deal to shape modern thinking about these enclosures.[8] Indeed, an emphasis on display has underpinned almost all comments made about the social character of parks and park-making, no doubt because it appears to offer an overarching explanatory tool, encompassing other, more particular, motivations. The supposed status-reinforcing quality of parks has been seen as an attraction for all sorts of individuals, including kings and great lords, although it is often thought to have been especially important to social climbers and parvenus, who may have had a special interest in asserting their high standing through the adoption of a particular lifestyle.[9] A preoccupation with status assertion is particularly evident in the field of landscape studies, where scholars have increasingly focused on the apparent integration of parks with castles and manor houses to create a kind of extended stage for gracious living and conspicuous consumption.[10]

This concern with display tends to be reinforced by much modern historical, art historical, and anthropological literature, which posits the reinforcement of social standing through the acquisition and use of expensive possessions and the pursuit of activities closely associated with high-status social groups.[11] Parks have been explicitly linked to other possessions interpreted at least partly as status-symbols, such as tombs and chantry chapels, with their strong chivalric imagery (at times taken up by those with limited military experience), and, above all, castles and houses themselves and their associated seigneurial features, such as ponds, dovecotes, orchards, and warrens.[12] It has even been suggested that royal permission to make a park, encapsulated in permanent and tangible form in a charter or letter patent, was a sought-after recognition of status, something which might in turn imply a parallel with the supposed cachet of receiving licence to fortify a residence.[13]

The perceived connection between status concerns and park-making has been given added depth and sophistication by being fed into larger analyses of the nature, formation, and growing stratification of the medieval aristocracy. For instance, certain key periods have been suggested when the role of parks as status-symbols was likely to have been particularly important, especially to groups or individuals newly self-conscious about their social status. Looking at the second quarter of the twelfth century, for example, some historians have linked the apparent emergence of more complex 'designed landscapes' around the residences of great lords, often incorporating parks, with a competitive reaction engendered

---

[8] Chisholm 1910–11 (ed.): 924; Rowley 1986: 129; Dyer 1994: 20; Harriss 2005: 154, 225.
[9] Cantor and Hatherly 1979: 78; Bond 1994: 134, 139; Carpenter 1992: 180; Williamson and Bellamy 1987: 70–1; Liddiard 2005: 106–7; Britnell 1997: 192–3; Richardson 2005: 14; Harriss 2005: 225.
[10] Richardson 2007; above, pp. 83–4.
[11] Blockmans and Janse 1999 (eds.); Coss and Keen 2002 (eds.).
[12] Carpenter 1992: 225–34, 240–1; Coulson 2003: 74–7, 83, 85; Liddiard 2000b: 182–3; Dyer 1994: 110–11; Coss 1991: 157–8.
[13] Cantor and Hatherly 1979: 79; Coulson 1982: 70–1.

by the challenge of 'new men' to the more established aristocracy.[14] On a broader level, it has been suggested that knights created parks as part of their assertion of aristocratic credentials in the later twelfth and thirteenth centuries. This may be seen as part of the same process of 'social diffusion' illustrated by knights adopting heraldic devices and improving their residences in the same period.[15]

On the other hand, many accounts of the later middle ages would seem to indicate that the later fourteenth and fifteenth centuries were in fact the time when parks truly came into their own as markers of high standing.[16] The post-Black Death period has, after all, often been characterized as one of social flux, witnessing the emergence of a new social order as old barriers were broken down.[17] Such an atmosphere could well have created particular concerns about status. The gentry in particular may have felt themselves faced by the prospect of social competition from increasingly literate and self-confident sections of the yeomanry and landowning burgesses, and within their own ranks there was ever-greater concern to distinguish between members, with the addition of a new bottom rung, the gentleman. As fourteenth- and fifteenth-century sumptuary laws demonstrate, those who sought to protect their social position feared that others were using expensive possessions, clothes, and food to assert greater distinction than was their due; at the same time, the very emergence of more complex hierarchies of dress and manners provided a tool for the sophisticated social climber.[18] The statutory restrictions on hunting in 1390 may appear as the same kind of attempted social 'closure'.[19] Guides to proper manners, dress, and hunting etiquette show a keenness to emulate accepted modes of gentle behaviour, and the later middle ages may well have seen the same kind of increased formalization and stylization in the gentle hunter's role that can be detected in fifteenth-century tournaments.[20] Malory, after all, saw Tristan as role model for the gentleman, who could distinguish himself from a yeoman partly by using proper hunting terms.[21] The fact that rising labour costs and reduced agricultural profits made parks more costly to construct and maintain may only have served to attach greater prestige to their possession.

LOOKING FOR STATUS

The perception of a strong, and developing, relationship between the act of park-making and the desire to proclaim high social standing certainly seems to

---

[14] Liddiard 2005: 67–8.   [15] Above, p. 8.   [16] Britnell 1997: 192; Harriss 2005: 154, 225.
[17] Du Boulay 1970: 66–7; Bennett 1987: 19–39; Rigby 1995: 195–205; Harriss 2005: 240, 242.
[18] Lachaud 2002: 119–23.
[19] 13 Ric. 2, Stat. 1 c. 13: *SR* ii. 65; Marvin 1999: 226–7; Rigby 1995 (closure theory); below, p. 145.
[20] Orme 1992: 138–42.   [21] Vinaver and Field (eds.) 1990: i. 375.

be supported by some of the features of parks themselves. It is notable, for instance, that the park was usually an impressive physical presence in the landscape (see Fig. 17). Park perimeters were typically constructed of substantial fences or (less often) walls mounted on one or two metre high banks with wide internal ditches.[22] The sheer length of these prominent boundaries attracted contemporary comment: the fifteenth-century antiquary John Rous remarked upon the length of the park wall at Woodstock, which he believed was already seven miles in circuit in Henry I's time.[23] In the mid-thirteenth century, one of Earl Warenne's Yorkshire parks was said to have a circuit of five leagues.[24] The larger gentry parks might also have perimeters of several miles. Such an enclosure would have demonstrated a considerable degree of social control and authority, providing an instantly recognizable sign of the wealth and lifestyle priorities of the owner, evident not least to the locals who were tasked to build or maintain a reserve which effectively kept large areas of woodland and pasture beyond communal control.[25]

Walled or fenced park boundaries would probably have reminded the viewer of castle defences and the kind of control and organization of space that these signified. Indeed, where the park surrounded a residence it effectively became its outer perimeter curtilage: in a well-known passage from the late fourteenth-century Gawain poem, the narrator speaks of the defensive ditches of Bertilak's admirable castle in almost the same breath as he mentions the surrounding park's palisade of close-set spikes.[26] Parks often had several gates and the main one was likely to be large, like the 'great gate' described in 1250 at 'Rigge' park, King's Somborne (Hampshire).[27] Such entrances might be approached across bridges or have smaller wicket gates set inside, in this way further resembling castle entrances.[28] By the end of the middle ages park gates seem to have reached an apogee of formalization, as with Henry VII's crenellated gates at Clarendon (Wilts.) or the still extant castellated stone 'Prior's Gate' at the abbey park at Peterborough (Northants.), constructed *c*.1510.[29] Impressive boundaries, close internal ordering, and physical and symbolic association with castles seem likely to have been evocative of power. It may be plausible then that medieval park creators thought in a similar way to the late seventeenth-century agriculturalist John Houghton, who, although he disliked parks as uneconomic, recognized that they brought their owners certain advantages, since 'they make or preserve a grandeur, and cause them to be respected by their poorer neighbours'.[30]

---

[22] See e.g. RCHM *Northants.*, i. 37, 46, 70, 72; ii. 129, 176–7, 186; RCHM *Dorset*, iv. 35, 95; Squires and Humphrey 1986: 103; Northumberland HER, 10723 (Newtown Park); Hants. HER, 25404 (Merdon); NMR, ID No. NZ80NW34 ('Cucket' park, near Mulgrave Castle, North Yorks.); Higham 2004: 121, 123.
[23] Hearne (ed.) 1745: 138.   [24] *Rot. Hund.* i. 113.   [25] Bettey 2000: 37; Steane 1993: 149.
[26] Barron (ed.) 1998: 72–3.   [27] MCO, King's Somborne 76.
[28] Fowler (ed.) 1937: 116–17; Slade and Lambrick (eds.) 1990 and 1992: i. 299–300.
[29] Richardson 2005: 116; Bond 2004: 176.   [30] Thomas 1983: 202.

Fig. 17. Merdon park, Hursley (Hants.), 1588. This park, first recorded in the early thirteenth century, spread out from the twelfth-century palace of the bishop of Winchester. The palace had been built on the site of an earlier motte and bailey, itself raised over an Iron-Age hillfort: HCCAHBR, 25400, 25401, 25404.
Source: original map, used by permission of IBM UK Ltd.

But of all the characteristics of parks, it was hunting and attitudes towards hunting which seem likely to have been crucial in projecting status. Hunting has never been a socially neutral pastime—if such a thing could ever exist—even when a wide cross-section of society has participated. Anthropological studies suggest a recurring pattern in which hunting is a means of integrating and ordering communities as well as gathering food.[31] The hunting of larger game is particularly significant, since it usually requires group participation. In more complex societies, hunting seems to have involved a range of status-reinforcing rituals, for instance those centring on the dismembering of the prey. Leadership of the hunt and possession of hunt objects seem likely to have allowed individuals to assert authority and gain prestige. In medieval England great men sometimes presided over grand hunts, bringing out large numbers of tenants and others to assist.[32] Such hunts helped to cement social relations within communities, and not just between lord and non-gentle tenants: men of knightly status might act as huntsmen for greater lords, and nobles

---

[31] Lee 1997: 252–3; Dean 2001.   [32] Orme 1992; *VCH Durham*, i (Boldon Book).

for the king.[33] Regular involvement in hunting was a way of demonstrating the possession of extensive leisure time, a traditional aristocratic characteristic. This is brought home by an anonymous late thirteenth-century poem, 'Contempt of the World', where the narrative voice, apparently that of a non-aristocrat, sees the worldly lives of the elite, including their hunting and hawking, as the source of their damnation.[34]

Medieval kings and aristocrats did not just take a leading role in hunting, they tried to preserve and control it too, in forests and other hunting preserves, and this linked the hunt more directly with the question of authority.[35] In this context possession of a hunting reserve seems likely to have been a mark of power. By allowing selected people to have some share in hunting opportunities and game meat a king or lord could demonstrate power and exercise patronage, strengthening social ties, both vertical and horizontal.[36] Parks themselves could be temporarily loaned out, giving other aristocrats the chance to hunt in fine style. Venison could not be readily purchased, but could only be obtained through hunting (legitimately or illegitimately) or as a gift from the owner of a forest or a park, for whom it took a good deal of effort and resources to produce. Not surprisingly, this meat was much sought after by those who did not have it, for celebrations and special occasions.[37] Being able to give venison away from one's own preserves was likely to have been a visible sign of social leadership; simply receiving it showed an individual's connections. Decisions about whom to give it to and whom not to can reveal a good deal about local relationships, as shown by analysis of Howard gifts from Framlingham park in the early sixteenth century.[38]

Occasionally the sources give us a more direct insight into the way parks and the hunting opportunities they could offer were sources of pride for their owners. Several English kings seem, for instance, to have thought of their parks as reflections of their power and splendour, as was also the case with their finest architecture. For example, the context of Henry III's permission for Gaucher de Châtillon to hunt in Elham park (Kent) shows that Henry wanted to show it off.[39] The proposed park visit was to follow on from the constable of Dover giving a tour demonstrating the nobility (*nobilitas*) of the castle a few miles away. Henry clearly wanted to impress Gaucher and thought that his deer-filled park at Elham would help to do this. In the later fifteenth century Edward IV's hospitality for the visiting Flemish nobleman Louis de Bruges had a distinctly ostentatious edge and much of the focus was on the delights of hunting in his Little Park at New Windsor.[40] Louis had played host to Edward

---

[33] Roberts 1988: 71; Baillie-Groham and Baillie-Groham (eds.) 1904.
[34] Davies (ed.) 1963: 56–9.   [35] Below, Chs. 5 and 6.
[36] Greenway and Sayers (eds.) 1989: 26; Roberts 1988: 71; *CCR, 1302–7*, 21; Cox 1905: 193–5; Watkins 1993: 23; Spencer 2008: 26–30.
[37] Above, p. 80; Rackham 1986: 135; Stamper 1988: 143; Roberts 1988: 72; Woolgar 1999: 115.
[38] MacCulloch 1986: 56–7.   [39] Coulson 1979: 75.   [40] Anon (ed.) 1836.

during his recent exile in the Low Countries and the English king, besides being grateful, was no doubt keen to convey a more suitably regal image than would have been possible in his straitened circumstances abroad.

PROBLEMS WITH THE STATUS-SYMBOL PARADIGM

It seems entirely plausible that parks played a part in concerns about familial and individual image, concerns which, after all, have been seen as influencing many aspects of medieval aristocratic life. There seems to be little doubt that display helped reinforce power: a fairly ostentatious, open-handed lifestyle was seen as a necessary part of a lord's standing or 'worship'.[41] The desire to demonstrate a suitably aristocratic lifestyle was given a sharper edge, no doubt, by the fact that there was a degree of fluidity within, and on the fringes of, landed society throughout the period. The reality of who held power, land, and wealth in particular localities was liable to shift.[42] Individual changes in fortune made image and the projection and assertion of social leadership significant, especially for the ambitious parvenu, but also, presumably, for the more established aristocrat.

Nonetheless, as many historians have recognized, understandings of the medieval aristocracy which focus on social mobility and the significance of display have their problems and limitations; and in the same way the link between the desire for a park and for social recognition has to be kept in perspective. Pomp and circumstance were doubtless an aid to social standing, but they were not its ultimate foundation. Kings became increasingly concerned about projecting an image of magnificence, but they did not rely on fine possessions to demonstrate their authority. Rather they carried in their crown and person a power and prestige that stemmed from their acknowledged and divinely sanctioned role as leaders and representatives of their people.[43] If the king had many fine houses, wide forests, and expensively enclosed parks this may have been more because he enjoyed a certain lifestyle rather than because he consciously acquired them to impress his power (for all that he might like to show them off occasionally). The same might have been true among the nobility, whose standing and prestige was hardly open to question and came from their great landholdings and power to resolve disputes and provide leadership. Status concerns might seem more plausibly influential lower down, but they were not necessarily paramount. It might also be suggested that since high status was not a finite commodity, the degree of competition for recognition can be exaggerated.

The part that status concerns may have played in park-making also has to be set alongside the popularity of hunting as a leisure activity. It might be argued

[41] Carpenter 1992: 198–211, 245.   [42] Crouch 1996.   [43] Watts 1996: 16–21.

that a good deal of the motivation for park creation was about the pleasure derived from having hunting facilities on hand; if this showed the owner's power over the use of the landscape and helped him to entertain in a more impressive manner, then that was all the better. Particular features of parks can be interpreted rather differently too, such as their boundaries. Their main purpose—keeping deer inside the park—actually ensured that park banks would often have been less impressive from the outside than some larger wood banks, since their ditches were usually internal rather than external.[44] And if parks were such status-symbols, it is perhaps rather odd that at any one time quite a number were likely to be in a poor state of repair, with faulty perimeters, depleted deer herds, and ill-tended woods and pastures. As estate accounts and inquisitions *post mortem* demonstrate, where lords' fortunes or residential patterns shifted, they were as willing to allow some of their parks to fall into decay as certain of their manor houses and castles, or to see their purpose shift towards stock-raising or wood production.

These kinds of objections and apparent limitations to the status-symbol approach clearly cannot be simply brushed aside. The question is how they can be reconciled with the case for status assertion outlined above. One way forward may be through an examination of the individuals who were actually responsible for their creation. One of the most significant barriers to a clearer understanding of the social role of parks is that the sociological context of park making remains only superficially explored, especially when compared with the much greater volume of work devoted to uncovering the form, utilization, and landscape setting of parks themselves. The people behind parks—those kings and lords who actually had them created—clearly ought to be close to the heart of any attempt to understand these important features of the medieval countryside. Yet many questions about these men and women (mainly men) remain unanswered. While the broad outlines of the distribution of park ownership are fairly well established, the extent to which this ownership moved down the landowning scale, and precisely when, remains open to debate. More significantly, active park-makers have seldom if ever been looked at as a group to try to discern whether they shared any common characteristics which might suggest a special interest in demonstrating prestige and power.

PARK OWNERSHIP

Park ownership was focused at the top of the social scale and extremely limited towards its lower end. Certainly no individual below the rank of manorial lord would have had the resources to create a park, but, equally, many manorial lords did not possess one. The king was by far the greatest single owner of

---

[44] For a good example see RCHM *Northants.*, iii. 11 (Badby).

parks, having many scores of them at any one time. Some were ancestral creations, others were acquired with estates escheated through failure of heirs, forfeited for treason, or temporarily in royal hands through vacancies of bishoprics. By the thirteenth century the greatest earldom, Lancaster, had several dozen parks and others, like Arundel and Norfolk, had fifteen to twenty; richer bishoprics like Winchester, Canterbury, and Durham had approximately twenty and lesser ones at least a small number; greater monastic houses, like Bury St Edmunds (Suffolk) had several.[45] Presumably most of the approximately two hundred members of the greater baronage in the thirteenth century had at least one park, and similarly most of the hundred or less parliamentary peers of the later fourteenth and fifteenth century. Below this high level things are less certain, although it seems likely that park owners were a minority amongst the gentry.

A closer examination of the situation in the early fourteenth century gives an idea of gentry park ownership, at the time when parks had probably reached their maximum numbers. According to one estimate there could have been up to 3,200 parks in existence at this time.[46] These parks, if indeed there were so many, seem to have been shared between a similar number of individuals: the king, great lords, bishops, large and middle-ranking religious houses, and greater gentry families (knights and richer esquires, of which there were about 70 per county).[47] Many of the parks belonged to the king and the two to three hundred greatest lay and ecclesiastical lords: one estimate suggests that they owned at least 50 per cent of the total.[48] If this is correct, then, besides this small elite group, almost 3,000 landowners had approximately 1,600 parks between them, which would equate to roughly one park to every two members of the richer gentry. But, in fact, things appear to have been considerably more restricted than this. It actually seems that in 1300 only around one in five of the greater gentry were park owners, although the picture no doubt varied somewhat from region to region.[49] The most likely explanation for this more limited gentry park ownership is that the total number of parks existing in 1300 was lower,[50] and that the proportion of parks owned by the king and great lords was rather higher when, as in Rackham's calculations, multiple parks in the same manor are counted separately.[51] In earlier periods there would have been fewer parks to go round, especially in the twelfth century, when the great growth in park numbers was only at its beginning.

---

[45] Cantor and Hatherly 1979: 77–8; Roberts 1988: 67; Cantor 1983.
[46] Rackham 1980: 191. [47] McFarlane 1973: 268; Given-Wilson 1987: 14–15, 71–4.
[48] Cantor and Hatherly 1979: 78.
[49] Cf. Mileson 2005b: 150–1 (a detailed study of Oxfordshire) to Cantor and Hatherly 1979: 78 and Cantor 1983 (regional differences in gentry park-ownership).
[50] See e.g. Rowe 2007: 128, on Hertfordshire park numbers. An estimate of around 3,000 parks existing at various times during the middle ages, rather than in 1300 alone, appears more realistic.
[51] Above, p. 3.

Although it is often said that park ownership moved down the landowning scale in the later medieval period,[52] the situation did not actually change that drastically in the fourteenth or fifteenth centuries. Great lords continued to own a large number of parks. The correspondence of John of Gaunt, duke of Lancaster, by far the greatest lay landowner in the late fourteenth century after the king, reveals that in the 1370s he possessed at least forty-six parks.[53] At lower levels, park ownership remained much less common: as before, only the wealthier gentry could generally hope to afford the costs of park creation and maintenance. In Staffordshire, for example, at least seventy parks are known by 1350, but almost half of them belonged to a mere five leading landowners.[54] Over the next 150 years the overall number of parks in England dropped somewhat, perhaps by somewhere between 20 and 30 per cent.[55] The circle of park owners must have been reduced as a result, and perhaps disproportionately so since greater lords tended to have the resources to maintain their parks. Nor was it normally possible to acquire full possession of a park by renting it, since active parks were not included in demesne leases.[56]

This continued exclusivity was the result of the cost of enclosing and maintaining a park, which set limits on imparkment as an assertion of status by the parvenu. But, of course, exclusivity may have been part of what attracted the wealthier among the socially ambitious to try to acquire their own parks. While few parks were available for rent or purchase and only the better-established man was likely to attract an heiress with a park, there was little to stop anyone creating their own once they had sufficient control over the land on which they wished to do so and enough funds or labour services to carry out construction. For the man who wished to assert his high standing and wealth these expenses were perhaps worth meeting. It might therefore seem likely that park-making would be particularly attractive for individuals who had newly risen up the ranks of the aristocracy, or those of a mercantile background who used their wealth to buy into country landowning and manorial lordship.

THE IDENTITY AND CAREERS OF PARK-MAKERS

Many hundreds of individuals were involved in establishing, extending and redesigning parks throughout the middle ages. Unfortunately, in the majority of cases very little is known about their activities and in many instances even their identity is a matter of speculation. Detailed research can sometimes reveal more, but all too often the documentary sources required for precise information are lacking, especially outside some of the more richly documented royal

---

[52] Dyer 1991: 236; Harriss 2005: 154, 225.   [53] Armitage-Smith (ed.) 1911: *passim*.
[54] Birrell 1990–1: 35.   [55] Cf. above, pp. 37–8.
[56] Roberts 1988: 81; Lomas 1978: 345; MCO, Otterbourne 72.

and ecclesiastical estates. This necessarily means that it is only possible to discuss a relatively small proportion of park-makers, with the sample being biased towards those about whom most is known, whose number includes those who obtained royal licences and those whose parks attracted particular contemporary comment or opposition. Both groups, however, we may suspect of being somewhat atypical.

Park licensees perhaps call for particular comment, since they are often the individuals who can be most easily identified as probable park-makers. First, there is the potential problem that park licences do not always coincide with actual park creation, but sometimes represent the legitimization of existing parks or merely mark the intention to impark.[57] In fact though, the majority of park licences do seem to relate fairly closely to actual park-making or at least refurbishment and restocking with deer. Secondly, there is the question of the motivation for obtaining a licence, given that complying with legal formalities was scarcely automatic for medieval landowners. In other words, it might be thought that park licensees were those who felt more need for recognition or, perhaps, protection from the jealousy of their neighbours, like the parvenus who were supposedly keenest to acquire crenellation licences. However, leaving aside this interpretation of crenellation licensing, which not everyone would agree with,[58] it seems safe to say that park licensing revolved around compliance with royal franchisal rights over forests, which were enforced, albeit variously.[59] This creates a straightforwardly pragmatic motivation for licensing, with other factors being secondary.

It can be said at once that the link between park-making and social ambition was not always clear-cut. Not all those who rose in wealth and social position made parks: many of the gentry did very well from some combination of royal service, the law, marriage, the profits of landholding, or even trade, without ever making or acquiring a park. More significantly, not all of those who did make parks were parvenus. Some lesser park-makers seem to have been fairly typical members of families of long-standing and relatively stable wealth and position in landed society. Of course, these men may have wished to augment their individual and family image by making a park, but this is difficult to prove.

Nonetheless, there are clear common themes in the careers of substantial numbers of known park-makers: rising social standing; wider improvements to and expansion of family estates; and emulation. Rising wealth and social standing is a frequently recurring part of the background of park creators, and this is evident even in very early periods. Warwickshire in the early twelfth century provides an interesting example. Here the arch 'new man' Geoffrey de Clinton, who owed his position entirely to royal favour, had established a castle, priory, and park at Kenilworth by c.1125, only three or four years after Henry I

---

[57] Below, p. 137. [58] Colvin 1997: 21. [59] Below, Ch. 5.

had made him sheriff of the county and installed him as a great lord there, more or less in opposition to the earl of Warwick.[60]

Succeeding centuries and other areas demonstrate similar trends. In the thirteenth, fourteenth, and fifteenth centuries a substantial number of park licensees were royal servants from families of relatively minor background, making a name and wealth for themselves. They included men like William Brewer, Hubert de Burgh (newly earl of Kent), and Stephen de Segrave in the thirteenth century; William Montagu, William de Clinton (both of whom were ennobled), and John Molyns in the fourteenth; and John Norbury, Sir Andrew Ogard (a naturalized Dane), and William, Lord Hastings in the fifteenth. Prominent among identifiable thirteenth-century park creators in Bedfordshire was Paulinus Pever, who rose from obscure origins to become steward of the royal household. In the fourteenth century, many park licensees were knights who had served with Edward III, some of whom, like Sir Thomas Breadstone, had made large profits in France. In the next century, royal household knights and esquires were particularly prominent, above all those who were greatly enriched by the free-flowing royal patronage of the 1440s. Across the period there were also a number of clerks of fairly humble origins come good through royal service, most obviously men like Robert Burnell (chancellor to Edward I and bishop of Bath and Wells), John Droxford (administrator for the first two Edwards, and also bishop of Bath and Wells), and Adam Moleyns (diplomat, councillor, and bishop of Chichester, d. 1450). Still other park creators were men who had increased their family wealth through advantageous marriages, like John de la Mare or William de Dives. Another notable feature was the creation of parks or the acquisition of park licences by individuals at times when their careers were reaching new heights, like Michael de la Pole, who, while Lord Chancellor, received a licence to impark at Wingfield and elsewhere in Suffolk just a few months before being made earl of Suffolk in August 1385. A particular feature of the fifteenth century was the new prominence of the merchant park-maker who had recently bought into landed society, especially in south-east England. Of course, some aristocrats had had trading interests in earlier centuries, but it was only in this period that those whose background was primarily grounded in commerce seem to have been actually creating parks in sizeable numbers.[61]

A closer look at individual localities in the late fifteenth century seems to do much to confirm this link between social rising and park-making. Warwickshire provides an especially interesting case study, suggesting that, here at least, there was an ever-closer correlation between social ambition and park construction.[62] Many of the imparkers in this county were men who were increasing or had already dramatically raised their personal and family status. Further detailed studies of other counties are required, but it is notable that in Yorkshire,

[60] Crouch 1982: 114–17   [61] Mileson 2005a: 32.   [62] Mileson 2005a: 32–3.

although longer established lords and gentry made many of the new parks, the park-makers included social risers like Sir Guy Fairfax, justice of the king's bench and lawyer come good (or perhaps his son), and William, Lord Conyers, who moved from one of the top knightly families of Yorkshire to the threshold of the peerage. In late fifteenth-century Norfolk too several new men made parks.[63]

As suggested already, the second pronounced feature of park-makers was their tendency to be individuals who were carrying out substantial improvements to their estates, above all major building works on their residences and remodelling of their local churches. This link between parks and building or rebuilding projects can be seen on the grandest scale in the activities of the crown. In and around Windsor royal residential building coincided with the development and extension of parkland from a very early date. This included Henry III's creation of a manor house in the Great Park in the 1240s; Edward II's construction of new houses and extension of the parkland; and Edward III's massive rebuilding of 1357–68, which was accompanied by substantial imparkment and the establishment and renovation of further park lodges.[64] The link between building and imparking was also close at Clarendon and other royal estates.[65]

But the same feature is just as visible with non-royal park-makers. Geoffrey de Clinton's park seems to have been set up along with his castle and priory as part of a package,[66] and the same pattern was repeated time and again. Richard of Cornwall rebuilt the castle at Oakham (Rutland), where he extended the park; Hugh de Courtenay built a stunning new domestic range at Okehampton (Devon) around the same time as he created a park in the 1290s; the Sir John Stonor who probably established the park at Stonor in the earlier fourteenth century was also responsible for major building works; Sir John Foxley set up a manor house at his new manor-park complex at Puckmere (Berks.) in the same period. The list could be greatly extended: William Cantilupe at Eaton Bray (Beds.) in the early thirteenth century; Pever at Toddington (Beds.) in the middle of the same century; John Wyard at Stanton Harcourt (Oxon.) in the late 1320s; the Beches at De La Beche in Aldworth (Berks.) in the 1330s; and de la Pole at Wingfield to name but a few. The link between building (or rebuilding) and imparking became even stronger in the fifteenth century, as we saw earlier.[67]

Finally, we come to the third common feature, emulation or competition relating to parks and other hunting reserves. Emulation of others who owned or were making parks is seldom possible to prove, but circumstantial evidence suggests that it would often have been significant, just as it probably was with many fine new castles and houses. Certainly by the fifteenth century the antiquary John Rous believed that Henry I's imparking at Woodstock led directly to

[63] Beresford 1954: 59–60; Pollard 1990: 90–1; Liddiard 2000*b*: 110.
[64] Astill 2002: 10–11; Harwood 1929: 124; *CPR 1364–7*, 95–6; *1367–70*, 136.
[65] Richardson 2007.   [66] Liddiard 2000*a*: 183.   [67] Above, pp. 88, 96.

park-making by Henry, earl of Warwick and other lords, following his example.[68] Rous's view may well reflect fifteenth-century attitudes more than twelfth-century realities in this case, but there is no reason to suppose that such emulation was a new feature in the late middle ages.[69] It seems likely, for instance, that the park-making of Abbot Samson of Bury St Edmunds in the late twelfth century was motivated by the desire to keep up with other Suffolk lords who were able to offer their guests good hunting opportunities.[70]

In some cases emulation seems to have focused around contact at the centre. This perhaps partly explains the exceptional amount of park licensing among (mainly northern) knights in the 1330s and early 1340s, most of whom were prominently involved in Edward III's military campaigns; among yeomen of the royal household and king's sergeants more generally; and, most obviously, among Henry VI's intimates and ministers in the 1440s (mainly in the Home Counties). Elsewhere it was probably more local, as in Gloucestershire where several gentry parks seem to have been established following the Clare imparkments at Thornbury in the late thirteenth century.[71] A similar situation perhaps existed in north Yorkshire in the later fifteenth century, where Richard of Gloucester's park-making may have acted as a spur to others, and where Sir William Gascoigne received licence to impark within a few years of his fierce rival Sir William Plumpton. Very likely, a lord's leisure pursuits and possessions could inspire his fellows or retainers.

For all the caveats about established lords making parks, this brief study of park-makers does suggest a genuine correlation between park-making and the desire of 'new men' to assert their place within landed society. We need not, of course, be hugely surprised that rising men were more likely to be park-makers—since they were, necessarily, less likely to inherit parks, or even acquire them by marriage—but this, if anything, reinforces the significance of park possession to high status and gracious living. The frequent relationship between park-making and general programmes of building further strengthens the idea of this link with social assertiveness, especially where house and park were conceived as part of a package. Indeed, by the early sixteenth century, some, like Sir Thomas Cokayne, whose tomb in Ashbourne church (Derbs.) explicitly referred to his house building and park-making activities, self-consciously presented the establishment of parks as an important part of the furthering of their family name.[72] In this light, we might wonder whether the creation of very large parks in the fifteenth century had a competitive element, as well as reflecting the availability of land in particular areas. Or perhaps it may even have been that the possession of a park could almost have become tarnished in the 1440s and 1450s by the sense that they were the vulgar acquisitions of disreputable upstarts? At any rate, we are not far here from Shakespeare's later idea, put in

[68] Hearne (ed.) 1745: 138. [69] *VCH Warks.*, viii. 467; Wallsgrove 2004/5: 239.
[70] Above, pp. 30, 34. [71] Franklin 1989: 154. [72] Mileson 2005*a*: 33.

the mouth of Bolingbroke in *Richard II*, that parks and forest woods were signs of gentlemanly status; signs, moreover, which required defending, since their destruction could imply a loss of that status.[73]

Any serious attempt to understand the cultural context of park creation clearly has to take into account considerable complexities. As has been seen, the range of those who created, inherited, or acquired parks was wide; their numbers included kings, lay and ecclesiastical lords, gentry, young and old, men and women, well-established landowners and parvenus. If all shared in the same aristocratic cultural world, their priorities and perspectives must have varied considerably. Parks themselves varied too: some were fairly small, others very large. The use owners made of their parks might differ according to their location, size, and internal arrangements, as well as being affected by the extent of the lord or lady's estates, their itinerary, leisure interests and estate management priorities (which could change over time). The degree to which parks were subject to agrarian exploitation, like livestock grazing or wood production, or other complementary uses, such as breeding horses, differed widely between time and place. While some of the functions of parks may seem to be compatible with a purported concern for projecting status and social power, such as hunting or acting as a landscape setting for a major residence, others, like pastoral farming and wood production, appear less obviously related.

Nonetheless, for all this, the strongly distinctive features of parks, above all the combination of separation, deer-rearing, and provision of facilities for hunting, suggest the possibility and relevance of a general analysis of social views and functions which incorporates the attempted expression of high standing. Parks were clearly close to many aristocrats' hearts and almost certainly played an important part in their sense of identity: they were among their biggest expenditures on their estates, often second only to building works; they were usually referred to among the major appurtenances of lordships, even in highly abbreviated documents;[74] they readily became elements in political disputes;[75] and they were seldom sold, except because of debt, and tended to be among the last possessions impoverished aristocrats clung on to.[76] The status-symbol idea has most to offer when approached through close attention to individual circumstances and particular local landscapes, economies, and societies. It is the cumulative delineation of local case studies, informed by a greater awareness of the kind of larger context outlined here, which ought to provide a fuller understanding of the social role of the park in the middle ages.

---

[73] See above, epigraph to this chapter. Cf. Casson (ed.) 1949: 9, 33, 35, for what seems to be a late 14th- or early 15th-cent. anticipation of this idea in the *Romance of Sir Degrevant*.
[74] e.g. see Stenton (ed.) 1933: 274 (Arundel, Sussex) and 1934: 60 (Higham Ferrers, Northants.).
[75] Hewlett (ed.) 1886–9: ii. 117; Warren 1961: 215–16; Treharne and Sanders (eds.) 1973: 271; below, Ch. 6, esp. p. 155.
[76] Coss (ed.) 1986: pp. xxiv–xxv; Coss 1991: 187; Crook 2003: 12–15; *CCR, 1318–23*, 596. For occasional alienations prompted by religious enthusiasm see above, p. 28.

II
Parks and Society

Introduction to Part II

Parks evoked strong responses, and their creation and continued existence might be highly contested. As well as being a source of pleasure and pride for their owners, they could be a focus for envy and conflict at all levels of society. Perhaps surprisingly, current writing does not fully convey this: there has been no sustained exploration of the social effects of park-making. Most of the focus has been on royal forests and how kings were affected by or responded to parks, and even here—as we shall see—there has been a good deal of misunderstanding. By contrast, less has been written about the considerable impact parks had on the surrounding nobility, gentry, peasantry and townsmen. This impact can, in a sense, be divided into three strands. First, there was the effect on hunting practices and the knock-on implications for social relationships. Secondly, the proliferation of parks and the retention of access to hunting were concerns for the self-image of all those who aspired to aristocratic standing, and perhaps for others too. Because parks were markers of status, their creation could to some extent change the 'landscape of lordship'. The third potential cause of contention was more tangible: park enclosure represented a significant assertion of private control over agrarian resources, often disrupting others' use of the land, and even threatening landholdings or whole areas of settlement.

But it is important not to be overschematic: in practice these factors, leisure, status, and the control of the landscape, were related and intermingled, rather than discrete. As shall become clear, different groups among those affected by parks had different priorities, but only a few aspects of the footprint left by parks solely concerned one group or another. The right to hunt, for example, seems to have been claimed as a facet of free as well as aristocratic status; and landlords as well as peasants were concerned about grazing rights. It might be helpful to picture a spectrum of interests among neighbours that ranged from the desire to have a supply of deer to the need for land, pasturage, timber, and fuel. Jealousy among landowners and popular discontent could both be strongly felt and violently expressed; where they closely coalesced serious disorder might result.

The goal of this second part of the book is to uncover how parks and park-making affected people in medieval England. For the sake of clarity, the discussion will be divided into three sections, looking in turn at the king, the aristocracy, and the peasantry and townsmen. Older studies of parks have often given the impression, explicitly or implicitly, that the king was the main party concerned about park-making by others. This section—and indeed this book as a whole—takes a different, and wider, approach to understanding parks; part of the aim has been to escape the shadow of the concerns of the king and his ministers that bulk so large in our thinking thanks to the output of chancery and exchequer clerks. But kings did have an interest in and authority over parks and this has to be understood, not least to correct the over-emphasis on the crown restricting park creation. An appreciation of the true nature of the royal interest and intervention also provides an important context for the kind of effects parks could have on other members of society.

5

Parks and the Crown

Royal claims over deer and hunting gave kings a direct interest in parks.[1] Control over game animals and the privileging of their habitat was considered a special attribute of kingship from a very early date.[2] The kings of the Franks and other Germanic peoples designated lands around their residences as forests, where they controlled hunting. Over time, probably from the late Carolingian period, it seems that this idea of forest was divorced from a specific tract of land under royal ownership and became a right that kings could claim anywhere or grant to others.[3] Anglo-Saxon kings were in touch with Frankish practices and claimed some sort of control over hunting on royal estates, but it seems that it was the Norman kings who really took up the more abstract and powerful implications of the forest concept.[4] As contemporaries lamented, they hugely expanded the areas under forest law and tightened their jurisdiction over wild beasts, especially deer, and the well-wooded tracts in which they were concentrated.[5] After a setback under Stephen, Henry II continued his predecessors' work and by the end of his reign the royal forest covered almost a third of the country, according to one estimate, including many aristocratic as well as royal estates within its bounds.[6] Since parks were a means of containing deer and enclosed their habitat, there was clear potential for conflict between subjects' possession of parks and the expanded ideas of royal control.

But the establishment of forests was not the limit of the crown's activity in this sphere: kings made an attempt to regulate parks as (permitted) intrusions upon a royal right.[7] At the centre of this regulation lay the system of park

---

[1] An examination of the royal regulation of park-making must be closely limited if it is to be kept within manageable proportions. This chapter will touch on the royal forests, but no attempt will be made at a potted history of their establishment, administration, and regulation. The standard works on forests are Turner (ed.) 1901: pp. i–cxxxix; Petit-Dutaillis 1930; Neilson 1940; Young 1979; Grant 1991. See also Winters 1999.

[2] Some of the context for this is discussed above, p. 106.   [3] Wickham 1994: 159–61.

[4] The old idea of forests and hunting regulations as entirely Norman innovations in England (Petit-Dutaillis 1913: 61–2) requires some moderation (e.g. as implied by Mew 2001: 159–60; McDonnell 1992: 113). Hooke 1989: 122–9 provides a balanced view of pre-Conquest hunting management and controls.

[5] Whitelock (ed.) 1961: 165 (under the year 1087).   [6] Poole 1955: 29.

[7] For a flavour of the usual view on this see Shirley 1867: 20; Bilikowski 1983: 3; Lasdun 1991: 18.

licensing, which is fully documented from the beginning of the thirteenth century, but apparently existed in some form considerably earlier. Modern writers have overwhelmingly suggested that royal licensing represented a serious and largely successful effort to control and limit park-making, but their interpretations of the nature and scope of the system have differed considerably. Some authors have asserted that all parks required licences;[8] others claim that licences were only necessary for parks located in or close to royal forests.[9] Almost all agree, however, that licences were costly and difficult to obtain and that the existence of forest law precluded park-making in large areas.[10] Within this broad picture of royal control, there is a common view that things changed over time, although little agreement about exactly when, or how. It is often suggested that the crown was strictest early on, and eased up later. Twelfth-century chroniclers and other sources suggest wide or even universal royal claims over hunting and hunting reserves,[11] and this has been swallowed more or less whole by a number of historians writing about this period.[12] Meanwhile, widespread disafforestations in the thirteenth and early fourteenth centuries supposedly allowed more parks to be created.[13] On the other hand, a few scholars have suggested that the crown tightened up its regulation of parks in the early thirteenth century,[14] or even the early fourteenth.[15]

These findings give an impression of strong royal regulation of parks, but their inconsistency and lack of detail leaves us with a number of uncertainties. Quite apart from the vexed issue of chronology, there has been little explanation of how the supposed regulation was actually carried out. Almost nothing has been written about forest rules concerning parks and how rigorously they were enforced. Likewise there has been hardly any indication of the kind of process by which a park licence was obtained and whether acquiring such a licence was really as arduous, or perhaps even as necessary, as has been assumed. Such serious gaps in our knowledge make it difficult to be fully confident about the standard image of royal control over park creation. Given the doubts that we might have, what really seems to be required is a clearer sense of the scope and chronology of royal claims and activities over the whole period c.1066–1500, looking at the situation both within the forest bounds and beyond them. As we shall see, once a more comprehensive view of this kind has been formulated, the traditional image of royal stringency over park-making begins to look rather

---

[8] Williamson and Bellamy 1987: 70–1; Rackham 1986: 123; Harding and Lambert 1994: 5.
[9] Turner (ed.) 1901: p. cxvi; Cantor and Hatherly 1979: 73; Bond 1998: 25.
[10] Cantor and Hatherly 1977: 432; 1979: 79; Stamper 1996: 5–6.
[11] Mynors et al. (eds.) 1998–9: i. 564–5; Chibnall (ed.) 1969–80: vi. 100; Markland (ed.) 1979: 6–7. Cnut's forest laws—actually a 12th-cent. forgery—do not make it clear whether sanctions against killing the royal beasts (deer and boar) applied everywhere, or just within the royal forest: Liebermann (ed.) 1894: 52–5 (nos. 19, 21, 24, 26, and 34).
[12] Gilbert 1979: 11–12; Green 1986: 130.
[13] Stamper 1988: 140; Crook 2002: 73; Short 2000: 139; Stamper 1996: 5–6.
[14] Rackham 1980: 191; 1986: 123; Lasdun 1991: 18.   [15] Gulley 1960: 310.

ROYAL REGULATION

A useful starting point may be to reconstruct, as far as possible, the formal regulations about park-making and the procedures by which these were enforced. The clearest part of the picture is that relating to the royal forests: within forest areas the rules about park creation can be set out with some precision, even in the early part of the period. It seems that throughout the middle ages all parks created on land which fell within the bounds of the forest technically required royal approval. At least from the codification of the forest law under Henry II there was a system of regulations which could be applied against unauthorized forest enclosures. In the Norman period there was less bureaucracy, but we must suspect that similar rules existed and that some attempt was made to enforce them. The main regulatory mechanism was provided by the duty of foresters to report the creation of traps, barriers, or enclosures in their jurisdiction, and these might either be ordered to be removed or paid for by fine at the forest eyre.[16] Some forest documents refer specifically to parks in this context.[17] Those parks which were authorized required a special kind of licence because forest rules on enclosures stated that all barriers should be low enough to permit the access of a doe and her foal.[18] Precisely how such a licence could be obtained and what form it took we shall consider later on.

The rules, if any, in areas outside of the forest jurisdiction are much less certain: there is more indication that here the situation really did shift over time, but not quite as usually assumed. It is difficult to say much about the late eleventh and twelfth century because of the survival of so much less written material and the lack of information about contemporary forest bounds. Nonetheless, surviving evidence of fines and charters for parks from this period apparently relates to areas that would then have been within the forest, rather than outside it. The picture, as usual, is clearer from the thirteenth century. The set of writings

---

[16] Stubbs (ed.) 1913: 188, nos. 10 and, perhaps, 16, although there is no medieval source for the latter (Douglas and Greenaway (eds.) 1981: 453 and nn. provide too narrow a definition for 'purpresture' in no. 10, and an inaccurate translation and improbable accompanying gloss for no. 16); Warren 1973: 602 and n. 5. See also the chapters of the regard of 1229 printed in Shirley (ed.) 1862–6: i. 346–8 (regulations on 'purprestures' inside or outside woods and earthworks outside the covert), and the second of the articles of the regard for Pamber forest (Hants.), *temp*. Edward II in TNA: PRO, E32/162. The dating of the composite surviving forest regulations is dealt with by Petit-Dutaillis 1930: 167–77; Richardson and Sayles 1963: 444–9; Holt 1971: 97–100.

[17] The third article of the regard for Lancashire *temp*. Edward III actually includes the stipulation that the regarders should check whether parks or closes had been thrown down as ordered in the previous eyre: TNA: PRO, E32/57.

[18] On this regulation see: TNA: PRO, C143/2, no. 1; C143/20, no. 17; CCR, *1288–96*, 163. For the manner in which licences gave exemptions see Johnson and Cronne (eds.) 1956: 273; CChR, *1226–57*, 114.

attributed to Bracton claims that kings were an exception to the general rule that wild beasts are common to all before their capture, but there is no necessary implication that this applied beyond the royal forests or that it affected park-making in non-forest areas.[19] In fact, thirteenth-century disafforestation charters often suggest that once land was removed from forest law it could be freely imparked, at least as far as the king was concerned.[20] It is also notable that the articles of the general eyre, as opposed to the forest eyre, did not include a specific question on how parks were claimed.[21] So too that in this period kings gave deer to many lords to stock parks outside forests for which no licences are recorded.[22] In 1313–14, during the Kent eyre, Justice Spigurnel pronounced that 'any lord may have a park on his own land, if it is not prejudicial to the rights of other people'.[23] This implied that the king's legal rights, like those of others, might not be affected by a park, in other words that they were limited, rather than universal. In this respect it is notable that there were no royal forests in Kent, suggesting that where there was no forest the king had no direct interest. Certainly, as the maps illustrate (Figs. 18.1–18.4), the great majority of thirteenth-century park licences were for areas in or very close to royal forests; those few outside seem to have related to road closures and diversions (kings claimed special rights over roads as well as forests).[24]

However, from the late thirteenth century there appear to have been significant changes in the powers the crown claimed over parks outside its forests. Edward I initiated a campaign of investigating and testing private liberties of many kinds, including parks. The groundwork for this was laid by the hundred roll enquiry of 1274–5 and was followed up by the requirement that all franchise holders should make claims of franchises at the start of each eyre, and by the issuing of writs of *quo warranto* (literally, 'by what warrant'). Sometimes the jurors on the hundred roll enquiries referred to parks outside the forest bounds as though they might require a licence,[25] and a number of investigations into park franchises were carried out in 1278–81. But it seems to have been in a short period rather later when the questioning of lords' rights to parks was taken to a new level. In 1329–31 dozens of lords (or their attorneys) were brought to court over their rights to parks in areas that had been disafforested and even in areas that had

---

[19] Thorne (ed.) 1968–77: ii. 166–7.   [20] Hardy (ed.) 1837: 132; *CChR, 1226–57*, 75.
[21] *Capitula Itineris: SR* i. 233–8. There were related articles on warrens set up without royal warrant, apparently introduced in 1246, and, from the reign of Edward I, on the appropriation of free chases or warrens without warrant and the undue extension of chartered ones: Meekings (ed.) 1961: 32–3; *SR* i. 235–6. These could potentially be used to enquire into parks, which, as exclusive hunting grounds, were sometimes regarded as warrens, but this did not happen as a matter of course: Turner (ed.) 1901: p. cxvi and n. 2.
[22] A couple of examples among very many are Caversham (Oxon.) and Ilkeston (Derbs.): *Rot. Litt. Claus.* 545; *CCR, 1234–7*, 399. Ilkeston park was actually claimed by prescriptive right (rather than royal licence) in 1330: *PQW* 137.
[23] Maitland *et al.* (eds.) 1910–13: i. 188.   [24] See e.g. *CPR, 1247–58*, 100.
[25] To take a couple of Oxfordshire examples, the jurors stated that they did not know by what warrant lords held parks at Ducklington (in an area made forest by Henry II but disafforested in the early 13th cent.) and Watlington (in the Chilterns, which had never been royal forest): *Rot. Hund.* ii. 700, 815.

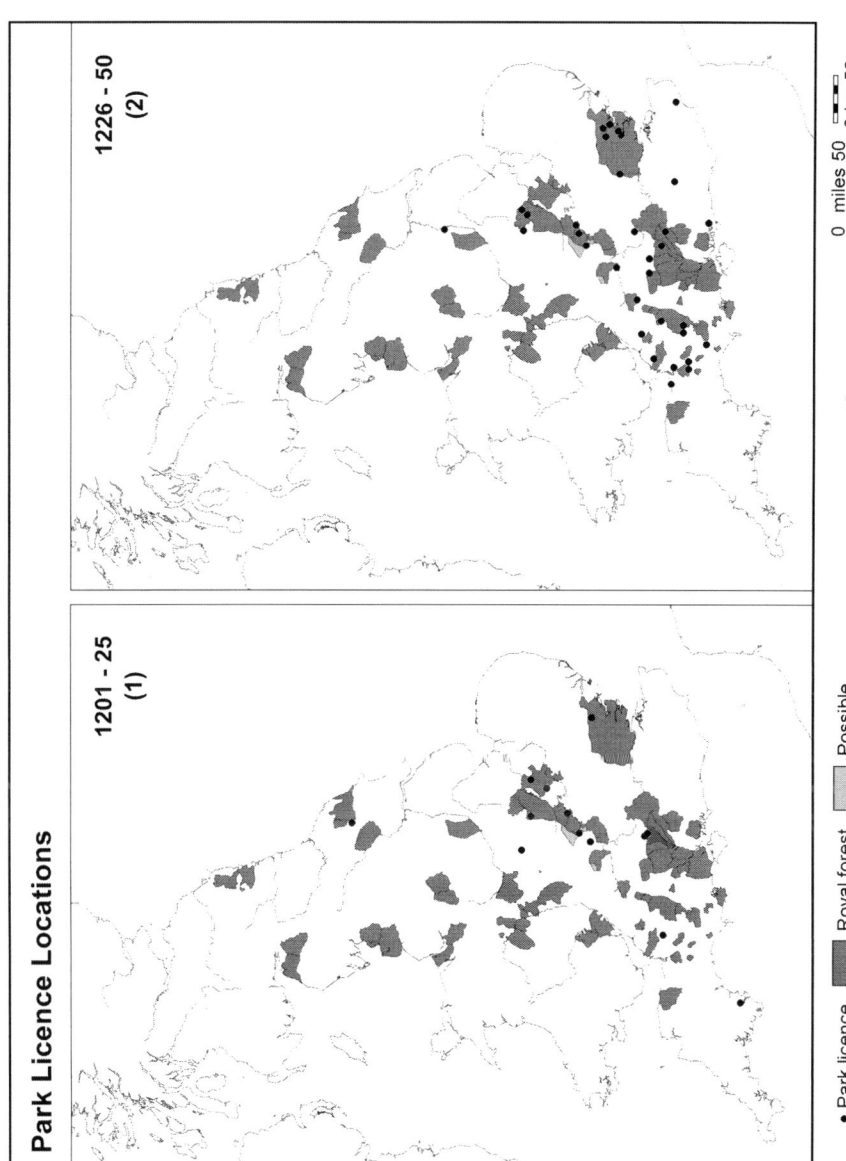

Fig. 18(1). Park licence locations and royal forests, 1201–25. The forests of east Derbyshire and south Lincolnshire, disafforested in the 1220s, are not included. (2) Park licence locations and royal forests, 1226–50.

Sources for maps: Forest bounds shown by Bazeley 1921 (map between 160–1) and Crook 1979: 42 (Notts.); licence locations plotted by author from place-names given in *CPR* and *CChR* and identified through EPNS volumes.

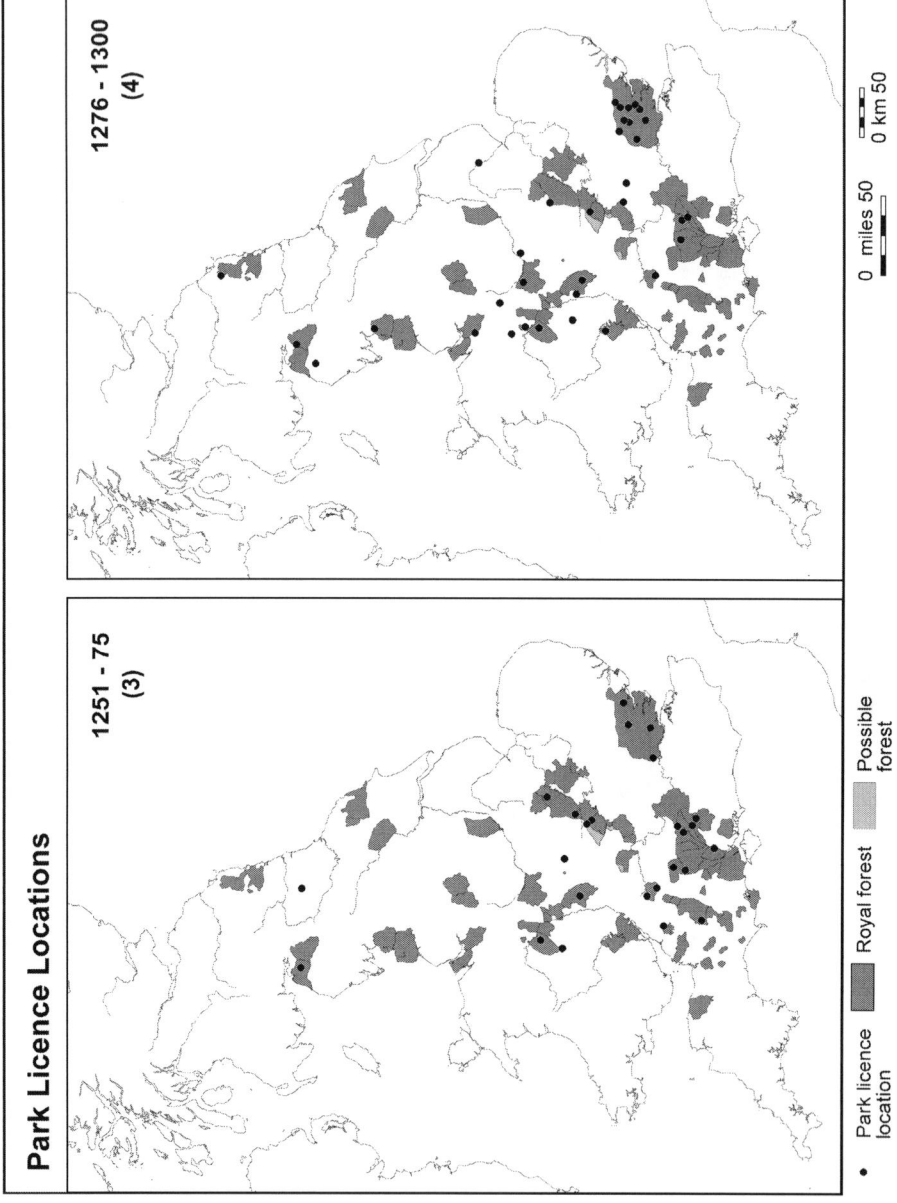

Fig. 18(3). Park licence locations and royal forests, 1251–75. (4) Park licence locations and royal forests, 1276–1300.

never been forest.[26] These enquiries doubtless played a part in prompting the single greatest spurt in medieval park licences in the 1330s and early 1340s (see Fig. 19).[27]

This questioning of rights to parks was probably associated with a final, serious, but ultimately failed, attempt to restore and even extend forest bounds, bounds that had effectively shrunk by around a third between the 1250s and 1320s.[28] No single ordinance seems to survive, but it is probable that Mortimer and Isabella and (after October 1330) Edward III, or their advisers, wanted assurance that the bounds of the forest were not being too much further eroded by the creation of parks or other reserves; this seems to have prompted some landowners to apply for licences for parks outside forests to demonstrate that they were indeed not encroaching on what was left.[29] Although some licences continued to be for areas within forests, quite commonly from the mid-1330s licences stated that they were granted as long as the area was *not* in the forest, borrowing from the standard phraseology of the much more common free warren licence. Some licences carrying this stipulation covered places near forests, others districts far away. In later periods the scale of licensing died down but a similar pattern continued: a few grants were for areas within the reduced bounds of the royal forests, the rest for areas a variable distance away (Figs. 20.1–20.8, below). The theme of stressing royal rights continued and was further clarified and strengthened: in 1501 Thomas Pygot asserted that unless a park was very old and could be claimed by (immemorial) prescription it required a royal licence.[30] Other Tudor and Stuart legal writings suggest that all new parks required licences.[31]

The actual means by which a licence was obtained can be reconstructed from thirteenth-century and later evidence. Potential licensees petitioned the king, either in person or through a friend or agent, and a few of the written petitions which were handed over to the king by these individuals still survive.[32] Early on, the decision about whether to grant a licence would have been quite a personal one, especially where tenants-in-chief were involved. In 1210 King John was outraged, or pretended to be outraged, with his chief forester Hugh de Neville for allowing Peter des Roches to enclose his park at Taunton (Som.) without the king's

---

[26] The chronology of the 90-odd known *quo warranto* cases involving parks (in *PQW*) is as follows: 1277–8, 1 case (Herts.); 1278–9, 11 cases (Surrey 9; Sussex 2) and 1278–81, 14 cases (Yorks.); 1291–2, 2 cases (Cumbl., Lancs.); 1292–3, 5 cases (Yorks. 3; Northumb. 2); 1312–13, 1 case (Kent); 1313–14, 1 case (Kent); 1329–30, 25 cases (Notts. 20; Northants. 5); 1330–1, 35 cases (Derbs. 32; Beds. 3).

[27] It is worth noting that licences to crenellate (or fortify) residences also reached their high point in the 1330s and 1340s (Emery 1996: 176, fig. 42). For other factors which may have contributed to this peak of park licensing see above, p. 112 (a fashion for park-making among particular groups), and below pp. 144, 156–7 (securing title in order to benefit from legal protection at a time of heavy poaching).

[28] Grant 1991: 165–9.

[29] The legal position was not clear-cut, however: one opinion recorded in relation to the 1329–30 Northamptonshire eyre stated that it was not necessary to claim a park at the eyre except where the park in question was within a forest: Sutherland (ed.) 1982–3: i. 114.

[30] Baker (ed.) 1997: 58.   [31] Turner (ed.) 1901: p. cxvi.

[32] e.g. TNA: PRO, SC8/175/8707 and C143/16, no. 26 (Henry Fitzaucher, 1291); C143/205, no. 7 (Waltham abbey, 1329); SC8/226/11289 (Robert de Bousser, 1336); Lyte 1926: 224 (William Carent, 1448).

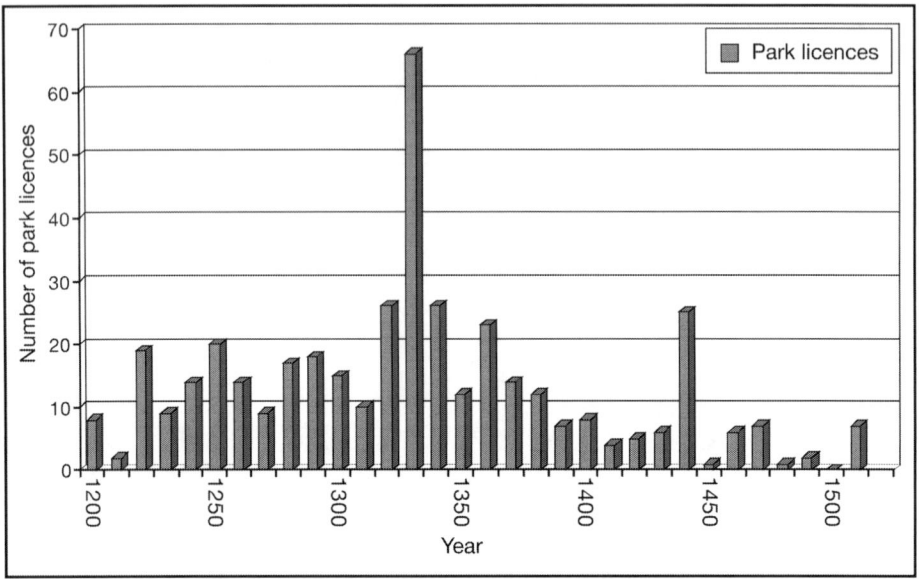

Fig. 19. The chronology of park licensing, 1200–1520. Over 400 licences were granted during this period.
Sources: CPR and CChR.

permission and threatened to fine him a staggering 1,000 marks.[33] Officially at least, kings continued to make the final decision about the granting of a licence—as with the granting of all other liberties—and it is notable that no perpetual park licences were granted during Henry III's minority.[34] However, by the end of the thirteenth century the processes involved had become more bureaucratic.

An ordinance of 1299 laid down a procedure for the handling of applications for park, mortmain, warren, and other licences. This presumably formalized or clarified existing processes, although no doubt some flexibility remained.[35] Those who wanted to make parks were to apply for a writ from chancery for the holding of an inquisition *ad quod damnum* into the proposed imparkment.[36] If the inquisition jury's findings were positive, the petitioner was to pay a fine to the exchequer, which notified the chancery; the chancellor or his deputy was then supposed to deliver the formal licence, in the form of a charter or letter patent, in return for a reasonable fee. The king, although not mentioned in the ordinance, would have had to sign off the issue of the writ for the inquisition, and the judgement that the return was favourable may possibly have involved him and the council, not just the exchequer. Nevertheless, the fact that perpetual park licences were granted during the early years of Richard II's reign and during Henry VI's

---

[33] Vincent 1992: 192–3.
[34] *CPR, 1216–25*, 135 and *CChR, 1226–57*, 114; *CPR, 1225–32*, 2.   [35] *SR* i. 131.
[36] The surviving examples of these inquisitions date from the mid-13th to the mid-15th cent., mainly from before 1350: TNA: PRO, C134.

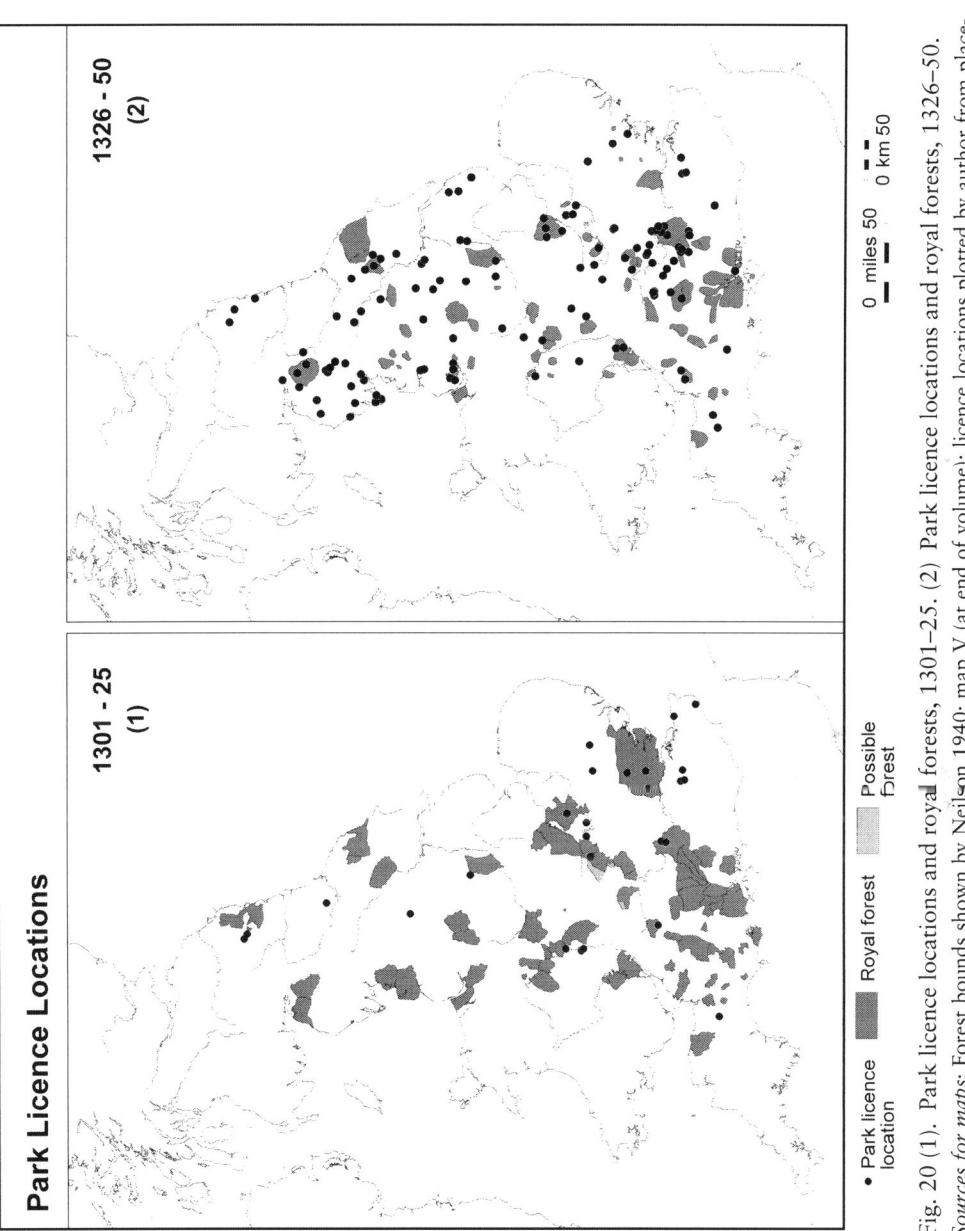

Fig. 20 (1). Park licence locations and royal forests, 1301–25. (2) Park licence locations and royal forests, 1326–50.

Sources for maps: Forest bounds shown by Neilson 1940: map V (at end of volume); licence locations plotted by author from place-names given in *CPR* and *CChR* and identified through EPNS volumes.

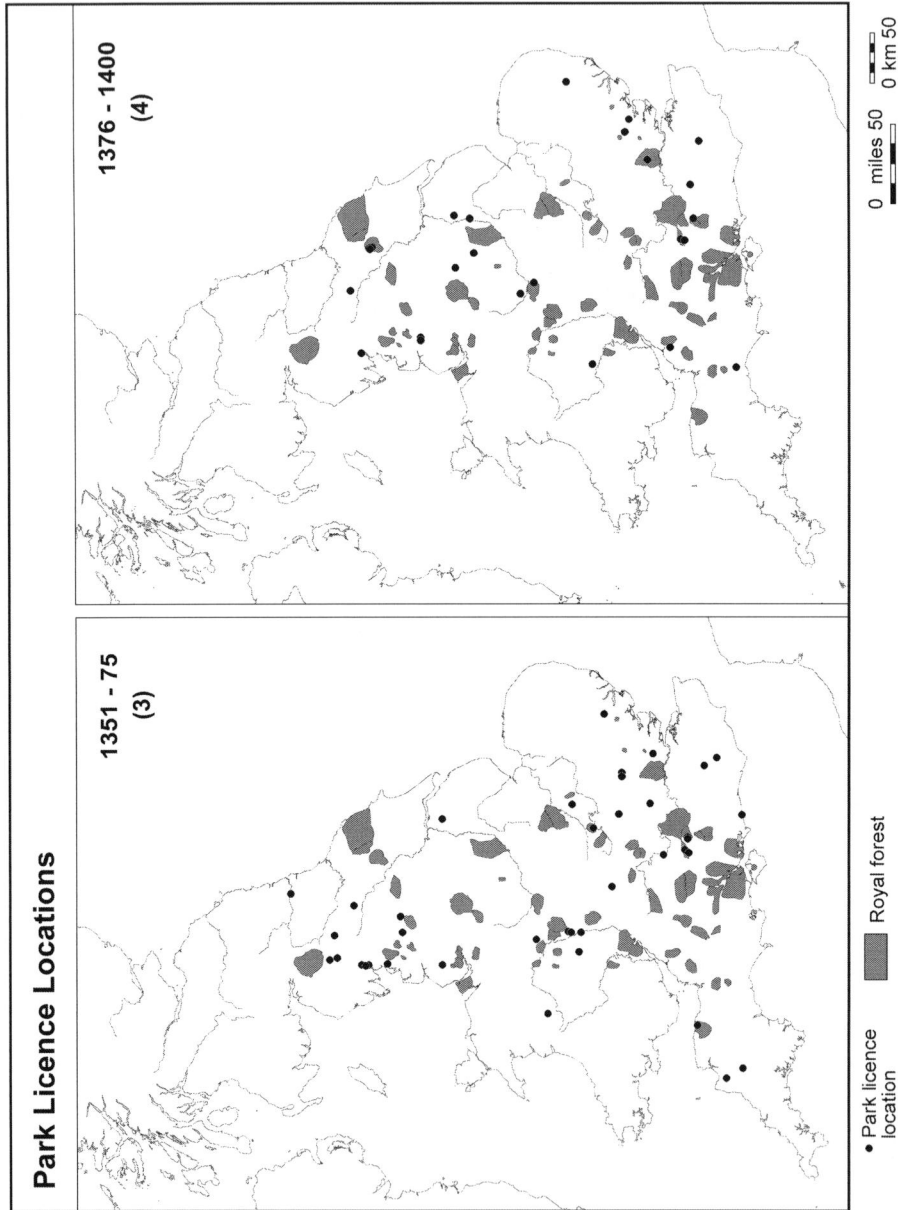

Fig. 20 (3). Park licence locations and royal forests, 1351–75. (4) Park licence locations and royal forests, 1376–1400.

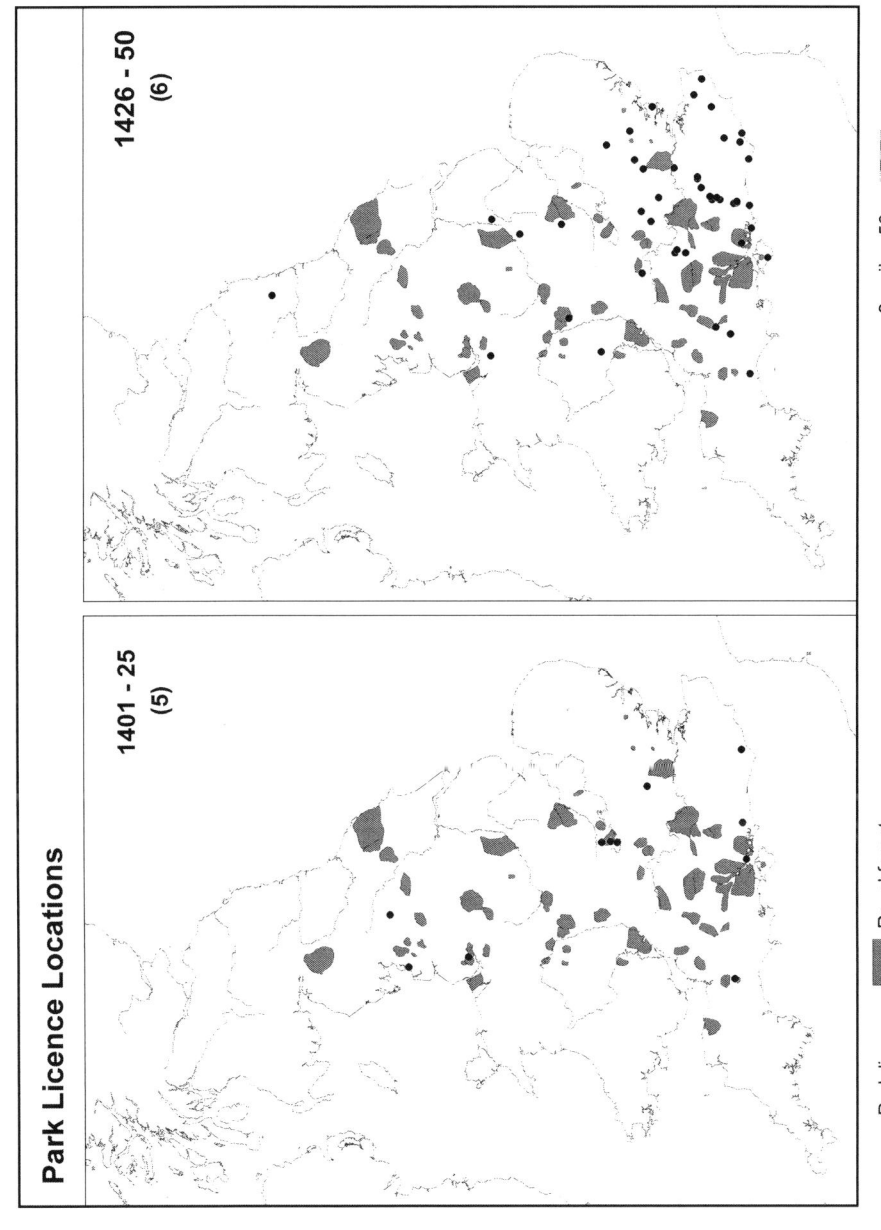

Fig. 20 (5). Park licence locations and royal forests, 1401–25. (6) Park licence locations and royal forests, 1426–50.

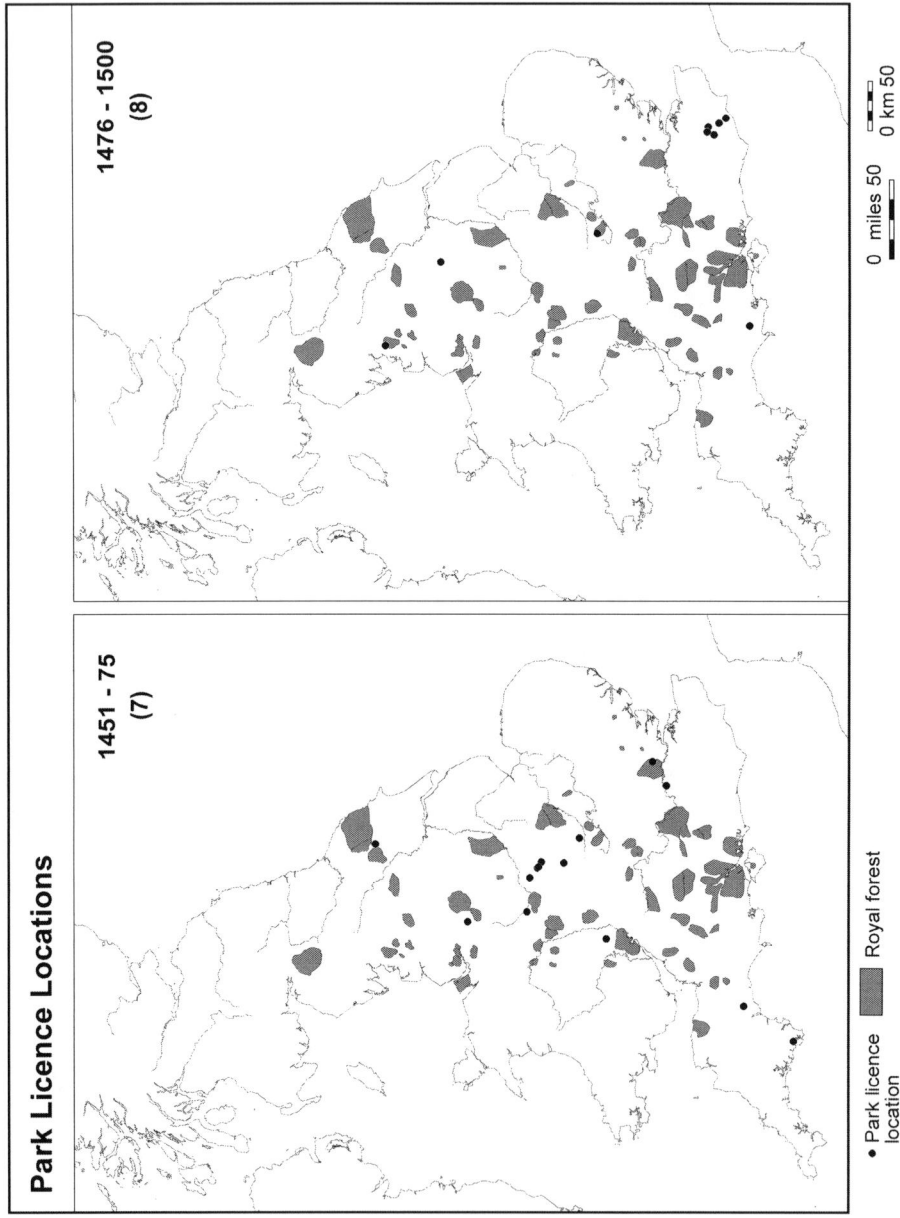

Fig. 20 (7). Park licence locations and royal forests, 1451–75. (8) Park licence locations and royal forests, 1476–1500.

minority reflects the declining importance of forest rights in the later middle ages, as well as (perhaps) greater conciliar authority.

The charges levied for licences varied considerably, especially before the mid-fourteenth century. A fairly typical fee was probably about £12–£15 in the thirteenth or fourteenth century. Chancery fees for the use of seals varied between a few shillings and £7, and the clerks would usually levy a further small fee for enrolment on the current charter or patent roll.[37] The exchequer charge was the main one. In the late twelfth and early thirteenth century payments to the exchequer for permissions to impark might typically amount to about £10. Such payments usually took the form of one or two palfreys (riding horses)—their money equivalent being about 5 marks each, or slightly more for a 'good palfrey'—topped up by a further fee of around £5.[38] Sometimes considerably larger sums were demanded. In 1204, for instance, the abbot of St Mary, York, owed 40 marks and a palfrey for the enclosure of his park at Overton.[39] In 1230 Ralph Hareng paid 50 marks for confirmation of his father's park licence.[40] Heavier fees naturally tended to be associated with the granting of multiple liberties: in 1204 Alan de Wilton paid 100 marks for a park licence for Thornton Riseborough and a whole raft of other privileges.[41] Fines might also be larger where previously unlicensed parks were given retrospective recognition: Matthew Columbers and Robert St John (in 1245) and Cirencester abbey (in 1315) were fined 100 marks (over £60) each for retrospective licences.[42] But fines for unauthorized parks might also be much smaller: sometimes as little as £2.[43]

ROYAL CLAIMS: A REASSESSMENT

The evidence presented above certainly illustrates the existence of formal rules about park-making—at least within the royal forests—as well as processes which could be used to test subjects' rights to parks. It also shows that, by obtaining a licence, lords could seek to exempt their reserves from potential interference or even destruction by foresters or other royal officials. Whether such a licence was issued seems to have depended ultimately upon the assent of the king. The same evidence might suggest an increasing pressure for the licensing of parks beyond the forest bounds. Heavy fines levied for some licences, meanwhile, could be interpreted as an attempt to discourage park creation.

But, in reality, to present a maximal view of royal control by focusing on the rules and the evidence that exists for their implementation would be highly misleading. The extent of royal interference was actually much more limited,

---

[37] For examples see TNA: PRO, E101/211/19 (accounts of the keeper of the hanaper of chancery, 10 and 11 Edward III).
[38] Stenton (ed.) 1932: 107 (1198–9); 1936: 240 (1201–2). [39] Stenton (ed.) 1940: 189.
[40] Roberts (ed.) 1835–6: ii. 194. [41] Stenton (ed.) 1936: 189.
[42] CChR, 1226–57, 282, 284; TNA: PRO, C143/11, no. 15 (dorse). [43] CPR, 1313–17, 362.

both in early periods and in later ones, and within forests and without. Notwithstanding the bursts of activity at particular times, the crown was generally permissive in its attitude to park creation, especially after the 1330s. This was partly because it lacked the means for any very effective policing, but more fundamentally because on the whole park-making did not seriously harm royal interests. In order to appreciate this properly, the more thoroughgoing royal claims and apparent peak periods of interference have to be looked at more closely and put into a larger context. Once this has been done we will have a much more realistic assessment of the purpose of crown regulations and the extent to which they were either meant to limit park creation or had the effect of doing so. It is easiest to uncover the picture in the better-documented period after 1200, but something can also be said about the period before by looking in a general way at early park-making and the conditions which allowed it to take place.

EARLY DAYS: THE LATE ELEVENTH AND TWELFTH CENTURIES

Written records from the period before 1200 are too scarce to allow a detailed investigation of royal interference with park-making, but it is nonetheless possible to show that factors other than the crown's attitude were central to the early progress of park numbers. As later, royal forest jurisdiction was not the most important consideration governing how many parks there were and who owned them.

To start at the beginning, there were few parks in pre-Norman England, but this had little or nothing to do with royal restrictions, since Anglo-Saxon kings did not claim anything like the same control over hunting as their Norman successors.[44] Twenty years after the Conquest, Domesday Book mentioned only a small number of parks (thirty-five),[45] mainly in the south and southeast of England. The fewness of parks in the later eleventh century was primarily explained by a lack of the most suitable kind of deer and also because there was still space in many areas of open countryside for hunting. Nevertheless,

---

[44] Liddiard 2003: 7 suggests that many Domesday 'hays' (or 'hedges') were simply Anglo-Saxon parks, but this does not seem likely. Those 'hays' which were used for hunting rather than for other purposes were associated with roe deer (Terrett 1962: 359; Saunders 1954: 140; Sykes 2007b: 70–1) and this solitary, territorial deer species has never very successfully adapted to being kept in captivity within parks (Whitehead 1950: 125, 172; Sykes 2007a: 60–1). In fact, rather than being full enclosures, the more permanent hays were probably linear or curving earthworks used to help retain game in certain wooded areas on major estates, or to trap animals during the final stages of the hunt; the less substantial were perhaps temporary fenced or netted traps (Hooke 1989: 122–9; Barlow 1983b: 129–32; Rackham 1986: 123; Hagen 1995: 135; Cummins 1988: 57–8; and cf. Harrop et al. (eds.) 2005: 19 and n.). A minority of the earliest parks may have been adapted from surviving hays but more often there was a disjuncture between these features in terms of both chronology and purpose. In some cases it is possible to show that earlier hays and later parks in a particular locality occupied quite different sites, as at Ducklington in Oxfordshire: Blair 1994: 131; VCH Oxon., xiii. 112–13.

[45] J. Palmer et al. (eds.), Domesday Explorer.

even at this time those lords with the inclination, and enough power and wealth, could create parks: the large majority of the parks mentioned in 1086 were held by great barons and leading churchmen, rather than the king,[46] and the Domesday inquiry almost certainly omitted some further non-royal parks.[47]

The first signs of a larger growth in park-making appear in the twelfth century: precisely the period when royal claims to control over hunting are thought to have been at their greatest and forest bounds at their most extensive. As we saw earlier in the book, it seems that this increase in parks was mainly explained by pressures on game and the importation of a new deer species, the fallow deer, which was particularly well-suited to surviving in an enclosed park environment.[48] Fallow deer bones can first be positively identified in England in the late eleventh century, but the number of these animals appears to have increased exponentially in the twelfth century.[49] The fifteenth-century antiquary John Rous was wrong when he said that Henry I's park at Woodstock was the first in England, but he was probably correct that it was among the first of a new and far greater wave of deer parks.[50] Whether or not the king's park-making was a direct inspiration for the earl of Warwick as Rous thought it was, Henry more probably started a fashion for *making* parks, rather than prohibiting them.[51] It certainly seems unlikely that, in a period when central government power and bureaucracy was so limited, royal policing of parks greatly prevented their growth, either under Henry I or Henry II, let alone in the intervening chaos of Stephen's reign.[52] The fact that there is surviving evidence of formal royal permission for only a small number of pre-thirteenth-century parks should not lead us to think that hardly any lords made parks in the twelfth century. On the contrary, twelfth-century references to parks and thirteenth-century and later evidence suggests the presence of a sizeable number of these reserves, including in areas under forest law.[53]

The increase in park numbers seems likely to have speeded up towards the end of the twelfth century (continuing at a high level into the thirteenth). This probably higher level of park-making can be explained in a variety of ways, and none of them relate directly to royal policy over forests or other hunting reserves. The shift to demesne farming from c.1180 tended to increase lords' interest in obtaining closer control of their lands and clearer delimitation of property bounds, creating a fertile environment for imparking.[54] At the same time, the move to direct farming gave many lords a higher money income, which they often spent on improvements to their estates. This was a great era for the

---

[46] Shirley 1867: 11–12.
[47] Liddiard 2003: 7 (where probable omissions are somewhat overstated).
[48] Above, Ch. 1, esp. pp. 27–9.   [49] Sykes 2007a: 59; Griffith *et al.* 1983: 341 (graph 1).
[50] Hearne (ed.) 1745: 138; *VCH Oxon.*, xii. 439.   [51] See above, pp. 113–14.
[52] Cf. Clanchy 1998: 81.   [53] Below, pp. 139–40.
[54] For the origins of demesne farming see Harvey 1974: 345: 353.

rebuilding of castles and manorial centres in more substantial style, with a greater emphasis on internal luxury and decoration, and, at the same time, seemingly more interest in outside facilities, like gardens, dovecotes, ponds, and parks.[55] The large rise in population in this period put more pressure on game animals and space for hunting, making enclosed game reserves more necessary.[56]

This short review of the early phases of park-making in England makes it very difficult to accept the usual picture of royal restriction of park-making before 1200. In the period after 1200 the limits of royal intervention can be set out in detail, rather than simply being inferred from the continued growth of park numbers, in forest areas and elsewhere.

THE THIRTEENTH TO FIFTEENTH CENTURIES

The main point to make about royal policy towards parks in the thirteenth century and later is that the seeming high points of royal interference revealed by a richer documentary record can be misconstrued all too readily. First of all it should be realized that the extraordinary investigations into parks which started in the late thirteenth century and the occasional earlier extortion of high fines for licences were fiscally rather than politically motivated. They were, in other words, small parts of a wider effort to obtain additional income, rather than representing an attempt to restrict park-making. The charging of higher fees for park licences and, later, the testing of park franchise were both most often associated with periods when the crown was dependent on casual income because taxation had either not been developed or was unavailable; parks were caught up along with a wide variety of minor judicial and other privileges which could be made to yield funds. In this sense, the royal attitude towards private parks reflected a general approach towards forest rights, which became prized mainly as a source of income.

This financial interest is first clearly illustrated in the early thirteenth century, when King John was particularly hard-pressed for money and deeply unscrupulous in how he obtained it: occasional high fines for park licences and other exactions based around royal forest rights were part of his *ad hoc* measures to secure extra money.[57] Later in the century, Edward I's enquiries into parks were part of a judicial campaign which was partly designed to assert royal control and correct abuses, but which was also in large measure about increasing royal

---

[55] Faith 1997: 193–4; Platt 1978: 45–7; Brown 1954: 31–2, 177–8; Jansen 2002: 105; Barker 1987: 54; McLean 1981: 93; Roberts 1986: 125–6.

[56] Above, p. 28.

[57] In 1209, for instance, he ordered the destruction of all houses and barriers in Essex forest, no doubt as a way of raising fines from the owners in the same way that he extracted them from the foresters themselves: Luard (ed.) 1866: 31.

revenue.[58] The latter consideration was doubtless at the forefront when it came to the questioning of minor non-jurisdictional perquisites such as parks. Similarly, although the subsequent *quo warranto* cases relating to parks in 1329–31 might have been in part designed to maintain the formalities of royal dignity in the aftermath of the first royal deposition (in this case by asserting strong control over hunting), the realization of additional sources of income must have been the main attraction. This was a time, after all, when the government was too weak to raise money by taxation, despite having military commitments.[59]

It is equally important to appreciate the limitations of these sorts of exactions and investigations. They were, by their very nature, short-term measures rather than continuous processes, and they affected only a small minority of park-makers. Charging heavy fines for park licences was unnecessary when the king had access to more regular forms of income and, as we have already seen, most licences were obtained for a fee which, if substantial, was far from exorbitant, especially when compared to the high cost of establishing a park.[60] Major judicial inquiries were rare events—since they were difficult to organize and unpopular—and they touched only a limited number of parks. The hundred roll inquiry of 1274–5 made very uneven reference to parks, turning up only a modest number of imparkments, with a significant bias towards more recent ones, partly since the inquiry itself was mainly concerned with losses after 1258.[61] The *quo warranto* cases involving parks numbered less than a hundred and they were mainly focused on areas in or near forests or in areas that had been disafforested, rather than in areas that had never been afforested at all. After the *quo warranto* flurry of the late 1320s and early 1330s died down, there is no further evidence of royal justices proactively inquiring into rights to parks outside forests (the great majority of which remained unlicensed).

When we turn to more ordinary processes and procedures, which, as we have seen, were more or less restricted to areas within the royal forests, the reality was that the crown simply did not have very effective mechanisms for keeping track of park-making. The main tool, the forest eyre, provided at best intermittent royal supervision over parks created in royal forests. So much is suggested by the retrospective licensing of certain parks created in forests without permission, one or two cases of which have already been referred to, but which actually occurred on a rather larger scale.[62] The majority of such cases date from the early to mid-thirteenth century and presumably reflect owners being caught out by royal justices at a time when forest eyres were at their most

---

[58] Sutherland 1963: 147–50; Carpenter 2003: 469.
[59] Buck 1983; Waugh 1991: 12–13, 184, 203–4; Ormrod 1990: 3–11. For instances of Edward III's strong assertion of royal rights, at least prior to the crisis of 1340–1, see Harriss 1975: 231–3.
[60] Above, p. 77.
[61] In Oxfordshire e.g. only the parks at Witney and Watlington were apparently questioned and local complaint about loss of common rights seems to have been the prompt in both cases: *Rot. Hund.* ii. 30, 33.
[62] *CChR, 1226–57*, 282, 284; *CPR, 1232–47*, 490 (bis), 502; *1247–58*, 18, 23, 95, 180; *1307–13*, 356, 385; *1313–17*, 362; *1330–4*, 118.

frequent.[63] But even here very often decades had passed since the parks had been created—a number of them were said to have been enclosed by the fathers of the licensees.[64]

Supervision often appears to have been lax as well as infrequent. Park-makers often ranked among the local forest officials since most of the more important landowners in and near royal forests held lands by forest serjeanty or had some other forest post, and being on the inside of the local forest administration must have helped circumvent the regulations.[65] For example, in Nottinghamshire the implementation of the rule against high fences in the forest seems to have been a new departure in 1278 thanks to an order by the head of the forests north of Trent.[66] Elsewhere, parks were sometimes created on the back of mere licences to enclose with low hedges.[67] The actions of powerful men, like royal justiciar Stephen de Segrave in the early 1230s, show just how little grip the king might have over what was going on in his forests.[68]

Forest law is therefore likely to have been less of a discouragement to park creation than has usually been assumed. Certainly foresters could sometimes be a nuisance to lords who had established parks within the royal forest, perhaps extracting bribes, entering parks, or trying to remove deer. In the earlier thirteenth century even important individuals occasionally faced difficulties, like William Montacute in John's reign,[69] and Joceline, bishop of Bath, in the late 1220s.[70] But the problems were seldom drastic. This is well illustrated by the consequences when a lord's rights to an unlicensed park were legally challenged. Justices in forest eyres or similar inquiries effectively accepted many long-established parks as existing by prescriptive right. These parks had supposedly always been appurtenant to manors from 'time out of mind', rather than being the subject of any specific, surviving royal grant. Such prescriptive claims were put on a sounder footing in 1290, when continuous exercise of a franchise ever since 1189 was accepted as title to that franchise, but even before 1290 actions might be dropped or deferred when such prescriptive claims were made, as seems to have happened at Colwick (Notts.).[71] Where claims based on long tenure failed to convince a jury, or could not plausibly be made at all, justices might pursue legal actions and sometimes take seisin of the park on behalf of the king, but formal possession would then be returned after a gracious royal

---

[63] *CChR, 1226–57*, 282; *PQW* 161; TNA: PRO, C66/175, m. 4.

[64] Detailed local research suggests that some other licences may also have been retrospective, even though this was not specified in the text: Dunning 1981: 126; Coss (ed.) 1986: 2; Winchester 1987: 105–6.

[65] For the general laxity of forest administration see e.g. *VCH Gloucs.*, v. 361–2 (Dean). Local worthies might well not be required to attend the common summons of the forest eyre: *CCR, 1288–96*, 274 (Essex, 1292).

[66] Crook 2002: 73.   [67] *VCH Wilts.*, iv. 411 (Despenser, 1305).

[68] *CCR, 1231–4*, 385; *CRR* xv. 237; Turner 1988: 131.

[69] *CChR, 1226–57*, 357; Rowley 1986: 132–3.   [70] *CCR, 1227–31*, 58.

[71] Crook 2002: 73. This park appears to have been given some kind of limited lifetime recognition in 1250 (*CPR, 1247–58*, 62), but in 1278 and 1287 it was claimed by prescriptive right and custom. For the acceptance of prescription as title more generally see Brand 1992: 427–34.

concession and payment of a fine.[72] No outraged king tore down the park palings in any of these cases and, in fact, the rare instances of parks actually being destroyed on royal orders mostly seem to relate to their owners being in open rebellion against the king, who helped them restock the parks once they returned to fealty.[73] In any case, for any potential problems in setting up a park in or near a forest there were also benefits, above all the prospect of securing an illicit supply of deer through deer-leaps.

The degree to which lords were willing and able to create parks in areas under forest law is best demonstrated by examining the evidence from a couple of counties in a little more detail, since it shows that sizeable numbers of parks were created in afforested areas before the mid-thirteenth century. Often enough this park-making may have occurred without royal licence. In Nottinghamshire, for example, there were certainly at least five parks in existence in the very large forest area north of the Trent well before extensive disafforestations in 1225–7, and for only two of these (both at Laxton) do we know of anything like specific royal permission.[74] Other parks in this area which happen to be first mentioned after the mid-1220s perhaps also existed before the disafforestations; their later appearance in the written record may simply reflect the increasing number of documents being produced, rather than to their recent creation. Later on, at the beginning of Edward III's reign, many further Nottinghamshire parks in remaining forest areas were claimed by prescription rather than royal licence. It seems implausible that all of these parks had actually been licensed but the licensees had failed to claim them as such.

Berkshire provides another good case study.[75] In Windsor forest, besides the royal parks, there were other parks by the thirteenth century at Remenham, Sonning, Whitley, Ashridge, Billingbear, Swallowfield, and possibly at Sheep Bridge. Further west, a park was created at Hungerford in the small part of Savernake forest that intruded into the county. Whitley, Hungerford, and Remenham were subject to royal licences, for the abbot of Reading in the 1160s, Simon de Montfort in 1246, and Peter de Montfort in 1248. Ashridge was licensed as an assart but was known as a park. No formal permission is known for Sonning (twelfth century, bishop of Salisbury), Billingbear (twelfth or early thirteenth century, bishop of Winchester), Swallowfield (pre-1316, John St John), or Sheep Bridge (which was enlarged by royal licence in 1368, when it belonged to the king's clerk Adam de Hertingdon). Besides Whitley and Sonning, several other parks in the western part of Windsor are first referred to in surviving

---

[72] Richard de Willoughby's park at Wollaton (Notts.) is a classic example: *PQW* 627–8.
[73] When Richard Marshall, Gilbert Basset, and their followers rebelled in 1233 Henry III ordered the destruction of their residences and parks at Hampstead Marshall (Berks.), Inkberrow (Worcs.), Wootton Bassett (Wilts.), and elsewhere: *CCR, 1231–4*, 542–3. When they returned to his fealty the king graciously permitted the re-enclosure of the parks (ibid. 441), even granting Marshall live deer to replenish his supply (ibid. 518).
[74] Crook 2002: 73.   [75] Hatherly and Cantor 1979–80: 72–9 (gazetteer and map).

documents post-dating the disafforestation there in 1227; like those parks in a similar situation already referred to in Nottinghamshire, they may or may not have been created after forest law was removed.[76]

In these and other forests the level of private park-making and location of subjects' parks probably depended as much upon patterns of landownership as rigorous enforcement of forest law. Royal demesne manors were at the heart of most forests and the crown's property rights preserved these from park-making by other lords.[77] It was here that crown parks were created and deer concentrated, often by the early to mid-twelfth century, if not before,[78] and these parks were far more efficient producers of venison for the royal household than areas of open forest.[79] If other landowners wanted to enclose certain of their own woods in the outlying parts of forests, this was of limited concern to the crown,[80] especially if this occurred away from the wooded core, or 'great covert', which formed the essential part of most lowland forests.[81] Kings who liked to hunt needed only so many places to do so and would hardly be refused access to private parks. Whether parks were actually created in the outlying parts of forests before they were disafforested largely depended, like park creation as a whole, on the presence of landowners with sufficient resources and inclination to create them.

This discussion has so far dealt mainly with the thirteenth and early fourteenth centuries, but all of the observations which have been made apply with equal or greater force to the later middle ages. This, after all, was a period when supervision

---

[76] Stratfield Mortimer (× 2), Shinfield, Wokefield (in Stratfield Mortimer), and Earley.

[77] Rackham 1986: 136; *VCH Wilts.*, iv. 391; Schumer 1999: 57; Bond 1994: 134.

[78] See e.g. Rowley 1986: 116 on Gillingham park (Dorset) as the nucleus of the wider forest of the same name.

[79] Above, p. 79.

[80] Surviving inquisitions into park-making rarely found that parks would be to the king's harm, and these almost all suggested only trifling losses of grazing for deer or fines for vert and venison trespasses: TNA: PRO, C143/1, no. 39; C143/16, no. 26. Even when inquisitions found that some harm would result from park-making, applications might still be accepted and licences granted: C143/1, no. 39 (Simon de Montfort, 1256, Shipley, Northumb.), licensed in 1257, without a deer-leap (*CChR, 1226–57*, 460); C143/5, no. 12 (Richard de Brus, 1280, Horsfrith in Writtle, Essex), licensed in 1280 (*CPR, 1272–81*, 378); C143/14, no. 8 (John Filliol, Wickhay, Essex, 1290), licensed in 1291 (*CPR, 1281–90*, 445). The draining of deer from the forest into parks through deer-leaps or faulty enclosure was a recurrent concern (TNA: PRO, E32/281), and could clearly anger a king if he chanced to see it, as apparently happened at Worksop (Notts.) in 1355 when Edward III himself supposedly saw a deer jump into the park (*CCR, 1354–60*, 121; this park was extremely conspicuous since very close to the highway between Worksop and Warsop). But foresters and forest justices were given the task of trying to ensure parks were properly sealed and had no unauthorized deer-leaps, at least nominally taking parks into royal hands and extracting fines until gaps were stopped (Grant 1991: 28; TNA: PRO, E32/13, rot. 25 (Essex forest eyre, 1292)). Sometimes the creation of parks in or near forests seems actually to have been regarded as beneficial, since they might stop the passage of deer to areas outside, where they would be lost to hunters, or remove hideouts for poachers (TNA: PRO, C143/57, no. 22).

[81] Many inquisitions reflect this, stating in favour of the proposed park that it was several leagues from the forest covert: TNA: PRO, C143/4, no. 28; C143/5, nos. 12–13; C143/23, no. 19; C143/29, no. 14; C143/32, no. 7; C143/35, no. 21; C143/58, no. 9; C143/77, no. 6; C143/142, no. 1. Note also the willingness to license woodland clearance in forest areas away from royal hunting lodges: Dyer 1994: 20.

of forests was further reduced, along with the forest bounds themselves. Central checks by justices on forest eyres became less and less regular after the late thirteenth century,[82] with special inquisitions nothing like a full replacement. Individual forests, many of which were farmed out to favoured lords, might go fifty or a hundred years without seeing a forest justice. The forest administration declined as its importance as a revenue source atrophied with the advance of regularized taxation. The spurt in park licensing in the 1440s was mainly caused by members of the royal household obtaining licences for parks created in the south-east, near London, and the several chases in Kent and Sussex which had by then come into royal hands; it was certainly not prompted by rigorous forest checks, since the forest administration at this time was in chaos.[83] After long decay, there was some revival of forest regulations under Edward IV and especially Henry VII,[84] but this just served to demonstrate how bad things had become.[85]

Not surprisingly, the creation of a certain number of unlicensed forest parks seems to have been just as much a feature of this period as the earlier one, although only very rarely do we glimpse what must have been going on in many forests. In Edward IV's reign investigations into duchy of Lancaster administration in the late 1470s picked up local complaints alleging that Thomas Molyneux was trying to impark a massive 4,000 acres in Fulwood forest (Lancs.).[86] Slightly later, some men close to a monarch as scrupulous about his rights as Henry VII seem to have been untroubled by making parks without licences (or at least did not bother to have their licences enrolled), including the Gowers in Yorkshire and Henry de Willoughby and Robert Throgmorton in Warwickshire.[87] Robert Throgmorton's apparently unlicensed park at Wyke (Warks.) was in Feckenham forest and, at a rare forest inquiry, his unauthorized construction of a deer-leap was found to have entrapped the queen's deer.[88]

THE PROCESS OF PARK LICENSING

Finally, it is worth saying something about park licensing, since the mechanics of the licensing process itself are highly revealing about royal attitudes

---

[82] Winters 1999: 21–4.

[83] Humphrey of Gloucester complained early in 1445 that he could no longer run the forests as he had been charged to do because of Henry's multiplicity of warrants and grants, made under different seals, which were doing 'grete hurt' in the royal forests and parks, damaging 'bokis, underwodde, vert and game' (TNA: PRO, E28/75, no. 13; *CPR, 1441–6*, 335). Part of Humphrey's concern was about his loss of influence over royal patronage at this time, but real problems can be well imagined in the context of Henry's lavish distribution of royal resources.

[84] For enquiries into unlicensed forest parks *temp*. Henry VII see *Calendar of Inquisitions Post Mortem, 2nd series, vol. III, 20–24 Hen. VII*, appendix III, 597 (Cumbl.), 598 (Notts., Derbs.); and cf. other entries on 598–9, 601.

[85] Above, p. 29; below, pp. 142–3.   [86] Myers 1985: 321, 336.

[87] Pollard 1990: 354–5; Carpenter 1992: 86 and n. 174 and 88 and n. 178.

[88] Carpenter 1992: 179–80.

throughout the middle ages. The first point here is that in all periods the initiative for park licensing, like other kinds of franchisal licensing, almost invariably came from the individual petitioner: the licence was sought, rather than demanded.[89] Just as importantly, for those who chose to follow proper procedure, obtaining a royal licence was not usually a difficult task. King John, after all, had no problem with Peter des Roches creating a park, but rather with Hugh de Neville overstepping his authority by authorizing it without the king's knowledge: the fine against Neville was not levied and John actually helped the bishop stock his park with deer.[90] By 1300, with the firm establishment of more bureaucratic processes, it seems likely that the king was often happy merely to rubber-stamp park licences as they passed before him, by which time they had usually already fulfilled any procedural requirements.[91] It is difficult to judge what proportion of park licence applications were successful, but certainly the large majority of the ninety-two surviving inquisitions *ad quod damnum* into imparkment were followed by the granting of royal licences. We cannot assume that all of the small number of these inquisitions which were not followed by licences necessarily failed; they may simply have been dropped by the applicants, for various reasons. Nor does there seem any reason to suppose that the surviving inquisitions are unrepresentative, for instance because inquisitions were less often preserved where licences were not granted. It seems more logical that, where royal administrators preserved inquisition findings for future reference, they would have filed them all away indifferently. Legal and other records provide no suggestion of large numbers of rejected applications.

That there were far fewer licences obtained in the later fourteenth and fifteenth century than earlier is certainly no evidence that this was because they were harder to obtain. In fact, there is some indication that inquisitions *ad quod damnum* were increasingly dispensed with. The survival of only small numbers of these inquisitions after the mid-fourteenth century might be ascribed to loss or destruction at some unknown stage, but there are actually more positive indications that procedure was slipping in the later middle ages. One licence of 1442 was apparently granted *before* inquisition, on the condition that the findings turned out to be positive.[92] Whether the inquisition was ever held is uncertain (no record survives), but another case strongly suggests that licences were by this time being granted without any proper investigation: in 1474 Sir William Plumpton was licensed to impark all his lands in Plumpton in Knaresborough forest (Yorks.), but in the following year the chancellor of the duchy of Lancaster was trying to prohibit him from imparking and enclosing within the manor because he was thereby interfering with the free run of the deer and the grazing of the tenants.[93] (There is no indication that his activities

---

[89] Coulson 1982: 70. [90] Above, p. 128 and n. 33.
[91] There is an obvious comparison here with crenellation licensing: Coulson 1994: 109–10.
[92] *CChR, 1427–1516*, 30. [93] *VCH Yorks.*, i. 509.

were significantly hindered: Leland reported a park near the house there in the early sixteenth century.[94])

The apparently rather routine nature of park licensing underlines the danger of assuming, as many have done, that park licences, or indeed other grace and favour licences, were granted as a form of patronage.[95] The king's generosity may largely have been limited to releasing favoured individuals from paying fees for licences, or reducing them, but then chancery fees at least were very commonly waived anyway.[96] The fact that royal ministers, householders, and regulars at court made up a large portion of all park licensees was probably because they were more in touch with proper process. After all, where they felt they needed them, some men of purely local significance obtained licences too,[97] and religious houses, with their careful record keeping, were often scrupulous about acquiring them.

It is also worth noticing that, although those who acquired licences were mainly concerned to avoid the risk of royal officials interfering with or fining unauthorized parks, some were probably also partly motivated by other secondary issues which did not relate to any royal interference. It may be, for instance, that licences were sometimes sought where rights over woods and wastes were still disputed, or to forestall local opposition,[98] even though the crown was keen to stress that its park licences were granted 'pertaining to the forest' or 'as far as the king can', 'as far as pertains to us'. For example, the prior of Coventry's 1332 licence was perhaps part of an attempt (albeit a failed one) to ward off Queen Isabella and her ministers' attack on his park as part of the struggle over the lordship of Coventry.[99] In the fifteenth century Sir Thomas Brook and Ralph Wolseley both seem to have tried to use royal licences as weapons in silencing the opposition of neighbours to new parks which blocked off roads and restricted access.[100] A certain amount of licensing was probably prompted by the desire to formalize agreements over land,[101] or to help secure title to parks in order to be able to benefit from special kinds of statutory protection against poachers, especially in periods of disorder.[102]

The foregoing sections have made it clear that the royal response to parks cannot be properly understood if reference is confined to forest law or tests of franchise.

---

[94] Toulmin Smith (ed.) 1964: i. 87.   [95] On parks in particular see Neave 1991: 5.
[96] For exemptions from chancery fees for the great or little seal for some park licences in the 1330s see: TNA: PRO, E101/211/15 (Molyns, Trussell, and Ros, 1331); E101/211/18 (Philip de la Beche, 1335); E101/211/18 (Richard Cogan, John de Molyns, William Scot, Robert de Bousser, Alice de Lisle, Sir Thomas Breadstone, 1336). By contrast, Henry Percy paid £7 11s. 8d. in 1332 (E101/211/16). See also CCR, 1346–9, 222.
[97] e.g. CChR, 1226–57, 98; 1341–1417, 72; 1427–1516, 98, 188; CPR, 1232–47, 490; 1266–72, 76; 1307–13, 356; 1354–8, 577; 1408–13, 425.
[98] Perhaps helping to explain Ralph de Dacre's 1338 licence (TNA: PRO, C66/193, m. 19). See below, pp. 153, 168–9, 171.
[99] Coss (ed.) 1986: 2.   [100] See below, pp. 154, 176.
[101] CPR, 1317–21, 431–2; 1348–50, 18; 1354–8, 40, 92–3; 1429–36, 250, 369.
[102] Below, pp. 144–5.

In fact, royal intervention was generally very restricted; the initiative for park licensing normally came from park owners; and obtaining royal permission to create a park was seldom difficult, where it was requested at all. It was never natural for kings to want to stop or strictly limit park creation. Besides the consideration that parks usually interfered little with royal interests, the greatest individual park-makers, apart from the king himself, were the magnates and bishops. These men were the monarch's relatives and natural companions and advisers. Knights and gentry soon wanted to have parks too and, although this may have somewhat challenged greater lords in the localities, it was no threat to the king's hunting, let alone his standing, since he had the most forests and the biggest and best-stocked parks. Besides, the gentry performed vital administrative duties in the localities. A secondary factor making private parks more appealing to kings was the resources and profits that they themselves could obtain from them. Other lords' parks and woods could be a source of materials, deer, and some minor financial profits when they escheated to the crown.[103] If woods were carefully protected inside parks their value was likely to be all the greater. What is more, we have already seen that fees could be charged for royal recognition of parks, and the crown also obtained the financial penalties imposed on those poaching or otherwise transgressing in private reserves, via a £10 forfeiture clause included in warren licences.

The crown, in fact, took a number of measures to help lords and gentry protect their parks and hunting privileges. Although in 1236 the crown resisted a baronial wish for self-policing and private prisons, in 1246 and 1275 parliament passed laws against trespassing in parks.[104] The punishments set out for trespasses in these reserves were far more severe than those for equivalent offences in forests, and in 1276 measures were put in place to help enforce this legislation. In 1293 there was specific protection from legal action for parkers, foresters, and warreners who killed malefactors who failed to surrender.[105] Even the twelfth-century pipe rolls have quite a few references to individuals fined for trespassing in lordly parks and by the second half of the thirteenth century large numbers of judicial commissions were seconded to investigate supposed breaches of royal and private parks. It seems to have been important to the king that the hunting privileges of the aristocracy were upheld, if only to prevent the public order problems that arose from unauthorized hunting.

After the Black Death concerns about disorder were magnified by changed demographic and economic circumstances: there was a new worry about

---

[103] Holt 1965: 303, 307; Treharne and Sanders (eds.) 1973: 271; Altschul 1965: 218; Waugh 1988: 233–4.
[104] Powicke 1953: 69; Turner (ed.) 1901: pp. cxviii–cxxii; Luard 1872–83: iii. 343 (on 1236), iv. 518, vi. 117 (1246); Westminster I, c. 20: *SR* i. 32.
[105] 21 Edw 1, Stat 1: *SR* i. 111–12.

unauthorized hunting as a form of lower-class unrest. Again, the crown was willing to respond in full measure. In 1390 the Commons petitioned the king about the damage done to lords' parks and warrens by 'butchers, shoemakers and tailors', who hatched 'plots and conspiracies of rebellion' under colour of hunting.[106] The result was legislation prohibiting the keeping of dogs for hunting or the use of ferrets, nets, or snares by laymen with lands worth less than £2 a year and clerks with benefices worth less than £10.[107] Fear of sedition associated with poaching continued, however, and in Henry VII's reign was reflected in further legislation. In 1485 there was a reissue of the statute of 1390, with a new clause prohibiting nocturnal and disguised hunting in forests, parks, and warrens. In 1503–4 further laws targeted unauthorized stalking and restricted possession of deer traps ('buck-stalls') and great nets (or 'hays') to the owners of parks and other reserves.[108]

On the whole, the royal attitude to parks should probably be seen as one of benign indifference, rather than hostility or a desire to limit park numbers. Kings might from time to time expect a certain due deference over their forest rights and want to milk some revenue from park-makers, but they made only sporadic and fairly toothless attempts to enforce their control over imparking. An occasional desire to bring in fines has to be put alongside the positive measures to protect parks as rightful perks of great subjects. There was a relatively laissez-faire attitude and a willingness to allow individuals to settle their concerns by agreement or litigation in the royal courts. This, in turn, had important implications for the way parks were established and the effects they had in local society, as the final two chapters show.

[106] *Rot. Parl.* iii. 273.
[107] 13 Ric 2, Stat.1 c. 13: *SR* ii. 65.
[108] 1 Hen 7, c. 7: *SR* ii. 505–6 and 19 Hen 7, c. 11: *SR* ii. 655; McIntosh 1986: 255–6; Pollard 2004: 90; below, Ch. 7. Actual disorder was particularly bad in Kent, Surrey, and Sussex, where gentry leadership was weak in the 15th cent.

6

Parks and the Aristocracy

[In April 1497 kinsmen and servants of Sir William Gascoigne] riotoselie assembled ... uppon Marston More ... to thentent to poule doon the pale of the parke of ... Milez [Wilstrop] at Willesthorp' ... [On the night of 9 January 1498] cccc persons and above ... pulled down [380] rode of pale of the said parke.[1]

Despite the well-recorded claims of the crown, the creation of parks by other lords probably raised considerably greater concerns for the nobility and gentry than they did for the king. For them much was potentially at stake. The most obvious issue was how parks affected access to hunting, and this question, in turn, had implications relating to perceptions of social standing. As a widely shared passion, hunting might unite the aristocracy, strengthening relationships as lords hunted and hawked together, allowed their fellows across their lands, or even gave them access to the game upon it.[2] But, as we have seen, hunting was more than a hobby: it could be a potent expression of power, of spare time, money, and the ability to go where one pleased.[3] Overtly the hunter revelled in the chase and slaughter of wild beasts; the undertones were of human war and male rivalry.[4] With so much vested in the hunt, with a limited space for hunting and, for many, a restricted supply of game, it seems hardly surprising that the creation of parks and other hunting reserves could cause a considerable strain within landed society. Added to this were more prosaic but nonetheless real concerns about the effects on farming and access to resources.

There is no doubt that the numerous parks in existence by the thirteenth century presented benefits to members of the aristocracy. These reserves brought not only potential hunting opportunities, but also provided a source of fees and perquisites. Some aristocrats gained very directly from the existence of royal or magnate parks in particular, by being appointed to sinecure positions as salaried parkers or stewards, or by acquiring a farm of the agricultural profits from parks, usually as part of the manors to which these

---

[1] An extract from Miles Wilstrop's bill of complaint in Star Chamber: Brown (ed.) 1909: 16–17.
[2] Orme 1992: 133. Lords sometimes asked their neighbours to watch over their game stocks in their absence: Kingsford (ed.) 1919: ii. 150.
[3] See Ch. 4 above.   [4] Hanawalt 1988; Birrell 1982: 15; Manning 1993: ch. 2.

enclosures were attached.[5] Such individuals—who included lords as well as gentry—were given special access to the reserve, receiving some opportunity to hunt and to have part of the venison which they or their servants took on the owner's orders. They might also be able to put some of their own domestic animals in the park, or take a certain amount of wood without charge.[6] The more senior of these men were usually absentees, but others lived locally, perhaps even in the park itself. Whichever was the case, they might exercise considerable control over these reserves, particularly in periods of royal or lordly weakness.[7]

By the fourteenth century, the hierarchy of royal forest and park officials seems to have been proliferating.[8] Having so many forests and parks, kings in particular became somewhat blasé about granting out offices and heedless of the loss of control over the less valuable ones.[9] This was encouraged by the regularization of taxation, which made forests unimportant sources of revenue, and by the shrinking of kings' itineraries into the south-east of England, which reduced the likelihood of visits to more far-flung parks.[10] Where the royal presence became less regular, local lords and gentry officeholders and their subordinates might take over effective ownership, milking the profits and perpetuating park and forest jobs simply to maintain and extend their own privileges. This occurred even at important properties by the fifteenth century, including Clarendon (Wilts.), Ridlington (Rutland), and certain duchy of Lancaster estates.[11] Only near the end of the period did overexploitation and waste bring large-scale rationalization, as when Henry VII disbanded all the official posts in Inglewood forest (Cumberland).[12]

Besides the minority with formal posts, a wider circle of aristocrats probably gained occasional access to royal and other parks as a favour.[13] John of Gaunt's letters suggest that he was happy to allow local worthies to enjoy an occasional hunt in certain of his parks in his absence, overseen by his parkers. For example, in a letter of 1373 written at Northbourne (Kent), Gaunt ordered the chief forester of Leicester Frith to prohibit hunting in two parks in the chase until his return, but this was only because stocks were low because so many deer there had died of disease.[14] That guests and visitors in particular might expect to be allowed a hunt in their host's park is suggested by a letter from an acquaintance of

---

[5] *VCH Oxon.*, v. 61–2 (Beckley); viii. 223 (Watlington); Dyer 2002: 113; *CPR, 1330–4*, 35; *1354–8*, 356; *1399–1401*, 90; Watney 1910: 45; Stenton (ed.) 1934: 23; *VCH Sussex*, ii. 304; *CIPM* viii. 465; *VCH Wilts.*, xv. 127; Young 1979: 159–61; *CFR, 1327–37*, 213–16. For the lesser men who were employed as working parkers (and who were the only officials at gentry parks) see above, p. 78, and below, pp. 178–9.

[6] Mosley 1832: 349; Watney 1910: 45; *CIPM* xxi, no. 280; xxiii, no. 714 (p. 379).

[7] Henry III, for instance, apparently struggled to retain control of timber and deer in royal forests, woods, and parks in the disorder of the later 1250s and 1260s: *CCR 1256–9*, 131; *1264–8*, 467.

[8] Young 1979: 165.   [9] Grant 1991: 169.   [10] Above, pp. 24, 141.

[11] Richardson 2005; Squires 2003: 106; Harper *et al.* (eds.) 1823–34: ii. 4.

[12] Above, p. 29.   [13] Above, pp. 35, 40.

[14] Armitage-Smith (ed.) 1911: ii. 208 (no. 1383). See also ii. 15 (no. 892).

the Stonor family, Henry Carnbull, in the late 1470s. In Sir William Stonor's absence his parker had apparently denied Carnbull a hunt in the park at Stonor (Oxon.) and had thereby made himself Carnbull's 'great enemy'.[15]

On the other hand, some lords and probably a majority of gentry were neither post-holders nor favoured guests and may well have had little or no legitimate access to local parks. Powerful resentment could result from this, especially where sinecure park posts were given to those with weaker local ties.[16] Tensions over park (and forest) offices might be played out through local riots and violence, as occurred most spectacularly in the West Riding of Yorkshire in the late 1380s. Here William Beckwith's failure to secure the office of parker of Bilton park began a murderous feud in which Beckwith and his followers were pitted against duchy officials, local landowners, and, above all, the unfortunate outsider whose appointment as forester of Knaresborough had apparently thwarted Beckwith's ambitions.[17] Sometimes in the later middle ages the issue of access to park perquisites even reached the national stage. In 1404 there was a well-known Commons petition in parliament about royal patronage: the profits from royal property were being granted out and yet the king was still providing for upkeep.[18] One of the key complaints was that in many places people were taking profits of herbage and trees in parks and woods and yet the king was paying for the enclosure of the same. The implication was that ultimately the wider taxpaying community was footing part of the bill for private profit.

But the issue was not simply one of patronage: a complex system of general hunting rights and personal arrangements had been built up among landowners, and park creation could dramatically cut across this, sometimes even severing long-standing traditions of mutual assistance. Where one lord, knight, or, later, esquire or even gentleman, erected a park fence, his neighbours could no longer hunt across his lands as freely as they did before and this bespoke the limits to their authority, as well as disrupting their leisure. In some cases the park owner might be creating a resource that had not been there before, a supply of deer, but it was still very much *his* deer herd. Most of the evidence of conflict over park-making comes from the thirteenth century, though some is later. This may partly represent the thickening up of evidence, although this century may have seen a scissor effect as parks became ever more numerous, and comparatively open hunting grounds were compromised by a rapidly growing population and expanding human activity.[19]

At the top end of the spectrum, new parks might pose particular problems for great lords, who would have expected to hunt in all the woods and open lands around their estates, and not just on their own demesnes. From soon after the

---

[15] Kingsford (ed.) 1919: ii. 93. [16] Payling 1987: 143; Rowney 1984: 141.
[17] Marvin 1999: 231–6 (where it is suggested that this episode may have helped prompt the hunting legislation of 1390); Bellamy 1965: 254–61. Beckwith, though called an 'esquire' by a chronicler, was perhaps of lower, fringe gentry status.
[18] *Rot. Parl.* iii. 523–4. [19] Above, p. 28.

Conquest many great lords had started to claim various kinds of hunting privileges, either by virtue of grants from the king or at first simply by asserting their own rights. The controls they set up varied from full forests, where they could control the use of trees and undergrowth as well as deer, to exclusive hunting on their lands.[20] Where a magnate possessed hunting rights and parks first, as happened in the majority of places where he had major residences, he must often have had mixed feelings about others setting up their own reserves. By the thirteenth century the claims of others to hunting rights, not least to parks, were becoming an issue, especially given the fact that even great magnates had far more limited potential hunting grounds than the king.

The increasing power of the king, the protective arm of his law, and the royal desire for easy profits combined to help large numbers of lesser landowners carve out their own exclusive hunting areas. In particular, from the early 1250s the crown started to sell very large numbers of warren charters for landowners' demesnes,[21] including those held by knights in and near baronial preserves.[22] Many grantees were content to reserve only the hunting of hares, foxes, badgers, cats, and so on in their awarrened land, or use warren rights to protect rabbit warrens (or 'coneygarths'). But some either fenced off land for these lesser game animals or saw warren rights as justifying the creation of deer parks, as is made clear in a number of *quo warranto* cases.[23] In this respect warren grants represented as much of a challenge for the nobility as for others who wanted to hunt freely. Great lords increasingly saw the importance of securing warren rights for themselves,[24] but they could hardly have been happy with their wider spread. The article in the Petition of the Barons (1258) against warrens represented a baronial concern as much as it tapped into a wider discomfort at the proliferation of hunting reserves.[25] Baronial worries were no doubt increased by the fact that the crown, although it came to be generally supportive of or neutral towards private parks, was, on the whole, no great proponent of baronial forest rights. In this respect it is probably significant that non-royal forests started to be called chases (*chacia*) rather than forests (*foresta*) in the thirteenth century.[26] This was presumably a facet of the king's desire to demarcate forest rights as a peculiarly royal prerogative.

Park enclosure caused particular problems by limiting the free range of hunting and, above all, draining precious deer from lords' forests and chases. Deer

---

[20] See *Rot. Hund.* and *PQW*. One writer has suggested that there were over seventy private forests (or 'chases') in the 13th cent. (Bazeley 1921: 140), and this may be an underestimate. These large reserves were mainly established in areas where population was low and royal interference limited, such as the north of England, the Welsh borders, and the Sussex rapes.

[21] For chartered rights of free warren see above, p. 4.

[22] A few examples are provided in *VCH Sussex*, ii. 317, 324–5. Note also Crook 2001: 42–8 on the close association between warren rights—so often allied with parks—and lordship in the mid-13th-cent. struggles of the abbot of St Albans with local knights over hunting rights.

[23] *PQW* 186, 190, 192, 196.   [24] Crook 2001: 37.   [25] Cf. Crook 2001: 33–4.

[26] Crouch 1992: 306; Turner (ed.) 1901: p. cix; Liddell 1966: 127–8.

in chases—like those in royal forests—might be lost through deliberately constructed deer-leaps which trapped deer inside parks and doubtless also by more active poaching by park owners eager to top up their own deer stocks by catching deer in the forest. Sometimes lords agreed to allow park-making: throughout the thirteenth century and later the great franchise holders (the earls of Lancaster and bishops of Durham) and other lords with lands throughout the country granted such permissions to feudal inferiors who held lands from them.[27] But these agreements were no easy matter. Lords were usually eager to reserve some limited hunting rights for themselves in the new parks and, especially, to make specifications against deer-leaps. These demands in turn might compromise the viability of the new park herd. In many cases no consensus about such park-making was possible at all, or was only eventually achieved after long dispute, and in some places there were extremely bitter conflicts. A good example of this is provided by Sussex, where several lords had large forests.

In that county, the forest of Arundel witnessed particular contention and it serves as a case study of how great lords fought a battle (albeit usually a losing one) to stop others from creating parks. The forest of Arundel—about twelve miles long by five wide—was partly in the demesne of the earl of Arundel, but also contained lands granted to a number of other lords, notably the archbishops of Canterbury, bishops of Chichester, and the knightly families of de Haia and St John, successive owners of the manor of Halnaker, in the middle of the forest.[28] In the late 1250s, at a time when the earldom estates were divided, a long dispute over the hunting rights of the lords of Arundel and the archbishop in Arundel forest and park reached arbitration, and it was agreed that the archbishop was not to hunt outside his own wood at Slindon except for one deer once a year, while, in return, John Fitzalan and his heirs were not to hunt in the archbishop's wood.[29] The earl was to ensure that the archbishop or his deputy were shown good hunting on that day and also given a payment of venison. Certain details show the seriousness of the situation: the constable of Arundel had to swear upon the souls of his lords to provide the hunting and venison and Fitzalan agreed that he and his heirs or assigns might be excommunicated and their lands laid under interdict if he failed to abide by the award; both parties agreed to secure confirmation from the pope and the king. Nonetheless, despite an agreement at the arbitration about keeping woods in the forest open, by the early fourteenth century the archbishops had made a park at Slindon.[30]

By the early 1290s the scene of conflict had shifted to the north-eastern edge of the forest and the bishop of Chichester's park of Houghton, which was such

---

[27] Examples of Lancastrian licences are: *CPR, 1361–64*, 38; *1401–05*, 470; some of those of the bishop of Durham are *CChR, 1257–1300*, 140–1, 481. For agreements between other lords see: Liddell 1966: 127; Hodder 1988–9: 40, 46, 49; Dugdale 1730: ii. 660, 910; *VCH Berks.*, iii. 397; *CPR, 1354–8*, 18.

[28] Much of the following is based on *VCH Sussex*, ii. 303–5 (although it almost certainly dates the creation of some of the parks too early). For the location of Arundel forest see Fig. 9.

[29] *CChR, 1257–1300*, 187–8.   [30] *VCH Sussex*, iv. 235.

a large preserve that it was sometimes itself called a 'forest', or 'chase'. Earl Richard (Fitzalan) was determined to do as his ancestors had done and hunt throughout his forest, including in the bishop's park. On the bishop's complaint the earl asserted that 'he had hunted and would hunt there again, notwithstanding the rights of the bishop'. The bishop went so far as to excommunicate him; the dispute was only eventually resolved some time later when the earl climbed down and agreed to a penance and pilgrimage to a local shrine.

Other parks set up in the forest became sore points too, notably the St Johns' park at Halnaker.[31] In the second half of the thirteenth century, John St John seems to have added sixty acres of land there to his park, 'to the prejudice of Arundel chase'. In 1283 an inquiry was held to investigate this addition to the 'old' park, which had been enclosed so that deer could get in by a deer-leap. The enquiry was carried out on the orders of the king, acting for Richard Fitzalan, then his ward, since an inquest held by the sheriff had shown that on the death of the young Richard's father this park had been fully sealed, so that deer could neither get in, nor out.[32] No doubt the earls did not much like the park being there at all. Around the same time, Henry Hussey's park at Harting was also referred to as being harmful to the same chase of Arundel.

The situation facing the earls of Arundel was far from unique: the circumstances of the earls of Warwick in Sutton chase (Staffs.) in the thirteenth century provide an obvious parallel;[33] so too the long-running feud between Edmund, earl of Cornwall, and Walter Bronescombe, bishop of Exeter (1258–80), over the bishop's Cornish parks;[34] and likewise the disagreements between Gilbert de Clare, earl of Gloucester, and Godfrey Giffard, bishop of Worcester (1268–1302), and others.[35] The many cases of resistance by great men to the wider ownership of parks show how much they saw them as a nuisance. In some places lords seem to have been bent on the complete destruction of others' parks, quite unlike the king. In the 1230s Earl Warenne forced William de Say to remove his apparently well-established park at Hamsey (Sussex) by claiming common rights there and made him promise that he would not hunt deer or other game in the earl's nearby chase (called Cleres) or in his Sussex warrens. Say's only compensation was Warenne's recognition of his right to a fishery and rabbit warren at Hamsey.[36] Similarly, in the late 1280s, Gilbert de Clare succeeded in convincing judges that the two deer-leaps of William Poer's park at Farley (Worcs.) were trapping deer from his chase of Malvern, about half a mile away; Poer was ordered to remove not only the leaps but also the park

---

[31] In 1253 Robert St John was granted free warren for his demesne lands in Halnaker and elsewhere. The standard stipulation that these lands were to be 'outside the limits of the forest' did nothing to protect the earl's chase (*CPR, 1247–58*, 245).
[32] *CPR, 1281–92*, 67.   [33] Hodder 1988–9: 39, 49, 50.   [34] Henderson 1935: 157–8.
[35] *CChR, 1257–1300*, 401; *Rot. Hund.* ii. 173.
[36] Maitland (ed.) 1887: no. 806; Salzman (ed.) 1903: nos. 341, 371.

enclosure.[37] Elsewhere, recognition of rights to a park probably had to be squeezed from a reluctant lord, including perhaps in Gilsland (Cumberland), where in 1254 the prior of Lanercost extracted the concession from Thomas de Moulton that he and his monks could have a park in Thomas's lordship, so long as it did not include a deer-leap.[38]

These kinds of issues remained potentially divisive throughout the middle ages: lords retained their chases (if often reduced in size and much permeated by other property ownerships and land uses) and others continued to make parks. In Yorkshire in the early fourteenth century Nicholas de Meynill had apparently been unable to stop Robert de Coleville creating a huge 2,200-acre park at Ingleby Arncliffe, adjacent to Nicholas's chase of Whorlton. In 1317 Robert had arranged for an inquisition *ad quod damnum*, which had found that the imparkment would not harm the king or others, and obtained a royal licence;[39] but in 1319 Nicholas was complaining that an unauthorized deer-leap in the park perimeter was draining the deer belonging to his chase.[40] Back at Halnaker (Sussex), the park remained and possibly even grew, being estimated at three miles in circumference in the 1330s. In 1404 Hugh, the elder son of Lord St John, was licensed by the king to complete a 300-acre imparkment, 'according to the bounds of the lordship', so long as the land was not in the forest. The latter phrase was standard, but the former was no doubt a nod to the local problems.[41] Henry Fitzhugh's 1391 licence for a park at Ravensworth (Yorks.) might be interpreted in the same light: here he was careful to specify that he was enclosing 'land of his own fee round his castle'.[42]

However, great lords were far from the only ones likely to be concerned about park creation. New parks could also cause serious problems for pre-existing gentry hunting practices. The case of Simon de Pierpont against Thomas de Poynings at the 1240 Suffolk eyre is a good example. Simon claimed to be able to hunt throughout his and Thomas's fiefs, and challenged Thomas's right to hunt throughout the whole vill of Wrentham. For his part, Thomas said that he had reciprocal rights to hunt wolves and hares in Simon's fief as in his own. The judgement was that Simon had the right to hunt throughout Thomas's fief, including in his park until it was enclosed (which it currently was not); Thomas could only hunt in his park.[43] Similar kinds of issues remained throughout the period, showing the potential difficulties in balancing exclusivity with courtesy to neighbours in a society acutely conscious of hierarchy and proper behaviour. In 1388, for example, Lettice Kyriel took John French and William Patching to

---

[37] Turner (ed.) 1901: p. cxviii; *VCH Worcs.*, iv. 140; *Abbrev. Plac.*, 214, 222, 283.
[38] Todd (ed.) 1997: no. 201.   [39] TNA: PRO, C143/120, no. 4; *CPR, 1317–21*, 2.
[40] TNA: PRO, SC8/127/6321; *CPR, 1317–21*, 374.
[41] This licence was renewed by new owners in 1517: *Letters and Papers Henry VIII*, ii./2. 1517–18 (no. 3311).
[42] *CPR, 1388–92*, 395 (index incorrectly identifies as Durham).
[43] This is based on a transcription supplied by John Gallagher.

court over hunting in her park of Westenhanger (Kent).[44] John claimed that Lettice had made a common place for hunting in the park for 'knights and esquires of the neighbourhood', including him; William that he had chased a wounded deer in nearby Postling park (where he was parker), but it had entered Lettice's park, and she had given him permission to pursue the deer and sent some villeins of hers with him to kill it. Lettice denied both claims.

Some landowners could suffer losses more directly material than simply in terms of free access for hunting. This was especially likely to be an issue in areas of wood or waste where boundaries between lordships and fees might be uncertain.[45] Not surprisingly, the less powerful were particularly at risk of losing land to the more powerful. For instance, in the twelfth century Sele priory claimed that William, third lord of Bramber, had taken some of its land for the enlargement of his park at Knepp (Sussex).[46] The park of John, duke of Bedford, at Fulbrook (Warks.) incorporated land and tenements worth 18s. a year which had belonged to Pinley priory,[47] and the licensing by Humphrey, duke of Gloucester, of his new park at Greenwich in the 1430s was probably at least partly designed to clear up a dispute with Sheen priory over ownership of pasture and heath land in the park area.[48] Landowners affected in this way might have to struggle long and hard for any kind of recompense, as seems to have occurred where Stephen de Segrave carved out a park from land claimed by the Le Brets near Coventry in the early thirteenth century, Stephen having received the support of the earl of Chester, the territorial lord.[49] Even where some kind of agreement and exchange of lands took place, this might often be one-sided or forced.[50]

If new imparkments did not cause the loss of land title, they could bring concerns for other lords in terms of agrarian profits where common rights (access to another's land for pasturage and wood) were involved. Farming disputes will be examined more closely in the next chapter, but it is clear that park-making could entail the loss of pasture and wood-gathering rights in waste areas nominally covered by others' title deeds but which had formerly been freely accessed. Once a park was made, use of these resources would usually have to be paid for and could be much more closely controlled by the owner.

---

[44] Arnold (ed.) 1985 and 1987: i. 272–3.

[45] The place-name Flitteris (Rutland), 'brushwood region of disputed ownership', is particularly suggestive, reflecting a long history of uncertain ownership in an area on the county boundary, where Richard of Cornwall was licensed to create a park in the mid thirteenth century (Cox 1994 (ed.): 125–6; Squires 1992: 50–1).

[46] *VCH Sussex*, ii. 306.   [47] TNA: PRO, C139/77/36, m. 44.

[48] *CPR, 1429–36*, 250, 369; Emery 1996: 175.   [49] Coss 1991: 93, 95, 97–8.

[50] Loyd and Stenton (eds.) 1950: no. 431 (Odo of Bayeux, earl of Kent (the king's half-brother) and Christ Church, Canterbury, 1071–82); Eyton 1854–60: x. 113 (John le Strange and Shrewsbury abbey, c.1195); *CCR, 1234–7*, 35 (the earl of Chester and Hulton abbey, early 13th cent.); *CChR, 1226–57*, 465–6 (William de Valence (the king's half-brother) and Hyde abbey, 1256; *CPR, 1317–21*, 431–2 (Hugh le Despenser, the elder and the abbots of Stanley and Malmesbury, 1320).

Finally, it is worth noting that the disruption of local roads and paths could be highly inflammatory, especially, as with all these possible disagreements, where there were pre-existing local rivalries. In the later 1420s Sir Thomas Brook enclosed a large part of his manor of Weycroft in Axminster (Devon) as a deer park. His new fences seem to have blocked three roads and restricted the access of Sir William Bonville of Chute and his tenants to their own lands.[51] In February 1427 he had managed to have an *oyer et terminer* commission set up against Bonville and his men for supposed forcible entry and assaults. Brook alleged that Bonville and other malefactors arrayed in manner of war broke his close, houses, and park at Axminster, hunted in the park without licence, carried off deer and dogs, lay in wait to kill him, and assaulted his men. They had apparently cut the gates, pales, and posts of the park into small pieces. The circumstantial details give his allegations the ring of truth. At any rate, he then put the manor in the hands of a powerful set of feoffees, in whose name he obtained a charter to crenellate the house and impark 800 acres. In the end, however, his court connections and park charter proved insufficient: it was decided in arbitration in August 1428 that all the obstructions he had set up had to be removed.

The Brook–Bonville dispute, like many other conflicts over parks, seems likely to have been linked to concerns about lordship and social standing. The park could be a powerful symbol of authority and power, and provide a focus for lords' sense of group identity.[52] Given this, it would not be surprising that displays of wealth invested in traditional symbols of lordship like parks could cause friction, especially where parvenus were involved, or where there were long-standing disputes over land, politics, or office.[53] Where there was discord in a local community, a park's status as a signifier of lordship could readily bring it into dispute and thereby escalate conflict.

A concern about status perhaps informed the aggression of William de Valence, Henry III's half-brother, against Hugh of Northwold, bishop of Ely (1229–54) in the early 1250s. In 1252 Valence set out with some companions from his castle at Hertford on a hunting trip to nearby Hatfield. According to Matthew Paris, when Valence reached Hatfield he 'violently' entered the bishop's park and hunted there without permission, against the law of the land and the knightly code, before causing great tumult at the palace, breaking open the buttery and doling out wine to mere grooms.[54] The chronicler was at pains to point out the tyrannies practised by the king's unpopular relatives, but the situation may actually have been more complex. Perhaps Valence felt that the bishop had no right to claim an exclusive hunting ground only four miles from his own castle? Or perhaps he simply felt slighted because his party had

---

[51] Roskell *et al.* 1992 (eds.): ii. 376–7. Cf. Henderson 1935: 157–8.   [52] Ch. 5 above.
[53] Rigby 1995: 199; Carpenter 1992: 244–5.
[54] Luard (ed.) 1872–83: v. 343–4; *VCH Herts.*, iii. 99.

been refused access to it? This might explain his use of the bishop's wine: he was showing that he too could disturb the social order. As in other areas, great lords could be touchy about wanting their inferiors, or perceived inferiors, to act with due deference. This may also help explain Waltham abbey's opposition to Henry Fitzaucher's proposed imparkment at Copped Hall (Essex) in 1291.[55]

Throughout the middle ages, attacking park fences or slaughtering deer seems to have been a significant way of challenging another aristocrat's standing. The clearest example of this comes from the mid-fifteenth-century struggle between Ralph, Lord Cromwell and Lord Grey of Codnor in the north Midlands. In 1440, when Grey wanted to insult his enemy Cromwell, he had his servants carry out a very careful attack on Cromwell's park at West Hallam (Derbs.).[56] Rather than cause general havoc and slaughter the whole deer herd, his followers killed a single animal, took out its organs (in contemporary hunting terms the 'curée', supposed to be ceremoniously handled and fed to the dogs as their reward for the successful chase), and placed them at the gates of the park, 'in despictu' of Cromwell, perhaps comparing him to a dog. Such an act would have been meaningless had the park and its game supply not been seen as a powerful symbol of lordship, which made it an appropriate target in what was a long-standing conflict over political power. In the previous decade Cromwell had taken over Grey's position as the leading magnate in the region and the two were locked in a protracted and bitter struggle: Grey's attack came just a month after a thoroughly one-sided *oyer and terminer* commission had been issued against him at Cromwell's behest, a commission that was to gravely weaken Grey's local authority.

Many other similar examples could be cited. For instance, in 1321, Bohun, the Mortimers, Mowbray, Damory, and their friends and armed followers missed no opportunity to hunt in and destroy Despenser parks as part of a wider campaign of retribution, theft and destruction.[57] In the 1330s, attacks on the prior of Coventry's park were an important part of the struggle for local power between the priory and Queen Isabella's followers.[58] In the early fifteenth century, Reginald, Lord Grey of Ruthin, broke into Eleanor Lady St Amand's park at Millbrook, near Ampthill (Beds.), from his nearby base at Wrest, apparently as part of his general and prolonged molestation of a woman whose magnificent castle, estates, and fine hunting grounds he seems to have coveted. For Reginald large-scale poaching raids were seemingly a key element in a campaign of intimidation which allegedly included threatening and assaulting her servants and tenants.[59]

The question remains as to how we should measure the overall impact of parks on aristocratic society. Clearly there were limits to the effects one lord's park-making had on his fellows, especially since lords were not everywhere and

---

[55] TNA: PRO, C143/16, no. 26, m. 3d.; *VCH Essex*, v. 122.   [56] Payling 1987: 144.
[57] *CCR, 1318–23*, 541–6 (at 542 and 544).   [58] Coss (ed.) 1986: 2.
[59] *CPR, 1416–22*, 78–9; *Rot. Parl.* iv. 92–3; Payling 1989: 889.

at all times in a state of fierce competition. Where one lord stated his credentials by making a park, this did not necessarily stop his neighbour from doing the same. One lord's assertion of high status did not have to be damaging to others, especially where those others were obviously superior, possessing far more extensive estates, and more impressive lineage. Because of this, alleged attacks on parks have to be treated with some care. 'Violence' and 'force and arms' were standard legal phrases, used to bring certain types of legal actions. Park 'breaks' occurred for a variety of reasons and need to be related to specific local circumstances. If some raids were reactions against more or less recent imparkments, others were apparently the result of high-spirited hunters transgressing agreed norms, and a number were carried out by organized gangs, motivated by theft of venison, valuable livestock, or timber.[60] Non-aristocrats, including local tenants, townsmen, and even monks, were responsible for a considerable amount of the recorded poaching, apparently without any noble or gentry involvement.[61] In this respect it is notable that a fair proportion of poaching episodes in parks in and around Oxfordshire seem to have resulted from the fact that unruly Oxford scholars regarded them as a kind of illicit leisure resource.[62]

Similarly, we must not overstate frictions arising from the economic impact of park-making on other landowners. Any lands lost to others' parks would tend, by definition, to be peripheral to the manor since they would be on the edge of someone else's lordship where they could be hived off. If some lesser lords struggled to secure timber, fuel, and pasturage, which they had to beg, steal, or borrow, others were generally able to secure these materials adequately within their own manors. Even where parks were created, initial disagreements could be overcome and arrangements made allowing reservation or sharing of wood or waste.[63] Certain disputes over relatively low-value pasture-rights might have had more to do with a striving to display pre-eminence than a real struggle over resources.[64]

Outright attacks on parks were not continuous but peaked in times of political instability and disorder, like other crimes. The absence of nobles in Edward I's second Welsh war encouraged many attacks on their parks, as 'malefactors' grew bold with the king and great men out of the country.[65] In June 1304 a commission was sent to investigate poaching in Walter de Huntercombe's park of Huntercombe (Oxon.) while he was on the king's service in Scotland and under his protection.[66] In the first half of the fourteenth century, political crises produce noticeable peaks in recorded park-breaking, in other

---

[60] Birrell 1990–1: 28–9; Bellamy 1964: 708; Franklin 1996: 181.
[61] This is discussed further in Ch. 7 below.
[62] *CPR, 1272–81*, 451; *CCR, 1413–19*, 75–6; *Rot. Parl.* iv. 131; TNA: PRO, SC8/24/1158.
[63] Farrer and Clay (eds.) 1913–65: iii. 381–2; Salter (ed.) 1906–7 and 1908: i, no. 200; *VCH Shrops.*, i. 493; *VCH Wilts.*, viii. 221; Riley (ed.) 1870–1: i. 254–61.
[64] Wright 1983: 120. [65] Prestwich 1988: 281; *CPR, 1281–92*, 66.
[66] *CPR, 1301–7*, 278. There were similar commissions at this time into breaks into Bohun and Warenne parks, while the owners were likewise engaged.

words 1315–18, 1328–30, 1340–1.[67] The generally high levels in the 1330s may well have been a result of Edward III's early inattention to disorder in the localities, disorder that was partly caused by his cronies, men like John Molyns. The greatest single peak came in 1329, a year of great instability as Mortimer and Isabella's regime tottered.

Nonetheless, with these kinds of caveats in mind, aristocrats could certainly be deeply concerned about others' park-making, especially where a monopoly on hunting reserves was challenged for the first time, or where large areas of wood and waste were being carved up. In particular, there seems to have been a phase in the thirteenth century when great lords felt themselves pressured in this respect by lesser landowners, albeit they increasingly focused their own hunting and deer-keeping inside their own parks. But the issue of access to game and hunting did not go away thereafter: the use and abuse of parks remained a contentious issue, even in years which did not witness notable disorder, as demonstrated by a petition from the Commons in 1417 complaining about 'violent' park breaks and unauthorized hunting in parks and other reserves.[68] If there was more available land on which to establish parks in the later middle ages, the deer inside were just as important to a suitable hunting and venison-eating lifestyle. Indeed, as deer outside parks were concentrated into smaller areas of remaining royal forests and noble chases, the deer within parks would have become increasingly vital.

In this light, the high points in generally lower-level violence involving parks might plausibly be seen as the periodic expression of underlying tension over hunting and land use. For example, almost half of the parks in Oxfordshire and Bedfordshire are known to have suffered poaching raids or other damage at some stage in their existence. Others were no doubt affected without records surviving. The involvement of the gentry in many of these attacks suggests the significance of parks as potential flash-points in local disputes. At a national level, the local gentry certainly led many of the hundreds of recorded poaching raids and thefts from parks that resulted in *oyer et terminer* commissions from the later thirteenth century onwards.[69] Sometimes no doubt they were acting for more senior lords, but at other times almost certainly on their own initiative.

Not all was discord, nor was there everywhere division, but these reserves and their role in regulating access to hunting and venison could be a cause of contention amongst lords throughout the middle ages. A desire to hunt and to have the power to hunt played a part in the great majority of aristocratic poaching forays and attacks on parks: it was what made the attacks and the parks themselves so meaningful. In this respect, further study of particular conflicts involving parks has the potential to shed all sorts of new light on medieval aristocrats' self-image and social relationships.

---

[67] Statistics in Way 1997: 112–13.   [68] *Rot. Parl.* iv. 111–12.
[69] Hanawalt 1988: 75; Way 1997: 76–7; Saul 1986: 191–2; Naughton 1976: 77; *CPR, 1446–52*, 236.

7

Parks and the Community

For all the possible tensions among the elite, the impact of the park was likely to be more direct and material lower down the social scale, closer to subsistence level. Yet the wider social effects of park-making have attracted scant attention from historians. There has been no general assessment of the scale of the problems caused by park enclosure, no sustained analysis of the land-use practices, or even the land, that individuals and communities may have lost.[1] Often, in fact, it has been implied that parks made hardly any impression on locals at all. The traditional picture of the high medieval park downplays its position in the landscape: it was set up on poor and remote land on the edge of manor and parish, away from settlement and agriculture.[2] Such parks, carved out of areas of woodland and waste, supposedly interfered little with pre-existing land uses or property rights.[3] Where they did, it has sometimes been suggested that lords were scrupulous in providing compensation.[4] Later medieval park-making has attracted somewhat more attention as part of the wider social problems associated with the enclosure of arable land, conversion to grazing, and rural depopulation in this period, but there is no clear sense of how significant deer parks were in these developments.[5]

Earlier parts of this book, although looking at things from the lord's point of view, have already cast doubt on this generally anodyne view of park-making. We have seen that woods and wastes were a diminishing and potentially valuable resource in the high middle ages and that park creation laid claim to large areas of this terrain; that parks caused considerable disruption to existing farming by taking in areas of arable land, meadow, and pasture and by impeding the further spread of cultivation; and that they could ensure the blocking or redirection of roads.[6] In other words, even if a lord's motivation in making a park was not directly economic, the effects on others could be. But the effects did not stop there. As will become clear, high as well as later medieval parks could actually interfere with the growth of settlements or bring about their decline or even destruction; and in all periods park-making also had a major

---

[1] See above, p. 9. [2] Cantor and Hatherly 1979: 74; above, p. 2.
[3] Beresford 1971: 197 (discussing Fountains Park, Yorks., 13th cent.).
[4] Lasdun 1991: 18–19; Rackham 1990: 172; Stamper 1988: 135 (on common rights in general).
[5] Below, p. 172. [6] Above, pp. 28, 51–9, 154.

effect on peasant, as well as aristocratic, hunting, which was partly a material concern, but also increasingly a social and cultural one. In all sorts of ways then, it seems likely that parks would have had a direct impact on many ordinary people. These reserves therefore merit investigation as an element in the wider process of medieval enclosure and privatization of land use.

Carrying out such an investigation is no easy task given the evidence at our disposal. To put the problem simply, the documentary sources were typically written at the behest of those indifferent to local concerns or with a strong interest in concealing conflicting priorities and opposition. As a result, most of them are either blandly factual or present an image of consensus and agreement. Tensions tended only to emerge in a fully developed and articulated form during large-scale revolts, which were rare,[7] and on the whole we are left to try to identify latent or simmering discontents, which are much harder to measure.[8] In this sense, the problem of comprehending peasant reactions to parks is part of a wider problem: before the later fourteenth century especially we have almost nothing of peasants' own attitudes, towards parks or anything else.[9] This has, inevitably, done a good deal to shape the modern study of parks, focusing interest on why lords may have wanted to make these reserves and what they used them for, rather than on the impact of park-making on others, particularly lesser locals. By contrast with the paucity of evidence on the peasant mentality, the poems and literary works written for a courtly, chivalric audience extolling the pleasures of parks and hunting, and offering other scattered clues about noble attitudes, appear a rich source of information.

Where conflict was recorded the story was typically presented from the perspective of the landholding class and its officials. For instance, attempts to gain access to parkland to exercise previously held common grazing or wood-gathering rights were often silently redesignated in court rolls as encroachments or petty crimes to be clamped down on or fined and paid for.[10] Free men could, of course, take their grievances to the king, and from the later twelfth century there were standardized legal actions available which could be used to claim access to land, but for many people legal action would have been too risky and expensive, especially if group backing could not be secured. As a result, while a significant number of cases over common rights were heard in royal courts, they probably only represent the tip of an iceberg.[11] This is especially the case since around half of the population was legally unfree and had no right to use any court other than their lord's own manorial court, which was hardly a sympathetic venue for challenging enclosure by the lord of the manor or another landowner.[12] The records of the royal forest administration, meanwhile, provide

---

[7] Hatherly and Cantor 1979–80: 75; Davies 1978: 123–7.
[8] Modern parallels of furtive resistance and non-cooperation by peasant groups are instructive. See e.g. Scott 1985–6; Guha and Gadgil 1989: 163 ff.
[9] Hallam 1988b: 845. [10] Cf. VCH Oxon., x. 50; Birrell 1987: 45.
[11] Dyer 2006: 27–30. [12] On the unfree see e.g. Hyams 1980: 49–65.

evidence on the creation of hundreds of parks, but their concern was with royal prerogative rights and possible damage to the king's deer stocks, not local common rights, which, in any case, since they were based on custom and prescription, had a rather uncertain legal standing.[13] Similarly, when the crown set up wide-ranging investigations into local government, like the hundred rolls inquiry, these focused on judicial privileges and landholding rather than tenant welfare. Even the more systematic early sixteenth-century enclosure inquiries were at first intended to omit deer parks and we must suspect that only a minority of the most flagrant recent abuses emerged from the final inquiry even after its remit was extended to include parks.[14]

This chapter sets out, as far as possible, to circumvent these problems of evidence and present a fuller picture of the effect of parks on the population at large. Besides looking at the impact of park-making, it seeks to recover the way individuals and communities responded to the changes brought about, whether by passive resistance or by tearing down park fences. The discussion is divided into two parts, the first dealing with the period up to the Black Death, and the second looking at the impact of parks in the very different demographic, economic, and social circumstances of the later middle ages. A short concluding section then provides an assessment of the overall scale of the disturbance and distress that was caused.

THE HIGH MIDDLE AGES

A useful starting point for this analysis may be to look at the impact of earlier parks on settlements and farmland, since this is an area which has been particularly neglected. In the lowlands especially, settlement was already relatively dense by the twelfth century and, as we saw in Chapter 2, from the earliest periods parks were often located close to manorial and settlement centres and their associated roads, cart-tracks, fields, meadows, and pastures.[15] Castle building, borough foundation, and park-making were often part of a package of developments in the Norman and Angevin periods and the same lords who encouraged the growth of towns or villages by granting civic or market rights also often created deer parks for their nearby residences.[16] Not surprisingly, it actually appears that in many places park-making interfered with settlements and farming landscapes.

Urban communities were amongst those which felt the effects of park enclosure, and where parks and towns grew up in close proximity park fences could actually cause a hindrance to the physical expansion of streets and houses. At Woodstock (Oxon.), for instance, the settlement of Old Woodstock developed

---

[13] See e.g. TNA: PRO, C143/3, no. 7.   [14] 7 Hen. 8, c. 1: *SR* iii. 176–7.
[15] Above, pp. 53–8.   [16] Liddiard 2000b: *passim*.

in the shadow of the early royal park, and the new borough Henry II established there in the later twelfth century was planted right up against the enclosure.[17] This kind of direct proximity can be clearly demonstrated in a number of other cases. At Devizes (Wilts.) the town was established in the early twelfth century immediately next to a castle and its associated parkland, a position which prevented any expansion to the west or north (see Fig. 21).[18] Likewise, the potential development of Coventry was partly limited by the presence of Cheylesmore park to the south. Although the northern part of the park was given over to development in the later twelfth and thirteenth century, this only allowed so much space: Much Park Street had to veer off at right angles to run parallel to the (relocated) park paling.[19] At Sheffield (Yorks.) a huge deer park limited expansion of the town east of the River Sheaf until after the middle ages.[20] At Ludgershall, in Wiltshire, the crown's development of extensive parkland around the castle in the thirteenth century stopped the expansion and commercial growth of the small borough to the south of the castle.[21] The park created at Dunster (Som.) by the later thirteenth century blocked the line of the old road from Gallox Cross to Carhampton and burgage tenements in the high street ran along the park fence.[22] Imparking occurred close to many other urban centres too, including Nottingham, Leicester, and Bath, and in most cases it probably had some effect in limiting or at least directing expansion.[23] Where towns flourished under other favourable conditions the impact was probably relatively limited; but, for a variety of reasons, many planned boroughs failed, and it would not be surprising to find that where a park was present it played at least some part in this. In an era of expansion would-be entrepreneurs could choose to set up operations in more promising centres.

The effect of parks on smaller settlements could be just as significant, and many more villages and hamlets were affected than towns. In some cases these settlements seem to have been restricted from developing. At Tankersley (Yorks.), for instance, the creation of a park apparently 'stifled the development of the village'.[24] Similar effects may have been felt at Hanley Castle (Worcs.), a village nucleus to surrounding hamlets: by the thirteenth century the park attached to the castle impinged on the south-west of the settlement, its fence running close to the church and market.[25] In other places the effects seem to have been more radical, with major reorganization of settlements. At Somersham (Hunts.) the bishops of Ely appear to have moved almost the entire village in the twelfth or thirteenth century in order to extend their palace and surround it with a garden and park complex.[26] At Godmanchester (Hunts.) a small part of the village

---

[17] Bond 1997: 29; above, Fig. 10.   [18] Below, Fig. 21.
[19] VCH Warks., viii. 9, 13, 18–19; Lilley 1998.   [20] Creighton 2002: 185–6.
[21] Stevenson 1992: 78–9.   [22] Lyte 1909: ii. 342–3.   [23] Creighton 2002: 191.
[24] Hey 1975: 111.   [25] Toomey (ed.) 2001: pp. xiv–xix.   [26] Taylor 1989: 223.

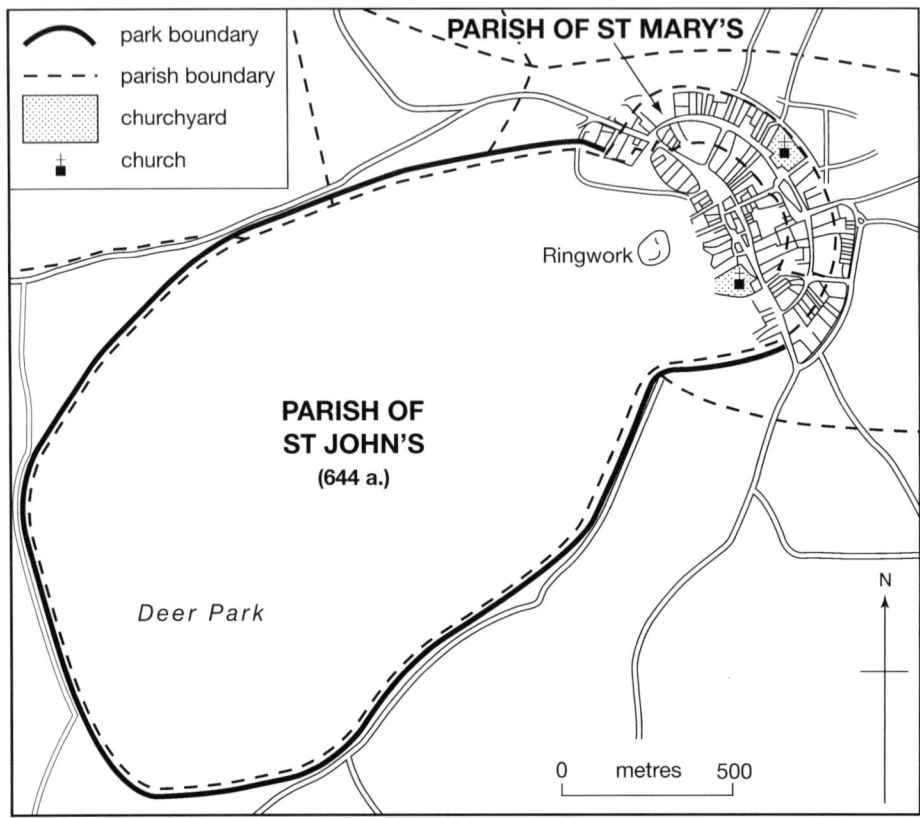

Fig. 21. Devizes (Wilts.). The planned town of Devizes, probably established by Roger, bishop of Salisbury (d. 1139), was located immediately next to a castle and its associated parkland. The castle, to the west of the town, was situated at the eastern edge of a large park (shown here); to the north was a second, smaller, park at Roundway.
Source: Liddiard 2005: 102. See also *VCH Wilts.*, x. 226, 232, 237–8, 245.

was removed and the rest restructured; and at Spaldwick (Hunts.) the village seems to have been replanned in the twelfth century as part of the reorganization of the bishop of Lincoln's residence, gardens, and park.[27] Sometimes existing settlements were even completely destroyed to make way for parks. At Osmerley (Worcs.), the establishment of a park and grange by Bordesley abbey in the late twelfth and early thirteenth century seems to have resulted in the desertion of the settlement after the acquisition of land from local landowners and the expulsion or buying out of tenants.[28] The creation of a park at Nether Stowey (Som.) in the early thirteenth century apparently led to the enclosure and destruction of most of the settlement at nearby Budley, cutting off

---

[27] Way 1997: 228.
[28] Dyer 1982: 21. Domesday listed fourteen tenants on the manor, but no settlement is referred to in later records.

its remnants from the church and from the new town under the castle walls.[29] The enclosure of Okehampton park in the late thirteenth century seems to have led to the abandonment of a group of dispersed farmsteads at Byrham, on the northern edge of the Dartmoor uplands.[30] Other possible examples of total destruction from a similar period include the hamlets at Nuthill, in Holderness (Yorks.), Shottle and Wallstone (Derbs.), and Ree, in Westbury (Shrops.).[31]

Besides the possibility of direct interference with streets and houses, many parks affected agricultural land and cultivation, and this could have damaging effects on peasants (and townsmen).[32] Given the land hunger that characterized most of the period from the twelfth to the early fourteenth century, the enclosure of arable and other farmland into parks was likely to have had a significant local impact, especially since tenants held much of the land which was affected. The poor and the unfree were particularly vulnerable to arbitrary action. Occasionally it seems that sitting tenants were simply expropriated and evicted, as at Segenhoe (Beds.), where a number of *rustici* were ejected from their lands in the twelfth century.[33] Elsewhere, as at Princes Risborough (Bucks.) in the late thirteenth century, villeins had to pay for the losses of others (presumably free men) for lands taken into the park.[34] The unfree might sometimes receive compensation, especially if they were the men of another lord, as seems to have happened with the men of Hensington after an extension of Woodstock park, but this was probably only because their lord's interests were affected (in this case the Templars).[35] Kings especially—and no doubt other lords where they could—tended to think of their park first and their tenants later,[36] if they had to or it was made worth their while.[37] On the whole, free men (like those at Princes Risborough) were more likely to be given alternative lands or money compensation,[38] but even where compensation was given there was no guarantee that it would be fair or timely: the bland and soothing words of charters should not always be taken at face value. Many land swaps or purchases probably involved pressure being exerted, and where the king or powerful local lords were concerned others possibly had little choice in the agreements made. And even where solely demesne land was enclosed—for instance where this already formed a consolidated block rather than being held as strips in common fields—parks tended to cause problems for tenants since they lost their access to much prized post-harvest grazing rights on any imparked arable.[39]

---

[29] Dunning 1981.   [30] Austin 1978: 196–7; Hinton 1990: 171.
[31] Neave 1991: 11; Wiltshire *et al.* 2005: 98; *VCH Shrops.*, viii. 298, 306.
[32] Above, pp. 51–9.   [33] See above, p. 56.   [34] *CIPM* iii. 463–4.   [35] Above, p. 54.
[36] Crook 2002: 73 provides a useful instance of this.
[37] For an example of a fine levied by King John for recovery of pasture rights see Crook 1976: 36.
[38] Mason (ed.) 1980: 151–2 (William Mauduit IV, earl of Warwick, and various free tenants, 1260s); *CPR, 1334–38*, 101–2 (William de Clinton, 1335). Occasionally a tenancy might become available for imparking through escheating back to the lord for lack of heirs: Stamp (ed.) 1930–3: i. 142 (Edward, the Black Prince, 1347).
[39] Ault 1972: 15–17; Vanderzee (ed.) 1807: 172; *CPR, 1348–50*, 148–9.

Churchmen, meanwhile, might lose their tithes where land was taken out of cultivation for parks, whether it was demesne or tenant land.[40]

We should also remember that arable farming was not just affected by the imparkment of land which was already incorporated into fields and closes: the enclosure of 'wastes' had an important impact on this too, by blocking the path of the plough, especially as population expanded in the twelfth and thirteenth centuries. As we have already seen, many park sites or considerable parts of them were of a cultivable quality but were retained as wood-pasture (see Fig. 22).[41] Detailed landscape and documentary research can sometimes suggest just how much potential farmland could be involved. At Woodham Walter in Essex, for example, although most of the parish was comprised of similar terrain, peasant holdings were restricted to the north: much of the south of the parish was taken up by a park created before the 1230s.[42] In places, the presence of parks could prevent any further expansion of the open fields, as at Cippenham (Bucks.),[43] or Burton Lazars (Leics.), where field strips abutted their boundaries.[44] Elsewhere, they represented an equally firm barrier to woodland clearance for creating farmland in more outlying parts of parishes and townships: in places it was only parks that were entirely free from peasant assarting, as is shown by a reconstruction of woodland clearance at Eccleshall (Staffs.).[45] Likewise, at Watlington (Oxon.), the park was formed, around the middle of the thirteenth century, at a time when settlement and farming had for quite some time been spreading into the higher ground around it in the eastern part of the parish.[46] There are plenty of other thirteenth- and early fourteenth-century references to crofts near parks, including at Myerscough (Lancs.) and elsewhere, but not, of course, within them.[47]

The presence of a park had other negative side effects on arable cultivation and mixed farming. Fallow deer are voracious eaters and must have been a menace to crops as much as young trees and grass.[48] While park-making could reduce the damage caused by deer by enclosing them, it was not always a complete solution.[49] Many parks must have been poorly enclosed, since park perimeters decayed over time: wood rotted, walls crumbled and fell down.[50] Enclosure was expensive and neglect common, especially by absentee lords,

---

[40] Beresford 1954: 302; Munby 1977: 132.   [41] Above, pp. 51–3.
[42] Ryan 1999: 178, 182, 183.   [43] Cantor and Hatherly 1977: 437.
[44] Cantor 1970–1: 20 ('Park End').   [45] Spufford 2000: 295. See also Squires 1992: 49 (fig. 2), 50.
[46] *VCH Oxon.*, viii. 224, 225, 215 (map).
[47] Higham 2004: 123. See also Godber (ed.) 1964: ii. 242; MCO, Basingstoke 12.
[48] *Rot. Parl.* ii. 313a; Coates 1964–9: 138. Cf. Manning 1993: 117, 125.
[49] For the problems caused by deer in open chases see Stamp (ed.) 1930–3: iv. 471. At Petworth (Sussex) in the mid-14th cent. there were arrangements for a reap-reeve to guard the lord's corn at night against injury by deer from the forest of Arundel, particularly the oats on the hill by the forest: Salzman (ed.) 1955: 78, 84.
[50] *CPR, 1247–58*, 21; *1281–90*, 382; Stamp (ed.) 1930–3: iv. 81; Linnard 2000: 56 (a vivid description of decayed palings and deer straying outside Marsley park in Denbigh in 1595). Cf. Steane 1994: 459–60.

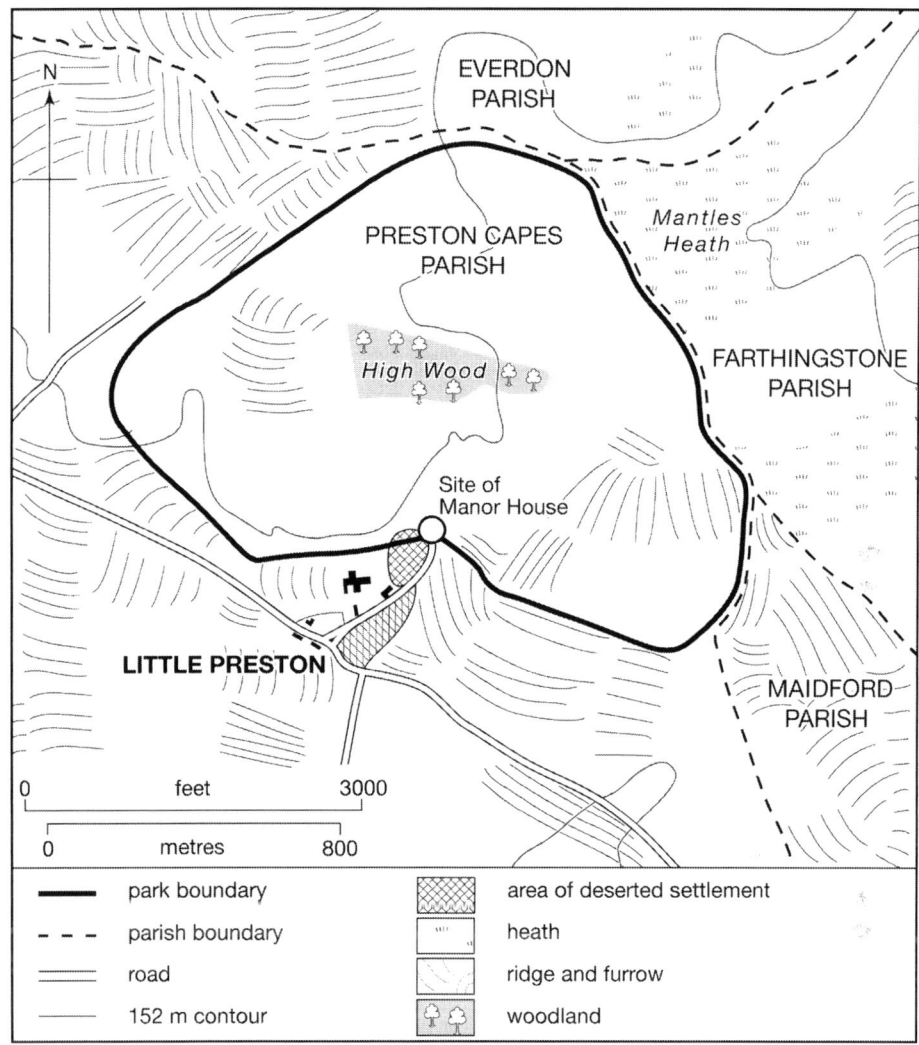

Fig. 22. Little Preston park, Preston Capes (Northants.). This 350-acre park was created to the east of the village of Preston Capes and immediately north of the smaller settlement of Little Preston. The area of the former park includes blocks of ridge and furrow, at least some of which may be from cultivation prior to the creation of the park, rather than after its abandonment. The establishment of the park, perhaps partly from farmland as well as waste, almost certainly had a limiting effect on the potential development of the adjacent settlements, particularly Little Preston.

Source: RCHM Northants., iii. 167. © Crown Copyright. NMR.

including kings themselves.⁵¹ Where tenants were supposed to carry out repairs or pay for them they were no doubt reluctant; Henry III used the threat of damage to crops by animals escaped from Woodstock park to encourage locals to maintain the park walls.⁵² Parks that were part of wider forests or chases caused particular problems. Deer were sometimes let out of the park for hunting, and gates might be opened to mix up the deer stock, perhaps to prevent inbreeding.⁵³ At Wyre (Shrops.) in the 1270s it was said that Roger Mortimer had made it so that for a distance of some three miles deer could easily get in and out of his park, to the great harm of the whole area; he had created a large chase in the woods round about, preventing their owners and others from hunting there.⁵⁴ Similar porosity can be seen at Woodstock around the same time.⁵⁵ Where rabbit warrens were associated with parks the destruction by game animals would tend to be increased.

Besides the impact on farmland, parks could also cause disruption to roads and communications, which affected tenants as much as landowners.⁵⁶ Park-makers usually wanted to stop or at least strictly control access through their parks: small gates and paths for entry to perform labour services or enter with stock might be created, but larger roads and cart ways were often removed. The hundred rolls provide some fifteen complaints about road stoppages, mostly from the 1250s to 1270s, and inquisitions *ad quod damnum* give some thirteen further examples of disruption to access, especially from the fourteenth century.⁵⁷ Inquisitions often suggest that little harm resulted from stoppages and diversions, but this was not always the case. Sometimes access through the park area was entirely blocked;⁵⁸ on other occasions those passing through were charged for the privilege.⁵⁹ Disruption of access to fields, mills, or to routes between settlements could be anticipated.⁶⁰ For instance, the rather nugatory compensation given to the men of Ludgershall (Wilts.) on the extension of the royal park there in 1348 was partly to recompense revenue lost because 'the paths and ways leading to the town through the field from the north are now closed, whereby men and merchants no longer come to the town to do business there'.⁶¹ Where park-makers provided alternative routes these must often have been less direct and locals would have had to travel further to reach their

---

⁵¹ After a period of neglect, escapes of deer prompted royal orders for repairs to the broken down boundaries of Clarendon park, c.1327–31: CCR 1327–30, 18, 269, 329, 332, 341; 1330–3, 185.
⁵² CCR, 1227–31, 500. Local people were much exercised about poor repairs to the enclosure in the 1250s, towards which they had financially contributed: *Rot. Hund.* ii. 41.
⁵³ Bond 1997: 31.   ⁵⁴ *Rot. Hund.* ii. 108. Cf. Birrell 1994: 44–5.
⁵⁵ TNA: PRO, C143/3, no. 34.   ⁵⁶ Above, p. 154.
⁵⁷ TNA, PRO, C143/2, no. 5 (1257); C143/2, no. 38 (1268); C143/11, no. 10 (1287); C143/28, no. 7 (1298); C143/71, no. 18 (1308); C143/95, no. 10 (1313); C143/142, no. 1 (1318); C143/149, no. 3 (1321); C143/259, no. 11 (1341); C143/377, no. 17 (1372); C143/384, no. 10 (1374); C143/445, no. 9 (1413); C143/450, no. 32 (1445); *Rot. Hund.* i. 41, 46, 113, 133, 175, 179, 192, 200, 205, 237 (cf. apparently the same case in ii. 50).
⁵⁸ *Rot. Hund.* i. 41.   ⁵⁹ Ibid. i. 46.
⁶⁰ *CPR, 1247–58*, 100; TNA: PRO, SC8/155/7720.   ⁶¹ *CPR, 1348–50*, 148–9.

properties or adjoining settlements.[62] The amount of litigation over closures or diversions was, unsurprisingly, limited but topographical evidence of roads skirting park perimeters and depression marks in parkland marking the route of former lanes raises the possibility of diversions and destructions in many other places where no documentary record survives.[63] A good example appears to be at De La Beche in Aldworth (Berks.), where the enclosure of a park in the early fourteenth century seemingly led to the closure of two roads and the construction of alternative routes up much steeper gradients.[64]

This kind of disruption to settlements, fields, roads, and tracks was important enough, but the enclosure of woods, scrub, and rough grazing within parks also had a serious impact in itself, on peasants and townsmen alike. Woods and wastes were as important to ordinary people as to their social betters and the manifold uses they made of this terrain demonstrate its continuing value.[65] Arable farming was almost everywhere supplemented by the keeping of livestock and, since animals' food needs could not necessarily be satisfied by fallow fields, meadows, or pasture closes alone, woodland and waste provided much-prized additional grazing and fodder.[66] At the same time, timber and underwood was vital for building and farm use, for rural crafts and industries, and for fuel.[67] Nuts and berries were gathered for food; honey acted as a sweetener; thistledown was collected for pillows and mattresses; young buds were eaten; and herbs were used as medicines, toiletries, and dyes.[68] Wild animals and birds provided a source of additional protein, often captured in traps or snares.[69]

Lordly attempts to regulate access to this common ground had a long history and their controls took many forms besides park-making. Already from the ninth century the establishment of more local lordship and administration may have put new restrictions on lesser locals' use of this terrain, as land was more closely parcelled up.[70] Measures to control the use of untilled ground contributed to unrest in Normandy as early as 966.[71] Nonetheless, the twelfth and thirteenth centuries saw a step-change in the intensity of land use and in lords' corresponding imposition of control; 'rights' to hunting and fishing, pasturing, and wood-gathering were 'constantly encroached upon by the growing definition and development of lordship'.[72] Parks, although specialized in function, were an important part of this development.

---

[62] This is illustrated by Hey 1975: 111; Franklin 1989: 165; MacGregor 1983: 16 (alignment of Roman road altered by early royal park); Way 1997 on Godmanchester (1135–54) and Wimpole (1302); Cantor and Hatherly 1979: 81; *VCH Oxon.*, v. 65.

[63] Beresford 1971: 193; Cantor and Hatherly 1979: 81; *VCH Staffs.*, x. 40.

[64] Above, Fig. 13.   [65] Britnell 2004: 311.

[66] Hoskins and Stamp 1963: 36; Neilson 1940: 447; Trow-Smith 1957: 98–105; Michelmore 1979: 7.

[67] Birrell 1969.

[68] Birrell 1987: 26–7; Thomas 1983: 71–3; Hoskins and Stamp 1963: 44–9 (where Hoskins sets out the long-lasting ethos of thrift and self-sufficiency in the peasant economy).

[69] Birrell 1996: 71–4.   [70] Biddick 1984: 111–13; Faith 1997: 3–4, 153–4.

[71] Hilton 1973: 70–1.   [72] Neilson 1942: 59.

In all sorts of ways, the enclosure of uncultivated land within parks was inherently likely to cause tension. For all the growing layers of restrictions, woods and the wastes remained in a real sense the last resort from lordship. They had a special aura as the hideout of a counter-society of rebels and criminal gangs, who sometimes obtained a romantic, even heroic, status, which could appeal to the independent-minded spirit of ordinary folk.[73] There seems to have been a strong sense of a kind of 'public domain' beyond the fields where everyone ought to have access to the fruits of nature,[74] and significant elements of communal organization of the use of this land remained in place.[75] There was also a long-standing idea that wild creatures should be free targets for all huntsmen:[76] custom seems to have allowed local people of all social levels to hunt and trap unmolested, as long as they did not do it in privileged hunting reserves, damage property, or enter closes.[77] As remaining woods and rough pastures came to be more intensively used, they were more valued, by peasants as much as by lords. In fact, according to one pair of economic historians, there was 'something like a battle' over common rights between lords and tenants by the thirteenth century.[78] And since peasants were actually involved in enclosure as well, one might add 'between tenant and tenant' too.[79]

There can be little doubt that the local impact of parks in restricting the use of these resources was significant. A high park fence, locked gates, and on-site parker would have given a much greater degree of control over wood-pasture than had usually been exercised hitherto.[80] Park-makers typically made every attempt to exclude others from claiming grazing, gathering, and hunting rights in their parks: only favoured individuals or religious houses normally retained any privileges, and these privileges were often focused on 'outwoods' or other areas remaining outside the park proper.[81] In this respect, parks were much

---

[73] Keen 2000: ch. 11; Holt 1982: ch. 6.   [74] Hilton 1973: 40.
[75] Vinogradoff 1892: 276.
[76] Bartlett 2000: 674; Hilton 1973 40: 70–1; Marvin 1999: 235; Hoppitt 1992: i. 160, 166.
[77] Turner (ed.) 1901: p. cxxiii; *VCH Sussex*, ii. 295; Marvin 1999: 229 and n. 26.
[78] Miller and Hatcher 1978: 39. Cf. Stamper 1988: 147–8 on shortage of pasture for tenant animals.
[79] Dyer 2005: 58–66.
[80] For examples of locks and other efforts to control access see Slade and Lambrick (eds.) 1990 and 1992: i. 299–300; Kerr 1925: 68; Mosley 1832: 349, 351, 353.
[81] Van Caenegem (ed.) 1990 and 1991: ii. 671; Reedy (ed.) 1995: 145, 165; *Extenta Manerii: SR* i. 242–3; MCO, King's Somborne A122; Hilton 1966: 120; *CPR, 1232–47*, 234; Hunter (ed.) 1835: 49, 84; Todd (ed.) 1997: no. 202; *Catalogue of Ancient Deeds*, iv. 338; Hallam 1981: 148–9; Lyons (ed.) 1884: 184; Rees (ed.) 1985: nos. 139, 140; Stevenson (ed.) 1987: no. 207; Bennett (ed.) 1999: no. 1011 (p. 128); *VCH Sussex*, vi/2.106–7; *CIM* iv, no. 396; TNA:PRO, C66/48, m. 1; E32/249; SC8/35/1716; SC8/47/2336. The following complaints about park-making causing the loss of common rights are recorded in the hundred rolls: *Rot. Hund*. i. 41 (appropriation of 200 acres of common), 133 (enclosure of a large part of the common of the sokemen of Knaresborough), 169 (enclosure of a wood where many men had common rights), 175 (enclosure of 60 acres of common pasture in two parks), 190 (appropriation of a park in a wood where there was common), 428 (park and pond on land that ought to be common); ii. 14 (enclosure of wood which ought to have been common), 33 (enclosure of park where local free men should have chase and common), 50 (imparking of 5 acres of common pasture and wood), 54 (imparking of a wood in the forest, which ought to be common).

more exclusive than surrounding forests, where substantial common rights were preserved.[82] Once the park was established lords or their estate managers could decide on the level of grazing or other uses which would be permitted and set fees and periods of use unfettered by any previous custom, in contrast to areas of common wood or pasture where tenants typically had a certain amount of animal grazing and wood-gathering free of charge or for a small payment.[83] Lords' courts handed out fines for unauthorized use of park resources,[84] and although some apparent fines for theft may have been simple payments for casual use, the time and money spent on policing and prosecuting offenders suggests a real desire to limit access, especially where fines were set at a level several times higher than the market price.[85] The craftsmen and charcoal burners who operated in wooded areas were often excluded from parks, including where they were allowed to rent the use of nearby coppices.[86] Even those officials or tenants who were granted or purchased some access might be shut out at particular times of the year, for example when deer were rutting or fawning.[87]

Tenants were occasionally compensated for loss of access to imparked woods and wastes, but this was less common than compensation for loss of tenancies or common rights in the cultivated fields. Most often 'compensation' took the form of confirming existing access in the untilled ground that was left elsewhere in the manor, and more substantial free tenants were better able to secure this than others.[88] The experience of the archbishop of Canterbury's tenants at Bexley (Kent) in the 1280s was probably fairly typical: the tenants claimed that they used 'of old' to feed their pigs in West Wood, summer and winter, but that 'now that the woods are in part destroyed [presumably by assarting] and in part lie in the park they have none of these things'.[89] What is unusual is that their complaint was recorded in a rental and survey and thus survives.

A closer look at one particular example may help to give a flavour of the kinds of difficulties that could be experienced, and Plumpton in Inglewood forest (Cumberland) provides a well-recorded instance of the impact of park-making on a neighbouring community, in this case an upland, pastoral one. The park here seems to have been created and extended in the thirteenth and earlier fourteenth century in the teeth of considerable local opposition. In 1268 an inquiry was held into men illegally entering ('breaking') the park.[90] It seems likely that they were trying to exercise or reclaim long-held pasture rights, an explanation which is strengthened by the findings of an inquisition of the same

---

[82] See, e.g. Schumer 1999: 49; Bazeley 1910: 269; Birrell 1988: 163.
[83] Birrell 1987: 38–9. Birrell points out that pig pannaging was exceptional in almost always being subject to a 'significant direct payment' wherever it was allowed, including in common woods.
[84] e.g. TNA: PRO, SC6/955/4; Ridgard (ed.) 1985: 11.
[85] May 1973: 391; Alston 1992: 5; Rimington 1971: 12. Cf. also Birrell 1988: 152–4.
[86] Moorhouse 1981: 687–9. [87] Stamp (ed.) 1930–3: iv. 82.
[88] See e.g. CPR, 1374–7, 183–4; TNA: PRO, C143/387, no. 13. [89] Du Boulay 1966: 137, 215.
[90] TNA: PRO, C47/12/1/3.

year into a proposed extension of the park. The inquiry found that putting a certain new area 'in defence' and adding it to the park would harm the grazing rights of locals by precluding use of two areas, one apparently three miles by eighty perches and the other around three quarters of a mile by ten perches; access of livestock to river water in the summer would also be hindered. The jury of knights, foresters, and other men cautiously stated that the king could carry out the extension in so far as he was the owner of the land; as for the harm to locals, they were uncertain as to whether the king had enfeoffed them with these rights.[91] The difficulties rumbled on: in the early 1270s justices were commissioned to hear a case of trespass in the park involving the steward of the northern forests and the king of Scotland and his men of Penrith.[92] In August 1274 a further commission was sent to inquire whether Alexander, king of Scotland and his men of Penrith and Salkeld had been accustomed to have common of pasture in any part of the park.[93] By $c.$1309 the park was in a state of decay, but this only served to change the nature of the grievances, rather than remove them: the locals requested the park be properly enclosed to stop them being fined for their animals which wandered into it from adjacent forest commons.[94] Finally, in the early 1330s, a large wall was built around the park,[95] forming a formidable physical barrier and a powerful reminder of the English king's control over the landscape. By the mid-fourteenth century local men were paying sizeable sums for grazing and wood-gathering in the park,[96] their access very much on the terms determined and price demanded by the king and his officers.

The sensitive political circumstances of this border region have left us with an unusual concentration of evidence, but it is the extent of surviving information that is exceptional, not the situation. Other similar tensions seem to have existed in many places, including in the lowlands. A good example is Ducklington (Oxon.), where detailed legal evidence suggests how the new park of William de Dives interfered with the agricultural arrangements of the wealthy and well-connected abbot of Eynsham and his tenants in the 1240s.[97] A number of Edward II's park enclosures seem to have been equally contentious and some were documented because complaints were made to the new regime after his deposition, for instance regarding Clipstone park (Notts.),[98] and Windsor, where new imparkment supposedly removed the common pasture rights of the 'poor gentz', making it hard for them to make ends meet and pay their rents.[99]

But besides its effects on farming and woodland use, park-making also represented a dramatic privatization of hunting. Parks did not cover such large areas as

---

[91] TNA: PRO, C143/2, no. 38.   [92] TNA: PRO, C47/12/1/4.
[93] *CPR, 1272–81*, 69.   [94] TNA: PRO, SC8/164/8167.
[95] Young 1979: 116.   [96] Winchester 2007: 176.
[97] *VCH Oxon.*, xiii. 129; Salter (ed.) 1906–7 and 1908: i, nos. 250–1; TNA: PRO, JUST 1/699, m. 22v.; *CRR, 1249–50*, 179–80. For some idea of the number of tenants see *Rot. Hund.* ii. 700–1.
[98] Crook 1976: 36–9, 41–4.   [99] TNA: PRO, SC8/201/10005.

forests and chases, but the enclosed park was probably easier to maintain and police as a private hunting ground. All free men expected to be able to hunt at least lesser game freely outside forests and other reserves, and the unwonted establishment or extension of private hunting grounds through rights of free warren was by far the single greatest abuse by lords reported in the hundred rolls.[100] Parks themselves were sometimes complained about in this respect,[101] and many other complaints about 'warrens' may have also related to parks, at least in part, even where these are not specifically mentioned.[102] Parks and warren rights were very often combined and the resulting reserve could attract considerable opposition in some circumstances, as at Isleworth (Middx.) where the park and warren was seen as an infringement upon Londoners' civic rights.[103]

Given all the potential causes of conflict over parks, it is not surprising that detailed local studies suggest that parks could engender widely felt and long-lasting opposition. An analysis of the court rolls from the Clare manor of Thornbury (Glos.), for example, suggests that the enclosure of around 1,200 acres of parkland in the late thirteenth century created a dispute over pasture rights there that rumbled on over a period fifty years and more and particularly involved middling and lesser tenants.[104] In the mid-thirteenth century, the townsmen of Beverley (Yorks.) had made an agreement with the archbishop of York to remove common rights to allow him to create a deer park, but were apparently unhappy with the exchange. From the 1260s many expressed their displeasure by trespassing and poaching in the park; the tensions appear to have recurred until the sixteenth century.[105] At Somersham (Hunts.) there were persistent attempts to burn down the park fences in the early fourteenth century.[106] Although organized attacks on parks were often gentry-led, they too normally relied on local collusion and involvement and large numbers of people sometimes participated, not all of whom could have the ringleaders' tenants or direct dependants.[107] Some poachers were members of more or less professional

---

[100] Above, p. 168; *Rot Hund.*, passim. In 1280 a rare, if not unique, inquisition *ad quod damnum* into a proposed grant of free warren rights reported that the new reserve would be harmful to all those in the vicinity, 'both rich and poor alike', who had previously hunted with dogs after hares, foxes, rabbits, and pheasants on the land in question: TNA: PRO, C143/5, no. 9 (Snorscombe, Northants.). Such concerns were irrelevant to the king's right to create an exclusive hunting area, of course, and licence was subsequently granted: *CChR, 1257–1300*, 198.

[101] *Rot. Hund.* i. 168 (enclosure of a wood where king and local free men ought to be able to hunt), 169 and 181 (appropriation of rights of chase in enclosed wood), 541 (appropriation of chase in two parks); ii. 30 (enclosure of a park where there was common chase of the king), 33 (enclosure of park where local free men should have chase and common).

[102] e.g. there was a complaint in 1275 about William Raleigh, bishop of Norwich (1239–43), enclosing a wood in Gaywood (Norf.) and claiming warren there (*Rot. Hund.* i. 543); elsewhere this is referred to as a park (*CCR, 1237–42*, 193).

[103] *Rot. Hund.* i. 404, 414, 417, 428, 429, 432. On the claims of London's citizens to extensive privileges in hunting lesser game by the later 12th cent. see Douglas and Greenaway (eds.) 1981: 1029–30.

[104] Franklin 1989: 158, 160; 1996: 179.   [105] Neave 1991: 11–12.   [106] Way 1997: 75.

[107] See, e.g. Marvin 1999; Harvey 2004; *CPR, 1313–17*, 598 (Haynes park, Beds., 1316), *CPR, 1327–30*, 277 (Marston Moretaine, Beds., 1328).

gangs and others were probably involved for the thrill of an activity which could, paradoxically, bridge social divides and join together family and household groups against local rivals. But many park-breakers were perhaps simply trying to take a share of what they felt they had been unfairly denied. As suggested earlier, the link between political crisis and park breaks was clear, but there was also a broad connection with high grain prices, especially in the period up to the early fourteenth century.[108]

THE LATER MIDDLE AGES

The period after the Black Death was a profoundly different one, characterized by demographic collapse and continued low population, rather than land hunger and growing numbers of mouths to feed. In this respect parks could not have had quite the same kind of impact. However, their potential social effects in this period should certainly not be discounted. If overall standards of living were perhaps somewhat higher, the benefits were unevenly shared and poverty remained common.[109] Many smaller villages and hamlets, particularly in champion areas, suffered from declining population and wealth and some historians have seen lordly enclosures and evictions as strongly contributing to the social problems in these places.[110]

Contemporary criticism of enclosure, including deer parks, was certainly more strongly expressed from the later fifteenth century than ever before. John Rous, a chantry priest and antiquary, complained about the evils of enclosure to the Coventry parliament in 1459 and later compiled a list of some fifty-eight deserted Warwickshire villages. As he saw it, villages were destroyed to make way for parks and great pastures and these blocked roads and water courses; where there had been fields around towns there was now wood, undergrowth, and hideouts for robbers and criminals; where there had been people there was only the nourishment of sheep and cattle or wild beasts, such as rabbits, hares, foxes, and deer.[111] Chancellor John Russell picked up on a similar theme in a draft of his speech for the opening of the parliament proposed for November 1483, pointing to the selfishness of members of the body politic, each looking only to their own interests, including by carrying out 'closures and enparkynge' which led to the 'driving away of tenants and letting down of tenantries'.[112] A number of sixteenth-century commentators saw park-making as a social travesty, trampling established rights, hindering farming, and causing rural poverty.[113]

---

[108] Above, pp. 156–7; Way 1997: 112 (fig. 8.1).
[109] Britnell 1996: 229 (table 6); Dyer 1994: 349–62; Hatcher 1996: 259–63.
[110] See, e.g. Fryde 1996: 185–208.   [111] Hearne (ed.) 1745: 123–6.
[112] Watts 2002: 36–8; Chrimes (ed.) 1936: 180–1.
[113] Ellis (ed.) 1807–8: i. 343–6; Edelen (ed.) 1968: 256–9.

These comments did have some basis in reality. The hundreds of new deer parks created and existing parks extended in the post-Black-Death period did often cause the conversion of arable to parkland and this was sometimes controversial. The extensive later fourteenth-century royal imparking of arable near castles and houses in the south-east, for example, seems often to have required sitting tenants to be bought out and caused clergy to lose tithes, with compensation being apparently retrospective and reluctant.[114] Such actions tended to cause secondary damage to settlements, as at Castle Bolton in the Yorkshire Pennines where new imparkment in 1379 seems to have brought an end to arable farming,[115] or at Windsor (Berks.), where by 1466 'certain tenements in the town are threatened with ruin and the inhabitants have come to great poverty, and two hundred acres of land ... adjoining the town, which they held at fee farm for pasture and cultivation for payment of the farm of the town, have been lately enclosed by the king for a park' (see Fig. 23).[116] Many of the proposed new parks of the fifteenth century were large and some truly enormous.[117] Such huge parks would have carved out large parts of parishes and most would probably have resulted in the dispossession of at least some tenants, as apparently occurred at Thornbury (Glos.) when the earl of Buckingham greatly enlarged his parkland in the early sixteenth century.[118] Big parks were also particularly likely to affect communications, as at Castle Bolton, where the Richmond to Bolton road was diverted.[119]

However, the overall effect of late medieval park-making on settlements and arable farming was limited and has to be put into context. For a start, we ought to realize that if Rous and others were self-consciously reflecting a new conception of a wider 'public' or 'commonwealth', they did not fully understand the causes of decay. They knew little of the particular local circumstances and gave too much weight to lordly action instead of recognizing it as a secondary factor after initial changes.[120] The disappearance of the overwhelming majority of the 2,000 or more villages and large number of hamlets and isolated farms that were lost in the period c.1370–1520 and the contraction of many other places had absolutely nothing to do with deer parks. Nor were other more common forms of enclosure, like stock grazing grounds, the primary cause of settlement decay.[121] Overall population remained low thanks to recurrent epidemics and low birth rates, with depopulation worse in smaller, less prosperous settlements, which people left to look for better opportunities elsewhere. In

---

[114] The following references are to park-making by Edward III, unless otherwise stated: *CCR, 1354–60*, 218–21, 633; *CPR, 1354–58*, 137–8 (Black Prince), 489; *1361–4*, 439 (Queen Philippa); *1364–7*, 95–6, 221; *1367–70*, 101–2, 136, 233, 239; *1370–4*, 273, 328–9; *1374–7*, 179.

[115] Beresford 1971: 195.   [116] *CPR, 1461–7*, 551; Fig. 23, overleaf.

[117] *CPR, 1401–05*, 164; *1422–9*, 477; *1429–36*, 446; *CChR, 1427–1516*, 94–5, 112–13, 137, 242, 268; *CPR, 1476–85*, 203–4; *1485–94*, 367. Note also those grants that allowed for the imparking of whole manors: *CPR, 1441–46*, 282–3; *1467–77*, 184, 421; *CChR, 1427–1516*, 242; *CPR, 1476–85*, 151, 162.

[118] Finberg 1975: 90; Chandler (ed.) 1993: 186; Harding and Lambert 1994: 5; Rawcliffe 1978: 64–5.

[119] Rowley 1986: 137 (caption).

[120] Dyer 1982: 25; Lomas 1992: 161–2; Bolton 1980: 218–19.   [121] Dyer 2002: 350–3.

Fig. 23. Norden's map of Windsor Little Park (1607), showing the proximity of the park to the east of the town. The Little Park was established by Edward III and extended by Edward IV.
Source: BL, Harley 3749, ff. 5v–5. © British Library Board. All rights reserved.

many places lords tried for a long time to retain tenants and only eventually enclosed land when locals no longer wanted it, as in parts of the west Midlands or at Ampthill and Millbrook (Beds.).[122]

Although park-making could lead to fairly brutal evictions, these were not widespread or on a large scale and new parks were often only one aspect of landowners' larger landscape reorganizations. My search has revealed only some thirty-odd places where imparking certainly or almost certainly contributed to evictions or desertions over the whole period c.1400–1520.[123] Some

---

[122] Dyer 1991: 80–1; Jack (ed.) 1965: 107–8. See also Cantor 1987: 108.
[123] Wilde, in Hampstead Norris, Berks.; Great Woolstone, Bucks.; Castle Camps, Cambs.; 'Hallendaves' and 'Penbruglith' in Lanhadron, St Ewe, Corn.; Thornbury, Glos.; Highclere, Hants.; Pendley, Herts.; Staunton Harold and Bradgate, Leics.; Hanworth, Twickenham, and Hampton, Middx.; Peterborough, Easton Neston, and Wicken, Northants.; Sutton Passeys and Wiverton, Notts.; Stourton and Great Sandon, Staffs.; Cestersover, Charlecote, Compton Wynyates, and Stoneleigh, Warks.; Wittenham, Wilts.; and East Lilling (Sheriff Hutton Park), Gawthorpe, Steeton, Hornby, Stittenham, Thornton Bridge, Wilstrop, and Brandsby (where the village was destroyed and a smaller settlement created further west), Yorks. Less clear cases include Liscombe, in Soulbury, Bucks.; Linton, Cambs.; Washingley, Hunts.; Lathom, Lancs.; Althorp, Boughton, and Charwelton, Northants; Baddesley Clinton, Budbrooke, and Fulbrook, Warks.; Shap, Westml.; and Bashall Eaves, Yorks.

parks seem to have been associated with substantial depopulation, like those at Pendley (Herts.), Wiverton (Notts.), and Hornby and Wilstrop (Yorks.),[124] but mostly it was small and struggling settlements that were affected.[125] Of the fifty-one instances of enclosure for deer parks alleged in the 1517 reports, thirteen (a quarter) apparently involved depopulation.[126] In all it was alleged that 188 people had been evicted from these places, although often only tenants were referred to and this figure would have to be multiplied several times to include their families.[127] Rous's figures, although not to be trusted too far, suggest that the situation was similar earlier in the fifteenth century: his list of fifty-eight places partly or wholly depopulated within, roughly, a twelve-mile radius of Warwick in the first three-quarters of the century included only five cases (or 9 per cent) of destructions relating to imparking—exactly the same percentage as after 1489 in this county. No doubt some cases have escaped record, but almost certainly deer parks were only a small cause of the shifts in settlement experienced in some parts of England in the later middle ages.

Nonetheless, for all these caveats, parks did continue to cause widespread social tensions: it is simply that these are not to be understood solely in terms of depopulation or the conversion of arable to grassland, which was only one dimension of the economic problem. Perhaps more significant was the issue of common rights to grazing land in pastoral areas, areas that were left out of the remit of the 1517 enclosure inquiry, with its focus on lost arable husbandry.[128] As we saw earlier, parks continued to tie up valuable non-arable resources, which were not fully exploited within their bounds.[129] Despite a reduction in population and some spread of woods and wastes, there was still demand for the products they could offer. The issue of common rights was only 'partly defused by demographic collapse':[130] there was no longer the pressure that a high population put on the products of wood and waste, but there was, in places, continued or even increased demand for pasture from other lords and peasants who were expanding their cattle and sheep herds, especially in the later fourteenth and earlier fifteenth centuries.[131] Even in the mid-century slump, demand cannot be measured solely in terms of the mixed and often slack rental market for pasture, since many animals were traditionally grazed for little or no

---

[124] Beresford 1954: 147–8, 210, 302–6; 1971: 205; Fryde 1996: 199; Leadam (ed.) 1904: 51; Dodsworth (ed.) 1904: 232.
[125] For interesting case studies see Cameron 1977: 56–8; Stevenson and Squires 1999: 12, 14, 25, 28, 29.
[126] Places allegedly affected were Wilde, in Hampstead Norris (Berks.); Great Woolstone (Bucks.); Worthington and Staunton Harold (Leics.); Peterborough, Easton Neston, and Wicken (Northants.); Wiverton (Notts.); Compton Wynyates and Stoneleigh (Warks.); and Hendon, Hanworth, and Hampton (Middx.).
[127] Wilde, 4; Great Woolstone, 3; Worthington and Staunton Harold, 24; Peterborough, 50 (with other non-park enclosures probably leading to a further 34 evictions); Easton Neston, 34; Wicken, c.13; Compton Wynyates, 20; Stoneleigh, 20; Wiverton, c.20; Hanworth, 12; Twickenham, 4; Hampton, 12.
[128] Thirsk 1967: 214–16. [129] Above, pp. 72–6. [130] Birrell 1987: 49.
[131] Dyer 2002: 331, 338, 343, 348–9, 360; Campbell 2000: 171.

charge in woods and wastes and on the fallow open fields, and in depressed areas access to fuel or feed for a few animals could be extremely important to struggling locals. In places, especially near urban areas, wood remained a valuable commodity too.[132] New enclosure of parkland thus continued to play a potentially significant role in restricting access to wood-pasture resources, putting them more firmly under kings' or lords' control, as at East Worldham (Hants.) in the 1370s,[133] or at Holt in Leicestershire in the 1440s.[134] The enclosure of meadowland, like at Hertingfordbury (Herts.), could have a particularly pronounced effect on local tenant farming.[135] And although sometimes parts of existing parks were farmed out to tenants as pasture in the later middle ages, as at Beckley (Oxon.),[136] as well as agistment going on as before, and some parks were poorly maintained and policed, considerable swathes of parkland remained carefully reserved for deer and demesne use.

Even in areas that might be assumed to have contained considerable untilled ground, it is clear that free access to pasture in particular could be in demand and that imparkment was still seen as an affront to pre-existing customary uses. The most serious—and best-recorded—incidents of conflict tend to come where important local landlords lined up behind their aggrieved tenants, as occurred at Wolseley (Staffs.) in the 1460s when Sir John Gresley and the bishop of Coventry opposed the park-making of Ralph Wolseley.[137] But even without a lordly lead, tensions could erupt into violence or at least formal protest. At Stoke Gifford (Glos.) in the late 1390s new imparkment by Sir Maurice Berkeley provoked a riot over the alleged loss of common pasture rights.[138] In 1412 copyholders at Great Barrington (Glos.) complained that the prior of Llanthony's new park had deprived them of land and animals in the open fields.[139] Likewise, in 1448 tenants at Pendley (Herts.), where a park was licensed in 1440, made it known that they were being prevented from exercising common grazing rights over eighty acres.[140] And nor was it simply new imparkments that were the issue. Long existing parks remained unpopular too, like the prior's park at Whitmore, near Coventry. The citizens of the town seem to have regretted their earlier decision to renounce their claims to the land in the park: locals continued to trespass in it throughout the fifteenth century, breaking fences and taking wood, in open defiance of the priors.[141]

But, besides all these economic issues, there were the old questions of hunting, leisure, and status: in this period in particular the impact of parks has to be

---

[132] Carpenter 1992: 180–1; Wright 2003: 73.

[133] Edward III's 30-acre extension of East Worldham park apparently left tenants of the vill of Binswood with insufficient pasture: TNA: PRO, C143/387, no. 13.

[134] The park which Thomas Palmer was licensed to create here in 1448 would have enclosed all or part of one of the largest wooded areas in eastern Leicestershire: CChR, 1427–1516, 100; Acheson 1992: 59–61.

[135] Rowe 2009: 124.   [136] VCH Oxon., v. 67.
[137] Mander (ed.) 1935: 78–9.   [138] CPR, 1396–99, 365.   [139] VCH Glos., vi. 19.
[140] Munby 1977: 133.   [141] VCH Warks., viii. 201–2; Harris (ed.) 1907–13: ii. 444–6, 455.

understood in more than simply material terms. Parks were also highly significant as a social, perhaps now a class, concern. The elite privileging of game and hunting seems to have rankled more than ever before thanks to the heightened aspirations of many increasingly literate and self-confident ordinary folk. With more leisure time on their hands than their predecessors, these men were angered by exclusion from an activity which was becoming an increasingly important expression of independence and social standing. This applied most notably to some disgruntled yeomen, who stood on the fringes of political society, but who were in many ways denied a full role in it; these men could afford hunting dogs and had some leisure to hunt, but could not afford their own hunting reserves.[142] The economic issue was focused in particular areas, but the social tension was more universal, although perhaps particularly strongly felt in the more prosperous and politically aware south-east.

Parks and other hunting reserves were an affront to popular culture. Strong resentment of landowners' reservation of the privilege of hunting was clearly demonstrated in 1381 when the rebels' demands included the specification that 'all game, whether in waters or in parks and woods should become common to all, so that everywhere in the realm, in rivers and fishponds, and woods and forests, they might take the wild beasts, and hunt the hare in the fields and do many other things without restraint'.[143] Despite the harsh repression of the revolt and subsequent legislation against lesser men keeping dogs for hunting,[144] tensions over hunting between lesser and greater remained very much alive and well. In 1419 the knights and burgesses in the Commons were again complaining about 'artificers, labourers, servants and grooms (*garcions*)' spending feast days, 'when good Christians are at church hearing divine service', hunting in parks, warrens and coneygarths of seigneurs and others, to their very great destruction,[145] and there were periodic indictments of illegal hunting under the legislation of 1390 throughout the fifteenth century.[146] Parks remained both one of the main sources of game and one of the principal methods of restricting access to it.[147] Although some poaching in parks must have gone undetected, these reserves continued to be policed by their owners' officials and illicit hunters and trappers who were apprehended were fined heavily, especially those who took deer rather than smaller game.[148] In periods

---

[142] Harriss 2005: 253; Harvey 2004: 175–7.

[143] Martin (ed.) 1995: 219. See Faith 1984: 65–8 for the symbolic trespass in the warren at St Albans during the Peasants' Revolt, and, more generally, on poaching as one of the most frequent kinds of challenge to aristocratic privilege in the late 14th cent.

[144] Above, p. 145.   [145] *Rot. Parl.* iv. 121–2.

[146] Pollard 2004: 89. Numerous cases were brought in Kent in the 1420s: personal communication from Andrew Prescott.

[147] It seems unlikely, contrary to some suggestions, that game was in abundant supply in the open countryside: above, pp. 6, 29.

[148] See e.g. Scrope 1852: 163, 165–6, 208, 243; Harris (ed.) 1907–13, ii. 446, 458; Preece 1991: 58.

of unrest poaching by yeomen and husbandmen in parks and other reserves could become a form of sedition, as in Kent in 1450,[149] and the fact that parks were targeted reinforces the idea that ordinary people resented them as symbols of aristocratic privilege.

In many ways then, later medieval imparking was far from marginal or uncontentious. Hunting and venison eating remained key markers of fine living and fifteenth-century parks often stood at the centre of attempts by new men to assert their aristocratic credentials in the locality. The parks themselves had a significant impact, much of which is to be understood in terms of social relations, cultural norms, and expectations as well as economics. Grandeur and social tension were inextricably mixed together. By blocking roads or restricting access to fields and pastures the park-maker was seen to be cocking a snook at the established practices of the community, even its very existence—this was what so animated critics of enclosure and imparking like Bishop Russell. Little wonder that parks remained tempting targets for aristocratic rivals, aggrieved locals, and criminal gangs. Or that sometimes aristocratic feud and local discontent could unite in spectacular fashion, as at Wolseley, or at Wilstrop (Yorks.) in the late 1490s, where a small-scale war was waged over depopulation, enclosure of fields, and a new park encroaching on the common.[150]

MEASURING THE FOOTPRINT OF PARKS

The evidence in this chapter suggests that the creation of several thousand parks over the course of the middle ages had a far more considerable social effect than usually appreciated. Large as well as small settlements were affected in a number of ways, from the restriction of the growth of streets and tofts, the more effective limitation and policing of access for pasture and fuel, the restriction of farming expansion, the disruption of communications, and the seizure of land or at least its removal from productive use. Of course, levels of disruption varied, and some of it was overcome: parks were unevenly distributed, and sometimes park-makers lacked the power to override existing local land uses.[151] A certain amount of authorized and unauthorized access continued after parks were created: a degree of poaching and removal of trees, branches, and herbage was difficult to stop, especially where landowners were absentee or parks in decay.[152] A few lesser locals even gained employment as (sub-)parkers

---

[149] Virgoe (ed.) 1964: 217–18; Du Boulay 1966: 190; Harvey 2004: 176. Note also the poaching raid in the early 1430s on William Scott and Archbishop Kempe's park at Birling (Kent): *CPR, 1429–36*, 273. For fear of sedition as a motivation behind legislation aimed to curb poaching in Henry VII's reign see above, p. 145.

[150] Brown (ed.) 1909: 16–17; Coates 1964–9: 137.   [151] See e.g. Saul 1986: 190.

[152] Bond 1998: 24, 27, 30; Acheson 1992: 60–1; Saltman (ed.) 1962: no. 264; McIntosh 1986: 4, 163; Crook 1976: 36, 38; Franklin 1989: 155, 158.

or gate-keepers (with more serious duties than their betters), receiving pay, land, and perks in return.[153] But these men usually formed a very small minority of the local population, and for others parks more often caused inconvenience and distress. For many local communities, these large, exclusive enclosures must have been among the least positive aspects of lords' reorganization of the landscape.

Just occasionally we can catch distant glimpses of what ordinary men and women may have felt about parks. In the Chiltern parish of Fingest (Bucks.), the park-making activities of Henry Burghersh, bishop of Lincoln (1320–40), apparently evoked such strong negative feelings as to become the stuff of local legend. Fingest was the location of an episcopal manor house, which the bishops occasionally visited,[154] and it seems that Burghersh's park of over 300 acres took in large areas of arable land, including tenant plots, probably in the early 1330s.[155] Very unusually, a monastic chronicler, Walsingham, recounts a local tale that reveals much about how the inhabitants felt about the new park.[156] Burghersh (*cupidus et avarus*) had offended God in hurting the poor people with his park-making and because of this his soul could not rest. He was condemned to walk as a ghostly keeper of his own park, dressed in green, with huntsman's horn and bow and arrows.

[153] For some examples see Kerr 1925: 64–5; Slade and Lambrick (eds.) 1990 and 1992: i. 299–300; VCH Oxon., xiii. 130 (Ducklington); Franklin 1989: 154–5.
[154] VCH Bucks., iii. 42.
[155] Vanderzee (ed.) 1807: 334; CPR, 1330–34, 16; C66/174, m. 30; Parker 1903: 470–1; VCH Bucks., iii. 43–4; Holborow 1999: 174–5. Traces of ridge and furrow and possible lynchets are visible on the slopes to the west of Hanger wood and the land in the surrounding valley bottoms is stony, but by no means infertile: personal observation, 2004. See also above, Fig. 7.
[156] Riley (ed.) 1863–4: i, 254–5. Walsingham's abbey (St Albans) was situated a dozen or so miles to the north-east of Fingest; the house had possessed the manor until handing it over to the bishops in the 1160s (VCH Bucks., iii. 42).

Conclusion

The preceding chapters should have made it clear that parks were far from marginal to medieval life, but deserve a prominent place in the social history of the middle ages. These reserves were much more important to the concerns of the aristocracy than has usually been suggested, and they had a strong, and often negative, effect on many rural communities and some urban ones. Their significance was social and cultural, as well as jurisdictional and economic. The park was an obvious bastion of individual privilege that in the right circumstances could provoke outright aggression, whether it was newly established or a long felt presence. And parks neither perished in the later middle ages, nor were totally transformed in that period, as often supposed. These insights stem from a closer definition of parks themselves and the purposes which they served. It is by making an argument for aristocratic deer hunting as the central rationale behind the great bulk of medieval park-making that it has been possible to put the other functions of parks in clearer context.

By reasserting the key importance of hunting in aristocratic social life it can be shown that parks had an integrity of purpose that lies at the heart of their significance, and this takes us closer to understanding why they were set up and how others reacted to them. In particular, it helps us to see that the idea of earlier and later medieval parks being totally different in character is wrong. Recent studies suggest that an interest in landscape setting was sometimes present much earlier than the late fourteenth or fifteenth century, and this is something which this research to some extent reinforces. But they still display a familiar tendency to see a shift away from practicalities (like hunting and deer-keeping) towards more abstract representation and reinforcement of ideas in the later middle ages ('landscaping' and status assertion). In this way, newer narratives have retained the old divisions between periods and between practical and symbolic elements, despite having undermined their foundations.

Of course, we must recognize that the park was not a monolithic and unvarying phenomenon. Not only were there differences between parks in terms of size and character, but the use made of individual parks could shift over time, as has been effectively demonstrated by Richardson's recent study of the great royal park at Clarendon. Elements of variation and change cannot be ignored and underline the ever-present dangers for the historian in attempting to filter out the 'essential' from the 'peripheral' in understanding social phenomena. In other words, if there were probably differing contemporary views about the purpose of something like the castle,[1] the same must apply to the park. But to focus solely on nuance, variety, and subjectivity in meaning is to risk a similar foreshortening of insight as that which comes from antiquarian description of individual examples. There are common patterns and they need to be identified and used in understanding individual cases, even if each example remains unique and open to contrasting interpretations. It is only when we properly appreciate the role of hunting that we can capture the important continuities in the character of many parks across the middle ages.

This does nothing to diminish the wider insights that parks can offer: it simply gives them a centre of gravity. As major, and perhaps increasingly pre-eminent, hunting reserves, deer parks occupied a unique position in the social landscape as a meeting point for a variety of groups and a range of often conflicting ideas. These enclosed areas seem to have roused particular sensitivities in contemporaries because of the way in which they helped their owners to define who was to be involved with and, just as importantly, who was to be excluded from hunting—an activity closely associated with the assertion of social leadership and high standing. It was this role which made the properly ordered public hunt such a valued but also potentially abrasive assertion of lordship, and which made poaching an emotionally charged and symbolically rich activity which had the potential to unite the excluded, even where they were members of different social groups. It also served to give the non-aristocratic hunt servant, forester, or parker a special, almost contradictory and no doubt awkward social position as a bridge between the building of aristocratic cultural values and their subversion.

These unique characteristics of parks gave them a rich and significant role in more general developments in social relations in the countryside, rather than in any way separating them from them. The negotiations and confrontations that surrounded parks emerge as an important part of the early history of enclosure, a process that involved the shaping of social norms as well as of agrarian practices. Most obviously, as very strong assertions of possession over tracts of land, parks can help us to chart shifts in lordship and the organization and control of the landscape. In particular, park-making throws light on a larger and longer running definition of rights of individual ownership over woods and uncultivated ground, and disputes and litigation over hunting and land use show how controversial and how complex this process could be. Royal franchise, perceived rights of lordship, and, later, the proprietary rights of landownership were at stake as much as traditional practices and customary freedoms. Park-makers staked all sorts of powerful claims, which local aristocrats and communities had to respond to, whether by assimilation, negotiation, or outright

---

[1] Austin 1984: 69; Johnson 2002: 10–11.

opposition. The various reactions of wider groups to parks thus help us to uncover popular views on lordship and customary rights and the nature of the potential tension between lord and tenant over land use. Conflicts over parks provide a window not only on changing attitudes to ownership of the landscape, especially that beyond the tilled fields, and the growth of more clearly defined legal concepts of property (over land, beasts, and activities), but also on the developing relationships between classes.

From the lords' point of view, parks also shed an interesting side light on more recent research emphasizing the rational, flexible, market-focused aspects of much medieval farming and estate management.[2] In other words, if lords and their officials could be concerned with efficiency and profits, the culture of the aristocracy and their leisure interests ensured that non-economic considerations also had a strong influence, which has sometimes been in danger of being overlooked. Historians are now becoming more alive to the role of culture in influencing economic behaviour,[3] and this book provides a contribution to this. The presence of so many large and expensively enclosed deer parks across the medieval countryside reminds us of the great differences between medieval landlords and their eighteenth-century successors, and, more generally, between the medieval world and our own.

Studies of medieval society often operate through a relatively limited range of sources and this has a strong influence on the kind of picture that emerges. By focusing instead on one feature of medieval life in depth, over a long period and through a wide variety of evidence, novel approaches can be opened up to a host of social, economic, and even political history topics. Parks may in this way be used as a vantage point on such fundamental matters as the distribution of resources, social controls over the use of space, and, ultimately, the construction and expression of an increasingly differentiated social hierarchy. Such a methodology underlines the benefits of adopting techniques that have traditionally been largely alien to a particular discipline, for example, using map-making to explore legal history or prosopography to understand the context of landscape features. The findings of this kind of thematic and interdisciplinary study may help promote a still richer appreciation of medieval social dynamics.

[2] Mate 1985: 30–1; Campbell 2000: 1, 10, 12; Stone 2005.
[3] A good recent example is Rosser 2003.

Bibliography

MANUSCRIPT SOURCES

Bedfordshire and Luton Archives

H/DE 433 (Survey of Brogborough Park, 1728).
THOMPSON, J. S. (ed.), 'Bailiffs' Accounts, 1382–97: Willington, Haynes, Shirehatch in Beds., and Wing in Bucks.', unpublished transcript (1978).

Berkshire Record Office

D/EZ 77 (Records of Chamberhouse manor, Thatcham, 1306–1800).

Bibliothèque nationale de France, Paris

MS Fr. 616 (Gaston de Foix, *Livre de Chasse*).

Bodleian Library, University of Oxford

MS Douce 335 (15th-century manuscript of the *Master of Game*).

British Library, London

Harley 1885 (Dunstable Cartulary).
Harley 2278 (Lives of Saints Edmund and Fremund, presentation copy for Henry VI).
Harley 3749 (Description of the Honor of Windsor, John Norden, 1607).
Add. Roll 32141.

Buckinghamshire Record Office

AR1/93/1/2 (15th-century court rolls of Fawley manor).

Hampshire Record Office

11M59/B1 (Bishopric of Winchester Pipe Rolls, 1208–1711).

Magdalen College, Oxford

Otterbourne 10.
Otterbourne 72.
King's Somborne 76.
King's Somborne A 122.

Oxfordshire Record Office

ORO, P328/F/1 (typed abstract of expenses of Humphrey Stafford of Grafton, 15th-century).

St John's College, Oxford

Kirtlington Survey, 1750.

The National Archives: Public Record Office

C1 (Chancery, Six Clerks' Office, Richard II to Philip and Mary).
C132–139 (Chancery, inquisitions *post mortem*, Henry III to Henry VI).
C143 (Chancery, inquisitions *ad quod damnum*, Henry III to Richard III).
C145 (Chancery, inquisitions miscellaneous).
C47 (Chancery, miscellanea).
C53 (Chancery, charter rolls, 1199–1517).
C66 (Chancery, patent rolls, 1201–).
CP23 (Court of Common Pleas, rex rolls, 1327–1409).
CP40 (Court of Common Pleas, plea rolls, 1273–1874).
E13 (Exchequer of Pleas, plea rolls, 1236–1875).
E28 (Exchequer, Treasury of the Receipt, council and privy seal records, *c.*1327–*c.*1603).
E32 (Justices of the Forest, records formerly in the treasury of the receipt of the exchequer, etc., 1180–1672).
E101 (King's Remembrancer, accounts various, *c.*1154–*c.*1830).
JUST 1 (Justices in eyre, of assize, of oyer and terminer, of the peace, etc., rolls and files, 1198–1528).
KB27 (Court of King's Bench, plea and crown sides, coram rege rolls, 1273–1702).
SC6 (Special Collections, ministers' and receivers' accounts, Henry III to 18th century).
SC8 (Special Collections, ancient petitions, Henry III to James I).

PRINTED PRIMARY SOURCES

ANON. (ed.), 1836, 'Narrative of the Reception in England of Louis Seigneur de la Gruthuyse', *Archaeologia*, 26 (London), 275–80.

ARMITAGE-SMITH, S. (ed.), 1911, *John of Gaunt's Register, 1372–1376*, 2 vols., Camden Society, 3rd ser. 20–1 (London).

ARNOLD, M. S. (ed.), 1985 and 1987, *Select Cases of Trespass from the King's Courts 1307–1399*, 2 vols., Selden Society, 100 and 103 (London).

BAIGENT, F. J. (ed.), 1891 for 1890, *A Collection of Records and Documents Relating to the Hundred and Manor of Crondal*, Hampshire Record Society (London).

BAILLIE-GROHMAN, WM A. and F. (eds.), 1904, *The Master of Game by Edward, Second Duke of York: The Oldest English Book on Hunting* (London).

BAKER, J. H. (ed.), 1997, *Spelman's Reading on Quo Warranto*, Selden Society, 113 (London).

BARRON, W. R. J. (ed.), 1998, *Sir Gawain and the Green Knight*, rev. edn. (Manchester).

BATES, R. (ed.), 1998, *Regesta Regum Anglo-Normannorum: The Acta of William I (1066–1087)* (Oxford).

BENNETT, N. (ed.), 1999, *The Registers of Bishop Henry Burghersh, 1320–1342: I*, Lincoln Record Society, 87.

BENSON, L. D. (ed.), 1987, *The Riverside Chaucer*, 3rd edn. (Oxford).

BIRRELL, J. R. (ed.), 2006, *Records of Feckenham Forest, Worcestershire, c.1236–1377*, Worcestershire Historical Society, NS 21.

BOND, E. A. (ed.), 1866–8, *Chronica Monasterii de Melsa*, 3 vols., Rolls Series (London).

BOTFIELD, B. (ed.), 1841, *Manners and Household Expenses of England in the Thirteenth and Fifteenth Centuries* (London).

BROWN, W. (ed.), 1909 for 1908, *Yorkshire Star Chamber Proceedings*, YAS, Record Series, 41.

BYERLY, B. F. and C. R. (eds.), 1977, *Records of the Wardrobe and Household, 1285–1286* (London).

—— —— (eds.), 1986, *Records of the Wardrobe and Household, 1286–1289* (London).

CANNON, H. L. (ed.), 1918, *The Great Roll of the Pipe, 26 Henry III, AD 1241–2* (New Haven).

CASSON, L. F. (ed.), 1949, *The Romance of Sir Degrevant*, EETS 221 (London).

Catalogue of Ancient Deeds, 1890–1915, 6 vols. (London).

CHANDLER, J. (ed.), 1993, *Leland's Itinerary: Travels in Tudor England* (Stroud).

CHIBNALL, M. (ed.), 1969–80, *Orderic Vitalis: The Ecclesiastical History*, 6 vols. (Oxford).

CHRIMES, S. B. (ed.), 1936, *English Constitutional Ideas in the Fifteenth Century* (Cambridge).

CLOUGH, M. (ed.), 1969, *Two Estate Surveys of the Fitzalan Earls of Arundel*, Sussex Record Society, 67.

COSS, P. R. (ed.), 1986, *The Early Records of Medieval Coventry* (London).

DAHLBERG, C. (ed.), 1995, *The Romance of the Rose. Guillaume de Lorris and Jean de Meun*, 3rd edn. (Princeton).

DALE, M. K. (ed.), 1950, *Court Roll of Chalgrave Manor, 1278–1313*, Bedfordshire Historical Record Society, 28.

DAVIES, R. T. (ed.), 1963, *Medieval English Lyrics: A Critical Anthology* (London).

DICKENS, A. G., and MYERS, J. N. L. (eds.), 1951, *The Register or Chronicle of Butley Priory* (Winchester).

DODSWORTH, R. (ed.), 1904, *Yorkshire Church Notes, 1619–31*, Yorkshire Archaeological Society Record Series, 34.

DOUGLAS, D. C., and GREENAWAY, G. W. (eds.), 1981, *English Historical Documents, 1042–1189*, 2nd edn. (London).

DU BOULAY, F. R. H. (ed.), 1964, 'The Pipe Roll Account of the See of Canterbury During the Vacancy after the Death of Archbishop Pecham, 1292–5', in F. R. H. Du Boulay (ed.), *Documents Illustrative of Medieval Kentish Society*, Kent Records, 18, 41–57.

EDELEN, G. (ed.), 1968, *The Description of England by William Harrison* (New York).

ELLIS, H. (ed.), 1807–8, *Holinshed's Chronicles of England, Scotland and Ireland*, 6 vols. (London).

—— (ed.), 1809, *Hall's Chronicle, containing the History of England during the Reign of Henry the Fourth and the succeeding Monarchs*, collated from the 1548 and 1550 edns. (London).

—— (ed.), 1846, *Polydore Vergil's English History*, i, Camden Society, OS 36 (London).

Farrer, W. (ed.), 1907, *Lancashire Inquests, Extents, and Feudal Aids, Part II, AD 1310–1333*, Record Society of Lancashire and Cheshire, 54.

Fedrick, A. S. (ed.), 1970, *Beroul, The Romance of Tristan* (London).

Field, R. K. (ed.), 2004, *Court Rolls of Elmley Castle, Worcestershire, 1347–1564*, Worcestershire Historical Society, ns 20.

Fisher, J. L. (ed.), 1946, *Cartularium Prioratus de Colne*, Essex Archaeological Society, Occasional Publications, 1 (Colchester).

Fowler, G. H. (ed.), 1935, *Records of Harrold Priory*, Bedfordshire Historical Records Society, 17.

—— (ed.), 1937, 'Calendar of Inquisitions Post Mortem. No. II', *Bedfordshire Historical Record Society*, 19, 111–70.

Giles, J. A. (ed.), 1845, *The Chronicles of the White Rose of York* (London).

Godber, J. (ed.), 1964, *The Cartulary of Newnham Priory*, 2 vols., Bedfordshire Historical Record Society, 43.

Gray, D. (ed.), 1985, *The Oxford Book of Late-Medieval Verse and Prose* (Oxford).

Greatrex, J. (ed.), 1978, *The Register of the Common Seal of the Priory of St. Swithun, Winchester, 1345–1497*, Hampshire Record Ser. 2 (Winchester).

Greenway, D., and Sayers, J. (eds.), 1989, *Jocelin of Brakelond: Chronicle of the Abbey of Bury St. Edmunds* (Oxford).

Greenwell, W. (ed.), 1857 for 1856, *Bishop Hatfield's Survey*, Surtees Society, 32.

Hallam, E. M. (ed.), 1984, *The Itinerary of Edward II and his Household, 1307–28*, List and Index Society, 211.

Halliwell, J. O. (ed.), 1839, *Warkworth's Chronicle*, Camden Society, 10 (London).

Hands, R. (ed.), 1975, *English Hawking and Hunting in the Boke of St. Albans* (Oxford).

Hardy, T. D. (ed.), 1837, *Rotuli Chartarum in Turri Londinensi Asservati*, i/1 (London).

Harper, R. J., Caley, J., and Minchin, W. R. (eds.), 1823–34, *Ducatus Lancastriae*, 3 vols. (London).

Harris, M. D. (ed.), 1907–13, *The Coventry Leet Book*, 4 vols., Early English Text Society, 134–5, 138, 146 (London).

Harrop, P., Booth, P., and Harrop, S. (eds.), 2005, *Extent of the Lordship of Longdendale*, Record Society of Lancashire and Cheshire, 140.

Hart, W. H., and Lyons, P. A. (eds.), 1884–93, *Cartularium Monasterii de Rameseia*, 3 vols., Rolls Series (London).

Harvey, J. H. (ed.), 1969, *William Worcestre: Itineraries* (Oxford).

Hearne, T. (ed.), 1745, *Johannis Rossi, Historia Regum Angliae* (Oxford).

Hector, L. C., and Harvey, B. F. (eds.), 1982, *The Westminster Chronicle, 1381–1394* (Oxford).

Hewlett, H. G. (ed.), 1886–9, *Rogeri de Wendover liber qui dicitur Flores Historiarum*, 3 vols., Rolls Series (London).

Hog, T. (ed.), 1845, *F. Nicholai Triveti, de Ordine Frat. Praedicatorum, Annales Sex Regum Angliae* (London).

Hollings, M. (ed.), 1934–50, *The Red Book of Worcester*, 4 vols., Worcestershire Historical Society.

Hull, P. L. (ed.), 1971, *The Caption of Seisin of the Duchy of Cornwall (1337)*, Devon and Cornwall Record Society, ns 17 (Exeter).

HUNTER, J. (ed.), 1833, *Magnum Rotulum Scaccarii vel Magnum Rotulum Pipae de Anno Tricesimo-Primo Regni Henrici Primi* (London).
—— (ed.), 1835, *Pedes Finium* (London).
JACK, R. I. (ed.), 1965, *The Grey of Ruthin Valor* (Sydney).
JAMES, M. R., BROOKE, C. N. L., and MYNORS, R. A. B. (eds.), 1983, *Walter Map. De Nugis Curialium. Courtiers' Trifles* (Oxford).
JOHNSON, C., and CRONNE, H. A. (eds.), 1956, *Regesta Regum Anglo-Normannorum, 1066–1154*, ii. *Regesta Henrici Primi, 1100–1135* (Oxford).
KEKEWICH, M. L., RICHMOND, C., SUTTON, A. F., VISSER-FUCHS, L., and WATTS, J. L. (eds.), 1995, *The Politics of Fifteenth-Century England: John Vale's Book* (Stroud).
KINGSFORD, C. L. (ed.), 1919, *The Stonor Letters and Papers, 1290–1483*, 2 vols., Camden Society, 3rd ser. 29–30 (London).
KIRBY, J. W. (ed.), 1996, *The Plumpton Letters and Papers*, Camden Society, 5th ser. 8 (Cambridge).
LEADAM, I. S. (ed.), 1897, *The Domesday of Inclosures, 1517–1518*, 2 vols. (London).
—— (ed.), 1904, *The Domesday of Inclosures for Nottinghamshire*, Thoroton Society, Record Ser. 2.
LE PATOUREL, J. (ed.), 1957 for 1956, *Documents Relating to the Manor and Borough of Leeds*, Thoresby Society, 45.
LIEBERMANN, F. (ed.), 1894, *Über Pseudo-Cnuts Constitutiones de Foresta* (Halle).
LOCK, R. (ed.), 1998, 2002, *The Court Rolls of Walsham le Willows, I and II*, 2 vols., Suffolk Record Society, 41 and 45.
LOYD, L. C., and STENTON, D. M. (eds.), 1950 for 1942, *Sir Christopher Hatton's Book of Seals*, Northamptonshire Record Society, 15.
LUARD, H. R. (ed.), 1866, *Annales Monastici*, iii. *Annales Prioratus de Dunstaplia (A.D. 1–1297); Annales Monasterii de Bermundeseia (A.D. 1042–1432)*, Rolls Series (London).
—— (ed.), 1872–83, *Matthaei Parisiensis, Monachi Sancti Albani, Chronica Majora*, 7 vols., Rolls Series (London).
LUCE, S., and RAYNAUD, G. (eds.), 1869–99, *Chroniques de Froissart*, 11 vols. (Paris).
LUMBY, J. R. (ed.), 1889–95, *Chronicon Henrici Knighton*, 2 vols., Rolls Series (London).
LYONS, P. A. (ed.), 1884, *Two Compoti of the Lancashire and Cheshire Manors of Henry de Lacy, Earl of Lincoln, 24 and 33 Edward I (1294–6; 1304–5)*, Chetham Society, OS 112.
LYSONS, S. (ed.), 1814, 'Copy of a Roll of Purchases made for the Tournament of Windsor Park, in the Sixth Year of King Edward the First, Preserved in the Record Office at the Tower', *Archaeologia*, 17, 297–310.
MAITLAND, F. W. (ed.), 1887, *Bracton's Note Book: A Collection of Cases Decided in the King's Courts During the Reign of Henry III* (London).
—— HARCOURT, L. W. V., and BOLLAND, W. C. (eds.), 1910–13, *The Eyre of Kent 6 & 7 Edward II, A.D. 1313–1314*, 3 vols., Selden Society, 24, 27, 29 (London).
MANDER, G. P. (ed.), 1935 for 1934, *History from the Wolseley Charters*, in Collections for a History of Staffordshire, William Salt Archaeological Society (Kendal), 53–94.
MARKLAND, M. F. (ed.), 1979, *John of Salisbury, Policraticus* (New York).
MARTIN, G. H. (ed.), 1995, *Knighton's Chronicle, 1337–1396* (Oxford).

Mason, E. (ed.), 1980 for 1971–3, *The Beauchamp Cartulary Charters, 1100–1268*, Pipe Roll Society, ns 43.

Meekings, C. A. F. (ed.), 1961 for 1960, *Crown Pleas of the Wiltshire Eyre, 1249*, Wiltshire Archaeological and Natural History Society, Records Branch (Devizes).

Midgley, L. M. (ed.), 1942 and 1945, *Ministers' Accounts of the Earldom of Cornwall, 1296–1297*, 2 vols., Camden Society, 3rd ser. 66 and 68 (London).

Monro, C. (ed.), 1863, *Letters of Queen Margaret of Anjou*, Camden Society, os 86 (London).

Morris, J. (ed.), 1978, *Domesday Book: Buckinghamshire* (Chichester).

Myers, A. R. (ed.), 1959, *The Household of Edward IV* (Manchester).

Mynors, R. A. B., Thomson, R. M., and Winterbottom, M. (eds.), 1998–9, *William of Malmesbury, Gesta Regum Anglorum*, 2 vols. (Oxford).

Newton, K. C. (ed.) 1960, *Thaxted in the Fourteenth Century*, Essex Record Office Publications, 33 (Chelmsford).

Offord, M. Y. (ed.), 1959, *The Parlement of The Thre Ages*, EETS 246 (London).

Oschinsky, D. (ed.), 1971, *Walter of Henley and Other Treatises on Estate Management and Accounting* (Oxford).

Page, M. (ed.), 1996, *The Pipe Roll of the Bishopric of Winchester, 1301–2*, Hampshire Record Ser. 14 (Winchester).

—— (ed.), 1999, *The Pipe Roll of the Bishopric of Winchester, 1409–10*, Hampshire Record Series, 16 (Winchester).

Palmer, J. et al. (eds.), *Domesday Explorer*, Hull University electronic database: http://www.domesdaybook.net

Pullen, B. (ed.), 1966, *Sources for the History of Medieval Europe from the Mid-Eighth to the Mid-Thirteenth Century* (Oxford).

Purvis, J. S. (ed.), 1936, *The Chartulary of Healaugh Park*, YAS Record Ser. 92.

Raban, S. (ed.), 2001, *The White Book of Peterborough*, Northamptonshire Record Society, 41.

Reedy, W. T. (ed.), 1995 for 1989–91, *Basset Charters, c.1120–1250*, Pipe Roll Society, ns 50 (London).

Rees, U. (ed.), 1985, *The Cartulary of Haughmond Abbey* (Cardiff).

Ridgard, J. (ed.), 1985, *Medieval Framlingham. Select Documents 1270–1524*, Suffolk Records Society, 27 (Woodbridge).

Riley, H. T. (ed.), 1863–4, Thomas Walsingham, *Historia Anglicana*, 2 vols., Rolls Series (London).

—— (ed.), 1870–1, *Amundesham, Annales Monasterii S. Albani*, 2 vols., Rolls Series (London).

Roberts, C. (ed.), 1835–6, *Excerpta è Rotulis Finium*, 2 vols. (London).

Safford, E. W. (ed.), 1974–7, *Itinerary of Edward I*, 3 vols., List and Index Society, 103, 132, 135.

Salter, H. E. (ed.), 1906–7 and 1908, *Eynsham Cartulary*, 2 vols., Oxford Historical Society, 49 and 51.

—— (ed.), 1947–8, *The Thame Cartulary*, 2 vols., Oxfordshire Record Society, 25–6.

Saltman, A. (ed.), 1962, *The Cartulary of Tutbury Priory*, Royal Commission on Historical Manuscripts, 2 (London).

SALZMAN, L. F. (ed.), 1903, *An Abstract of Feet of Fines Relating to the County of Sussex, 2 Rich. I–33 Hen. III*, Sussex Record Society, 2.

—— (ed.), 1955, *Ministers' Accounts of the Manor of Petworth, 1347–1353*, Sussex Record Society, 55.

SHIRLEY, W. W. (ed.), 1862–6, *Royal and Other Historical Letters Illustrative of the Reign of Henry III*, 2 vols. (London).

SLADE, C. F. (ed.), 1962 for 1960, 'Whitley Deeds of the Twelfth Century', in P. M. Barnes and C. F. Slade (eds.), *A Medieval Miscellany for Doris Mary Stenton*, Pipe Roll Society, NS 36, 235–46.

—— and LAMBRICK, G. (eds.), 1990 and 1992 for 1988–9 and 1990–1, *Two Cartularies of Abingdon Abbey*, 2 vols., Oxford Historical Society, NS 32 and 33.

SNEYD, C. A. (ed.), 1847, *A Relation of the Island of England about the Year 1500*, Camden Society, OS 37.

STACY, N. E. (ed.), 2001, *Surveys of the Estates of Glastonbury Abbey, c.1135–1201* (Oxford).

STAGG, D. J. (ed.), 1983, *A Calendar of New Forest Documents: The Fifteenth to the Seventeenth Centuries*, Hampshire Record Ser. 5.

STAMP, A. E. (ed.), 1930–3, *The Black Prince's Register*, 4 vols. (London).

STAPLETON, T. (ed.), 1839, *Plumpton Correspondence*, Camden Society, OS 4 (London).

STENTON, D. M. (ed.), 1932, *Pipe Roll 10 Richard I*, Pipe Roll Society, NS 9 (London).

—— (ed.), 1933, *Pipe Roll 1 John*, Pipe Roll Society, NS 10 (London).

—— (ed.), 1934, *Pipe Roll 2 John*, Pipe Roll Society, NS 12 (London).

—— (ed.), 1936, *Pipe Roll 3 John*, Pipe Roll Society, NS 14 (London).

—— (ed.), 1940, *Pipe Roll 6 John*, Pipe Roll Society, NS 18 (London).

STENTON, F. M. (ed.), 1922 for 1920, *Charters of Ghilbertine Houses*, Lincoln Record Society, 18.

STEVENSON, J. H. (ed.), 1987 for 1986, *The Edington Cartulary*, Wiltshire Record Society, 42 (Devizes).

STUBBS, W. (ed.), 1913, *Select Charters*, 9th edn., rev. by H. W. C. Davis (Oxford).

SUTHERLAND, D. W. (ed.), 1982–3 for 1981–2, *The Eyre of Northamptonshire*, 2 vols., Selden Society, 97 and 98.

THORNE, S. E. (ed.), 1968–77, *Bracton on the Laws and Customs of England*, 4 vols. (Cambridge, Mass.).

TILANDER, G. (ed.), 1956, *La Vénerie de Twiti*, Cynegetica, 2 (Uppsala).

TODD, J. M. (ed.), 1997, *The Lanercost Cartulary*, Cumberland and Westmorland Antiquarian and Archaeological Society Record Ser. 11, Surtees Society, 203.

TOOMEY, J. P. (ed.), 2001, *Records of Hanley Castle, Worcestershire, c.1147–1547*, Worcestershire Historical Society, NS 18.

TOPHAM, J. (ed.), 1787, *Liber Quotidianus Contrarotulatoris Garderobae Anno Regni Regis Edwardi Primi Vicesimo Octavo* (London).

TOULMIN SMITH, L. (ed.), 1964, *The Itinerary of John Leland in or about the years 1535–1543*, re-edn., 5 vols. (Carbondale, Ill.).

TREHARNE, R. F., and SANDERS, I. J. (eds.), 1973, *Documents of the Baronial Movement of Reform and Rebellion, 1258–1267* (Oxford).

TRIGG, S. (ed.), 1990, *Wynnere and Wastoure*, EETS 297 (Oxford).

TURNER, G. J. (ed.), 1901 for 1899, *Select Pleas of the Forest*, Selden Society, 13 (London).

VAN CAENEGEM, R. C. (ed.), 1990 and 1991, *English Lawsuits from William I to Richard I*, 2 vols., Selden Society, 106 and 107 (London).
VANDERZEE, G. (ed.), 1807, *Nonarum Inquisitiones in Curia Scaccarii Temp. Regis Edwardi III* (London).
VINAVER, E., and FIELD, P. J. C. (eds.), 1990, *The Works of Sir Thomas Malory*, 3rd edn., 3 vols. (Oxford).
VIRGOE, R. (ed.), 1964, 'Some Ancient Indictments in the King's Bench Referring to Kent, 1450–1452', in F. R. H. Du Boulay (ed.), *Documents Illustrative of Medieval Kentish Society*, Kent Records, 18, 214–65.
WARNER, G. (ed.), 1912, *Queen Mary's Psalter* (London).
WHITELOCK, D. (ed.), 1961, *The Anglo-Saxon Chronicle* (London).
WOOLGAR, C. M. (ed.), 1992–3, *Household Accounts from Medieval England*, 2 vols., British Academy, Records of Social and Economic History, NS 17 and 18 (Oxford).
WRIGHT, T. (ed.), 1839, *The Political Songs of England*, Camden Society, OS 6 (London).
—— (ed.), 1863, *The Historical Works of Geraldus Cambrensis* (London).
WROTTESLEY, G. (ed.), 1885, 'Extracts from the Plea Rolls, A.D. 1272 to A.D. 1294', *Collections for a History of Staffordshire*, William Salt Archaeological Society, VI, part 1 (London), 37–300.

SECONDARY WORKS

ACHESON, E., 1992, *A Gentry Community. Leicestershire in the Fifteenth Century, c.1422–c.1485* (Cambridge).
ADAMS, I. H., 1976, *Agrarian Landscape Terms: A Glossary for Historical Geography* (London).
ALEXANDER, J. J. G., 1983, 'Painting and Manuscript Illumination for Royal Patrons in the Later Middle Ages', in V. J. Scattergood and J. W. Sherborne (eds.), *English Court Culture in the Later Middle Ages* (London), 141–62.
ALLMAND, C., 1997, *Henry V* (New Haven and London)
ALMOND, R., 2003, *Medieval Hunting* (Stroud).
—— and POLLARD, A. J., 2001, 'The Yeomanry of Robin Hood and Social Terminology in Fifteenth-Century England', *Past and Present*, 170, 52–77.
ALSTON, L., 1992, 'Lamarsh Park (The Origin and Management of a Medieval Deer Park)', *Colchester Archaeological Group Annual Bulletin*, 35, 3–16.
ALTSCHUL, M., 1965, *A Baronial Family in Medieval England: The Clares, 1217–1314* (Baltimore).
ASTILL, G., 2002, 'Windsor in the Context of Medieval Berkshire', in L. Keen and E. Scarff (eds.), *Windsor: Medieval Archaeology, Art and Architecture of the Thames Valley*, British Archaeological Association Conference Transactions, 25 (Leeds), 1–14.
ASTON, M., 1988, 'Land Use and Field Systems', in M. Aston (ed.), *Aspects of the Medieval Landscape of Somerset* (Somerset CC), 83–98.
—— 2000, *Monasteries in the Landscape* (Stroud).
ATKIN, M. A., 1994, 'Land Use and Management in the Upland Demesne of the de Lacy Estate of Blackburnshire c.1300', *AgHR*, 42/1, 1–19.

AULT, W. O., 1972, *Open-Field Farming in Medieval England* (London).
AUSTIN, D., 1978, 'Excavations at Okehampton Deer Park, Devon, 1976–1978', *Proceedings of the Devon Archaeological Society*, 36, 191–239.
—— 1984, 'The Castle and the Landscape: Annual Lecture to the Society for Landscape Studies, May 1984', *Landscape History*, 6, 69–81.
BAILEY, M., 1988, 'The Rabbit and the Medieval East Anglian Economy', *AgHR* 36/1, 1–20.
—— 2007, *Medieval Suffolk. An Economic and Social History, 1200–1500* (Woodbridge).
BARKER, P. A., 1987, 'Hen Domen Revisited', in J. R. Kenyon and R. Avent (eds.), *Castles in Wales and the Marches: Essays in Honour of D. J. Cathcart King* (Cardiff), 51–4.
BARLOW, F., 1983a, 'Hunting in the Middle Ages', in F. Barlow, *The Norman Conquest and Beyond* (London), 11–21.
—— 1983b, *William Rufus* (London).
—— 2006, review of E. Mason, *William II: Rufus, the Red King* (Stroud, 2005), *EHR* 492, 827–9.
BARTLETT, R., 2000, *England under the Norman and Angevin Kings* (Oxford).
BAZELEY, M. L., 1910, 'The Forest of Dean in its Relations with the Crown During the Twelfth and Thirteenth Centuries', *Transactions of the Bristol and Gloucestershire Archaeological Society*, 33, 153–286.
—— 1921, 'The Extent of the English Forest in the Thirteenth Century', *Transactions of the Royal Historical Society*, 4th ser. 4, 140–72.
BEAN, J. M. W., 1958, *The Estates of the Percy Family, 1416–1537* (Oxford).
BELLAMY, B., FOSTER, P., and JOHNSTON, G., 1983, 'The Royal Deer Parks of Brigstock, an Archaeological Landscape Survey', *South Midlands Archaeology Newsletter*, 13, 16–19.
BELLAMY, J. G., 1964, 'The Coterel Gang', *EHR* 79, 698–717.
—— 1965, 'The Northern Rebellions in the Later Years of Richard II', *Bulletin of the John Rylands Library*, 47, 254–74.
BENNETT, M. J., 1987, 'Careerism in Late-Medieval England', in J. Rosenthal and C. Richmond (eds.), *People, Politics and Community in the Later Middle Ages* (Gloucester), 19–39.
BERESFORD, M. W., 1954, *The Lost Villages of England* (London).
—— 1971, *History on the Ground*, rev. edn. (London).
BETTEY, J., 2000, 'Downlands', in Thirsk 2000: 27–49.
BIDDICK, K., 1984, 'Field Edge, Forest Edge: Early Medieval Social Change and Resource Allocation', in K. Biddick (ed.), *Archaeological Approaches to Medieval Europe* (Kalamazoo), 105–18.
BIDDLE, M., BARFIELD, L., and MILLARD, A., 1959, 'Excavation of the Manor of the More, Rickmansworth, Hertfordshire', *Archaeological Journal*, 116, 136–99.
BIGMORE, P., 1979, *The Bedfordshire and Huntingdonshire Landscape* (London).
BILIKOWSKI, K., 1983, *Hampshire's Countryside Heritage, V. Historic Parks and Gardens* (Winchester).
BIRRELL, J. R., 1962, 'The Forest Economy of the Honour of Tutbury in the Fourteenth and Fifteenth Centuries', *University of Birmingham Historical Journal*, 8, 114–34.
—— 1969, 'Peasant Craftsmen in the Medieval Forest', *AgHR* 17/2, 91–107.

BIRRELL, J. R., 1982, 'Who Poached the King's Deer? A Study in Thirteenth-Century Crime', *Midland History*, 7, 9–25.

—— 1987, 'Common Rights in the Medieval Forest: Disputes and Conflicts in the Thirteenth Century', *Past and Present*, 117, 22–49.

—— 1988, 'Forest Law and the Peasantry in the Later Thirteenth Century', in P. R. Coss and S. D. Lloyd (eds.), *Thirteenth Century England II* (Woodbridge), 149–63.

—— 1990–1, 'The Forest and the Chase in Medieval Staffordshire', *Staffordshire Studies*, 3, 23–50.

—— 1992, 'Deer and Deer Farming in Medieval England', *AgHR* 40/2, 112–26.

—— 1994, 'A Great Thirteenth-Century Hunter: John Giffard of Brimpsfield', *Medieval Prosopography*, 15/2, 37–66.

—— 1996, 'Peasant Deer Poachers in the Medieval Forest', in R. H. Britnell and J. Hatcher (eds.), *Progress and Problems in Medieval England: Essays in Honour of Edward Miller* (Cambridge), 68–88.

—— 2001, 'Aristocratic Poachers in the Forest of Dean: Their Methods, their Quarry and their Companions', *Transactions of the Bristol and Gloucestershire Archaeological Society*, 119, 147–54.

—— 2006, 'Procuring, Preparing and Serving Venison in Late-Medieval England', in C. Woolgar, D. Serjeantson, and T. Waldron (eds.), *Food in Medieval England: History and Archaeology* (Oxford), 176–88.

BLAIR, J., 1994, *Anglo-Saxon Oxfordshire* (Stroud).

BLANNING, T., 2007, *The Pursuit of Glory: Europe 1648–1815* (London).

BLOCKMANS, W., and JANSE, A., 1999 (eds.), *Showing Status: Representations of Social Positions in the Late Middle Ages* (Turnhout).

BOLTON, J. L., 1980, *The Medieval English Economy, 1150–1550* (London).

BOND, C. J., 1981, 'Otmoor', in *The Evolution of Marshland Landscapes* [no editor], University of Oxford Department for External Studies, 113–35.

—— 1986, 'The Oxford Region in the Middle Ages', in G. Briggs, J. Cook, and T. Rowley (eds.), *The Archaeology of the Oxford Region* (Oxford), 135–59.

—— 1994, 'Forests, Chases, Warrens and Parks in Medieval Wessex', in M. Aston and C. Lewis (eds.), *The Medieval Landscape of Wessex*, Oxbow Monograph, 46 (Oxford), 115–58.

—— 1997, 'Woodstock Park in the Middle Ages', in C. J. Bond and K. Tiller (eds.), *Blenheim. Landscape for a Palace*, 2nd edn. (Stroud), 22–54.

—— 1998, *Somerset Parks and Gardens: A Landscape History* (Tiverton).

—— 2004, *Monastic Landscapes* (London).

BOOTH, P. H. W., 1981, *The Financial Administration of the Lordship and County of Chester, 1272–1377*, Chetham Society, 3rd ser. 28 (Manchester).

BRADLEY, J. and GAIMSTER, M., 2004 (eds.), 'Medieval Britain and Ireland in 2003', *Medieval Archaeology*, 48, 229–350.

BRAND, P., 1992, *The Making of the Common Law* (London).

BRANDON, P. F., 1974, *The Sussex Landscape* (London).

BRENTNALL, H. C., 1949–50, 'Venison Trespasses in the Reign of Henry VII', *Wiltshire Archaeological Magazine*, 53: 191–212.

BRITNELL, R. H., 1977, 'Finchingfield Park under the Plough, 1341–2', *Essex Archaeology and History*, 9, 107–12.

―― 1987, 'Minor Landlords in England and Medieval Agrarian Capitalism', in T. H. Aston (ed.), *Landlords, Peasants and Politics in Medieval England* (Cambridge), 227–46.

―― 1996, *The Commercialisation of English Society, 1000–1500*, 2nd edn. (Manchester).

―― 1997, *The Closing of the Middle Ages? England, 1471–1529* (Oxford).

―― 2004, *Britain and Ireland 1050–1530: Economy and Society* (Oxford).

BROOKE-LITTLE, J. P., 1970 (ed.), *Boutell's Heraldry* (London).

BROWN, A. E., and TAYLOR, C. C., 1974, 'The Earthworks of Rockingham and its Neighbourhood', *Northamptonshire Archaeology*, 9, 68–79.

BROWN, H. PHELPS, and HOPKINS, S. V., 1981, *A Perspective of Wages and Prices* (London).

BROWN, R. ALLEN, 1954, *English Medieval Castles* (London).

BUCK, M., 1983, *Politics, Finance and the Church in the Reign of Edward II: Walter Stapeldon, Treasurer of England* (Cambridge).

BUCKLEY, C., n.d., 'Ewelme Park: The Story of a Royal Tudor Deer Park', unpublished article, Centre for Oxfordshire Studies.

BUTLIN, R. A., 2003 (ed.), *Historical Atlas of North Yorkshire* (Otley).

CAM, H., 1930, *The Hundred and the Hundred Rolls* (New York).

CAMDEN, W., 1610, *Britannia* (London).

CAMERON, A., 1977, 'The Deserted Medieval Village of Sutton Passeys', *Transactions of the Thoroton Society of Nottinghamshire*, 80, 47–62.

CAMPBELL, B. M. S., 2000, *English Seigniorial Agriculture, 1250–1450* (Cambridge).

―― 2005, 'The Agrarian Problem in the Early Fourteenth Century', *Past and Present*, 188, 3–70.

―― and BARTLEY, K., 2006, *England on the Eve of the Black Death: An Atlas of Lay Lordship, Land and Wealth, 1300–49* (Manchester).

―― GALLOWAY, J. A., and MURPHY, M., 1992, 'Rural Land-Use in the Metropolitan Hinterland, 1270–1339: The Evidence of *Inquisitiones Post Mortem*', *AgHR* 40/1, 1–22.

CANADINE, R. M., 2003, 'The Bishop of Lincoln's Residential Manors in the East Midlands During the Later Medieval and Early Tudor Period', University of Cambridge Master of Studies thesis.

CANTOR, L. M., 1962, 'The Medieval Deer-Parks of North Staffordshire', *North Staffordshire Journal of Field Studies*, 2, 72–7.

―― 1964, 'The Medieval Deer-Parks of North Staffordshire, II', *North Staffordshire Journal of Field Studies*, 4, 61–6.

―― 1970–1, 'The Medieval Parks of Leicestershire', *Leicestershire Archaeological and Historical Society*, 46, 9–24.

―― 1982, 'Forests, Chases, Parks and Warrens', in L. M. Cantor (ed.), *The English Medieval Landscape* (Philadelphia), 56–85.

―― 1983, *The Medieval Parks of England: A Gazetteer* (Loughborough).

―― 1987, *The Changing English Countryside, 1400–1700* (London).

―― and HATHERLY, J. M., 1977, 'The Medieval Parks of Buckinghamshire', *Records of Buckinghamshire*, 20/3, 431–7.

―― ―― 1979, 'The Medieval Parks of England', *Geography*, 64, 71–85.

―― and MOORE, J. S., 1963, 'The Medieval Parks of the Earls of Stafford at Madeley', *North Staffordshire Journal of Field Studies*, 3, 37–58.

CANTOR, L. M., and SQUIRES, A. E., 1997, *The Historic Parks and Gardens of Leicestershire and Rutland* (Newtown Linford).
—— and WILSON, J. D., 1961–9, 'The Mediaeval Deer-Parks of Dorset: I–IX', *Proceedings of the Dorset Archaeological and Natural History Society*, 83, 109–16; 84, 145–53; 85, 141–52; 86, 164–78; 87, 223–33; 88, 176–85; 89, 171–80; 90, 241–8; 91, 196–205.
CARPENTER, C., 1992, *Locality and Polity: A Study of Warwickshire Landed Society, 1401–1499* (Cambridge).
CARPENTER, D. A., 2003, *The Struggle for Mastery: Britain 1066–1284* (London).
CASELDINE, C. J., 1999, 'Environmental Setting', in R. Kain and W. Ravenhill (eds.), *Historical Atlas of South-West England* (Exeter), 25–34.
CHALMERS, P., 1936, *The History of Hunting* (London).
CHAPELOT, J., 1994, *Le Château de Vincennes: Une Residence Royale au Moyen Âge* (Paris).
CHAPMAN, D. and N., 1975, *Fallow Deer* (Lavenham).
CHISHOLM, H., 1910–11 (ed.), *The Encyclopaedia Britannica*, 11th edn., 29 vols. (London).
CLANCHY, M. T., 1998, *England and its Rulers, 1066–1272*, 2nd edn. (Oxford).
CLARK, G. N., 1977, *Elsfield Church and Village* (Oxford).
COATES, B. E., 1964–9, 'Parklands in Transition: Medieval Deer Park to Modern Landscape Park', *Transactions of the Hunter Archaeological Society*, 9, 132–50.
COLVIN, H. M., 1997, review of A. Emery, *Greater Medieval Houses*, i, *TLS* 13 (June), 21.
COSS, P. R., 1991, *Lordship, Knighthood and Locality: A Study in English Society c.1180–c.1280* (Cambridge).
—— 2003, *The Origins of the English Gentry* (Cambridge).
—— and KEEN, M., 2002 (eds.), *Heraldry, Pageantry and Social Display in Medieval England* (Woodbridge).
COULSON, C. L. H., 1979, 'Structural Symbolism in Medieval Castle Architecture', *Journal of the British Archaeological Association*, 132, 73–90.
—— 1982, 'Hierarchism in Conventual Crenellation: An Essay in the Sociology and Metaphysics of Medieval Fortification', *Medieval Archaeology*, 26, 69–100.
—— 1994, 'Freedom to Crenellate by Licence: An Historiographical Revision', *Nottingham Medieval Studies*, 38, 86–137.
—— 2003, *Castles in Medieval Society: Fortresses in England, France and Ireland in the Central Middle Ages* (Oxford).
COULTON, G. G., 1960, *Medieval Village, Manor and Monastery* (New York).
COX, B., 1994 (ed.), *The Place-Names of Rutland*, EPNS (Nottingham).
COX, J. C., 1875–9, *Notes on the Churches of Derbyshire*, 4 vols. (Chesterfield).
—— 1905, *The Royal Forests of England* (London).
CRAWFORD, O. G. S., 1953, *Archaeology in the Field* (London).
CREIGHTON, O. H., 2002, *Castles and Landscapes* (London).
CROOK, D., 1976, 'Clipstone Park and "Peel"', *Transactions of the Thoroton Society of Nottinghamshire*, 80, 35–46.
—— 1979, 'The Struggle over Forest Boundaries in Nottinghamshire, 1218–1227', *Transactions of the Thoroton Society*, 83, 35–45.

—— 2001, 'The "Petition of the Barons" and Charters of Free Warren, 1227–58', in P. R. Coss and M. Prestwich (eds.), *Thirteenth Century England VIII* (Woodbridge), 33–48.

—— 2002, 'The Development of Private Parks in Medieval Nottinghamshire', *Transactions of the Thoroton Society*, 106, 73–80.

—— 2003, 'The Early History of Wollaton Park and its Lords, 1283–1345', in J. Beckett (ed.), *Nottinghamshire Past: Essays in Honour of Adrian Henstock* (Cardiff), 7–20.

CROUCH, D., 1982, 'Geoffrey de Clinton and Roger, Earl of Warwick: New Men and Magnates in the Reign of Henry I', *BIHR* 55, 113–23.

—— 1992, *The Image of Aristocracy in Britain, 1000–1300* (London).

—— 1996, 'The Local Influence of the Earls of Warwick, 1088–1242: A Study in Decline and Resourcefulness', *Midland History*, 21, 1–22.

—— 2005, *Tournament* (London).

CUHN, S. M., 1981 (ed.), *Middle English Dictionary: P* (University of Michigan Press).

CUMMINS, J., 1988, *The Hound and the Hawk* (London).

—— 2002, '*Veneurs s'en vont en Paradis*: Medieval Hunting and the "Natural" Landscape', in J. Howe and M. Wolfe (eds.), *Inventing Medieval Landscapes: Senses of Place in Western Europe* (Gainesville, Fla.), 33–56.

CURRIE, C. K., 1991, 'The Early History of Carp and its Economic Significance in England', *AgHR* 39/2, 97–107.

—— 1997, 'The Boundaries of the Medieval Park at North Stoneham', *Hampshire Field Club and Archaeological Society Newsletter*, NS 27, 13–18.

DARBY, H. C., 1977, *Domesday England* (Cambridge).

DAVIES, R. R., 1978, *Lordship and Society in the March of Wales, 1282–1400* (Oxford).

—— 1987, *Conquest, Coexistence and Change: Wales 1063–1415* (Oxford).

DAVIS, R. H. C, 1989, *The Medieval Warhorse* (London).

DEAN, R. M., 2001, 'Social Change and Hunting during the Pueblo III to Pueblo IV Transition, East–Central Arizona', *Journal of Field Archaeology*, 28, 271–85.

DENHOLM-YOUNG, N., 1932–4, 'The Yorkshire Estates of Isabella de Fortibus', *YAJ* 31, 389–420.

DRAGE, C., 1989, *Nottingham Castle: A Place Full Royal*, Transactions of the Thoroton Society of Nottinghamshire, 93.

DRURY, J. L., 1976, 'Early Settlement in Stanhope Park, Weardale, c.1406–79', *Archaeologia Aeliana*, 5th ser. 4, 139–49.

—— 1978, 'Durham Palatinate Forest Law and Administration, Specially in Weardale up to 1400', *Archaeologia Aeliana*, 5th ser. 6, 87–105.

DU BOULAY, F. R. H., 1966, *The Lordship of Canterbury* (London).

—— 1970, *An Age of Ambition: English Society in the Late Middle Ages* (London).

DUGDALE, W., 1730, *The Antiquities of Warwickshire*, 2nd edn., 2 vols. (London).

DUNNING, R. W., 1981, 'The Origins of Nether Stowey', *Somerset Archaeology and Natural History*, 125, 124–6.

DUNSFORD, H. M., and HARRIS, S. J., 2003, 'Colonization of the Wasteland in County Durham, 1100–1400', *EcHR* 2nd ser. 56, 34–56.

DYER, C., 1980, *Lords and Peasants in a Changing Society: The Estates of the Bishopric of Worcester, 680–1540* (Cambridge).

DYER, C., 1982, 'Deserted Medieval Villages in the West Midlands', *EcHR* 2nd ser. 35, 19–34.
—— 1988, 'The West Midlands', in Hallam 1988*a*: 369–83.
—— 1989, *Standards of Living in the Later Middle Ages: Social Change in England, c.1200–1520* (Cambridge).
—— 1991, 'The West Midlands', in Miller 1991: 77–92.
—— 1994, *Everyday Life in Medieval England* (London).
—— 2000, 'Woodlands and Wood Pasture in Western England', in Thirsk 2000: 97–121.
—— 2002, *Making a Living in the Middle Ages: The People of Britain, 850–1520* (New Haven and London).
—— 2005, *An Age of Transition? Economy and Society in England in the Later Middle Ages* (Oxford).
—— 2006, 'Conflict in the Landscape: The Enclosure Movement in England, 1220–1349', *Landscape History*, 28, 21–33.
EAMES, E. S., 1980, *Catalogue of Medieval Lead-Glazed Earthenware Tiles in the Department of Medieval and Later Antiquities in the British Museum*, 2 vols. (London).
—— 1985, *English Medieval Tiles* (London).
ELLIOTT, R. J., 1975, *The Story of Windsor Great Park* (St Ives).
EMERY, A., 1996–2006, *Greater Medieval Houses of England and Wales*, 3 vols. (Cambridge).
EMERY, F., 1974, *The Oxfordshire Landscape* (London).
EVERSON, P., and BARNWELL, P. S., 2004, 'Landscapes of Lordship and Pleasure: The Castle and its Landscape Setting', in J. Clark, *Helmsley Castle* (London), 24–5.
—— BROWN, G., and STOCKER, D., 2000, 'The Castle Earthworks and Landscape Context', in P. Ellis (ed.), *Ludgershall Castle, Wiltshire* (Devizes), 97–119.
EVERSON, P. L., TAYLOR, C. C., and DUNN, C. J., 1991, *Change and Continuity: Rural Settlement in North-West Lincolnshire* (London).
EYTON, R. W., 1854–60, *Antiquities of Shropshire*, 12 vols. (London).
FAITH, R., 1984, 'The "Great Rumour" of 1377 and Peasant Ideology', in R. H. Hilton and T. Aston (eds.), *The English Rising of 1381* (Cambridge), 43–73.
—— 1997, *The English Peasantry and the Growth of Lordship* (London).
FARMER, D. L., 1991, 'Marketing the Produce of the Countryside, 1200–1500', in Miller 1991: 324–430.
—— 1995, 'Woodland and Pasture Sales on the Winchester Manors in the Thirteenth Century: Disposing of a Surplus, or Producing for the Market?', in R. H. Britnell and B. M. S. Campbell (eds.), *A Commercialising Economy. England 1086 to c.1300* (Manchester), 102–31.
FENNER, A., 1990, 'A Documentary Study of Hales and Loddon', in A. Davison (ed.), *The Evolution of Settlement in Three Parishes in South-East Norfolk*, East Anglian Archaeology, 49, 41–57.
FIELD, J., 1993, *A History of English Field Names* (London).
FINBERG, H. P. R., 1975, *The Gloucestershire Landscape* (London).
FORD, W. J., 1979, 'Some Settlement Patterns in the Central Region of the Warwickshire Avon', in P. H. Sawyer (ed.), *English Medieval Settlement* (London), 143–63.

FOWLER, K., 1969, *The King's Lieutenant: Henry of Grosmont, First Duke of Lancaster, 1310–1361* (London).
FRANKLIN, P., 1989, 'Thornbury Woodlands and Deer Parks, Part 1: The Earls of Gloucester's Deer Parks', *Transactions of the Bristol and Gloucester Archaeological Society*, 107, 149–69.
—— 1996, 'Politics in the Manorial Court Rolls: The Tactics, Social Composition, and Aims of a Pre-1381 Peasant Movement', in Z. Razi and R. Smith (eds.), *Medieval Society and the Manor Court* (Oxford), 162–98.
FRYDE, E. B., 1996, *Peasants and Landlords in Later Medieval England* (Stroud).
—— GREENWAY, D. E, PORTER, S., and ROY, I., 1986 (eds.), *Handbook of British Chronology*, 3rd edn. (London).
FRYDE, N., 1979, *The Tyranny and Fall of Edward II* (Cambridge).
GAIMSTER, D. R., MARGESON, S. and BARRY, T., 1989 (eds.), 'Medieval Britain and Ireland in 1988', *Medieval Archaeology*, 33, 161–241.
GALLOWAY, J. A., KEENE, D., and MURPHY, M., 1996, 'Fuelling the City: Production and Distribution of Firewood and Fuel in London's Region, 1290–1400', *EcHR* 2nd ser. 49, 447–72.
GARDINER, M., 1999, 'The Medieval Rural Economy and Landscape', in K. Leslie and B. Short (eds.), *An Historical Atlas of Sussex* (Chichester), 38–9.
GELLING, M., 1953–4 (ed.), *The Place-Names of Oxfordshire*, 2 vols, EPNS 23–4 (Cambridge).
GERMANY, M., 2001, 'Fieldwalking at Crondon Park, Stock', *Essex Archaeology & History*, 32, 178–88.
GILBERT, J. M., 1979, *Hunting and Hunting Reserves in Medieval Scotland* (Edinburgh).
GIROUARD, M., 2000, *Life in the French Country House* (London).
GIVEN-WILSON, C., 1986, *The Royal Household and the King's Affinity* (New Haven and London).
—— 1987, *The English Nobility in the Late Middle Ages* (London).
GLASSCOCK, R. E., 1973, 'England *circa* 1334', in H. C. Darby (ed.), *A New Historical Geography of England* (Cambridge), 136–85.
GODBER, J., 1969, *History of Bedfordshire, 1066–1888* (Bedford).
GOVER, J. E. B., MAWER, A., STENTON, F. M., and HOUGHTON, F. T. S., 1936 (eds.), *The Place-Names of Warwickshire*, EPNS 13 (Cambridge).
GOWLAND, T. S., 1936–8, 'The Honour of Kirkby Malzeard and the Chase of Nidderdale', *YAJ* 33, 349–96.
GRANT, R., 1991, *The Royal Forests of England* (Stroud).
GREEN, J. A., 1986, *The Government of England under Henry I* (Cambridge).
—— 2006, *Henry I. King of England and Duke of Normandy* (Cambridge).
GRIFFITH, N. J. L., HALSTEAD, P. L. J., MACLEAN, A. C., and ROWLEY-CONWY, P. A., 1983, 'Faunal Remains and Economy', in P. Mayes and L. A. S. Butler (eds.), *Sandal Castle Excavations 1964–1973: A Detailed Archaeological Report* (Wakefield), 341–8.
GUHA, R., and GADGIL, M., 1989, 'State Forestry and Social Conflict in British India', *Past and Present*, 123, 141–77.
GULLEY, J. L. M., 1960, 'The Wealden Landscape in the Early Seventeenth Century and its Antecedents', University of London Ph.D. thesis.
GWYNN-JONES, P., 1988, *The Art of Heraldry: Origins, Symbols and Designs* (London).
HAGEN, A., 1995, *A Second Handbook of Anglo-Saxon Food and Drink: Production and Distribution* (Hockwold cum Wilton).

HAGOPIAN VAN BUREN, A., 1986, 'Reality and Literary Romance in the Park of Hesdin', in E. B. Macdougall (ed.), *Medieval Gardens*, Dumbarton Oaks Colloquium on the History of Landscape Architecture, 9 (Washington, DC), 115–34.

HALLAM, H.E., 1981, *Rural England, 1066–1348* (Brighton).

—— 1988*a* (ed.), *The Agrarian History of England and Wales*, ii. *1042–1350* (Cambridge).

—— 1988*b*, 'The Life of the People', in Hallam 1988*a*: 818–53.

—— 1988*c*, 'Population Movements in England, 1086–1350', in Hallam 1988*a*: 508–93.

HANAWALT, B. A., 1988, 'Men's Games, King's Deer: Poaching in Medieval England', *Journal of Medieval and Renaissance Studies*, 18/2, 175–93.

HARDING, S., and LAMBERT, D., 1994, *Parks and Gardens of Avon* (Bristol).

HARRISON, W., 1901, 'Ancient Forests, Chases, and Deer Parks in Lancashire', *Transactions of the Lancashire and Cheshire Antiquarian Society*, 19, 1–37.

HARRISS, G. L., 1975, *King, Parliament and Public Finance in Medieval England to 1369* (Oxford).

—— 2003, 'The Court of Lancastrian Kings', in J. Stratford (ed.), *The Lancastrian Court: Proceedings of the 2001 Harlaxton Symposium* (Donington), 1–18.

—— 2005, *Shaping the Nation: England 1360–1461* (Oxford).

HARVEY, I. M. W., 1991, *Jack Cade's Rebellion of 1450* (Oxford).

—— 1997, 'Bernwood in the Middle Ages', in J. Broad and R. Hoyle (eds.), *Bernwood: The Life and Afterlife of a Forest*, Harris Paper 2 (University of Central Lancashire), 1–18.

—— 2004, 'Poaching and Sedition in Fifteenth-Century England', in R. Evans (ed.), *Lordship and Learning: Studies in Memory of Trevor Aston* (Woodbridge), 169–82.

HARVEY, J., 1981, *Mediaeval Gardens* (London).

HARVEY, P. D. A., 1974, 'The Pipe Rolls and the Adoption of Demesne Farming in England', *EcHR* 2nd ser. 27, 345–59.

HARVEY, S., 1988, 'Domesday England' in Hallam 1988*a*: 45–136.

HARWOOD, T. E., 1929, *Windsor Old and New* (London).

HATCHER, J., 1970, *Rural Economy and Society in the Duchy of Cornwall, 1300–1500* (Cambridge).

—— 1993, *The History of the British Coal Industry*, i. *Before 1700* (Oxford).

—— 1994, 'England in the Aftermath of the Black Death', *Past and Present*, 144, 3–35.

—— 1996, 'The Great Slump of the Mid Fifteenth Century', in R. H. Britnell and J. Hatcher (eds.), *Progress and Problems in Medieval England: Essays in Honour of Edward Miller* (Cambridge), 237–72.

—— and BAILEY, M., 2001, *Modelling the Middle Ages: The History and Theory of England's Economic Development* (Oxford).

HATHERLY, J. M., and CANTOR, L. M., 1979–80, 'The Medieval Parks of Berkshire', *Berkshire Archaeological Journal*, 70, 67–80.

HENDERSON, C., 1935, *Essays in Cornish History*, ed. A. L. Rowse and M. I. Henderson (Oxford).

HEPPLE, L. W., and DOGGETT, A. M., 1994, *The Chilterns*, 2nd edn. (Chichester).

HERRING, P., 2003, 'Cornish Medieval Deer Parks', in R. Wilson-North (ed.), *The Lie of the Land: Aspects of the Archaeology and History of the Designed Landscape in the South-West of England* (Exeter), 34–50.

HEY, D., 1975, 'The Parks at Tankersley and Wortley', *YAJ* 47, 109–19.
—— 1986, *Yorkshire from AD 1000* (London).
HIGHAM, M. C., 2003, 'Take it with a Pinch of Salt', *Landscape History*, 25, 59–65.
HIGHAM, N. J., 2004, *A Frontier Landscape: The North-West in the Middle Ages* (Macclesfield).
HILTON, R. H., 1966, *A Medieval Society: The West Midlands at the End of the Thirteenth Century* (London).
—— 1973, *Bond Men Made Free: Medieval Peasant Movements and the English Rising of 1381* (London).
HINTON, D. A. 1990, *Archaeology, Economy and Society: England from the Fifth to the Fifteenth Century* (London).
HODDER, M. A., 1988–9, 'Medieval Parks in Drayton Bassett, Shenstone, and Weeford (Staffordshire)', *South Staffordshire Archaeological and Historical Society Transactions*, 30, 39–52.
—— 1992, 'Continuity and Discontinuity in the Landscape: Roman to Medieval in Sutton Chase', *Medieval Archaeology*, 36, 178–82.
HOLBOROW, J., 1999, *Fingest: Stony Ground* (London).
HOLLISTER, C. WARREN, 1985, 'Henry I and the Invisible Transformation of Medieval England', in H. M. Mayr-Harting and R. I. Moore (eds.), *Studies in Medieval History Presented to R. H. C. Davis* (London), 119–31.
HOLLOWELL, S., 2000, *Enclosure Records for Historians* (London).
HOLMES, G. A., 1957, *The Estates of the Higher Nobility in Fourteenth-Century England* (Cambridge).
HOLT, J. C., 1965, *Magna Carta* (Cambridge).
—— 1971, 'The Assizes of Henry II: the Texts', in D. A. Bullough and R. L. Storey (eds.), *The Study of Medieval Records: Essays in Honour of Kathleen Major* (Oxford), 85–106.
—— 1982, *Robin Hood* (London).
HOOKE, D., 1989, 'Pre-Conquest Woodland: Its Distribution and Useage', *AgHR* 37/2, 113–29.
HOPPITT, R., 1992, 'A Study of the Development of Parks in Suffolk from the Eleventh to the Seventeenth Century', UEA Ph.D. thesis, 2 vols.
—— 1999, 'Deer Parks, 1086–c.1600', in D. Dymond and E. Martin, *An Historical Atlas of Suffolk*, rev. edn. (Ipswich), 66–7.
—— 2007, 'Hunting Suffolk's Parks: Towards a Reliable Chronology of Imparkment', in Liddiard 2007: 146–64.
HOSKINS, W. G., 1955, *The Making of the English Landscape* (London).
—— and STAMP, L. D., 1963, *The Common Lands of England and Wales* (London).
HOWES, L. L., 2002, 'Narrative Time and Literary Landscapes in Middle English Poetry', in J. Howe and M. Wolfe (eds.), *Inventing Medieval Landscapes: Senses of Place in Western Europe* (Gainesville, Fla.), 192–207.
HUCHARD, V., ANTOINE, E., LAGABRIELLE, S., LE POGAM, P., n.d., *The Musée National du Moyen Age: Thermes de Cluny, Paris*, Musées et Monuments de France (n.pl.).
HUNT, J., 1997, *Lordship and the Landscape: A Documentary and Archaeological Study of the Honour of Dudley c.1066–1322*, BAR, British Ser. 264.
HUTCHISON, W., 1794–7, *The History of the County of Cumberland*, 2 vols. (London).

HYAMS, E., 1971, *Capability Brown and Humphry Repton* (London).
HYAMS, P. R., 1980, *King, Lords and Peasants in Medieval England: The Common Law of Villeinage in the Twelfth and Thirteenth Centuries* (Oxford).
HYDE, P., 1955, 'The Winchester Manors at Witney and Adderbury, Oxfordshire, in the Later Middle Ages', University of Oxford B.Litt. thesis.
JAMES, T. B., 1990, *The Palaces of Medieval England* (London).
JANSEN, 2002, 'Henry III's Windsor: Castle-Building and Residences', in G. Astill, 'Windsor in the Context of Medieval Berkshire', in L. Keen and E. Scarff (eds.), *Windsor: Medieval Archaeology, Art and Architecture of the Thames Valley*, British Archaeological Association Conference Transactions, 25 (Leeds), 95–110.
JOHNSON, M., 2002, *Behind the Castle Gate: From Medieval to Renaissance* (London).
JONES, M. K., and UNDERWOOD, M. G., 1992, *The King's Mother* (Cambridge).
JONES, R., and PAGE, M., 2003, 'Characterizing Rural Settlement and Landscape: Whittlewood Forest in the Middle Ages', *Medieval Archaeology*, 47, 53–83.
—— 2006, *Medieval Villages in an English Landscape. Beginnings and Ends* (Macclesfield)
KEEN, M., 1995, 'Nobles' Leisure: Jousting, Hunting and Hawking', in S. Cavaciocchi (ed.), *Il tempo libero: Economia e societa, Sec. XIII–XVIII*, Atti delle 'settimane di studio' e altri convegni, 2nd ser. 26 (Florence), 307–22.
—— 2000, *The Outlaws of Medieval Legend*, rev. edn. (London).
KERR, W. J. B., 1925, *Higham Ferrers and its Ducal and Royal Castle and Park* (Northampton).
KIFT, M., FALLOWFIELD, M., and PREECE, P., 1989, 'In Search of Applehanger', *South Midlands Archaeology*, 19, 59–61.
KING, D. J. CATHCART, *Castellarium Anglicanum*, 2 vols. (London, 1983).
KLEINEKE, H., 2009, *Edward IV* (London).
KOSMINSKY, E. A., 1956, *Studies of the Agrarian History of England in the Thirteenth Century* (Oxford).
LACHAUD, F., 2002, 'Dress and Social Status in England before the Sumptuary Laws', in P. Coss and M. Keen (eds.), *Heraldry, Pageantry and Social Display in Medieval England* (Woodbridge), 105–23.
LANDSBERG, S., 1995, *The Medieval Garden* (London).
LASDUN, S., 1991, *The English Park: Royal, Private and Public* (London).
LATHAM, R. E., 1965 (ed.), *Revised Medieval Latin Word List* (London).
—— and HOWLETT, D. R., 1975– (eds.), *Dictionary of Medieval Latin from British Sources* (London), fasc. iv.
LEE, R., 1997, 'Hunting', in T. Barfield (ed.), *The Dictionary of Anthropology* (Oxford), 252–3.
LIDDELL, W. H., 1966, 'The Private Forests of S. W. Cumberland', *Transactions of the Cumberland and Westmorland Antiquarian and Archaeological Society*, NS 66, 106–30.
LIDDIARD, R., 2000a, 'Castle Rising, Norfolk: A "Landscape of Lordship"?', in C. Harper-Bill (ed.), *Anglo-Norman Studies XXII: Proceedings of the Battle Conference 1999* (Woodbridge), 169–86.
—— 2000b, *'Landscapes of Lordship': Norman Castles and the Countryside in Medieval Norfolk, 1066–1200*, BAR, British Ser. 309.
—— 2003, 'The Deer Parks of Domesday Book', *Landscapes*, I, 4–23.

—— 2005, *Castles in Context: Power, Symbolism and Landscape, 1066 to 1500* (Bollington).

—— 2007 (ed.), *The Medieval Park. New Perspectives* (Macclesfield), including 'Introduction' by editor, 1–8.

LILLEY, K. D., 1998, 'Urban Design in Medieval Coventry: The Planning of Much and Little Park Street within the Earl of Chester's Fee', *Midland History*, 23, 1–20.

LINNARD, W., 2000, *Welsh Woods and Forests: A History*, 2nd edn. (Llandysul).

LOMAS, R. A., 1978, 'The Priory of Durham and its Demesnes in the Fourteenth and Fifteenth Centuries', *EcHR* 31, 339–53.

—— 1992, *North-Eastern England in the Middle Ages* (Edinburgh).

LONDON, H. S., 1959, 'The Greyhound as a Royal Beast', *Archaeologia*, 97, 139–64.

LYTE, H. C. MAXWELL, 1909, *A History of Dunster and of the Families of Mohun and Luttrell*, 2 vols. (London).

—— 1926, *Historical Notes on the Use of the Great Seal of England* (London).

LYTH, P., 1986, 'The Deer Parks of the Archbishops of York at Southwell', *Transactions of the Thoroton Society of Nottinghamshire*, 90, 14–29.

MACCULLOCH, D., 1986, *Suffolk and the Tudors: Politics and Religion in an English County, 1500–1600* (Oxford).

MCDONNELL, J., 1992, 'Pressures on Yorkshire Woodland in the Later Middle Ages', *Northern History*, 28, 110–25.

MCFARLANE, K. B., 1973, *The Nobility of Later Medieval England* (Oxford).

MACGREGOR, A., 1991, 'Antler, Bone and Horn', in J. Blair and N. Ramsay (eds.), *English Medieval Industries* (London), 355–78.

MACGREGOR, P., 1983, *Odiham Castle, 1200–1500: Castle and Community* (Gloucester).

MCINTOSH, M. K., 1986, *Autonomy and Community: The Royal Manor of Havering, 1200–1500* (Cambridge).

MCKENDRICK, S., 1995, 'Tapestries from the Low Countries in England during the Fifteenth Century', in C. Barron and N. Saul (eds.), *England and the Low Countries in the Late Middle Ages* (Stroud), 43–60.

MCLEAN, T., 1981, *Medieval English Gardens* (London).

MANNING, R. B., 1993, *Hunters and Poachers: A Social and Cultural History of Unlawful Hunting in England, 1485–1640* (Oxford).

MARKS, R., and WILLIAMSON, P., 2003 (eds.), *Gothic: Art for England, 1400–1547* (London).

MARTIN, A. F., and STEEL, R. W., 1954 (eds.), *The Oxford Region: A Scientific and Historical Survey* (London).

MARTIN, C. TRICE, 1982, *The Record Interpreter*, facsimile of 2nd edn. (1910) (Chichester).

MARVIN, W. P., 1999, 'Slaughter and Romance: Hunting Reserves in Late-Medieval England', in B. Hanawalt and D. Wallace (eds.), *Medieval Crime and Social Control* (Minneapolis), 224–52.

MATE, M., 1984, 'Agrarian Economy after the Black Death: The Manors of Canterbury Cathedral Priory, 1348–91', *EcHR* 2nd ser. 37, 341–54.

—— 1985, 'Medieval Agrarian Practices: The Determining Factors?', *AgHR* 33/1, 22–31.

MAY, A. N., 1973, 'An Index of Thirteenth-Century Peasant Impoverishment: Manor Court Fines', *EcHR* 2nd ser. 26, 389–402.

MERTES, K., 1994, 'Aristocracy', in R. Horrox (ed.), *Fifteenth-Century Attitudes* (Cambridge), 42–60.

MEW, K., 2001, 'The Dynamics of Lordship and Landscape as Revealed in a Domesday Study of the *Nova Foresta*', in J. Gillingham (ed.), *Anglo-Norman Studies*, 23 (Woodbridge), 155–66.

MICHELMORE, D. J. H., 1979, 'The Reconstruction of the Early Tenurial and Territorial Divisions of the Landscape of Northern England', *Landscape History*, 1, 1–9.

MILESON, S. A., 2005*a*, 'The Importance of Parks in Fifteenth-Century Society', in L. Clark (ed.), *The Fifteenth Century V* (Woodbridge), 19–37.

—— 2005*b*, 'Landscape, Power and Politics: The Place of the Park in Medieval English Society', University of Oxford D.Phil. thesis.

—— 2007, 'The Sociology of Park Creation in Medieval England', in Liddiard 2007: 11–26.

MILLER, E., 1964, 'The English Economy in the Thirteenth Century', *Past and Present*, 28, 21–40.

—— 1991 (ed.), *The Agrarian History of England and Wales*, iii. *1348–1500* (Cambridge).

—— and HATCHER, J., 1978, *Medieval England: Rural Society and Economic Change, 1086–1348* (London).

MOORHOUSE, S. A., 1979, 'Documentary Evidence for the Landscape of the Manor of Wakefield during the Middle Ages', *Landscape History*, 1, 44–58.

—— 1981, 'Woodland', in M. L. Faull and S. A. Moorhouse (eds.), *West Yorkshire: An Archaeological Survey to A.D. 1500*, 4 vols. (Wakefield), iii. 681–94.

—— 2003*a*, 'Anatomy of the Yorkshire Dales: Decoding the Medieval Landscape', in T. G. Manby, S. A. Moorhouse, and P. Ottaway, *The Archaeology of Yorkshire: An Assessment at the Beginning of the 21st Century*, YAS Occasional Paper, 3, 293–362.

—— 2003*b*, 'Medieval Yorkshire: A Rural Landscape for the Future', *ibid.*: 181–214.

—— 2007, 'The Medieval Parks of Yorkshire: Function, Contents and Chronology', in Liddiard 2007: 99–127.

MOSLEY, O., 1832, *History of the Castle, Priory, and Town of Tutbury* (London).

MUIR, R., 2004, *Landscape Encyclopaedia: A Reference Guide to the Historic Landscape* (Macclesfield).

—— 2006, *Ancient Trees: Living Landscapes* (Stroud).

MUNBY, L. M., 1977, *The Hertfordshire Landscape* (London).

MUSTY, J., 1986, 'Deer Coursing at Clarendon Palace and Hampton Court', *Antiquaries Journal*, 66/1, 131–2.

MYERS, A. R., 1985, *Crown, Household and Parliament in Fifteenth-Century England* (London).

NAUGHTON, K. S., 1976, *The Gentry of Bedfordshire in the Thirteenth and Fourteenth Centuries*, Leicester University Department of English Local History, Occasional Papers, 3rd ser. 2 (Leicester).

NEAVE, S., 1991, *Medieval Parks of East Yorkshire* (Beverley).

—— 1996, 'Medieval Parks', in S. Neave and S. Ellis (eds.), *An Historical Atlas of East Yorkshire* (Hull), 60–1.

NEILSON, N., 1940, 'The Forests', in J. F. Willard and W. A. Morris (eds.), *The English Government at Work, 1327–1336*, 3 vols. (Cambridge, Mass., 1940–50), i. 394–467.

—— 1942, 'Early English Woodland and Waste', *Journal of Economic History*, 2, 54–62.

NICHOLSON, J., and BURN, R., 1777, *The History and Antiquities of the Counties of Westmorland and Cumberland*, 2 vols. (London).

OGGINS, R. S., 2004, *The Kings and their Hawks: Falconry in Medieval England* (New Haven and London).

OOSTHUIZEN, S., and TAYLOR, C. C., 2000, '"John O'Gaunt's House", Bassingbourn, Cambridgeshire: A Fifteenth-Century Landscape', *Landscape History*, 22, 61–76.

ORME, N., 1983, 'The Education of the Courtier', in V. J. Scattergood and J. W. Sherborne (eds.), *English Court Culture in the Later Middle Ages* (London), 63–85.

—— 1984, *From Childhood to Chivalry* (London).

—— 1992, 'Medieval Hunting: Fact and Fancy', in B. Hanawalt (ed.), *Chaucer's England: Literature in Historical Context* (Minneapolis), 133–53.

ORMROD, W. M., 1990, *The Reign of Edward III* (New Haven and London).

ORR, J., 1916, *Agriculture in Oxfordshire* (Oxford).

PAGE, W., 1898 for 1895–6, 'Some Notes on Hatfield', *St Albans and Hertfordshire Architectural and Archaeological Society Transactions*, ns 1/1, 334–56.

PANTIN, W. A., 1941, 'Notley Abbey', *Oxoniensia*, 6, 22–43.

PARKER, J., 1903, 'Delafield's Manuscript Notes on Fingest', *Records of Buckinghamshire*, 8, 463–75.

PARRY, J. D., 1833, *An Historical and Descriptive Account of the Coast of Sussex* (Brighton).

PAYLING, S. J., 1987, 'Law and Arbitration in Nottinghamshire, 1399–1461', in J. T. Rosenthal and C. Richmond (eds.), *People, Politics and Community in the Later Middle Ages* (Stroud), 140–60.

—— 1989, 'The Ampthill Dispute: A Study in Aristocratic Lawlessness and the Breakdown of Lancastrian Government', *EHR* 104, 881–907.

PEARMAN, M. T., 1894, *Historical Notices of Caversham*, Oxfordshire Archaeological Society Transactions, 32 (London).

PETIT-DUTAILLIS, C., 1913, 'Les Origines Franco-Normandes de la "Forêt" Anglaise', in *Mélanges d'Histoire Offerts à M. Charles Bémont* (Paris), 59–76.

—— 1930, 'The Forest', in C. Petit-Dutaillis and G. Lefebvre, *Studies and Notes Supplementary to Stubbs' Constitutional History* (Manchester), 147–251.

PETT, D. E., 1998, *The Parks and Gardens of Cornwall* (Penzance).

PITTMAN, S., 1990, *Kerrybullock: The Evolution of the Royal Deer Park in Stoke Climsland* (Stoke Climsland).

PLATT, C., 1978, *Medieval England* (London).

PLUSKOWSKI, A., 2007, 'The Social Construction of Medieval Park Ecosystems: An Interdisciplinary Perspective', in Liddiard 2007: 63–78.

POLLARD, A. J., 1990, *North-Eastern England during the Wars of the Roses: Lay Society, War and Politics, 1450–1500* (Oxford).

—— 2004, *Imagining Robin Hood* (London).

POOLE, A. L., 1955, *From Domesday Book to Magna Carta, 1087–1216*, 2nd edn. (Oxford).
POWICKE, F. M., 1953, *The Thirteenth Century* (Oxford).
PREECE, P. G., 1991 for 1990, 'Mediaeval Woods in the Oxfordshire Chilterns', *Oxoniensia*, 55, 55–72.
PRESTWICH, M., 1988, *Edward I* (London).
—— 2005, *Plantagenet England, 1225–1360* (Oxford).
PRINCE, H., 1967, *Parks in England* (Shalfleet).
RACKHAM, O, 1976, *Trees and Woodland in the British Landscape* (London).
—— 1980, *Ancient Woodland: Its History, Vegetation and Uses in England* (London).
—— 1986, *The History of the Countryside* (London).
—— 1989, *The Last Forest: The Story of Hatfield Forest* (London).
—— 1990, *Trees and Woodland in the British Landscape*, rev. edn. (London).
—— 2002, 'The Medieval Countryside of England: Botany and Archaeology', in J. Howe and M. Wolfe (eds.), *Inventing Medieval Landscapes: Senses of Place in Western Europe* (Gainesville, Fla.), 13–32.
RAHTZ, S., and ROWLEY, T., 1984, *Middleton Stoney: Excavation and Survey in a North Oxfordshire Parish, 1970–1982* (Oxford).
RAWCLIFFE, C., 1978, *The Staffords, Earls of Stafford and Dukes of Buckingham, 1394–1521* (Cambridge).
RCHM, 1975–84, *Northamptonshire*, by Adeane and commissioners, 6 vols. (London).
RIALL, N., 1997, 'A Medieval Tile Kiln in Farnham Park', *Surrey Archaeological Collections*, 84, 143–68.
RICHARDSON, A., 2005, *The Forest, Park and Palace of Clarendon, c.1200–c.1650: Reconstructing an Actual, Conceptual and Documented Wiltshire Landscape*, BAR, British Ser. 387.
—— 2007, ' "The King's Chief Delights": A Landscape Approach to the Royal Parks of Post-Conquest England', in Liddiard 2007: 27–48.
RICHARDSON, H. G., and SAYLES, G. O., 1963, *The Governance of Medieval England* (Edinburgh).
RIGBY, S. H., 1995, *English Society in the Later Middle Ages: Class, Status and Gender* (London).
RIMINGTON, F. C., 1970, 'The Early Deer Parks of North-East Yorkshire, Part I: Introduction', *Transactions of the Scarborough and District Archaeological Society*, 2/13, 3–16.
—— 1971–8, 'The Early Deer Parks of North-East Yorkshire, Part II: The Catalogue', *Transactions of the Scarborough and District Archaeological Society*, 2/14, 1–16; 2/15, 33–6; 2/16, 21–4; 2/17, 5–10; 2/18, 9–13; 2/19, 23–6; 2/20, 31–8; 2/21, 24–8.
ROBERTS, B. K., 1968, 'A Study of Medieval Colonization in the Forest of Arden, Warwickshire', *AgHR* 16/2, 101–13.
—— 1987, 'Landscape Archaeology', in J. W. Wagstaff (ed.), *Landscape and Culture: Geographical and Archaeological Perspectives* (Oxford), 77–95.
—— and Wrathmell, S., 2002, *Region and Place: A Study of English Rural Settlement* (London).
ROBERTS, E., 1986, 'The Bishop of Winchester's Fishponds in Hampshire, 1150–1400: Their Development, Function and Management', *Proceedings of the Hampshire Field Club and Archaeological Society*, 42, 125–38.

—— 1988, 'The Bishop of Winchester's Deer Parks in Hampshire, 1200–1400', *Proceedings of the Hampshire Field Club and Archaeological Society*, 44, 67–86.

—— 1993, 'William of Wykeham's House at East Meon, Hampshire', *Archaeological Journal*, 150, 456–81.

—— 1995, 'Edward III's Lodge at Odiham, Hampshire', *Medieval Archaeology*, 39, 91–106.

ROBERTS, J., 1997, *Royal Landscape: The Gardens and Parks of Windsor* (New Haven and London).

RODEN, D., 1968, 'Woodland and its Management in the Medieval Chilterns', *Forestry*, 41, 59–71.

—— 1969, 'Demesne Farming in the Chiltern Hills', *AgHR* 17/ 1, 9–23.

ROGERS, J. E. THOROLD, 1866–1902, *A History of Agriculture and Prices in England*, 7 vols. (Oxford).

ROONEY, A., 1993, *Hunting in Middle English Literature* (Woodbridge).

ROSKELL, J. S., CLARK, L., and RAWCLIFFE, C., 1992 (eds.), *The House of Commons 1386–1421*, 4 vols. (Stroud).

ROSSER, G., 2003, 'The Quality of Life', in R. Griffiths (ed.), *Short Oxford History of the British Isles: The Fourteenth and Fifteenth Centuries* (Oxford), 31–58.

ROTHWELL, W., STONE, L. W., and REID, T. B. W., 1992 (eds.), *Anglo-Norman Dictionary* (London).

ROWE, A., 2007, 'The Distribution of Parks in Hertfordshire: Landscape, Lordship and Woodland' in Liddiard 2007: 128–45.

—— 2009, *The Medieval Parks of Hertfordshire* (Hatfield).

ROWLEY, T., 1986, *The High Middle Ages, 1200–1550* (London).

—— 1997, *Norman England: An Archaeological Perspective on the Norman Conquest* (London).

ROWNEY, I., 1984, 'Resources and Retaining in Yorkist England: William, Lord Hastings and the Honour of Tutbury', in A. J. Pollard (ed.), *Property and Politics: Essays in Later Medieval English History* (Gloucester), 138–55.

RYAN, P., 1999, 'Woodham Walter Hall: Its Site and Setting', *Essex Archaeology and History*, 3rd ser. 30, 178–95.

RYDER, P., 1979, 'Ravensworth Castle, North Yorkshire', *YAJ* 51, 81–100.

SAUL, N., 1986, *Scenes from Provincial Life: Knightly Families in Sussex, 1280–1400* (Oxford).

—— 1994 (ed.), *Historical Atlas of Britain: Prehistoric and Medieval* (Stroud).

—— 1997, *Richard II* (New Haven and London).

SAUNDERS, C. J., 1993, *The Forest of Medieval Romance* (Cambridge).

SAUNDERS, V. A., 1954, 'Shropshire', in H. C. Darby and I. B. Terrett (eds.), *The Domesday Geography of Midland England* (Cambridge), 113–59.

SAVAGE, H. L., 1933, 'Hunting in the Middle Ages', *Speculum*, 8, 30–41.

SCATTERGOOD, V. J., 1983, 'Literary Culture at the Court of Richard II', in V. J. Scattergood and J. W. Sherborne (eds.), *English Court Culture in the Later Middle Ages* (London), 29–43.

SCHUMER, B., 1999, *Wychwood: The Evolution of a Wooded Landscape*, 2nd edn. (Charlbury).

SCOTT, J. C., 1985–6, 'Everyday Forms of Peasant Resistance', *Journal of Peasant Studies*, 13, 5–35.

SCROPE, G. POULETT, 1852, *History of the Manor and Ancient Barony of Castle Combe, in the County of Wilts* (London).
SHIRLEY, E. P., 1867, *Some Account of English Deer Parks* (London).
SHORT, B., 2000, 'Forests and Wood-Pasture in Lowland England, in Thirsk 2000: 122–49.
SOMERVILLE, R., 1953, *History of the Duchy of Lancaster*, 2 vols. (London).
SPENCE, R. T., 1994, *The Shepherd Lord of Skipton Castle* (Skipton).
SPENCER, A., 2008, 'Royal Patronage and the Earls in the Reign of Edward I', *History*, 93/309, 20–46.
SPUFFORD, M., 2000, 'Eccleshall, Staffordshire', in Thirsk 2000: 290–306.
SQUIRES, A. E., 1992, 'Flitteries and Cold Overton: Two Medieval Deer Parks', *Rutland Record*, 12, 47–52.
—— 1996, *Donnington Park and the Hastings Connection* (Newtown Linford).
—— 2003, 'The Medieval Park of Ridlington', *Rutland Record*, 23 (2003), 105–13.
—— and HUMPHREY, W., 1986, *The Medieval Parks of Charnwood Forest* (Wymondham).
STAMPER, P. A., 1983, 'The Medieval Forest of Pamber, Hampshire', *Landscape History*, 5, 41–52.
—— 1988, 'Woods and Parks', in G. Astill and A. Grant (eds.), *The Countryside of Medieval England* (Oxford), 128–48.
—— 1996, *Historic Parks and Gardens of Shropshire* (Shrewsbury).
—— 1998, review of T. WAY, 1997, *Medieval Archaeology*, 42, 222–3.
STANSFIELD, M. M. N., 1987, 'The Holland Family, Dukes of Exeter, Earls of Kent and Huntingdon, 1352–1475', University of Oxford D.Phil. thesis.
STEANE, J.M., 1975, 'The Medieval Parks of Northamptonshire', *Northamptonshire Past and Present*, 5 (1975), 211–33.
—— 1993, *The Archaeology of the Medieval English Monarchy* (London).
—— 1994, 'Stonor: A Lost Park and a Garden Found', *Oxoniensia*, 59 (1994), 449–70.
—— 2001, *The Archaeology of Power* (Stroud).
STENTON, D. M., 1965, *English Society in the Early Middle Ages, 1066–1307*, 4th edn. (London).
STEVENSON, J., and SQUIRES, A. E., 1999, *Bradgate Park: Childhood Home of Lady Jane Grey*, 2nd edn. (Newtown Linford).
STEVENSON, J. H., 1992, 'The Castles of Marlborough and Ludgershall in the Middle Ages', *Wiltshire Archaeological and Natural History Magazine*, 85, 70–9.
STONE, D., 2005, *Decision-Making in Medieval Agriculture* (Oxford).
STRATFORD, J., 1993, *The Bedford Inventories* (London).
SUMNER, H., 1917, *The Ancient Earthworks of the New Forest* (London).
SUTHERLAND, D. W., 1963, *Quo Warranto Proceedings in the Reign of Edward I, 1278–1294* (Oxford).
SUTTON, A. F., and VISSER-FUCHS, L., 1997, *Richard III's Books: Ideals and Reality in the Life and Library of a Medieval Prince* (Stroud).
SYKES, N., 2005a, 'The Animal Bones', in R. Poulton (ed.), *A Medieval Royal Complex at Guildford*, Surrey Archaeological Society (Guildford), 116–28.
—— 2005b, 'Hunting for the Anglo-Normans: Zooarchaeological Evidence for Medieval Identity', in A. Pluskowski (ed.), *Just Skin and Bone? New Perspectives*

on Human–Animal Relations in the Historical Past, BAR International Series, 1410 (Oxford), 73–80.

—— 2007*a*, 'Animal Bones and Animal Parks', in Liddiard 2007: 49–62.

—— 2007*b*, *The Norman Conquest: A Zooarchaeological Perspective*, BAR International Series, 1656.

SYSON, L., and GORDON, D., 2001, *Pisanello. Painter to the Renaissance Court* (London).

TAYLOR, C. C., 1980, *Northamptonshire: An Archaeological Atlas*, RCHM, Supplementary Series (London).

—— 1989, 'Somersham Palace, Cambridgeshire: A Medieval Landscape for Pleasure?', in M. Bowden, D. MacKay, and P. Topping (eds.), *From Cornwall to Caithness: Some Aspects of British Field Archaeology. Papers Presented to Norman V. Quinnell*, BAR, British Ser. 209, 211–24.

—— 1998, *Parks and Gardens of Britain* (Edinburgh).

—— 2000, 'Medieval Ornamental Landscapes', *Landscapes*, 1/1, 38–55.

—— 2004, 'Ravensdale Park, Derbyshire, and Medieval Deer Coursing', *Landscape History*, 26, 37–57.

TERRETT, I. B., 1962, 'Cheshire', in H. C. Darby and I. S. Maxwell (eds.), *The Domesday Geography of Northern England* (Cambridge), 330–91.

THIÉBAUX, M., 1967, 'The Mediaeval Chase', *Speculum*, 42, 260–74.

—— 1974, *The Stag of Love: The Chase in Medieval Literature* (Ithaca, NY).

THIRSK, J., 1967, 'Enclosing and Engrossing', in J. Thirsk (ed.), *The Agrarian History of England and Wales*, iv. *1500–1640* (Cambridge), 200–55.

—— 2000 (ed.), *Rural England: An Illustrated History of the Landscape* (Oxford).

THOMAS, K., 1983, *Man and the Natural World: Changing Attitudes in England, 1500–1800* (London).

THOMPSON, M. W., 1995, *The Medieval Hall* (Aldershot).

—— 1998, *Medieval Bishops' Houses in England and Wales* (Aldershot).

TIGHE, R. R., and DAVIS, J. E., 1858, *Annals of Windsor*, 2 vols. (London).

TILLER, K., 2000, 'Hook Norton, Oxfordshire: An Open Village', in Thirsk 2000: 277–89.

TITOW, J. Z., 1962, 'Some Differences between Manors and their Effects on the Condition of the Peasantry in the Thirteenth Century', *AgHR* 10/1, 1–13.

TOUT, T. F., 1920–33, *Chapters in the Administrative History of Medieval England*, 6 vols. (Manchester).

TROW-SMITH, R., 1957, *A History of British Livestock Husbandry to 1700* (London).

TUPLING, G. H., 1927, *The Economic History of Rossendale* (Manchester).

TURNER, R. V., 1988, *Men Raised from the Dust: Administrative Service and Upward Mobility in Angevin England* (Philadelphia).

TURVILLE-PETRE, T., 1982, 'The Lament for Sir John Berkeley', *Speculum*, 57/2, 332–9.

VALE, M., 2001, *The Princely Court: Medieval Courts and Culture in North-West Europe, 1270–1380* (Oxford).

VEALE, E. M., 1957, 'The Rabbit in England', *AgHR*, 5/2, 85–90.

VENABLES, E., 1851, 'The Castle of Herstmonceux and its Lords', *Sussex Archaeological Collections*, 4, 125–202.

VINCENT, N. C., 1992, 'Hugh de Neville and his Prisoners', *Archives*, 20/88, 190–7.

VINOGRADOFF, P., 1892, *Villainage in England. Essays in Mediaeval History* (Oxford).
WADE-MARTINS, P., and YAXLEY, D., 1980, *Excavations in North Elmham Park, 1967–1972*, 2 vols., East Anglian Archaeology Report, 9 (Dereham).
WAITES, B., 1997, *Monasteries and Landscape in North East England: The Medieval Colonisation of the North York Moors* (Oakham).
WALLSGROVE, S., 2004/5, 'Wedgnock Park, Warwick: Its Creation and Loss', *Warwickshire History*, 12/6, 239–52.
WARREN, W. L., 1973, *Henry II* (London).
—— 1961, *King John* (London).
WATKINS, A., 1989, 'Cattle Grazing in the Forest of Arden in the Later Middle Ages', *AgHR* 37/1, 12–25.
—— 1993, 'The Woodland Economy of the Forest of Arden in the Later Middle Ages', *Midland History*, 18, 19–36.
—— 1997, 'Landowners and their Estates in the Forest of Arden in the Fifteenth Century', *AgHR* 45/1, 18–33.
WATNEY, V. J., 1910, *Cornbury and the Forest of Wychwood* (London).
WATTS, J. L., 1996, *Henry VI and the Politics of Kingship* (Cambridge).
—— 2002, 'The Policie in Christen Remes: Bishop Russell's Parliamentary Sermons of 1483–84', in G. W. Bernard and S. J. Gunn (eds.), *Authority and Consent in Tudor England: Essays presented to C. S. L. Davies* (Aldershot), 33–59.
WATTS, K., 1996, 'Wiltshire Deer Parks: An Introductory Survey', *Wiltshire Archaeological and Natural History Magazine*, 89, 88–98.
—— 1998, 'Some Wiltshire Deer Parks', *Wiltshire Archaeological and Natural History Magazine*, 91, 90–102.
WAUGH, S. L., 1988, *The Lordship of England: Royal Wardships and Marriages in English Society and Politics, 1217–1327* (Princeton).
—— 1991, *England in the Reign of Edward III* (Cambridge).
WAY, T., 1997, *A Study of the Impact of Imparkment on the Social Landscape of Cambridgeshire and Huntingdonshire from c.1080–1760*, BAR, British Ser. 258.
WHITEHEAD, G. K., 1950, *Deer and their Management in the Deer Parks of Great Britain and Ireland* (London).
WICKHAM, C., 1994, 'European Forests in the Early Middle Ages: Landscape and Land Clearance', in C. Wickham, *Land and Power: Studies in Italian and European Social History, 400–1200* (London).
WIGHT, J. A., 1975, *Mediaeval Floor Tiles* (London).
WILLIAMSON, T., 1998, *The Archaeology of the Landscape Park: Garden Design in Norfolk, England, c.1680–1840*, BAR, British Ser. 268 (Oxford).
—— 2000, *Suffolk's Gardens and Parks: Designed Landscapes from the Tudors to the Victorians* (Macclesfield).
—— 2003, *Shaping Medieval Landscapes: Settlement, Society, Environment* (Macclesfield).
—— and Bellamy, L., 1987, *Property and the Landscape* (London).
WILSON, C., 2002, 'The Royal Lodgings of Edward III at Windsor Castle: Form, Function, Representation', in L. Keen and E. Scarff (eds.), *Windsor: Medieval Archaeology, Art and Architecture of the Thames Valley*, British Archaeological Association Conference Transactions, 25 (Leeds), 15–94.

WILSON, J. D., 1970–4, 'The Mediaeval Deer-Parks of Dorset: X–XIV', *Proceedings of the Dorset Archaeological and Natural History Society*, 92, 205–11; 93, 169–75; 94, 67–9; 95, 47–50; 96, 76–80.

WILTSHIRE, M., WOORE, S., CRISP, B., and RICH, B., 2005, *Duffield Frith* (Ashbourne).

WINCHESTER, A. J. L., 1987, *Landscape and Society in Medieval Cumbria* (Edinburgh).

—— 2000, 'Hill Farming Landscapes of Medieval Northern England', in D. Hooke (ed.), *Landscape: The Richest Historical Record*, Society for Landscape Studies (Amesbury), 75–84.

—— 2007, 'Baronial and Manorial Parks in Medieval Cumbria', in Liddiard 2007: 165–84.

WINGFIELD DIGBY, G., 1971, *The Devonshire Hunting Tapestries* (London).

WHITEHEAD, D., and PATTON, J., 2001, *A Survey of Historic Parks and Gardens in Herefordshire* (Hereford).

WINTERS, J. F., 1999, 'The Forest Eyre, 1154–1368', University of London Ph.D. thesis.

WITNEY, K. P., 1990, 'The Woodland Economy of Kent, 1066–1348', *AgHR* 38/1, 20–39.

WOLFFE, B. P., 2001, *Henry VI*, new edn. (New Haven and London).

WOODGER, L. S., 1974, 'Henry Bourgchier Earl of Essex and his Family (1408–83)', University of Oxford D.Phil. thesis.

WOODWARD, F., 1982, *Oxfordshire Parks* (Woodstock).

WOOLGAR, C. M., 1999, *The Great Household in Late Medieval England* (London).

WRATHMELL, S. and S., 1974–5, 'Excavations at the Moat Site, Walsall, Staffs., 1972–4', *South Staffordshire Archaeological and Historical Society Transactions*, 16, 19–53.

WRIGHT, L. M., 2003, 'Woodland Continuity and Change: Ancient Woodland in Eastern Hertfordshire', *Landscape History*, 25, 67–78.

WRIGHT, S. M., 1983, *The Derbyshire Gentry in the Fifteenth Century*, Derbyshire Record Society, 8.

WYLIE, J. H., 1968, *The Reign of Henry V*, 3 vols. (New York).

YAXLEY, D., 1994, 'Medieval Deer-Parks', in P. Wade-Martins (ed.), *An Historical Atlas of Norfolk*, 2nd edn. (Norwich), 54–5.

YOUNG, C. R., 1979, *The Royal Forests of Medieval England* (Leicester).

Index

Note: Places are identified by the counties they were located in before the local government reorganisation of the 1970s.

abbeys 20
Agincourt (France) 27
agistment 45, 64, 65, 73, 176; *see also* grazing; pasture
Aldworth (Berks.) 53 n. 38, 86, 87, 113, 167
Alexander III, king of Scotland 170
Alston (Cumbl.) 96
Althorp (Northants.) 174 n. 123
Alvechurch (Worcs.) 36, 67
Alveston (Glos.) 54
Ampthill (Beds.) 73 n. 168, 155, 174
Anne of Burgundy 41
Applehanger, in Goring (Oxon.) 70 n. 150
arable land 3, 10, 28, 47, 51, 53–9, 61, 62, 63, 64, 70, 72, 158, 163–4, 167, 173, 175, 179
Arrow (Warks.) 40 n. 174
arrows 22, 25, 27, 40, 179; *see also* bows
Artois, Robert II, count of 92
Arundel (Sussex) 67 n. 122, 115 n. 74
  earl of 109, 150
Ashbourne (Derbs.) 44, 114
Ashdown (Berks.) 53 n. 34
Ashridge (Berks.) 139
assarting 60, 61, 62, 139, 164, 169
Aston Cantlow (Warks.) 73 n. 173
Axminster (Devon) 154

Badby (Northants.) 108 n. 44
Baddesley Clinton (Warks.) 174 n. 123
badgers 4, 149
Badmondisfield (Suffolk) 73 n. 168
Bampton (Oxon.), hundred of 60
Banbury (Oxon.) 61
  hundred of 61
Barnard Castle (Durham) 46, 91
Bashall Eaves (Yorks.) 174 n. 123
Basset, family 56
  Gilbert 139 n. 73
  Robert 26
Bath, bishop of 51, 53
Bath (Somerset) 161
Bayeux Tapestry 18
Bearpark (Durham) 89, 95
Beauchamp, William, earl of Warwick 30
Beaudesert, in Henley-in-Arden (Warks.) 89
Beaufort, Henry, bishop of Winchester 40
Beaufort, Lady Margaret 41, 95
Beche, family 113

Nicholas de la 34
Philip de la 143 n. 96
Beckley (Oxon.) 38 n. 160, 56, 57, 64 n. 99, 65 n. 102, 76, 77, 93, 147 n. 5, 176
Beckwith, William 148
Bedford, John of Lancaster, duke of 41, 88, 153
Beere, Richard, abbot of Glastonbury 91
Bek, Anthony, bishop of Durham 25
Belvoir (Leics.) 75 n. 193
Beoley (Worcs.) 30
Berkeley, Sir John 27
  Sir Maurice 176
Berkhamsted (Herts.) 24, 88 n. 42
Beverley (Yorks.) 66, 171
Bexley (Kent) 169
Billingbear (Berks.), 139
Bilton (Yorks.) 78 n. 217, 148
Binswood (Hants.), 176 n. 133
birds 167
  cranes 80
  game birds 4, 27, 32
  herons 1
  partridges 42 n. 192
  pheasants 42 nn. 191–2, 171 n. 100
Birling (Kent) 178 n 149
Bishop Auckland (Durham) 65, 67
Bishop's Sutton (Hants.) 77
Bishop's Waltham (Hants.) 65 n. 106
Bishopstoke (Hants.) 64 n. 97
Black Prince, Edward, the 33, 37, 64, 66, 93, 163 n. 38
Blackley, in Manchester (Lancs.) 34, 53
Bladon (Oxon.) 54, 60
Blockley (Worcs.) 36
boar 27, 122 n. 11
Boconnoc (Cornwall) 85
Bohun, Humphrey de, earl of Hereford and Essex 99, 155, 156 n. 66
Boldon Book, the 25, 105 n. 32
Bolney, in Harpsden (Oxon.) 51 n. 29
Bolsover (Derbs.) 70
bones and bone finds 42, 80, 135
Bonville, William 25 n. 65
  Sir William 154
Book of the Duchess, the 18
Bordesley abbey (Worcs.) 162
Boughton (Northants.) 174 n. 123
Bousser, Robert de 127 n. 32, 143 n. 96

bows 18, 22, 25, 31–2, 39, 40, 41, 42, 78, 179;
    see also arrows; crossbows
Bracton (or Bratton), Henry de 124
Bradgate (Leics.) 26, 174 n. 23
Brandsby (Yorks.) 174 n. 123
Breadstone, Sir Thomas 112, 143 n. 96
Bret, le, family 153
Brewer, William 112
Brigstock (Northants.) 33, 53 n. 34, 92
Brocas, Bernard 89
Bromley (Staffs.) 25 n. 65
Bronescombe, Walter, bishop of Exeter 151
Bronsil, in Eastnor (Herefs.) 88 n. 45
Brook, Sir Thomas 143, 154
Bruges, Louis de, lord of Gruuthuse 40, 106
Brus, Richard de 140 n. 80
Brussells (Flanders) 92
Buckden (Hunts.) 41, 74, 93
Buckenham (Norf.) 36 n. 146
Bucknell (Oxon.) 62
Budbrooke (Warks.) 174 n. 123
Budley (Somerset) 162
Burdett, Thomas 40 n. 174
Burgh, Hubert de, earl of Kent 112
Burghersh, Henry, bishop of Winchester 34, 179
Burgundy, dukes of 92
Burnell, Robert, bishop of Bath and Wells 112
Burton Lazars (Leics.) 164
Bury St Edmunds abbey (Suffolk) 30, 109, 114;
    see also Samson, abbot of
Byfleet (Surrey), 66
Byrham (Devon) 163

Cainhoe (Beds.) 67 n. 121
Canterbury, archbishop of 71, 109, 150, 169
    cathedral, 19, 20
Cantilupe, William 113
Carent, William 127 n. 32
Carhampton (Somerset) 71, 161
Carnbull, Henry 148
Castle Bolton (Yorks.) 88, 173
Castle Camps (Cambs.) 174 n. 123
Castle Donnington (Leics.) 40
castles and manor houses 1, 5, 8, 23, 34, 42, 54,
    82–98, 99, 102, 104, 106, 108, 111, 113, 114,
    136, 152, 154, 155, 160, 161–3, 173, 181
Catherine of Aragon 20
cats, 4, 149
cattle 3, 76, 172, 175
Caus (Shrops.), lords of 65 n. 106
Caversham (Oxon.) 38 n. 160, 124 n. 22
Cestersover (Warks.) 174 n. 22
Chamberhouse (Berks.) 73 n. 171
champion countryside 2, 3, 44, 49, 58, 172
charcoal and charcoal burners 64, 70, 169
Charlecote (Warks.) 174 n. 123
Charwelton (Northants.) 174 n. 123
chases 3, 4, 5, 29 n. 98, 38, 96, 124 n. 21, 141,
    149–52, 157, 164 n. 49, 166, 171
    Arundel (Sussex) 150–1, 164 n. 49
    Cannock (Staffs.)

Charnwood (Leics.) 26, 29
Cleres (Sussex) 151
Duffield Frith (Derbs.) 63
Hampton Court (Middx.) 98
Houghton (Sussex) 150–1
Leicester Frith (Leics.) 147
Malvern (Worcs.) 151
Needwood (Staffs.) 63
Sutton (Staffs.) 151
Whorlton (Yorks.) 152
Witney (Oxon.) 61
Yardley (Northants.) 26
Châtillon, Gaucher de 106
Chaucer, Geoffrey 18
    Thomas 27, 42
Chester, chamberlain of 33
    earl of 153
Chichester, bishop of 150
Chilterns, the, 43, 49, 51, 60, 61, 62, 68,
    124 n. 25, 179
Chisbury, in Little Bedwyn (Wilts.) 91
Christ Church priory, Canterbury (Kent) 153 n. 50
churches 20
Chute (Devon) 154
Cippenham (Bucks.) 164
Cirencester abbey (Glos.) 133
Cistercians 80
Clare, family 114, 171
    Gilbert de 26
    Gilbert de, earl of Gloucester (d. 1295) 151
Clarendon (Wilts.) 22, 32, 36 n. 146, 38 n. 160,
    66, 91, 92, 93, 104, 113, 147, 166 n. 51, 180
climate 7, 77
Clinton, Geoffrey de 86, 111, 113
    William de 112, 163 n. 38
Clipstone (Notts.) 77, 170
Cnut, king of England, supposed forest laws
    of 122 n. 11
Cockermouth (Cumbl.) 89
Cogan, Richard 143 n. 96
Cokayne, Sir Thomas 44, 114
Coldharbour (London) 95
Coleville, Robert de 152
Collyweston (Northants.) 95
Columbers, Matthew 91, 133
Colwick (Notts.) 138
common rights 54, 59, 62, 80, 124, 137 n. 61,
    151, 153, 158 n. 4, 159–60, 167–71, 175–7,
    178; see also livestock; pasture
Compton Wynyates (Warks.) 174 n. 123,
    175 nn. 126–7
'Contempt of the World' 106
Conyers, William, Lord 113
Copped Hall (Essex) 155
coppices 32, 65–7, 69 n. 142, 70, 72, 73, 81, 169;
    see also woodland and wood-pasture; wood
    and underwood
Cornbury (Oxon.) 37, 38 n. 160, 60, 77
Cornwall, duchy of 76
    earls of, see Edmund and Richard
    parks in 51, 76

Courtenay, Hugh de 54, 91, 113
Coventry (Warks.) 74 n. 176, 143, 153,
    161, 172, 176
  bishop of 79, 176
  prior of 143, 155, 176
covert 33, 98, 123 n. 16, 140
cows 46, 72, 73 n. 171, 77
crenellation and crenellation licences
    88, 102, 111, 127 n. 27, 142 n. 91, 154
Cromwell, Ralph, Lord 88, 155
Crosby Ravensworth (Westml.) 40, 65 n. 107
crossbows 40, 41; see also bows

Dacre, Ralph de 143 n. 98
Damory, Sir Roger 155
Dartmoor 54, 163
De La Beche, in Aldworth (Berks.),
    see Aldworth
Débat des héraulx d'armes 39, 41
deer 5, 6, 27–33, 38–9, 46–7, 76–80, 98, 149–50,
    157, 166; see also venison
  bucks 24, 35, 36, 145
  'curée' of 155
  disease among 7, 38, 147
  does 26, 123; barren 99, 101, 102 n. 5
  eating habits of 164
  fawning time of 24, 169
  feeding of 77–8
  foals 123
  inbreeding among 166
  rutting of 169
  species of: fallow 1, 20, 27, 28, 30, 42, 77, 79,
    135, 164; red 26, 28, 29, 30; roe 4 n. 22, 28,
    29, 30 n. 104, 134 n. 44
  stud animals 39
  'time of grease' 24
deer-courses 41, 42
deer-leaps 33, 34, 39, 42 n. 192, 77, 140 n. 80,
    141, 150, 151, 152
demesne farming 46, 48, 58, 64, 71, 135
depopulation 158, 173, 175, 178
Despenser, family 155
  Hugh le, the elder, earl of Winchester 153 n. 50
Devizes (Wilts.) 38 n. 160, 89, 161, 162
Dives, William de 112, 170
dogs, 19, 22, 25, 27, 31, 32, 35, 41, 145, 154, 155,
    171 n. 100, 177
  food for 37
  kennels for 25, 35
  types of: buckhounds 40; greyhounds
    32, 40, 41;
    hart-hounds 17
Domesday Book (1086) 25, 48, 62, 134, 135,
    162 n. 28
Domesday of Enclosures (1517) 42,
    160, 175
dovecotes 75 n. 188, 102, 136
Dover (Kent) 106
Downton (Wilts.) 64 n. 99
Droxford, John, bishop of Bath
    and Wells 112

Ducklington (Oxon.) 42 n. 199, 60, 124 n. 25,
    134 n. 44, 170, 179 n. 153
Dunster (Somerset) 71, 161
Dürer, Albrecht 92
Durham
  bishop of 65, 74, 109, 150
  prior of 89, 95
  wasteland in 63

Earley (Berks.) 140 n. 76
East Lilling (Yorks.) 174 n. 123
East Worldham (Hants.) 176
Easthampstead (Berks.) 24
Easton Neston (Northants.) 174 n. 123,
    175 nn. 126–7
Eaton Bray (Beds.) 56, 81 n. 239, 113
Eccleshall (Staffs.) 25 n. 65, 164
Edmund, earl of Cornwall 58, 151
Edward the Confessor, king of England 22
Edward I, king of England 21, 30 n. 105, 32, 78,
    99, 124, 136, 156
Edward II, king of England 32, 33, 92, 93,
    113, 170
Edward III, king of England 21, 24, 33,
    34, 77, 93, 112, 113, 114, 127,
    137 n. 59, 140 n. 80, 157, 173 n. 114,
    174, 176 n. 133
Edward IV, king of England 20, 21, 27, 40, 76,
    106, 141, 174
Elham (Kent) 106
Elizabeth of Rhuddlan 99
Elsfield (Oxon.) 60
Eltham (Kent) 24
Ely, bishop of 93, 161
enclosure 9–10, 163–4, 168, 172–5, 181
Enfield (Middx.) 67 n. 120
estate management, treatises on 71
Eu, countess of 8, 100
Eustace, Saint 19
Everswell, in Woodstock park 93
Ewelme (Oxon.) 27, 42
excommunication 150–1
Eynsham (Oxon.) 60
  abbot of 170

Fairfax, Sir Guy 113
Fareham (Hants.) 64 n. 99
Farley (Worcs.) 151
Farnham (Surrey) 67 n. 120
Fawley (Bucks.) 75 n. 188
Ferrers, family 63
fields 4, 7, 53, 54, 56, 58, 59, 60, 62,
    70 n. 150, 163–4, 166, 167, 172, 176,
    177, 178
Fiennes, Sir Roger 1
Filliol, John 140 n. 80
Fingest (Bucks.) 43, 179
Finmere (Oxon.) 62
fish and fishponds 1, 3, 42 n. 192,
    64, 70, 83, 95, 98, 102, 136, 151,
    168 n. 81, 177

Fitzalan, family 150
  Richard, earl of Arundel 151
Fitzaucher, Henry 127 n. 32, 155
Fitzhugh, Henry 152
Fitzralph, Ralph son of William 26
Flintshire (Wales), parks in, 33, 37
Flitteris (Rutland) 153 n. 45
floor tiles 20
Foix, Gaston de, 31, 32, 39
forests, 3–5, 8, 9, 17, 22, 23, 24, 25, 26, 27, 28, 29, 34, 38, 39, 49, 65, 77, 79, 83, 96, 106, 107, 111, 119, 121–45, 149, 157, 159, 166, 169, 170, 171, 177; *see also* covert; chases
  Clarendon (Wilts.) 65
  Dean (Glos.) 138 n. 65
  Derbyshire, 125
  Essex 79, 136 n. 57, 140 n. 80
  Feckenham (Worcs.) 31, 141
  Fulwood (Lancs.) 141
  Gillingham (Dorset) 140 n. 78
  Inglewood (Cumbl.) 29, 141, 169
  Knaresborough (Yorks.) 142, 148, 168 n. 81
  Lancashire 123 n. 17
  Lincolnshire 125
  New Forest (Hants.) 24, 41
  Northamptonshire 26
  Nottinghamshire 138, 139, 140 n. 80
  Pamber (Hants.) 123 n. 16
  Rockingham (Northants.) 33
  Rutland 24
  Savernake (Wilts.), 139
  Whittlewood (Northants.) 49
  Windsor (Berks.) 26, 139
  Wychwood (Oxon.) 37, 49, 60, 61 n. 75, 62
Fountains Abbey (Yorks.) 158 n. 3
foxes 4, 32, 149, 171 n. 100, 172
Foxley, Sir John 113
Framlingham (Suffolk) 54, 106
Franks, the 121
free warren, rights of 4, 42 n. 192, 124 n. 21, 127, 144, 149, 151 n. 31, 171
Freefolk (Hants.) 79
French, John 152
Fulbrook (Warks.) 73 n. 173, 88, 153, 174 n. 123
Furness abbey (Lancs.) 65
Furtho, William 79

gambling 21, 41
gardens 6, 8, 71, 82, 83, 84, 85, 86, 89, 90, 91, 92, 93, 94, 95, 96, 97, 98, 136, 161, 162
Garter, Order of the 83 n. 16
Gascoigne, Sir William 114, 146
Gaunt, John of, duke of Lancaster 33, 110, 147
Gawthorpe (Yorks.) 174 n. 123
Gaywood (Norf.) 171 n. 102
Gerald of Wales 82 n. 8
Giffard, Godfrey, bishop of Worcester 151
gifts 25, 106, 124
Gillingham (Dorset) 140 n. 78
Gilsland (Cumbl.) 152

Gloucester, earl of 65
  sheriff of 54
Godfrey of Crowland, abbot of Peterborough 34
Godmanchester (Hunts.) 161, 167 n. 62
Goito, near Mantua (Italy) 92
Goltho (Lincs.) 88
Gonzaga, family 92
Goring (Oxon.) 70 n. 150
Gough Map, the (*c.*1360) 23
Gower, family 141
grain, price of 172
grazing 28, 32, 36, 46, 47, 63, 65, 67, 72, 73, 92, 97, 115, 119, 142, 158, 159, 163, 167–70, 173, 175–6; *see also* pasture
Great Barrington (Glos.) 176
Great Sandon (Staffs.) 174 n. 123
Great Woolstone (Bucks.) 174 n. 123, 175 nn. 126–7
Greenwich (Kent) 153
Gresley, Sir John 176
Grey, Edmund, earl of Kent 26
Grey of Codnor, Henry, Lord 155
Grey of Ruthin, Reginald, Lord 155
Greystoke (Cumbl.) 73 n. 173, 89
Guildford (Surrey) 88

Haia, de, family 150
Halnaker (Sussex) 150, 151, 152
Halton (Ches.) 73 n. 170
Hampstead Marshall (Berks.) 139 n. 173
Hampton (Middx.) 174 n. 123, 175 nn. 126–7
  Hampton Court in 98
Hamsey (Sussex) 151
Hanborough (Oxon.) 60
Hanley Castle (Worcs.) 161
Hanworth (Middx.) 174 n. 123, 175 nn. 126–7
Hareng, Ralph 133
hares 4, 27, 32, 42 n. 192, 101, 149, 152, 171 n. 100, 172, 177; *see also* rabbits
Harrold (Beds.) 67 n. 121
  priory 56
Harting (Sussex) 151
Hartlebury (Worcs.) 36
Hastings, William, Lord 112
Hatfield (Herts.) 154
Haverah (Yorks.) 77 n. 208, 78 n. 217
Havering (Essex) 24, 79
hawks and hawking 17, 19, 22, 25, 27, 106, 146
Haynes (Beds.) 65, 171 n. 107
hays 31, 33, 65, 77, 134 n. 44, 145
headlands 53
heath 3, 4, 153
Helmsley (Yorks.) 89, 91, 93
Henbury (Glos.) 36
Hendon (Middx.) 175 n. 126
Henley-on-Thames (Oxon.) 51, 58, 68
Henley-on-the-Heath (Surrey) 24
Henry I, king of England 21, 97, 104, 111, 113, 135

Index

Henry II, king of England 21, 93, 121, 124 n. 25, 135, 161
Henry III, king of England 8, 88, 91, 100, 106, 113, 128, 139 n. 73, 147 n. 7, 166
Henry IV, king of England 17
Henry V, king of England 17, 18, 31, 92, 93
Henry VI, king of England 20, 39, 114, 128, 141 n. 83
Henry VII, king of England 40, 41, 104, 141, 145, 147
Henry VIII, king of England 20, 98
Hensington, in Bladon (Oxon.) 54, 163
heraldry 8, 18, 103
Hereford, countess of 40
  earl of 67 n. 120
Herstmonceux (Sussex) 1, 8, 88, 100
Hertingdon, Adam de 139
Hertingfordbury (Herts.) 176
Hesdin (France) 92
Higham Ferrers (Northants.) 38 n. 160, 40, 115 n. 74
Highclere (Hants.) 174 n. 123
Holt (Leics.) 176
Hook Norton (Oxon.) 62
Hornby (Yorks.) 174 n. 123, 175
horns, hunting 15, 16, 20, 22, 25, 32, 179
horses 3, 16, 20, 30, 40, 42, 53, 73 n. 171, 115
  palfreys 133
  studs 64, 68
Horsfrith, in Writtle (Essex) 140 n. 80
Horton (Oxon.) 56
Houghton, John 104
Houghton (Sussex) 150
household accounts 17
Howard, family 106
  John, duke of Norfolk 40
Hoxne (Suffolk) 88
Hugh of Avranches, earl of Chester 32
Hulton abbey (Staffs.) 153 n. 50
Humphrey of Lancaster, duke of Gloucester 141 n. 83, 153
hundred rolls (1274–5) 124, 137, 160
Hungerford (Berks.) 139
Huntercombe, Walter de 156
Huntercombe (Oxon.) 42, 156
hunting 3–4, 5, 6, 8, 9,10, 15–44, 51, 69, 70, 76, 80, 98, 99–101, 105–6, 107–8, 114, 115, 119, 121, 134, 136, 137, 140, 144, 145, 146, 147, 148–53, 154, 155–7, 159, 166–8, 177–8, 180, 181; *see also* nets; poaching
  bow and stable (the 'drive') 31, 32, 33, 41, 42
  coursing 30, 31, 32, 40
  female participation in 26–7, 41
  legislation restricting 103, 145, 148 n. 17, 177
  manuals 17, 30
  'par force' 30, 32, 42
  seasons 24
  stalking 31, 32
Huntington (Herefs.) 99–101
Hussey, Henry 151
Hyde abbey (Hants.) 153 n. 50

Ilkeston (Derbs.) 124 n. 22
Ingleby Arncliffe (Yorks.) 152
Inkberrow (Worcs.) 139 n. 73
inquisitions *ad quod damnum* 128, 142, 152, 166, 171 n. 100
inquisitions *post mortem* 38, 71, 73 nn. 168 and 173, 75 n. 191, 81 n. 239, 108
Isabella of France, queen 34, 127, 143, 155, 157
Isleworth (Middx.) 171

Joceline, bishop of Bath 138
John, king of England 21, 22, 24, 34, 127, 136, 142, 163 n. 37
John of Lancaster, duke of Bedford, *see* Bedford
John of Salisbury 21

Kempe, John, archbishop of Canterbury 178 n. 149
Kendal (Westml.) 88
Kenilworth (Warks.) 86, 92, 111
King's Langley (Herts.) 24, 54
King's Nympton (Devon) 44 n. 201
King's Somborne (Hants.) 104
Kirtlington (Oxon.) 53 n. 38, 56
Knepp (Sussex) 153
Kyriel, Lettice 152

'La Leigh' (Lee, in Souldrop?) (Beds.), lord of 56
labour services 78–9
Lacy, Henry de, earl of Lincoln 25
Lake District, the 51
Lake Geneva 44 n. 202
'Lament for Sir John Berkeley' 27
Lancaster, duchy of 73 n. 171, 141, 142
  earl of 77, 109, 147, 150
  Great Park 33
Lanercost (Cumbl.), prior of 152
Lathom (Lancs.) 3 n. 17, 174 n. 123
Laughton (Sussex) 26, 36
Laxton (Notts.) 139
Leicester (Leics.) 161
Lewes (Sussex), prior of 26
Lichfield, bishop of 25 n. 65
Lincoln, bishop of 40, 56, 74, 79, 93, 162
Linton (Cambs.) 174 n. 123
Liscombe, in Soulbury (Bucks.) 174 n. 123
Lisle, Alice de 143 n. 96
Little Preston, in Preston Capes (Northants.) 165
Lives of Saints Edmund and Fremund 19
livestock 6, 64–5, 67–8, 72, 73, 97, 115, 156, 167, 170; *see also* common rights; pasture
Llanthony (Gwent), prior of 176
lodges, forest and park 1, 3, 22, 24, 26, 33, 34, 65, 69, 78, 82, 88, 92, 93, 94, 95, 96, 98, 113, 140 n. 81
London 24, 48, 74
  citizens of 171

Longchamp, Robert de 26
Lothbrok, king of the Danes 19
Louis XI, king of France 20
Lovell, Sir William 42
Lovet, John 26
Ludgershall (Wilts.) 38 n. 160, 91, 161, 166
Lydgate, John 27, 42
lynchets 179 n. 155

Madeley (Staffs.) 41
Malmesbury abbey (Wilts.) 153 n. 50
Malory, Sir Thomas 103
Manchester (Lancs.) 34
manor houses, *see* castles and manor houses
Manorbier (Pemb.) 82 n. 8
manorial accounts 17, 47, 48, 108
Marcher lords 26
Mare, John de la 112
Mares, Robert de 26
Margaret of Anjou 39
Markham, Gervase 32
Marmirolo, near Mantua (Lombardy) 92
marsh 60
Marshall, Richard 139 n. 73
Marsley (Denbigh) 164 n. 50
Marston Moretaine (Beds.) 171 n. 107
Master of Game 15, 17
Mauduit, William IV, earl of Warwick 163 n. 38
Meaux abbey (Yorks.) 28 n. 93
Melchet, in Clarendon forest (Wilts.) 65
Mells (Somerset) 91
meadow 32, 54, 55, 58, 59, 60, 62, 68, 70,
    73 n. 169, 78, 80, 82, 95, 97, 158, 160,
    167, 176
merchants 112
Merdon (Hants.) 32, 64 n. 99, 104 n. 22, 105
Meynill, Nicholas de 152
Middleton Stoney (Oxon.) 62, 67 n. 122
Mileham (Norf.) 67 n. 122, 69 n. 142
Millbrook (Beds.) 67 n. 120, 155, 174
Minster Lovell (Oxon.) 42
Minsterley, in Westbury (Shrops.) 65 n. 106
moats 78, 83, 93, 98
Mohun, family 71
Moleyns, Adam, bishop of Chichester 112
Molyneux, Thomas 141
Molyns, John 34, 112, 143 n. 96, 157
Monceux, family 1
    Waleran de 8
    William de 8
monks 25, 28, 30, 47, 95, 97, 156
Montacute, William 138
Montague, William 34, 112
Montfort, Peter de 139
    Simon de, earl of Leicester 8, 139, 140 n. 80
moor 2
Moor Park (Herts.) 40, 42
Mortimer, family 155
    Roger, earl of March (d. 1330) 34, 127, 157
    Roger, earl of March (d. 1398) 25
    Roger, lord of Wigmore 166

Moulton, Thomas de 152
Mowbray, John, Lord 155
Mulgrave Castle, near Lythe (Yorks.) 104 n. 22
Musbury (Lancs.) 77
Myerscough (Lancs.) 164

Nether Stowey (Somerset) 86 n. 31, 162
nets 27, 31, 78, 134 n. 44, 145
Neville, George, archbishop of York 40
    Hugh de 24, 127, 142
Newtown (Northumb.) 104 n. 22
Norbury, John 112
Norfolk, earls of 109
North Elmham (Norf.) 53 n. 34
Northbourne (Kent) 147
Northwold, Hugh of, bishop of Ely 34, 154
Nottingham (Notts.) 38 n. 160, 161
Nuthill, in Holderness (Yorks.) 163

Oakham (Rutland) 113
Odell (Beds.), lord of 56
Odiham (Hants.) 34, 35, 36 n. 146, 78, 93
Odo of Bayeux, earl of Kent 153 n. 50
Ogard, Sir Andrew 112
Okehampton (Devon) 54, 91, 113, 163
orchards 83, 92, 93, 98, 102
Osmerley, in Alvechurch (Worcs.) 162
otters 27
Oundle (Northants.) 34
outwoods 168
Overton (Yorks.) 133
Oxford (Oxon.), scholars of 156
oyer et terminer, commissions of 154, 155, 157

Palermo (Sicily) 92
Palmer, Thomas 176 n. 134
pannage 67, 68, 71, 169 n. 83
parkers 3, 31, 40, 73 n. 168, 75, 78, 144, 146,
    147, 148, 153, 168, 178, 181
parks; *see also* enclosure; lodges; parkers;
    woodland
    agriculture, impact of parks on 51–9, 163–6,
        169–70, 172–6
    boundaries of 6, 42, 69, 76, 77 n. 208,
        79, 82, 104, 107, 154, 155, 164,
        170, 171
    bowers and 'pleasances' in 93, 95, 97
    chronology of 7, 134–6
    compartments in 64, 65, 66–7, 70,
        73, 78
    conflict over 119, 148–57, 159,
        171–2, 176–8
    costs of 75–81
    creators of 110–14
    deer shelters in 77
    disparkment of 38, 53, 72, 76, 99
    economic exploitation of 45–6, 63–76
    function of 5–7, 44, 63–4, 115, 180–1
    gates of 77, 78, 104, 154, 166, 168
    landscaping of 5–6, 8, 82–98, 102, 180
    launds (clearings) in 32, 33, 35, 69, 72, 96

licensing of 9, 37, 48, 111, 121–45
'little parks' 89 n. 49, 93, 94, 95, 98
location of 2, 48–52, 82, 95–6, 158
lordship and high status, parks as expression
 of 6, 8, 99, 101–7, 154, 155, 180
monastic foundations in 28
number of 3, 37–8, 109, 134–5
ownership of 108–10
paradises, parks as 83, 92
peasant attitudes towards 101, 159, 171–2,
 177–9
post-medieval 10
roads, impact of parks on 1, 154, 161, 166–7,
 172, 173, 178
royal attitude towards 143–5
settlements, impact of parks on 160–3,
 172–5
Parlement of Three Ages, the 18, 83
pasture 28, 45, 60, 62, 64, 67, 68, 71, 73, 74, 75,
 78, 80, 97, 104, 153, 156, 158, 167, 168,
 169, 170, 171, 172, 173, 175, 176, 178;
 see also grazing
Patching, William 152
Peasants' Revolt (1381) 177
peat 64
Peckforton (Ches.) 64
Pendley, in Tring (Herts.) 174 n. 123, 175, 176
Penn (Bucks.) 67 n. 120
Penrith (Cumbl.) 170
Penshurst (Kent) 41
Percy, family 73
 Henry 143 n. 96
Peterborough (Northants.) 174 n. 123,
 175 nn. 126–7
 abbey and park 104
Petition of the Barons (1258) 149
Pever, Paulinus 112, 113
Philip, king of Castile 40
Philippa of Hainault 33, 93
Pierpont, Simon de 152
Pinley (Warks.) 88 n. 42
 priory 153
pipe roll, 144
place-names 35, 48, 61, 153 n. 45
Plumpton, Sir Robert 36
 Sir William 114, 142
Plumpton (Cumbl.) 169
Plumpton (Yorks.) 142
poaching 4, 8, 9, 38, 80, 97, 140 n. 80, 143, 144,
 145, 150, 155, 156, 157, 171–2, 177, 178, 181
Poer, William 151
Pole, Michael de la, earl of Suffolk 112, 113
pollarding 67
Pontes (Essex) 26
population 10, 28, 45, 47, 48, 49, 60–3, 148
Postling (Kent) 153
pounds 64
Poynings, Thomas de 152
Princes Risborough (Bucks.) 163
property rights 143, 153, 158, 181–2
Puckmere, in Bray (Berks.) 113

Puiset, Hugh du, bishop of Durham 25
Pygot, Thomas 127

Quincy, Roger de, earl of Winchester 26, 34, 56
quo warranto, writs of 124, 127 n. 26, 137, 149

rabbits and rabbit warrens 1, 3, 42 n. 192, 64, 70,
 74–5, 102, 149, 151, 166, 171 n. 100, 172,
 177; *see also* free warren; hares
Radley (Berks.) 66
Raleigh, William, bishop of Norwich 171 n. 102
Ravensworth (Yorks.) 89, 94, 152
Reading (Berks.), abbot of 139
Ree, in Westbury (Shrops.) 163
Remenham (Berks.) 139
Restormel (Cornw.) 85
Richard II, king of England 18 n. 18, 22, 24, 128
Richard, duke of Gloucester 114
Richard, earl of Cornwall 58, 113, 153 n. 45
Richard II, Shakespeare play 99, 115
Richmond (Yorks.) 173
Rickmansworth (Herts.) 42
ridge and furrow 53, 54, 165, 179 n. 155
Ridlington (Rutland) 33, 147
rivers and river transport 68, 177
Robert, count of Artois, *see* Artois
Roches, Peter des, bishop of Winchester 127, 142
Rockingham (Northants.) 42
Roger, bishop of Salisbury 162
Romance of Sir Degrevant, the 115 n. 73
Romance of the Rose, the 97
Romano-British farming and settlement 53
Ros, William de 143 n. 96
Rotherfield Greys (Oxon.) 51 n. 29, 61
Rotherfield Peppard (Oxon.) 51 n. 29, 61
Rous, John 104, 113, 114, 135, 172, 173, 175
Russell, John, bishop of Lincoln 172, 178
Ryther, Ralph 36
Ryther (Yorks.) 36

St Albans (Herts.) 177 n. 143
 abbey 179 n. 156;
 abbot of 149 n. 22; *see also* John of
  Wheathampstead
St Amand, Eleanor, Lady 155
St Clair, Sir John 26
St Ewe (Corn.) 174 n. 123
St John, family 150, 151
 Hugh 152
 John 139, 151
 Robert 133, 151 n. 31
St Mary, York, abbot of 133
St Valery, honor of 25
Salisbury (Wilts.), bishop of 139
Salisbury Plain, the 49
Salkeld (Cumbl.) 170
Samson, abbot of Bury St Edmunds
Say, William de 151
Scot, William 143 n. 96
Scott, William 178 n. 149
Segenhoe, in Ridgmont (Beds.) 56, 163

Segrave, Stephen de 112, 138, 153
Sele priory (Sussex) 153
Shakespeare, William 114
Shap (Westml.) 174 n. 123
Sheen (Surrey) 24, 93
   priory 153
sheep 46, 77, 172, 175
Sheep Bridge, in Swallowfield (Berks.) 139
Sheffield (Yorks.) 161
Sherborne St John (Hants.) 89
Shinfield (Berks.) 140 n. 76
Shipley (Northumb.) 140 n. 80
Shirburn (Oxon.) 25, 80 n. 238
Shottle (Derbs.) 163
Shrewsbury abbey (Shrops.) 153 n. 50
Shuttlewood (Derbs.) 70
Sir Gawain and the Green Knight 18, 83, 104
Slindon (Sussex) 150
Snorscombe, in Everdon (Northants.) 171 n. 100
Somersham (Hunts.) 93, 161, 171
Somery, Roger de 26
Sonning (Berks.) 139
Spaldwick (Hunts.) 162
Spigurnel, Sir Henry 124
Standlake (Oxon.) 60
Stanley abbey (Wilts.) 153 n. 50
Stansted (Essex) 39
Stansted (Sussex) 67 n. 122, 69 n. 142
Stanton Harcourt (Oxon.) 60, 113
Staunton Harold (Leics.) 174 n. 123, 175 nn. 126–7
Steeton (Yorks.) 174 n. 123
Stephen, king of England 121, 135
Stevington (Beds.) 56
Stittenham (Yorks.) 174 n. 123
Stoke Bishop (Glos.) 36
Stoke Gifford (Glos.) 176
Stockholt, in Akeley (Bucks.) 42 n. 193
Stoneleigh (Warks.) 174 n. 123, 175 nn. 126–7
Stonor, family 148
   Sir John 113
   Sir William 148
Stonor (Oxon.) 61, 113
Stort Valley 62
Stourton (Staffs.) 174 n. 123
Stow (Lincs.) 89
Strange, John le 153 n. 50
Stratfield Mortimer (Berks.) 140 n. 76
sumptuary legislation 103
Sutton Passeys (Notts.) 174 n. 123
Swallowfield (Berks.) 139
swords 18, 30 n. 105

Tankersley (Yorks.) 161
tapestries 18
Taunton (Somerset) 127
Templars, the 54, 163
Thame (Oxon.) 55
   abbot of 56

Thames Valley 24
Thaxted (Essex) 73 n. 168
Theodore of Antioch 21
Thornbury (Glos.) 65, 114, 171, 173, 174 n. 123
Thornton Bridge, in Brafferton (Yorks.) 174 n. 123
Thornton Riseborough, in Normanby (Yorks.) 133
Threlkeld, Sir Lancelot 40
Threlkeld (Cumbl.) 40
Throgmorton, Robert 141
timber 1, 3, 32, 36, 47, 59, 60, 64–5, 66, 68–9, 72, 73, 74, 75, 77, 80, 119, 147 n. 7, 156, 167; *see also* wood
tithes 56, 164, 173
Toddington (Beds.) 113
tombs 44, 102, 114
tournaments 21, 94, 103
Tristan 18, 93, 103
Trivet, Nicholas 30 n. 105
Trussell, William 143 n. 96
Tutbury, honor of 38 n. 160
Twickenham (Middx.) 174 n. 123, 175 n. 127
Twiti, William 17
Tyttenhanger, in Ridge (Herts.) 97

Valence, William de, earl of Pembroke 153 n. 50, 154
Vastern, in Wootton Bassett (Wilts.) 65
venison 36, 46, 47, 78, 79–80, 106, 140, 147, 150, 156, 157, 178
Vere, Robert de, earl of Oxford 26, 34
Vergil, Polydore 37, 39
Vernon, Richard de 56
Vieuxpont, Robert de 96
Vincennes, near Paris (France) 88

Wakefield, Henry, bishop of Worcester 36
wall-paintings 20
Wallstone (Derbs.) 163
Walsall (Staffs.) 88
Walsingham, Thomas 179
Waltham abbey (Essex) 127 n. 32, 155
Warenne, family 104, 151, 156 n. 66
Warre, de la, family 34
Warsop (Notts.) 140 n. 80
Warwick (Warks.) 175
   earl of 74 n. 176, 112, 114, 135, 151
Washingley (Hunts.) 174 n. 123
waste, 4, 22, 26, 28, 45, 46, 54, 59–63, 75, 80, 81, 143, 153, 156, 157, 158, 164, 165, 167–8, 169, 175–6
Watlington (Oxon.) 58, 67 nn. 120 and 122, 68, 124 n. 25, 137 n. 61, 147 n. 5, 164
Weald, the 49, 58
Wedergrave, Nicholas de 99
Wedgnock (Warks.) 74 n. 176
Welland Valley 95
West Hallam (Derbs.) 155
Westbury (Somerset) 53

Westenhanger, near Hythe (Kent) 153
Westminster Abbey 22
    abbot of 26
Westminster Palace 18, 20
Weycroft, in Axminster (Devon) 154
Wheathampstead, John of, abbot of
    St Albans 97
Whitley (Berks.) 139
Whitmore, near Coventry (Warks.) 176
Wicken (Northants.) 174 n. 123, 175 nn. 126–7
    Wick Hamon manor in 79
Wickhay (Essex) 140 n. 80
Wilde, in Hampstead Norris (Berks.)
    174 n. 123, 175 nn. 126–7
William I, king of England 21
William II (Rufus), king of England 21
William, lord of Bramber 153
Willoughby, Henry de 141
    Richard de 139 n. 72
Wilstrop, Miles 146
Wilstrop (Yorks.) 146, 174 n. 123, 175, 178
Wilton, Alan de 133
Wimpole (Cambs.) 167 n. 62
Winchester, bishop of 32, 48, 51, 58, 60, 71, 77,
    109, 139
Windsor (Berks.) 22, 24, 40, 68 n. 133,
    73 n. 171, 77, 83 n. 16, 88, 92, 94,
    106, 113, 170, 173, 174; see also forests,
    Windsor
Winfarthing (Norf.) 73 n. 168
Wingfield (Suffolk) 112, 113
Witney (Oxon.) 60, 62, 77, 78 n. 218,
    137 n. 61
Wittenham (Wilts.) 174 n. 123
Witz, Konrad 44 n. 202
Wiverton (Notts.) 174 n. 123, 175
Wollaton (Notts.) 139 n. 72
Wolseley, Ralph 42 n. 192, 143, 176
Wolseley (Staffs.) 42 n. 192, 176, 178

wolves 27
wood and underwood 3, 6, 36, 45, 59, 60, 64,
    65–6, 67 n. 118, 69–70, 71, 73–4, 80, 108,
    115, 147, 159, 167, 169, 170, 176;
    see also coppices; timber; woodland and
    wood-pasture
Woodham Walter (Essex) 164
woodland and wood-pasture 2, 3, 4, 5, 7,
    9 n. 63, 22, 26, 28, 42, 43, 44, 45, 46, 47,
    48–51, 59–63, 64 n. 96, 71, 74, 80–1, 96,
    104, 115, 140, 143, 144, 153, 157, 158, 164,
    167–70, 172, 176, 181
    extent of 28, 175
    trenches in 32, 33
Woodperry (Oxon.) 56
Woodstock (Oxon.) 24, 32, 33, 37, 38 n. 160, 54,
    55, 60, 77, 78 n. 213, 89, 91, 93, 94, 97, 104,
    113, 135, 160, 163, 166
Woodville, Richard 79
Wootton (Oxon.) 54
    hundred of 60
Wootton Bassett (Wilts.) 139 n. 73; see also
    Vastern
Worksop (Notts.) 140 n. 80
Worthington (Leics.) 175 nn. 126–7
Wrentham (Suffolk) 152
Wrest (Beds.) 155
Wyard, John 113
Wyke (Warks.) 141
Wynnere and Wastoure 35
Wyre (Shrops.) 166

Yanwath (Westml.) 40
Yardley (Northants.) 26, 33
yeomen 103, 177, 178
York, archbishop of 171
    Edward, duke of 15, 17, 39
Yorkshire Dales 74
Yorkshire Wolds 49

Printed and bound by CPI Group (UK) Ltd, Croydon, CR0 4YY